THE DEFINING DECADE
Identity, Politics, and the Canadian Jewish Community in the 1960s

The 1960s witnessed a radical transformation in the Canadian Jewish community. The erosion of long-standing antisemitism resulted in increased access for Jews to the economic, political, and social mainstream. Arguing that as Canadian society became more accepting, the Jewish community became more focused on its own identity, Harold Troper examines how the 1960s redefined what it meant to be a Canadian Jew and a Jewish Canadian.

Domestic events such as the Quiet Revolution, the eruption of Neo-Nazi activity, the election of Pierre Elliott Trudeau, and the promise of multiculturalism as well as international affairs such as the Six Day War, Arab rejectionism with regards to Israel, and the explosion of Soviet Jewish activism radically reshaped Canadian Jewish priorities. In tracing the rapid changes of this tumultuous decade, *The Defining Decade* draws upon a wealth of historical documentation, including more than eighty interviews, to demonstrate that the expression of Canadian Jewishness was an increasingly public – and political – commitment.

HAROLD TROPER is a professor in the Department of Theory and Policy Studies in Education at the Ontario Institute for Studies in Education, University of Toronto, and co-author of *None Is Too Many: Canada and the Jews of Europe 1933–1948*.

The Defining Decade

Identity, Politics, and the Canadian
Jewish Community in the 1960s

HAROLD TROPER

UNIVERSITY OF TORONTO PRESS
Toronto Buffalo London

© University of Toronto Press Incorporated 2010
Toronto Buffalo London
www.utppublishing.com
Printed in Canada

ISBN 978-1-4426-4114-3 (cloth)
ISBN 978-1-4426-1046-0 (paper)

Printed on acid-free, 100% post-consumer recycled paper
with vegetable-based inks.

Library and Archives Canada Cataloguing in Publication

Troper, Harold Martin, 1942–
The defining decade : identity, politics, and the Canadian Jewish
community in the 1960s / Harold Troper.

Includes bibliographical references and index.
ISBN 978-1-4426-4114-3 (bound).   ISBN 978-1-4426-1046-0 (pbk.)

1. Jews – Canada – Identity.   2. Jews – Canada – Social conditions –
20th century.   3. Jews – Canada – Politics and government – 20th
century.   4. Nineteen sixties.   I. Title.

FC106.J5T76 2010   305.892'40710904   C2010-903510-0

University of Toronto Press acknowledges the financial assistance to its
publishing program of the Canada Council for the Arts and the Ontario
Arts Council.

 Canada Council   Conseil des Arts   ONTARIO ARTS COUNCIL
for the Arts   du Canada   CONSEIL DES ARTS DE L'ONTARIO

University of Toronto Press acknowledges the financial support of the
Government of Canada through the Canada Book Fund for its publishing
program.

For Eydie. For everything. For always.

Contents

Acknowledgments

The Defining Decade took me a decade to research and write. Looking back, I now understand why it took so long. What I originally intended was a narrowly focused study of Canadian Jewish response to the 1967 Six Day War. But the deeper I probed the clearer it became that to fully appreciate the impact of the war, a pivotal moment in Canadian Jewish history, it is imperative to understand that moment in the larger Canadian Jewish context of the 1960s. As a result, my research program gradually expanded to include both examination of the Canadian Jewish community in the several years preceding the Six Day War as well as analysis of how and why the 1967 war so profoundly altered Canadian Jewish self-definition, even as it dramatically remade the communal Jewish agenda. This much expanded research program took a decade to complete.

Just as researching and writing *The Defining Decade* was a lengthy process, it was often a lonely one as well. Writing history is not a group enterprise. But in this case my work was made easier by the cooperation and encouragement I received from others. Of course, nothing is for nothing. Research costs money. I am grateful to the Ontario Institute for Studies in Education for providing me with seed money necessary to ensure there was sufficient research data available to undertake this study. Like many Canadian academics, I am also indebted to the Social Sciences and Humanities Research Council of Canada for its generous support. And I am thankful to my colleagues in Theory and Policy Studies for providing me with so positive a research environment.

There have been many other individuals – including some, I am embarrassed to admit, now lost to memory – who contributed to the success of this research. Not least of these are other scholars. I am unendingly indebted to the late and much-missed Robert Harney, who was not just a good friend but a singularly shaping influence on my career. If this study adds to the historiography of Canadian Jews, credit is also due the growing body of scholarly literature on the Canadian Jewish experience I was able to tap into. Among those whose scholarship proved foundational to my study are Mindy Avrich-Skapinker, Frank Bialystok, Hiam Genizi, Michael Marrus, Richard Menkis, Michael Oren, Tom Segev, Gerald Tulchinsky, Jim Walker, and Morton Weinfeld. Much as I'd like to also hold them responsible for any failings in this book, I can't. I reserve that for myself.

It is important to acknowledge the work of archivists, dedicated custodians of the historical record, without whom the writing of history in Canada would be far more difficult and the result far less rewarding. I am especially indebted to the staff at the Ontario Jewish Archives in Toronto now led by Ellen Scheinberg, to Janice Rosen and her crew at the Canadian Jewish Archives in Montreal, to the archival teams at both the Jewish Heritage Centre of Western Canada in Winnipeg and the Archives of the Jewish Historical Society of British Columbia in Vancouver for easing my research load. And a special note of thanks goes to the archivists at the National Archives of Canada in Ottawa. Without their assistance this study would have been almost impossible. Two National Archives staff members, now retired, Lawrence Tapper and Myron Momryk, deserve special thanks for directing me to valuable manuscript materials.

Some of the manuscript material examined for this study remains in the private domain. I am grateful to Cyril Levitt, Donald Carr, Lou Ronson, and Frank Dimant for allowing me privileged access to private papers. Similarly, I acknowledge the cooperation of those archives, institutions, and individuals who granted permission for me to reprint photographs in this book. Several graduate students assisted with the research for this volume. Among them are Arlis Peer, Eniko Pittner, Kamara Jeffrey, Carlos Parra, and Erica Simmons.

What stand out as my most rewarding research moments are the almost ninety interviews I conducted. Each of the individuals I spoke with intersects the story of the 1960s Canadian Jewish community at a different point, but each of these interviews, some offered in confidence, provided me with personal anecdotes and insights I could never have gleaned from archives. I am grateful to all those who shared their personal stories with me. I hope I have done justice to that trust.

My research called for me to be on the road far more than I had originally planned. But if I did not particularly enjoy being away from home so much, I did enjoy the hospitality so generously offered by Phyllis Zelkowitz and Morton Weinfeld, Richard Menkis and Cathy Best, Ralph and Miriam Troper, Sarah Troper and Lucy Sterezylo, Adina and Yackov Dayan, Willy and Rachelle Moll, Ana and Gabriel Kleiman, and Carla Troper and Kevin Dilamarter. And I was also blessed with another kind of hospitality. As I began pulling together the many storied threads that make up this book, I was several times invited to 'test market' the unfolding narrative in lecture form, often before audiences that included many with lived experience of the 1960s Canadian Jewish community. Discussion periods following my lectures repeatedly served up fresh insight into the Canadian Jewish mindset during that decade. I am especially grateful to Karen Sanders at Temple Emanu-El, Rabbi Edward Goldfarb at Holy Blossom Temple, and Ira Schweitzer at Temple Sinai, all in Toronto, and Rabbi Steve Garten at Temple Israel in Ottawa, for organizing these lecture opportunities.

In the past the only technical assistance I needed in order to write was a pencil sharpener. Now I write on a computer and, as a result, have become dependent for technical assistance on the computer services group in the OISE Education Common. They rescued me from computer hell more times than I care to admit and, as far as I'm concerned, they have earned a special place in techie heaven. I am equally indebted to the staff at University of Toronto Press – especially Len Husband and Frances Mundy – who showed nothing but goodwill in turning my rough-around-the-edges manuscript into a book, to John St James for his copy-edit, and to Mia Spiro for the index. I am also appreciative of the support offered by Jerry and Linda Silver, Cathy Lace, Ron Silvers, Paula Draper, Myer Siemiatycki, Howard Adelman, Gadi Hoz, Carole Ann Reed, Avi Glasner, George Wharton, Michael Moir, Stan Carbone, Abe Arnold, Barney Danson, David Levine, Hy Eiley, Ernie Rubenstein, Andrew Zeidel, and my Tuesday lunch gang. A special thanks to my agent Beverly Slopen for her continuing encouragement.

Research and writing can be a lonesome enterprise. But not for me. Not this time. My kids – Carla, Kevin, Sarah, and Lucy – may not always have known what I was doing, but each in his or her own way was there for me when it counted, and it counted for a lot. And to complete our family's circle of love they have recently given my wife, Eydie, and me three wonderful grandchildren, Jonah, Ella, and Simon. All it takes is a smile from any one of them to light up the darkest day. Finally, and most importantly, this book would not have been possible without Eydie's active support. My debt to her is as large as my love for her is deep.

THE DEFINING DECADE
Identity, Politics, and the Canadian Jewish Community in the 1960s

CHAPTER ONE

Of Faith and Thanksgiving

Popular memory recalls the 1960s as a permissive decade, the 'swinging sixties,' a time of youthful exuberance, political upheaval, and recreational drug use. Hair was long; skirts were short. The pill hit the market in 1960, pantyhose in 1965. Bullets snuffed out the life of an American president, a presidential candidate, and a Black leader with a dream of racial harmony. An American astronaut walked on the moon and the acrid smell of smoke hung over riot-scarred Detroit, New York, and Los Angeles. There was the Chicago Democratic Convention, Woodstock, the Prague Spring, the Bay of Pigs, the Second Vatican Council, the War on Poverty, the Tonkin Resolution, the Tet offensive, and *Hair*. Forty-one new member states were admitted to the United Nations. Closer to home, Canadians witnessed the introduction of universal health care, an acrimonious flag debate, deliberations of the Royal Commission on Bilingualism and Biculturalism, and the influx of American draft resisters. The news was full of teach-ins, sit-ins, sleep-ins, love-ins, and drop-outs, the Auto Pact, striking doctors and postal workers, Beatlemania, Trudeaumania, Expo 67, the Twist, bank credit cards, green garbage bags, hootenannies, exploding mailboxes, and the founding of the New Democratic Party, the Parti Québécois, the FLQ, and the Montreal Expos baseball franchise.

Canadian Jews share in this memory history, but they also share a uniquely proximate history, a narrative at once internal to Jews and the Jewish community yet deeply entwined with the unfolding Canadian narrative. Jewish entanglement in history is not new. Author Bernard Malamud has offered that Jews have always 'stepped into history more deeply than others.'[1] And it was certainly true for Canadian Jews during the 1960s. The decade was uniquely defining for Canadian Jews, a

time of profound transformation. It was a decade in which Canadian
Jews became both more invested in Canada and in their Jewish particularism. It was a decade in which barriers to Jewish participation in
the larger Canadian social, political, and economic mainstream slipped
away and Canadian Jewish organizational growth and communal activism spiked, in which Canadian Jews felt at once more at home in
Canada and more uneasy about the Canadian Jewish future. It was a
decade in which shadows of Holocaust memory and concerns for Israel
increasingly dominated the organized Canadian Jewish community
agenda and coloured individual Jewish encounters with surrounding
Canadian society. It was a decade in which Canadian Jewish understanding of what it meant to be a Canadian Jew and a Jew in Canada
was remade.

But all of this was still in the future when on the afternoon of 13 October 1959 a delegation of prominent Canadian Jews was ushered into Rideau Hall, the stately residence of Georges Vanier, governor general of
Canada. The delegation, led by Montreal whisky tycoon Samuel Bronfman, was in Ottawa to officially launch a year-long celebration marking two hundred years of Jewish settlement in Canada. As flashbulbs
popped, the delegation presented the governor general with a colour-
fully illustrated scroll entitled 'A Proclamation of Faith and Thanksgiv-
ing on the Occasion of the National Bicentenary of Canadian Jewry.'
The document, hand scribed in four languages – English, French, Yiddish, and Hebrew – was signed by Samuel Bronfman, president of the
Canadian Jewish Congress, and Lavy Becker, chair of the Congress's
National Bicentenary Committee. The scroll praised Canada for the
two hundred years it had afforded Jews a secure and peaceful home.
The document also expressed Jewish hopes for the continued growth
and development of a free, just, and democratic Canada.[2]

The timing of the Rideau Hall visit had been carefully worked out
between the bicentenary organizing committee and the governor general's staff. For bicentenary committee members, anxious to launch
their celebration early in the autumn of 1959, 13 October was the first
possible date an official Jewish delegation could meet with the governor general. Anything earlier would have collided with the cycle of
Jewish holy days that dominate the community calendar every fall. For
the governor general's staff, the October date conveniently cleared the
ceremonial transfer of vice-regal authority from one governor general
to another, from the retiring Vincent Massey to the newly appointed
George Vanier. Had the Jewish delegation arrived a few weeks earlier,

Vincent Massey, the first Canadian-born governor general, would have been their host. Given that the purpose of the visit was to launch a public celebration of Jewish life in Canada, it was probably best that Vanier, not Massey, greet the delegates. When it came to Jews, Vanier and Massey were cut from very different pieces of cloth. Massey, a formal and snobbish man with aristocratic pretensions, harboured a deep and personal distaste for Jews. It has been argued in his defence that Massey was no more antisemitic than the times in which he lived, no more antisemitic than others in the social set he enjoyed. Perhaps so, but this did not make Massey any less of an antisemite.[3] And his antisemitism, if discreetly screened off from the public during his tenure as governor general, certainly was very much to the fore during the Second World War, when Massey was Canadian high commissioner in London. As the crisis of European Jewry worsened and Jews desperate to escape the Nazis looked westward for haven, Massey fought any suggestion that Canada should offer Jews a new home. In diplomatic dispatches to Ottawa he repeatedly cautioned the government against easing up on immigration restrictions to admit Jewish refugees from Nazi Germany, a position he maintained through the war and into the post-war years.

Of course, when it came to keeping Jews out of Canada during the pre-war and war years and even into the immediate post-war years, the Liberal government of the day needed little encouragement from Massey or anyone else. The Mackenzie King government was dead set against any slackening of immigration restrictions that would allow Jews into Canada. Given the antisemitic temper of the Depression and war years in both French- and English-speaking Canada, the government concluded that any lowering of barriers to Jewish immigration could set off a firestorm of protest that could cost it dearly at the polls. With little to gain and potentially much to lose, the government rejected any and all efforts by the organized Jewish community and a small group of Canadian pro-refugee sympathizers to change Canada's restrictionist immigration policy. Canada remained closed to immigration, and to that of Jews in particular.

After the war Canada gradually reopened its doors to immigration, including that of Jews. It did not do so because of persistent yet always diplomatic Jewish lobbying for a reopening of immigration or out of humanitarian concern for refugees in need of a new home. Nor was the government responding to public revulsion at the excesses of Nazi racism, much less guilt at the consequences of its mean-spirited war-time restrictionist policy. Nothing of the kind. The government was moved by *gelt* not guilt. Post-war Canada's economy boomed. Labour-intensive industries cautioned the government that continued economic expansion was dependent on access to cheap and abundant imported workers. The government responded by instituting a program of labour recruitment from the displaced-persons camps of Europe and a gradual lowering of barriers to European immigration. For the first time since the mid-1920s, tens of thousands of immigrants began arriving in Canada, including a steady stream of Jews, most of them Holocaust survivors. With immigration now a government priority, in 1952, the same year that Vincent Massey was appointed governor general, parliament passed a new Immigration Act easing, if it did not entirely eliminate, racially and religiously based restrictions on immigration to Canada from Europe. But an end to remaining restrictions against immigrants from Europe was not long in coming.[4]

Less than a decade later, with approximately 37,000 Holocaust survivors admitted to Canada and Massey no longer governor general, Georges Vanier symbolically cut the ribbon initiating the bicentenary of Jewish life in Canada. Vanier was as different from Massey as day is from night.[5] In the pre-war years, Vanier, a man of compassion and of deep religious conviction, served as Canadian ambassador to France. From his vantage point in Paris, Vanier witnessed first hand the growing despair of terrified Jews. His office was besieged by Jewish refugees frantic to escape Europe. Moved by their plight, he joined a handful of Canadian public servants who worked from within to change the government's restrictionist immigration policy as regards Jewish refugees. It was to no avail. Canada's door remained closed to Jews.

With the fall of France in 1940, Vanier was removed from Paris to London, where he served as Canadian ambassador to all allied governments in exile. He also continued to press his government to ease its no-Jews policy. In 1940, for example, he put his weight behind a plan for Canada to admit a group of Jewish children interned in southern France who, if Canadian authorities worked quickly, might yet be saved from deportation eastward to the death camps that had already consumed their parents. In a rare moment of compassion the Canadian cabinet approved the plan, but Canadian immigration authorities deliberately created enough red tape to stall implementation of the rescue effort. In the end, the children selected for removal to Canada were shipped eastward, where they suffered the same fate as their parents.[6]

In 1944, with Paris liberated and the Allies well on the road to victory in Europe, Vanier reclaimed his post as Canadian ambassador in Paris.

In April 1945, a week after Buchenwald was liberated by Allied forces, Vanier accompanied a delegation of American and British officials to tour the camp. He was deeply shaken by what he saw. In a report on his visit to the death camp broadcast on the CBC, Vanier shared his shame at a world and a Canada that had been so callously indifferent to the suffering of those abandoned to the Nazis. 'How deaf we were then to cruelty and the cries of pain which came to our ears, grim forerunners of the mass torture and murder which were to follow.'[7]

In September 1959 Vanier succeeded Massey as governor general, and less than a month later it was a warm and gracious Vanier rather than the aloof patrician Massey who welcomed the Canadian Jewish delegation to Rideau Hall. The change in vice-regal appointment was matched by changes in the Canadian Jewish world. Even as Vanier greeted his guests, the organized Jewish community in Canada was a key coalition partner with liberal and progressive groups, including labour unions, socially engaged churches, the media, and forward-thinking politicians, in actively championing the enactment of laws to protect Canadians from racism and antisemitism. Their efforts were then being rewarded with success. But this had not come easily or fast. For fifty years, the Canadian Jewish community, largely composed of immigrant Yiddish speakers and their children, had cautiously and gently chipped away at the rock of antisemitism in Canada. In the wake of the Second World War, Jewish community leaders, emphasizing Jewish contributions to the national war effort, argued that Canada's Jews had earned relief from antisemitism. Law abiding and hard working, in the post-war they continued to contribute to the growth of a strong and prosperous Canada. Legally tolerated discrimination, Jewish leaders argued, was hurtful, hateful, and incompatible with the values for which Canadians had fought and died. Jewish demands for equal protection under the law were echoed by a coalition of groups which favoured Canadian governments, federal and provincial, enacting and enforcing human rights protections.

This situation was not unique to Canada. Western nations were increasingly being caught up in a human rights revolution. In December 1948 Canada became a signatory to the United Nations Universal Declaration of Human Rights. Rather than being a symbolic act, this helped further domestic debate about human rights protections in Canada. After several provincial governments moved to translate the spirit of the declaration into legislative action in their respective jurisdictions, the federal government in 1960 passed a Canadian Bill of Rights setting out the basic civil and political rights of Canadians. The bill of rights was not constitutional in nature, or binding in areas of provincial responsibility, nor did it have the kind of legal teeth, even at the federal level, that human rights advocates might have hoped for. It did, however, fuel demands by human rights advocates that governments enact sweepingly binding codes of human rights protections. Across Canada provincial governments responded by beefing up existing legislation or enacting new laws making it illegal to discriminate on the basis of race, religion, and national origin, particularly in the areas of housing, employment, and education. While somewhat conservative by nature, provincial and federal courts also began demonstrating an increased readiness to enforce these protections.[8]

Justly proud of the role Jews had played in entrenching human rights protections in Canadian law, the delegation Vanier welcomed to Rideau Hall was also concerned that Jews still had a long way to go. That's why they were there. The celebration of the Canadian Jewish Bicentenary was envisioned as yet another tool in the organized Jewish community's ongoing effort to push antisemitism further and further to the margins of Canadian civil society. How so? The elite of the organized Jewish community ushered in to meet with the governor general were concerned that, in spite of recent legislative advances in the protection of human rights in Canada, many Canadians, including those in positions of power and influence, continued to view Jews as outsiders, in Canada by sufferance rather than right. This was seen as no less true of English Canada than of French Canada. In English-speaking Canada of the late 1950s many held fast to a vision of Canada as both a Christian society and an outpost of British values in North America. On both counts Jews failed to measure up. For Jews in Montreal there were added concerns about entrenched antisemitism in the powerful Quebec Catholic Church and in a Quebec government that had a demonstrated record of contempt for minority rights.

So long as Jews were regarded by many as alien to the nation-building enterprise – legally Canadian citizens, yes, but incapable of ever truly engaging as Canadians – establishment Jewish leaders feared Jews would face exclusion from core Canadian social, economic, and political spheres. It only made sense. So long as Jews were seen as guests in the Canadian house – unwelcome guests in the eyes of some – they would be expected to behave as guests and know their place, rather than try to secure themselves a place at the national table.[9]

Believing this view of Jews as outsiders was widely held, what could the Jewish community do about it? Few would deny that advances in legal human rights protections, especially in English-speaking Canada, were a positive indication that Jews were making strides in their struggle for acceptance. Indeed, the very notion of Canadian society as a singular bulwark of Anglo-Christian values in North America was slowly losing ground. But it was far from gone, not on Main Street and certainly not in the Canada's plush-carpeted and *judenrein* corporate boardrooms, elite social clubs, and political backrooms where power decisions were made.

Jewish leaders such as Sam Bronfman, according to his biographer, Michael Marrus, much 'preoccupied with Jewish standing in his society,' regarded the battle against persistent social, corporate, and professional antisemitism as among the most pressing challenges facing Canadian Jews. Unlike egregious antisemitism in more publicly exposed areas of employment, accommodation, and education which fell within the purview of human rights legislation, discrimination among Canada's social, corporate, political, and professional elites was sheltered within closed networks of social interaction beyond the reach of human rights legislation or enforcement. In the absence of a toughening up of legislation, many Jewish leaders felt what was needed was a change in attitude. Canadians, and particularly the Canadian elite, needed to be convinced that antisemitism was not just wrong, it was un-Canadian. They needed to see Jews not as just a bunch of Hymie-come-latelys, but as historical partners in the Canadian state-building enterprise, committed stakeholders not alien interlopers.[10] And what better way was there to debunk the notion of Canadian Jews as outsiders, in Canada but not part of Canada, than to 'Mayflower' Jews, to establish in the Canadian mind an image of Jewish roots running long and deep into Canadian soil.

Serendipitously for Canadian Jewish leaders, the late 1950s offered a ready historical peg on which to hang their effort to recast Jews as Canadian patriots and pioneers. The year 1959 marked the two hundredth anniversary of the arrival in Canada of Aaron Hart, a colonial-era Jewish businessman and commercial purveyor to the British Army. Hart settled with his family in Trois-Rivières in 1759. He was soon among the colony's most successful early pioneers. Of course there might be historical purists who would quibble about whether or not the arrival of Aaron Hart deserved to be proclaimed day one for the Canadian Jewish community. After all, Hart was not the first Jewish merchant to set up shop in what would become Canada. He was preceded by a number of other Jewish merchants and adventurers who engaged in commerce in Nova Scotia, with the Hudson's Bay Company, and even in New France – although the record of their activities is at best sketchy. There is also the odd tale of French-born and Jewish Esther Brandeau, who at fifteen was rescued from a shipwreck on her way to Holland. Saved by one of the ship's crew, she is said to have spent most of the next five years dressed as a boy and working aboard French and Spanish ships. Still dressed in male clothing, in 1738 Esther landed in New France, by royal decree closed to the settlement of all but Catholics. Once discovered to be both female and Jewish, the young Jewish woman was promised she could remain in New France, but only if she embraced Catholicism. She was even tutored in Catholicism, but, after vacillating for almost a year, Esther Brandeau reportedly declared converting to Catholicism as too high a price to pay for being allowed to remain in the French colony. She was shipped back to France at crown expense.[11]

Esther Brandeau did not stay in New France, and little is known about other Jewish merchants and adventurers who reached what would eventually become Canada. But Aaron Hart's story is both known and documented. The public record offers ample detail about his life and influence and that of his heirs. Born in England in 1724, Hart served with the British Army in colonial America and was a commissary officer when Montreal fell to British forces. He settled at Trois-Rivières, downriver from Montreal, where he went on to become a successful merchant, land owner, and political figure. Hart's legacy endured. His children and grandchildren were much involved in the early growth and development of business and governance in Canada. They were also important players in the tiny nascent Jewish community of Canada. In and of itself, this might have been reason enough for Jewish leaders to honour Hart's place in Canadian and Canadian Jewish history. But Hart also offered Canadian Jewish leaders another and perhaps even more important reason to celebrate his arrival: good timing. Establishment Jewish leaders anxious to identify a founding narrative need look no further than Aaron Hart, Jewish nation builder. In 1959, two hundred years after Hart first set foot in Canada, Jewish leaders latched onto the bicentenary of his arrival as occasion to proclaim the Bicentenary of Canadian Jewry and trumpet the historical contribution of Jews to Canada.[12]

The Canadian Jewish Congress, the organizational hub of the Canadian Jewish community, approved a budget and set up a National Bicentenary Committee headed by Lavy Becker, Montreal businessman, rabbi, and founder of the first Reconstructionist synagogue in Canada. The committee organized a year-long and Canada-wide calendar of celebrations designed to profile not just Hart but two hundred years of Jewish contributions to Canada. And the goal was to do so where Jewish leaders felt it counted most – outside the Jewish community. With every effort made to impress the larger Canadian community with how deep Jewish roots ran into Canadian soil, little or no priority was given to engaging the Jewish street in the celebration. Nor is there much indication that the Jewish street was much interested in the Hart bicentenary. In a Jewish community then still dominated, at least numerically, by Yiddish-speaking European immigrant Jews and their children, the bicentenary barely resonated. Why should it? Hart, shmart. What did most Jews know or care about Hart, Trois-Rivières, or the beaver trade? Did it help pay the mortgage? Did it help get a son into McGill or a daughter into the University of Toronto? Of course, generating street-level Jewish community pride at two hundred years of continuous Jewish settlement in Canada was never the bicentenary's goal. The goal was to impress non-Jewish opinion leaders and the larger Canadian society with the notion that Jews were not all just off the boat. The goal was to portray Jews as part of the fabric of Canadian history, as nation builders invested in the Canadian enterprise for two hundred years. As such, Jews had as much a proprietary right as anyone to be thought of as bedrock Canadians committed to Canada. This being the goal, as far as the Jewish establishment was concerned, the less spotlight cast on the Yiddish-speaking immigrant Jewish majority in Canada the better.

For a full year, bicentennial events followed hard on the heels of one another. In addition to launching the year-long celebration with the presentation of the proclamation scroll to the governor general, the Canadian Jewish Congress commissioned an educational syllabus on the historical contribution of Jews to Canadian society for distribution to public schools and discussion groups across Canada. A *Canadian Jewish Reference Book and Directory* was also commissioned. Originally conceived as a comprehensive single-volume guide to Jews, Judaism, and Jewish contributions to Canadian society, when finally published in 1963 the more than 400-page aqua-green-covered book turned out to be a somewhat disjointed collection of separately authored and too often unrelated articles suffering the absence of a strong editorial hand.[13] Unpolished though it turned out, the book was widely distributed free to schools and libraries across Canada. Those opening the book might be moved to read a letter of congratulations from the governor general to the Canadian Jewish community on its bicentenary. The governor general referred back to the bicentenary scroll previously presented him by the Jewish community.

> From it I gained a new insight into the contribution of this people to the building of a new nation, free and in quest of justice.
>
>   The guiding tradition of our country has been and continues to be primarily Judaeo-Christian, emphasizing primacy of the spirit and the duty we have to each other. May Canadians always draw strength from such tradition.[14]

The governor general's sentiments were echoed in congratulatory speeches in the House of Commons and Senate by spokespersons from all political parties. Similar speeches were also delivered in a number of provincial legislatures and unanimous resolutions passed in praise of Jewish contributions to Canadian society. The government of Quebec, discreetly sidestepping the fact that Hart was part of the apparatus of British conquest, marked the bicentenary by erecting a commemorative plaque at the site of Aaron Hart's home in Trois-Rivières. Quebec premier Maurice Duplessis was originally scheduled to unveil the plaque, but he was too seriously ill to attend the event. In his absence, a contingent of Quebec's political and community elite joined Quebec Jewish leaders in a rare moment of togetherness at the Hart home to mark the event.[15]

Across Canada, newspapers published editorials, feature articles, and, in several cases, full supplements hailing two hundred years of continuous Canadian Jewish achievement. In Montreal, the Canadian Jewish Congress commissioned acclaimed McGill composer István Anhalt to write a symphony in honour of the bicentenary. His Symphony no. 1 premiered in November 1959 at a public concert.[16] *The Toronto Telegram* published a souvenir edition coinciding with the City of Toronto's official proclamation of 9 February 1960 as a day to honour the Canadian Jewish bicentenary. The souvenir edition was printed in blue and white, traditional Jewish colours. The day's events kicked off with a formal luncheon attended by a who's who of the city's political, media, and business elite. Several major retailers in the Toronto downtown core cleared their windows for displays 'demonstrating the contributions and achievements of the Canadian Jewish community to Canadian culture.' The day ended with a mass public reception in the ballroom of the Royal York Hotel to which the Toronto community elite – Jewish and especially non-Jewish – was invited.[17]

Also in honour of the year-long celebration, the mass-circulation *Maclean's Magazine* published a feature essay entitled 'The Jew in Canada: Where Does He Stand Today?' The essay, reprinted and widely distributed across Canada by the Canadian Jewish Congress, was fulsome in its praise for Canadian Jews and their many contributions to Canada. Beyond praise, the article sought to explain something of the dynamic tension between Jewish particularism and universalism. Why did Jews, even as committed Canadians, prioritize communal Jewish bonding one to the other, a bonding that transcends borders, differences in language, and divisions over religious observance and practice? And why do Jews seem haunted by history and possessed by fears for Jewish survival? Even as these questions begged answer, *Maclean's* allowed that it was difficult if not impossible to draw an inclusive circle around Canadian Jews and say 'This is them.'

> There is, of course, no such thing as a typical Jew any more than there is a typical Canadian. In general, our Jewish fellow-citizens are distinguished by keenness of intellect, love of learning, a good sense of humor and few illusions. They are usually energetic, industrious and creative, and place a high value on human freedom. They are Canadian in their hopes, aspirations, love of family, daily life. They are Jews in that they are a part of the Jewish nation and world Jewry. A cold wind blowing on a Jew halfway around the globe is a chill breeze on the Jew in Canada. If there is anti-Semitism in this country, Jews will also admit to anti-Gentilism. This is a heritage from their past, evincing itself in exclusiveness and inborn distrust of the stranger.

What of the future? According to *Maclean's*, the Canadian Jewish story since the end of the Second World War was one of educational and economic achievement played out against a backdrop of expanding human rights protections and widening acceptance of Jewish participation in the larger society. But the essay speculated that there might eventually be a Jewish price to pay for unfettered Jewish access to Canadian society and that price could be high. With the decline of antisemitism and a community of increasingly educated and prosperous Canadian Jews ready to engage with Canada, might there also be a corresponding distancing of Jews from their roots? Would an open door to Jewish participation in the mainstream precipitate a gradual Jewish slide towards assimilation? Would the unintended consequence of declining antisemitism and a corresponding increase in Jewish social acceptance eventually spell the beginning of the end of Jewish life in Canada? Raising these questions, *Maclean's* again posited no answers. Instead, it offered that if there might be dark clouds looming on the very distant Jewish horizon, the forecast into the foreseeable future was continued sunshine. This generation of Canadian Jews showed every intention of remaining Jews and preserving their faith and traditions. That, according to *Maclean's*, was cause for all Canadians to celebrate. 'Despite the blandishments of assimilation and a probable decrease in their population, no one can doubt that Canadian Jews will stay Jewish. Judaism is in their blood. By the beat of their hearts, by the oneness with their brethren and by their own deliberate choice, they will preserve one of the world's oldest religions and continue as Jews to make their rich and unique contribution to our national life.'[18]

When the year-long bicentenary ballyhoo finally subsided, Bronfman congratulated organizers for their efforts, but, in fact, neither he nor they knew if they had succeeded in impacting public perception of Canadian Jews. Perhaps the best that could be concluded was that, like chicken soup, the bicentenary couldn't hurt. What of *Maclean's'* caution that widening social acceptance of Jews might come at the cost of a decline in commitment to Jewish life? That was not part of Canadian Jewish discourse during the bicentenary or during the few years that followed. But in contrast to the Canadian Jewish experience of the day, it was very much an issue then troubling American Jewish leadership, religious and secular. Even as Canadian Jewish leaders hoped their bicentenary celebration would unlock the door to Jewish social acceptance in Canada, American Jewish leaders were pondering the consequences of what seemed a door standing wide open to Jewish assimilation.

Of course, assimilation was not the only issue on the American Jewish agenda. The early 1960s was a period of growing discord in America. The United States was increasingly racked by internal upheaval fuelled by a building Black revolt on inner-city streets, by growing protest against an expanding war in the rice paddies of Southeast Asia, by a disquieting malaise that infected the comfort of middle-class suburban strip malls, elite ivy league campuses, and the family dining room table, and by the murder of a president.

American Jews did not stand separate from the social upheaval sweeping across their land. How could they? After several decades of unprecedented economic, educational, and social advance, American Jews, both as individuals and as a collectivity, were as never before invested, and comfortable, in America. What happened in America and to America happened to them.

But as much as American Jews were caught up by immediate and compelling issues affecting the larger society, a growing number in the American Jewish leadership community were also beginning to look inward at an issue immediate to the Jewish heart – was there a secure and meaningful American Jewish future? For years the organized American Jewish community, like its Canadian counterpart, had prioritized the fight against antisemitism with its denial of Jewish access to full and equal participation in the economic, educational, political, and social mainstream. In the post-war years their campaign was crowned with increasing success as barriers to Jewish entrée into the larger American society gradually crumbled. Doors long closed to Jews were swinging open. But, in contrast to the mindset of Canadian Jewish community leaders, in the early 1960s American Jewish leaders were increasingly beset by disquieting questions about if or how much the expanded acceptance of Jews in America had set the American Jewish community on the slippery slope to assimilation.

The questions were simple. The answers were not. Growing Jewish acceptance into the larger American mainstream was expanding the circle of social interaction between Jews and non-Jews. An inevitable consequence was the wholesale flowering of romantic entanglements and a resulting increase in intermarriage. As intermarriage became more common – certainly far more common than it was in Canada at the time – its meaning changed. In an earlier day, when social barriers between Jews and non-Jews were more rigid, intermarriage was not just far less common. For many Jews and non-Jews alike it was widely regarded as taboo. Those few Jews who entered into a 'mixed' marriage often did so knowing that they might find themselves cut off from family and community. Some Jews may even have deliberately sought out intermarriage as a way to break free from what they regarded as the narrow constraints of Jewish particularism, deliberately entering into an inter-faith union as a final, irrevocable step in self-removal from Jewish contact.

By the late 1950s and early 1960s, however, out-marriage was far less likely to be the result of a desire, conscious or unconscious, to escape the Jewish fold than an act of love. And who could argue with love? Some regarded a growing rate of intermarriage as unavoidable. As barriers to social interaction between Jewish and non-Jewish Americans continued to give way and Jews were welcomed into the American mainstream, intermarriage was the result.[19] It was already happening. In an America where individuals were increasingly free to choose their partners and romantic marriage was idealized, the increasing commonality of inter-marriage might not be celebrated by religious leaders – Jewish or non-Jewish – but individual Jews who might hope intermarriage would not happen in their family increasingly responded to the phenomenon more with a shrug rather than a shudder. If not exactly welcomed with joy, intermarriage was also not exactly the end of the world.

In some cases intermarried couples sought to identify as Jews and participate in Jewish life. This was not always easy. Jewish institutional and familial supports to accommodate intermarried couples were of-ten lacking or religiously unwelcome. As a result, many saw their ties to faith and community gradually slip away. If a growing incidence of intermarriage was the inevitable albeit unintended consequence of successful Jewish access to the American mainstream, Jewish leaders had reason to fear intermarriage would degrade the American Jew-ish future. Could American Jews even intermarry themselves out of existence? What a sad irony that the success of the organized Jewish community in overcoming antisemitism and the success of individual America Jews in accessing America might portend the demise of the American Jewish community.

Of course it was easier to identify the problem than to solve it. So long taboo, some community leaders preferred not even to discuss intermarriage, at least not openly. Thus, it remained something of an elephant thumping in the American Jewish closet, a looming presence no one knew how to handle. Easier to pretend it was not there. Un-fortunately for Jewish leaders, the elephant was proving increasingly restless. In early 1960 *Fortune Magazine* published a lengthy feature ar-ticle about the Jews of New York entitled 'The Jewish Elan.' Pointing out that there were more Jews in New York than in Israel, the author argued, 'The great Jewish population gives New York much of the dynamism and vigor that makes the city unique among all the cities on earth. And surely it can be said that Jewish elan has contributed mightily to the city's dramatic character – its excitement, its original-ity, its stridency, its unexpectedness.' It was not so much, the author argued, that Jews added greatly to the cultural richness of New York, but that, in the process of striking a balance between a desire to preserve their Jewishness and a desire to accommodate to the pressure cooker of modern urban life that was New York, several generations of Jews in New York had made 'live-and-let-live' a prized New York value. And in the 1960s that Jewish balancing act continued. Still, the author suggested, holding onto Jewish identity while accessing the larger community might be getting harder. In fact, it might be impossible to remain both uniquely Jewish and fully integrated into American society. One might have to be sacrificed in order to ensure the other. In consequence, he asked, would Jews who had for so long helped make New York so open and accepting now find an open and accepting New York and America remaking Jews out of existence? Already confronting dramatic changes in their economic, cultural, organizational, and ritual activities, greater ease of Jewish/non-Jewish relations, and the social and culturally homogenizing impact of Jewish migration to the suburbs, the author suggested, Jews were uncertain about what the Jewish future might look like or, put another way, how Jewish the next generation of Jews would be.

> What is the future of the Jews in New York and in the U.S.? Will they, as some Jews fear, be assimilated and thus disappear as an ethnic group?
>   Herman Wouk thinks that American materialism may erase Jewish consciousness. In his book, *This Is My God*, he writes: 'The threat of Jewish oblivion in America is ... the threat of vanishing down a broad highway at the wheel of a high-powered station wagon, with golf clubs piled in the back.'[20]

The notion that American Jews were going to vanish – not as a result of some kind of Holocaust-like cataclysm, but because individual American Jews were voluntarily casting Jewishness aside in a headlong rush to embrace an affluent and welcoming mainstream America, diving head first into the melting pot – was one thing. The notion that Jews might vanish because more and more young Jews were melting into the arms of non-Jews was quite another. The elephant in the closet was now suddenly pounding on the door, and it was increasingly difficult for the Jewish leadership community to pretend it was not there.

Sounding the alarm bell, the director of information and research for the American Jewish Committee, sociologist Milton Himmelfarb, called on American Jews to acknowledge the presence of the elephant and deal with it before it soiled the communal carpet. In a 1963 article entitled 'The Vanishing Jew,' published in the widely read Jewish journal of opinion *Commentary*, Himmelfarb picked up on a newly released study on the decline in American Jewish population numbers by sociologist Erich Rosenthal. Published in the 1963 *American Jewish Yearbook*, Rosenthal's study was not the first to warn that the American Jewish population was shrinking. However, Himmelfarb explained, in the past blame for declining Jewish numbers was spread among a number of factors that contributed to a lowering of Jewish fertility rates or encouraged smaller families. Prime among them were a wilful Jewish embrace of birth control and emphasis on upward mobility which resulted in marriage delay and decreased family size. Quoting Rosenthal, Himmelfarb argued that in the end all this, while important, took second place to the one reigning causal factor responsible for Jewish population decline in the United States – intermarriage, the love child of increasing Jewish acceptance. Not only was America witnessing growing numbers of marriages between Jewish and non-Jewish partners, but in these unions, Himmelfarb warned, citing Rosenthal's statistics, 'Only about 30 per cent of the children … are raised as Jews or are considered to be Jews by their parents.'

If Jewish continuity was important, Himmelfarb argued, the problem of intermarriage had to be tackled. But how? Pretending it was not happening or that it would somehow solve itself was not going to work. Nor would wringing hands or declaring the problem was beyond solution. And for that matter, shouting from the rooftops that Jews should not intermarry was also pointless. Himmelfarb allowed that there was no shortage of American rabbis and others in the American Jewish community railing against the increased incidence of intermarriage, but their cries were falling on deaf ears. Obviously, 'few Jews are listening.' They didn't have time to listen. They were too busy dating non-Jews and intermarrying to pay naysayers any heed. For his part, Himmelfarb offered one suggestion. Given that intermarriage was increasingly a fact of American Jewish life, one thing that might make a positive difference to the slippage in Jewish numbers was to encourage non-Jewish partners to convert to Judaism. Could this happen? he asked. Maybe. If the American Jewish community and its rabbis were more open to conversion, more welcoming of converts, Himmelfarb argued, many a non-Jewish partner might sign on, and as a result, children of these unions would be raised as Jews. But again, for the immediate future Himmelfarb saw little prospect of that. Just as most American rabbis disapproved of intermarriage, he acknowledged, 'Most of them are unenthusiastic about conversion. They believe that it is untraditional, that the would-be convert is probably a disturbed personality, or that before trying to convert others to Judaism we should convert the Jews.'[21]

Himmelfarb's *Commentary* article let the assimilationist cat out of the Jewish bag, or, more correctly, set the assimilationist elephant loose in the Jewish parlor. The article set off a heated intra-community debate among Jewish leaders, both religious and secular, about what if anything should or could be done to save the 'vanishing Jew.' American rabbis in their pulpits, Jewish functionaries at communal gatherings, pundits at conferences, and academics in scholarly journals let go an avalanche of words. Most agreed that the statistics on intermarriage signalled a grave threat to the American Jewish future. Some, treating intermarriage as if it were an infectious disease, joined in debating the merits of this or that remedial course of action, insisting a way must be found to quarantine the American community against intermarriage or at least mitigate its impact if American Jewish life was to survive. Others agreed that the gradually increasing intermarriage rate was a threat to Jewish survival in America, but likely an irreversible one.[22] Confident that the Jewish community would not disappear on their watch, they regrettably saw no way to stem the growing tide of inter-marriage and resulting assimilation. Looking beyond the 'foreseeable future,' they could only hope that the last Jew to leave the fold would respectfully remember to turn off the lights.[23] Even at that, they were unsure anyone would care enough to do so. A cartoon in one Jewish publication depicted the sanctuary of a large synagogue, the rabbi looking out from the pulpit saying, 'And tonight I will speak to you on The Vanishing American Jew.' Except for the rabbi, the sanctuary is empty.[24]

Admittedly, not all American Jews regarded intermarriage as a singular threat. Those who were intermarrying certainly did not. There were also those American Jewish commentators who regarded all the warnings about 'the vanishing Jew' as little more than overblown fear mongering. Some challenged the negative statistics and offered a counterbalancing analysis to prove that 'sky-is-falling' warnings that Jews were becoming an endangered species were not only exaggerated but wrong.[25] A few even took comfort in suggesting that while intermarriage was a problem, it was a problem inseparable from the larger blessing that accompanied it. Prominent Conservative rabbi Robert Gordis, professor at the Jewish Theological Seminary, argued that intermarriage was just 'part of the price we must pay for freedom and equality in an open society.'[26] Would American Jews trade away the gift of Jewish acceptance in America, even with its attendant rise in intermarriage, if it meant a return to an earlier day of antisemitism in employment, accommodation, and education? Would it be better to lock oneself behind ghetto walls – physically and intellectually – rather than accept the welcoming embrace of America? You want one, you have to take the other.[27]

Jewish leaders who thought their intermarriage debate would stay in-house forgot the old American journalistic adage that 'Jews is news.' It did not take long for the 'vanishing Jew' debate to spill out into the popular media. *Newsweek* and *Time Magazine*, in mid-October 1963 and January 1964 respectively, ran articles on Jewish/Gentile intermarriage and American Jewish fears of wholesale population slippage. The *Newsweek* article began with a telling story. 'A Philadelphia rabbi was addressing a congregation of Quakers one day. Alluding dryly to a tendency among Jews to drift away from their religion, the rabbi said: "Some of my best Jews are Friends."'[28] In the spring of 1964, the popular mass-circulation weekly *Look Magazine* added to the public hubbub. Under the title 'The Vanishing American Jews,' *Look* ran a four-page feature on Jewish intermarriage. Much of the article focused on how the American campuses, with so high a percentage of Jewish youth, had become the crock pot for intermarriage. But the campus in and of itself was not the problem. In the end, *Look* told its readers, it was not even intermarriage per se that was the problem. The root problem, according to some Jews *Look* consulted, was a vacuum of Jewish consciousness, a failure by many Jewish young people to ascribe value to being Jewish. Why hang on to what you don't value? A Hillel rabbi was quoted as lamenting that many young Jewish men and women come to the campus with 'a staggering amount of Jewish illiteracy.' Whatever Jewish content there was in their lives, it proved little more than 'blurred reproductions of vague childhood notions of no significance as an active and compelling force in the life of Jewish students.' With no Jewish anchor, what was to hold these young Jews in the Jewish fold? Not much. Thus, intermarriage was not the problem. It was the consequence. 'In the end, as [sociologist Marshall] Sklare has said "… the defense against intermarriage will necessarily involve a coming to terms … with what one is defending."'[29]

For all the doomsday clamour about the impact of intermarriage among American Jews, the 'Vanishing Jew' debate reverberated surprisingly little in Canada, or at least little that surfaced in mainstream Canadian Jewish community discourse. A lone exception was a sermon by Rabbi W. Gunther Plaut of Toronto's senior Reform temple, Holy

Blossom. At a Friday evening service honouring the temple's 1963 confirmation-class graduates a little more than a week after *Look*'s 'The Vanishing American Jew' was published, Rabbi Plaut delivered a two-part sermon. He first addressed his adult parishioners, warning them against thinking that Holy Blossom Temple and the Canadian Jewish community more generally were immune from slippage. Pulling much of his message from the *Look* article as if it was inclusive of Canadian Jews, Plaut called on his congregants to re-commit to Jewish values and practice as the best defence against creeping assimilation and the best way to shelter their children from intermarriage.

Turning to the children in the confirmation class, Plaut called on them to buffer themselves against assimilation by actively engaging as Jews.

> If you want to belong to the core [of Judaism] tomorrow, and you do not want to stand at the periphery, if you do not want to be drawn into the maelstrom of those who may become vanished Jews, then make it your business to stay at the core, then make it your business to continue learning, to continue practicing, and make it your business to keep your ears open to the voice of the covenant. I pray that when the accounting is done a generation from now most of you will be found to be at the core, part of the *sh'erit*.[30]

How Plaut's effort to wedge Canadian Jews into the American 'vanishing Jew' debate was received by his Friday evening congregation is unknown. From the general absence of other Canadian reverberations of the vanishing Jew debate, one would be tempted to conclude that in the early 1960s most Canadian Jews were not nearly as possessed by the twin plagues of assimilation and intermarriage as were their American cousins.

This does not mean that Canadian Jews and their leaders were unaware of the American debate. On the contrary. They knew the American Jewish community. They were very much plugged into the American and American Jewish media. There were a multiplicity of cross-border organizational links; Canadian Jewish communal leaders, educators, and rabbis, many of them American born, attended meetings and conferences with their American counterparts. Many Canadian Jews had American family and vacationed in the United States. Like Rabbi Plaut, many also read *Look Magazine*.[31] It has been commonly offered that there is no substantive difference between the Canadian and American Jewish communities, or at least none that time would not eliminate. Ca-

nadian Jews, it has often been said, are just American Jews one generation removed. If Canadian Jews prove a little more 'Jewish' than their
American cousins, if they still retain a lingering closeness to old-world
Yiddishkeit and tend to be more traditional in religious observance, all
that can be assumed as temporary. As the author of a short 1966 *Commentary* article, 'The Un-American Jew,' put it, 'To the casual observer
the Jews of Canada resemble nothing so much as a slightly underdevel-
oped extension of the sprawling Jewish community of the northeastern
United States, with one difference: they have a dated air about them
– as if they had not yet entirely moved out of the 1930s.'[32] One generation closer to their immigrant roots, Canadian Jews were said to suffer a
time lag that would pass with the passing of the immigrant generation.
And, so what if it might take a little longer for Jews to the north to melt
into the great homogenizing caldron that is America or, from that point
of view, North America? No big deal. Canadian Jews today are American Jews tomorrow or maybe the day after tomorrow. The timing may
not be exact but the destination is certain. Canadian Jews were going
to end up in the same place as American Jews. America is destiny and,
given the options, is that so bad?[33]

Bad or not, for all the shared organizational and familial contacts,
Canadian Jews simply are not, and never were, a northern franchise of
the American Jewish experience, even though distinctions between the
two Jewish communities might sometimes have eluded observers on
both sides of the border. Canadian Jews of the early 1960s were no more
American Jews running a little late than Canadians more generally were
just tardy Americans. Far from it. The Canadian Jewish community had
a character unique unto itself and whatever its destiny might be, it was
certainly not preordained that it would eventually dissolve into some
larger North American Jewish whole. That is not to say that Canadian
and American Jews do not enjoy commonalities. They do share core
Jewish interests, concerns, and values. But for all the overlapping interests and concerns, and for all the interdependence of Canadian Jewish
organizational life with that of the American Jewish community, Canadian Jewish self-definition is grounded in Canadian experience. As
Rabbi Plaut later put it, 'In many respects Canadian Jews were, indeed,
much like their American counterparts, but on closer examination they
exhibited important differences and formed a community that had its
own characteristics and played its own separate role on the stage of
world Jewish life.'[34] Asked for an example of how the distinctive Canadian Jewish character had impacted Canadian Jewish behaviour, Rabbi

Plaut has commented: 'One of the great differences between Jews in Canada and the US was that asked to describe their identity, Jews in the US would say American. In Canada they would say Jew ... It took Jews a long time in Canada to say Canadian. It took Jews in the US no time at all.' When asked why this was the case, Rabbi Plaut allowed: 'Americans in general are patriotic. Canadians in general don't know what patriotism is.'[35]

Plaut's notion that Canadian Jews saw themselves as Jews first and Canadians second smacks of the then emerging vision of Canada as a mosaic of peoples rather than, as was often said of the United States, a melting-pot nation. But to the degree that Canadian Jews presented themselves as more self-consciously 'Jewish' than their American counterparts, this may have been as much a reflection of the interior life of the Jewish community as it was of any grand multicultural national vision.

So who were these Canadian Jews? What were they like? In 1961 Canada's approximately 250,000 Jews made up less than one and a half per cent of a Canadian population then nudging the 18,000,000 mark. Encouragingly, the number of Jews was up by more than 100,000 from 1931. On the down side, the growth of the Canadian Jewish community was not keeping pace with the larger pattern of Canadian growth. While there had been a 60 per cent increase in Jewish population numbers in the preceding thirty years, the total Canadian population had grown by 85 per cent during that same period. As a result, the proportion of Jews in Canada's population fell from 1.5 per cent of the national total in 1931 to just under 1.39 per cent in 1961. It was projected to slip still further to 1.28 per cent by the end of the 1960s – not because of spiking intermarriage but because of a declining Jewish birth rate.

The prospects for any significant increase in Canadian Jewish population numbers through a rise in the Jewish birth rate were remote at best. The Jewish population in the 1960s was slightly older than the national average, and less concentrated in the childbearing years. Like American Jews, Canadian Jews as a whole were also more embracing of birth control and disposed to smaller families than their fellow citizens. In fact, Canadian Jews were fully one-third less likely than other Canadians to have more than two children. This was especially so for the growing number of more secular, economically secure, and university-educated members of the Jewish community. With the percentage of Canadian Jews entering the professions increasing and many delaying marriage until they finished professional training and successfully established themselves in business or professional practices, Jewish numbers fell victim to the inverse relationship between economic success and family size. If the Canadian Jewish community was going to depend on natural increase to stave off falling numbers, the future did not look promising.[36]

Could the Canadian Jewish community compensate for its declining birth rate through imported growth – the immigration to Canada of Jews in their child-rearing years who could pick up the demographic slack? In the past, immigration was the key to community growth. With the exception of the 1930s and the war years, since the 1880s immigration represented the single most important factor accounting for Jewish community population growth. Post-war Canada also brought a welcome renewal of Jewish immigration. Thus, while the Canadian Jewish establishment trumpeted two hundred years of continuous Jewish life in Canada, the vast majority of Jews in Canada were recent immigrants and their children. The percentage of foreign-born among Canadian Jews was beginning to decline slightly, but in 1961 fully 40 per cent of all Canadian Jews were born outside of Canada. More than half of these foreign-born Canadian Jews arrived in Canada in the years after the end of the Second World War. Together, immigrants and their first-generation, Canadian-born children dominated the Jewish street. This was reflected in Jewish language use. Almost 30 per cent of all Canadian Jews claimed Yiddish as a mother tongue, and many who did not grew up in Yiddish-speaking homes and spoke, or at least understood, the language. And in the early 1960s Yiddish was still widely spoken in homes, on the Jewish street, and in Jewish institutional settings that were largely Yiddish free in the United States. When Rabbi Gunther Plaut arrived in Toronto from Minneapolis in 1961 to become spiritual leader at Toronto's Holy Blossom Temple, one of his big surprises was to find Yiddish being spoken at Temple board meetings, something by then unimaginable in Minneapolis.[37]

However, while Canada in the early 1960s remained a major immigrant-receiving country and the immigration restrictions which had previously barred Jewish entry were gone, the flow of Jewish immigration into Canada since the arrival of approximately 37,000 largely Eastern European Holocaust survivors in the late 1940s was not large. Notable exceptions were the 4500 or so Jews among the approximately 37,000 Hungarian refugees who came to Canada following the abortive Hungarian uprising of 1956 and, beginning in 1957, a largely Montreal-bound Sephardic influx from North Africa and the Middle East, particularly that of Moroccan Jews.[38] Why were there not more Jewish immigrants coming to Canada? Because many of those Jews who might have wanted to immigrate to Canada couldn't and those who could, wouldn't. Jews denied exit from behind the Iron Curtain might dream of escape to the West, but in the early 1960s there was no way that Eastern European authorities were about to permit it. After decades of systematic Soviet repression of Jewish religious expression, there were even doubts among Western Jewish leaders as to the degree of Jewish spirit that survived in the Soviet Union and its satellite states, particularly among the young. As one Canadian Jewish leader later recalled, 'The impression was that Soviet Jewry was to be written off.'[39] Unlikely as it seemed at the time, even if the Soviet Union allowed those with some residual spark of Jewish identity to leave, would Canada benefit? Farfetched as the proposition of a Soviet Jewish exodus might have seemed in the early 1960s, there was no reason to think that, given an option, Soviet Jews would choose to come to Canada rather the United States or Israel. Canadian Jews might take pride in their country as a land of second chance, but if asked, most Canadian Jews would agree that for Eastern European Jews Canada was likely to be regarded as a land of second choice.[40]

What about the immigration of Jews from elsewhere – from Israel, the United States, France, Argentina, South Africa? Of course there were always individual Jews who might decide to immigrate to Canada, but in the early 1960s a mass immigration of Jews to Canada just wasn't in the cards. Thus, barring some unforeseen event that would spark an outflow of Jews from somewhere to Canada or an unexpected turnaround in Canadian Jewish birth trends, the Canadian Jewish community seemed to be on a path of very slow numerical decline.

With dipping Jewish immigration numbers and a declining birth rate, one might expect that Canadian Jews would feel increasingly apprehensive that the shrinking percentage of Jews in the total Canadian population would eventually jeopardize the community's survival. Certainly, Jewish communal leaders were well aware of the population trends. The Canadian Jewish Congress's Bureau of Social and Economic Research, headed by demographer Louis Rosenberg, laid out the statistical picture clearly enough.[41] Jewish communal insiders knew that the impact of slow population decline would eventually need to be addressed, but there is little evidence that the larger Canadian Jewish community was particularly concerned about any decline in Jewish numbers. Why? Several possible answers suggest themselves. One lies at the street level. In 1961 approximately 55 per cent of all Canadians lived in cities with populations of 100,000 or more. Almost 95 per cent of all Jews did. What is more, almost four out of every five Canadian Jews lived in either Montreal (103,000) or Toronto (87,000). In 1961 only three other Canadian cities were home to more than 5000 Jews: Winnipeg with approximately 19,000, Vancouver with 7500, and Ottawa with 5500. Six other cities had Jewish populations of more than 1000 – Hamilton, Calgary, Edmonton, Windsor, London, and Halifax. Thirty-three towns and cities scattered across Canada were home to between 100 and 1000 Jews.[42]

What this meant is that while there were Jews to be found in many cities and towns across Canada, the vast majority of Canadian Jews were concentrated in two urban areas, Montreal and Toronto. What is more, the very heavy concentration of Jewish population in these two cities showed no sign of lessening. Just the opposite. After Canada reopened its doors to immigration in the mid-1940s after more than a decade and a half of severe restriction, tens of thousands of Jews arrived in Canada.[43] Approximately 37,000 of them were Holocaust survivors and their overseas-born children. As a result of this inflow, by 1961 survivors constituted approximately fifteen per cent of the entire Canadian Jewish community, more than four times the proportion of Holocaust survivors in the American Jewish population and second only to Israel as a percentage of the total Jewish population. It was said that one suburban housing division in north Toronto, Bathurst Manor, had the highest residential concentration of survivors anywhere in the world. Many of these survivors arrived in Canada during their fertile years and made reconstruction of family a priority. As a result, in this era of the baby boom, not only were there more survivors who came to Canada in the post-war years than there were children born into the Canadian Jewish community, but many of these Canadian-born Jewish children were also parented by recently arrived survivors.[44]

The vast majority of survivors who arrived in Canada eventually settled in either Montreal and Toronto. These survivors were joined by other Jewish immigrants to Canada and Canadian-born Jews from smaller communities who also gravitated to Toronto and, to a lesser extent, Montreal and Vancouver. As a result, far more than was true in the United States, where Jews were shifting out of their traditional centres of population in northeastern inner cities and into often distant suburbs or even into cities in the south, southwest, and on the Pacific coast, most Canadian Jews remained remarkably rooted in place.

Where there was movement of Canadian-born Jews, it was from areas of low Jewish concentration to those of high concentration. Canadian-born Jews, particularly younger Jews from smaller towns and cities, gradually relocated in Canada's largest cities, where the urban lifestyle, expanding educational and employment opportunities, and an ethno-religious comfort zone provided by a large and thriving Jewish community proved a big draw. In the main, the young did not leave Montreal or Toronto to attend out-of-town universities. Unlike in the United States, during the early 1960s and into the early 1970s it was not regarded a right of passage for university-bound Jewish youth in Montreal or Toronto to go elsewhere, at least not at the undergraduate level. With quotas restricting Jewish university admissions now history, the University of Toronto and McGill University in Montreal – regarded as Canada's flagship universities with fine professional schools – remained first-choice Jewish-draw institutions for both locally born Jewish youth and Jews from elsewhere in Canada. Toronto's York University and Montreal's Sir George Williams (later Concordia) University also attracted goodly numbers of both Jewish students and faculty.[45] In the case of Toronto, even young Jews who left the city to attend university likely ended up at one of the new or expanding nearby universities in Waterloo, Hamilton, London, St Catharines, Peterborough, or Guelph, all within an hour or two drive of Toronto – close enough for them to make it home for Friday night dinner with family while a week's worth of dirty laundry churned in the washing machine. After graduation, it was back to Toronto for most.

What is more, not only did Canadian Jews overwhelmingly concentrate in Montreal and Toronto, but they also tended to live in close proximity to one another. Contiguous Jewish neighbourhoods backed onto one another. While these neighbourhoods might be variegated by class, time of immigration, and propensity for religious observance, as a rule of thumb Jews tended to have other Jews as neighbours. Consequently, while there was a measured decline in the proportion of Jews in Canada, the experience of Jews in Toronto and Montreal, home to 80 per cent of all Canadian Jews, was that they worked, shopped, went to school, and socialized in the company of other Jews. Thus, in the early 1960s Canadian Jews saw around their immediate selves not a decline in Jewish population numbers but growth, even if this growth was not proportional to the growth of the surrounding city or country. And in absolute numbers there was growth in these two Jewish communities. Even as the percentage of Jews in Canada was slipping, the number of Jews in Montreal and Toronto grew by 25 per cent between 1951 and 1961.[46] And while the clothing industry, the *shmata* trade, that once dominated the Jewish economic landscape in Montreal and Toronto was in decline, with off-shore imports forcing industry contraction, Jews so recently slaves to sewing machines watched with pride as their children entered business and the professions. Buoyed by economic prosperity and education, many younger Jewish families moved 'uptown' into newer and often higher-end neighbourhoods. But overall proximity of Jew to Jews continued.[47]

In Winnipeg, Canada's third largest Jewish community in 1961, with a Jewish population of approximately 19,000, Jews were also inclined towards contiguous residential huddling, even as they migrated to new neighbourhoods. And as in Montreal and Toronto, post-war affluence spurred a Jewish population shift from working-class, inner-city neighbourhoods towards newer, more prosperous outlying neighbourhoods. In the Winnipeg case there was a gradual decamping from the now-legendary immigrant North End in favour of West Kildonan further to the north or, for those with greater financial means, to south of the Assiniboine River and into River Heights and eventually into Tuxedo to the west. Whether they moved north or south, Winnipeg Jews moved away but not apart. They tended to resettle and rebuild their institutional infrastructure cheek by jowl with one another. Unlike in Montreal and Toronto, however, by the early 1960s, even as they cleaved to one another, the Winnipeg Jewish community was undergoing slow population decline, not just as a percentage of the total city population but in absolute terms as Jewish numbers began to reflect the hemorrhaging of Winnipeg Jews, particularly young adults, outward to Toronto, the United States, or further west in Canada. Winnipeg, it was said, was a great place to come from.[48]

In the early 1960s Vancouver, on the Pacific coast, was Canada's fourth-largest Jewish community. It was also somewhat anomalous among larger Canadian Jewish communities in the absence of any tightly bound Jewish neighbourhoods. The Jewish community of about 7500 was growing apace, both as a result of an in-trickle of Jewish immigration from abroad and, more substantially, from the resettlement of young Jewish singles and families from eastern Canadian and the United States. Many were attracted to Vancouver's more temperate climate, beautiful natural setting, relaxed lifestyle, and, for some perhaps, the prospect of breaking free of family and community far to the east. Those who moved to Vancouver, whatever their personal agendas, proved somewhat less inclined to settle in close proximity to other Jews than was true of the older and more established eastern Canadian Jewish communities. Even as the number of Jews in Vancouver grew steadily to about 10,000 by the end of the decade, in the area Vancouver local Jews often called the 'Borsht Belt,' home to the heaviest concentration of Jewish institutional life in Vancouver, the residential ratio of Jew to non-Jew was only about one to five. Levels of Jewish institutional affiliation were also lower in Vancouver than in other Canadian Jewish centres. While some Jews may have been happily indifferent to Jewish branding, other new arrivals suffered a sense of loss at the absence of the kind of close and institutionally intense Jewish community they had left behind.[49]

Certainly as compared to Vancouver, Jewish organizational and institutional life was thick on the ground in the areas of heavy Jewish residential convergence in Toronto, Montreal, and Winnipeg, where Jewish streetscapes reflected an extraordinarily wide array of Jewish professional, commercial, religious, and institutional activity. Jewish community social, political, religious, welfare, and social service agencies were wedged side by side with commercial businesses attending to the Jewish community's particular needs and tastes. Jewish residential concentration spawned a correspondingly dense infill of Jewish institutional life, but that institutional life also reflected the high degree of internal division and even fractiousness that characterized Canadian Jews. Of course, there were many issues on which divergent and perhaps otherwise incompatible elements of the community were able to fold together in common cause. For example, there was widespread agreement on the need to maintain a well-ordered and professional Jewish social service and welfare infrastructure, to ensure Jewish education for all those who wanted it, and to maintain the struggle against antisemitism in Canada and abroad. This took coordination and money. In the larger Jewish communities in Canada, well-oiled internal federation-style leadership structures, coordinated community fundraising, administered budgeting allocations, and set priorities for the network of Jewish social service, welfare, and educational agencies serving the community. Unlike in the United States, however, there was also wide support in Canadian Jewish communities for a single organized community political voice, especially when dealing with government and the non-Jewish community. Equally true, there was a grumbling resentment in some quarters at the influence exerted on the Canadian Jewish Congress by a thin band of community leaders, the *machers*, those regarded as having money and power enough to make their voices heard.

Who were the *machers*, the upper end of the community leadership group? No surprise. In the early 1960s Jewish community strings were being pulled by a small elite group, in the main deep-pocketed businessmen and professionals motivated by a sense of *noblesse oblige*. Often members of older and more established Jewish families, they took pride in being the founders of major synagogues and the backbone of mainstream Jewish organizations and community social service agencies. They knew one another well and tended to socialize among themselves. They had the luxury of money, connections, and time to devote to meetings and the travel demanded of those in the upper reaches of Jewish organizational life. Their children often went to private schools or, given the up-market neighbourhoods in which they could afford to live, to better public schools and expensive summer camps. While they 'ran' the community, or at least funded much of its programming and infrastructure and dominated the local and national Canadian Jewish Congress and federation-like organizations, they were often at a distance from the day-to-day struggles of a largely immigrant Jewish population, the shop workers, tradespeople, small-store owners, and their children, in whose name the *machers* claimed to speak.

None of this was a secret to the Jewish street. But since the *machers* gave the money that paid the bills, who could be surprised that they called the shots and were rewarded with wall pride, their names gracing the façades of Jewish community buildings. That did not mean the *machers* were necessarily held in the highest esteem. One is reminded of monkeys in a tree. Those at the top look down on smiling faces. Those below look up and smile at seeing so many bare asses.

Generous as the wealthier in the community might have been with their time, money, and advice, rarely were they the ones who rolled up their sleeves and dirtied their hands with all the in-tight day-to-day work necessary to ensure delivery of community programs and services. That was left to two other groups – volunteers, who were the lifeblood of the many organizations that served the community, and a growing number of paid Jewish professionals, responsible for the orderly and fiscally responsible management of community institutions and organizations. If smaller Jewish communities across Canada might only have money enough to employ a single jack-of-all-trades rabbi, larger centres might boast a small army of Jewish public servants – along with any number of rabbis, cantors, and other religious functionaries, including synagogue administrators, parochial school educators, professional fundraisers, policy advisers, and social workers – many of whom proved closer to the Jewish pulse than their lay masters and often mediated between those who spoke for the community and those in whose name they spoke. Like public servants everywhere, these community professionals were not without considerable leverage in shaping community policy priorities and service delivery.

Throughout the 1960s two interdependent organizational structures dominated national and local Canadian Jewish institutional life. The first, though functioning by different names at different times and in different locations, was what is generally referred to today as the Federation. Through to the Second World War, larger Jewish communities were characterized by a jumble of well-intentioned but often overlapping and competing Jewish social service, educational, and health agencies, many suffering from a lack of professional management and stable funding. To bring order to this chaos and end competitive fundraising and disjointed or inept service delivery, larger Jewish communities across Canada gradually cobbled together a local coordinating body – the Federation – responsible for community fundraising, overall budget allocation, and ensuring fiscal accountability in the model of the United Way.

The second major organization was the Canadian Jewish Congress, widely acknowledged as the political voice of the Canadian Jewish community. Congress was not an individual membership organization. Rather, it was an organization of organizations, an umbrella coalition that publicly represented itself as the parliament of Canadian Jews, the representative voice of the Canadian Jewish community. If the organizational structure was open and democratic in form, actual policy-making power rested, not surprisingly, with a small group of generally moneyed Congress insiders, in many cases forming an overlapping directorate with the Federation. Through much of the 1960s Montreal liquor magnate Sam Bronfman ruled at the national level. Congress national headquarters was in Montreal, with regional offices in Jewish centres across Canada. These separate offices handled more local issues, especially as related to intergroup relations, matters related to provincial jurisdiction such as education, and oversight of local pan-Jewish community events.

Sam Bronfman, Mr Sam as he was often called, had been a singularly forceful voice in national Congress affairs since he took hold of its organizational reins in the late 1930s. By the early 1960s the now elderly

Mr Sam was still prepared to toss his weight around the Congress table as he felt necessary. Day-to-day policy control of the organization, however, was increasingly devolved into the hands of a small group of lay leaders and administrative officials headed by long-time Canadian Jewish Congress executive director Saul Hayes, working out of the organization's national headquarters in Montreal. Local Congress affiliates in larger Jewish communities across Canada each had their own lay leadership group and core of paid administrators and professionals who coordinated local activities, often in consultation with the national office in Montreal.[50]

However, as smaller Jewish communities across Canada struggled to support a range of Jewish services, the single most important demographic fact of Canadian Jewish life remained the overwhelming concentration of Jews in Montreal and Toronto. If the Canadian Jewish story of the 1960s was a tale of two cities, these two cities were very different from one another. Montreal, long characterized by lines of separation between linguistic and religious groups, remained a city of boundaries – territorial boundaries, boundaries of imagination, boundaries of language, and boundaries of possibility. Montreal's Jews lived very much within their geographic, linguistic, institutional, and mind space, at once part of the larger city yet in many ways separate and distinct from others with whom they shared the same urban complex.

Toronto, by contrast, was far more fluid. By the early 1960s the lines that once separated the Anglo-Protestant majority from others were blurring and the rules of Jewish engagement with the larger non-Jewish world were more open for negotiation. For Jewish leaders in Toronto, concern was less with working within fixed boundaries than it was with probing accessibility. As a result, many of the issues which occupied Jews in Montreal, both as individuals and as a community, were distinctly different from those of Toronto. Indeed, the two major Canadian Jewish populations did not always share a common understanding of their place in the surrounding urban complex or their options for the future. Differences in mindset and points of reference sometimes even coloured approaches to areas of concern which the two communities shared, such as support of Jewish immigrant integration and strategies for combating antisemitism.

Just as there were differences in tone and texture between the two major Jewish population centres in Canada, there was also internal discord within these two large Jewish communities. How could it be otherwise? Jews might live in close proximity to one another and local

Canadian Jewish Congress officials might claim to speak for the entire community, but that did not mean that all Jews saw eye to eye on all things at all times. There was much truth to the adage 'two Jews, three political parties.' If there was any Canadian Jewish political rule of thumb it was that if something could create discord, it did. Times were generally good, however, and arguably the majority of Canadian Jews, reserving the right to grumble about the state of Jewish leadership, were usually content to get on with their lives and leave political bickering to others. But for many committed and community-active Jews, fractiousness seemed a Jewish way of life. And fractiousness was seldom hard to find. Even as Jewish leaders preached unity of purpose, translated by some to mean 'Don't rock the community boat,' Canadian Jews were divided among themselves on any number of social, cultural, economic, generational, religious, and political issues. There were also telling differences in world view between Zionists, non-Zionists, and even anti-Zionists, over levels of support for Israel and modes of Jewish civil engagement with the larger society. And, in spite of the prominence of a moneyed elite, who, if anyone, had the authority to speak on behalf of the entire Jewish community? More often than not the popular answer was 'no one.' One recalls the story of the Jew cast away on a desert island who spends his time reconstructing the Jewish neighbourhood of his youth. When a ship arrives to rescue him, the castaway takes the ship's captain on a tour of his creation. As they finish the tour the captain, marvelling at all the castaway built, asks but one question. Why, when the Jew has built one of everything – one school, one butcher shop, one bakery, one doctor's office, one travel agency, one restaurant – has he built two synagogues? 'Very simple,' said the castaway. 'One synagogue I pray in. The other I wouldn't be caught dead in.'

While there were divisions aplenty, there were also areas of agreement. This was particularly so on the need to confront and combat antisemitism. But even on this key issue there was a core divide over priorities and tactics. On one side there were those, especially in the Jewish establishment, who advocated a moderate and incremental approach to solving the problem of antisemitism – working with like-minded groups, opinion leaders, educators, and the media to educate and lobby government for legislative remedies and, to whatever degree possible, avoiding the politics of confrontation. On the other side were those more at a distance from the Jewish establishment – including those identified with immigrant and Yiddishist groups and those with a more radical bent – who chafed at what they regarded as the Jewish establishment's 'cap in hand' *sha shtil* (hush hush) approach to combating antisemitism.. They favoured more direct action to deal with antisemitism and antisemites, which might include in-your-face confrontation, protest, and boycotts. In the early 1960s the still-moderate establishment held sway, but not without activists nipping at their heels. Open discord was generally kept in check by a self-censoring Jewish fear that hanging dirty community laundry out in public, a *shandeh far di goyim*, would only give comfort to those who wished the Jews ill. Acquiescence was not the same as accord, a truth that establishment Jewish leaders would soon learn.

Nevertheless, through the early 1960s, it is easy to conclude, the moneyed governed and the governed bickered. Certainly, if Congress did not have an entirely free hand in community governance, it and its more moderate and moneyed leadership did present themselves as the becalmed public face of the Jewish community. But as with the calm before the storm, below the surface were many often churning currents of political, religious, and social discord that gave the Canadian Jewish community an unsettled character. How long the established leadership's rule would go unchallenged and what issues might generate revolt from below remained to be seen. Of course, to Jews the presence in the community of alternative voices, even those pushing in diametrically opposite directions from one another, is hardly new. It may even be argued that, rather than indicating community weakness, early 1960s communal squabbling was a sign of Jewish community strength, a sign that Jews cared about things Jewish and, indeed, cared enough about things Jewish to argue with one another about what was important to them.

But this still begs the question of why, with so much intra-community debate going on within the Canadian Jewish community, there was so little reverberation from the American 'vanishing Jew' debate? In its article celebrating two hundred years of Jewish community life in Canada, *Maclean's* rubbed up against the American debate. The article pointedly asked whether success in overcoming antisemitism and the prospect of increased Jewish integration or assimilation into the Canadian mainstream would inevitably come at the cost of Canadian Jewish particularism, even survival as a distinct community within Canada. Would it, as in the United States, pave the way for a sharp rise in the numbers of intermarriages, a prospect many Canadian Jewish families would not welcome?

Perhaps one answer is that in Canada in the early 1960s, unlike in the United States, any discussion along these lines was hypothetical. Intermarriage, if not unknown, was hardly an everyday occurrence in Canadian Jewish circles. In Montreal, intermarriage in 1960 between a born Jew and someone not born Jewish and who had not converted to Judaism stood at less than 4 per cent of all marriages involving a Jew. It was only a little higher in Toronto. Thus, with approximately 80 per cent of all Jews living in Montreal and Toronto, the intermarriage rate among Canadian Jews in the early 1960s was but a fraction of that then confronting American Jews.[51] Admittedly, the intermarriage rate was high in the smaller Jewish centres of western and Atlantic Canada, where the pool of potential Jewish partners was limited. In Vancouver, for example, in the early 1960s about one in every eight Jews was marrying out. Even so, according to a Vancouver community leader, it was not entry into marriage with a non-Jew that in and of itself drew the Jewish partner, most often male, out of the Jewish fold. More often than not, he argued, the Jewish partner was already well removed from community before the marriage took place. Intermarriage was just a final step out the door.

> My personal observation is that intermarriage results in a net numerical loss to the Jewish community. While it is true that a number of non-Jews, almost entirely women, have come into the Jewish fold, following up a conversion ceremony with actual participation in Jewish life, the majority, in my opinion, including their mates, were either on the fringe of the Jewish community or outside it altogether. The next question is: Is intermarriage a cause or an effect of lack of interest in and identification with Jewish life. I am inclined to think that many of the men who intermarry have been all but lost to the Jewish community and intermarriage is a further step in the direction they have chosen to take.[52]

Perhaps so. But if marrying out was a final rather than a first step in removing one's self from the Jewish community, what was the first step and where was it taken? In the United States, as noted, many Jewish leaders felt one need look no further than American universities to find the incubator of intermarriage. The campus, they warned, offered a rarified atmosphere far from the constraints of family and conducive to personal experimentation. It was here that young Jewish students, without a cocooning Jewish family and community, were exposed 'to new ideas and contacts with people of different races, cultures, and religions with a loss of intellectual rigidity, parochialism and ethnocentrism and, therefore, a greater readiness for intermarriage.' As more and more American Jewish youth packed off to university in the early 1960s, the temptation to taste of forbidden fruit was only going to get stronger.[53]

Canada again was different. It was not that the temptation of biting into the forbidden apple was not there. Rather, as noted, the Jewish presence on the Canadian campus was of a different order than in the United States. With most university-bound Jewish youth staying in Montreal or Toronto, and Jewish youth from smaller Canadian centres, where opportunities to interact with a large Jewish peer group were limited, also gravitating towards Montreal or Toronto, for most Canadian Jewish university-age youth, 1960s campus life often represented less a rupture with home, friends, and Jewish community than was true in the United States. What is more, for those from smaller Canadian Jewish communities, going to university in Montreal or Toronto meant not a lessening but an intensification of Jewish contact. University College at the University of Toronto had more Jewish students than there were Jews in many of the smaller towns from which out-of-town Jewish students had come. If American Jewish parents might have reason for concern about how their children's Jewish sense of self might be eroded on campus and their social context become increasingly non-Jewish, Canadian Jewish parents could hope that big-city Canadian university life might serve as a Jewish dating service enabling their daughters to come away with both a BA and a Mrs. What is more, following graduation it was not unusual for Jews from small-town Canada to stay in Montreal or Toronto, build a career, and establish a family within the Jewish community, and for their parents to trail after them.[54]

Of course, Jews are Jews. No matter how positive their present reality, there was always room for worry about the Jewish future. Among American Jews in the early 1960s, that took the form of the 'vanishing Jew' debate. But it may be a burden of Jewish history that every generation of Jews has to ask themselves if they are the last committed Jewish generation, that those who come next will somehow be less Jewish, less Jewishly committed, and less determined to ensure that their own children will engage as Jews. In some ways this worry is also a measure of community strength. According to Brandeis University professor Simon Rawidowicz's often quoted 1948 essay 'Israel: The Ever Dying People,' so long as there are Jews who are convinced that their generation of Jews is the last in the Jewish line, then there will be committed Jewish life.

> Such a Jewish realism will also show us the real meaning of that fear of the end that is so inherent in us. A people dying for thousands of years means a living people. Our incessant dying means uninterrupted living, rising, standing up, beginning anew. We, the last Jews! Yes, in many respects it seems to us as if we are the last links in a particular chain of tradition and development. But if we are the last – let us be the last as our fathers and forefathers were. Let us prepare the ground for the last Jews who will come after us, and for the last Jews who will rise after them, and so on until the end of days.[55]

For Canadian Jewish communal leaders in the early 1960s, Rawidowicz's sense of 'inherent' Jewish fear for the future translated not so much into debate about slippage through intermarriage, as was the case in the United States, but into worries about whether the next generation of Canadian Jews, the post-immigration and post-Holocaust generation, would feel as deeply about their Jewish connection to community as did their parents. Addressing the challenge facing Jewish youth in a prosperous and welcoming 1960s Canada, a 1966 article over the signature of Canadian Jewish Congress board chairman Sam Bronfman called for a recommitment to Jewish values.

> In this milieu we have the difficulties of keeping our third generation interested in Jewish values. We must work hard at preserving our heritage. No blueprint is possible but all resources of the community, from the national to the most minute of local ones, must play their part by producing elements of strong Jewish life. If this is done, these are the guarantees of survival.
>
> In Canada, the Jews are, and always will be, a small minority group of persons individually integrated into the social, economic and political life of the country while as a group they strive to retain their religious and cultural identify in a democracy which permits them to worship and to live their lives in accordance with their traditions and religious principles. Our survival as Jews necessitates the maintenance of our cultural and religious identity as a group in an active and vital form.
>
> We have reached the stage when scattered and fragmented efforts alone – no matter how sincerely motivated and ably made – cannot be relied

upon to meet the needs of Canada's Jewish population. We can survive and continue to develop as Jews only by deliberate choice and not merely through the accident of birth and environment.[56]

If Bronfman was warning that the emerging generation of Canadian Jews was dangerously light on commitment to Jewishness, his concern would prove misplaced. Barely had he affixed his signature to the article than the Canadian Jewish world was convulsed by a cascade of events that would engage Canadian Jews as Jews in ways they could not have previously imagined. The results would remake the Jewish agenda and redefine what it meant to be a Canadian Jew and a Jew in Canada. Two hundred years after Jews first settled in Canada, that drama would be scripted largely as a tale of two cities – two very different cities.

CHAPTER TWO

A Third Solitude

It was a simple coincidence. During the bicentenary year of the Canadian Jewish community in 1959, Maurice Duplessis, the conservative and aristocratic premier of Quebec, died. Over fifteen years Duplessis successfully led his Union Nationale Party to five consecutive electoral victories. Ruthless in dealing with opponents, the life-long bachelor dominated Quebec through a period of unprecedented economic expansion. An outspoken champion of conservative Catholic values, Duplessis was privately known to brag that he had the Church in his pocket and it was comfortable there. While some remember the Duplessis era as one of 'social stability' and prosperity, others recall his years in office as *les années noires*, dark years that stifled progressive change and denied Quebec the machinery of a modern state even as Duplessis gladly ceded control of Quebec's natural resources to the highest bidder. Critics decried his iron-fisted rule, his intolerance of opposition voices, demonstrated disdain for individual human rights, and willingness to ignore craven corruption by his officials.

Duplessis's passing lifted a heavy stone off the back of long-overdue reform. A period of public mourning had barely ended before Quebec was caught up in a wave of social, economic, and political change that has come to be known as the Quiet Revolution. Of course Duplessis's death did not go unnoticed among Montreal Jews. If not greeted with dancing in the streets, there were likely few Jews who shed a tear at the premier's passing. He and his government were hardly regarded as friendly to the Jewish community. To the contrary. At best, the Duplessis regime was seen as distant and disengaged from issues that mattered to the Jewish community, even in areas of provincial jurisdiction such as the delivery of education and social services. At worst, many in the Montreal Jewish community were concerned that Duplessis and his government were tainted by antisemitism, and the less the Jewish community had to deal with the provincial government the better. Few expected this to change with Duplessis's passing. The vast majority of Jews in Quebec lived in Montreal, and as far as most were concerned, their Montreal world was in a different universe from the rest of the province.

Montreal was in many ways as much at odds with the rural Quebec Duplessis claimed to hold dear as it was unique within Canada. How so? To honour the centennial of Canadian confederation, in February 1967 the *Toronto Daily Star* published a supplement entitled *Century 1867–1967: The Canadian Saga*. Among the many articles in the supplement was one entitled 'Montreal Confessions' by Toronto-based, but Montreal-born, journalist Peter Desbarats. As if lusting after a lost love, Desbarats gushed passion for Montreal. 'I love this city,' he declared. There is none other like it in Canada. 'Where is the comparison? Halifax and Quebec City have character. Toronto, recently and strangely, a kind of bounce. Vancouver has the sea and mountains, a kohinoor setting occupied by a chunk of paste. The others are hesitant proposals for cities.' But Montreal, he declared, was in a class all its own. 'Montreal is sensual.' According to Desbarats, the source of that pulsing sensuality was the city's deeply ingrained tradition of Catholicism. Even as Desbarats acknowledged the Quiet Revolution was eroding the historical power of the Church in Montreal and Quebec, 'Catholicism,' he argued, 'gave Montreal the gift of sinfulness. Other Canadian cities in other provinces received a Protestant tradition of puritanism. Montreal was blessed with a religious current of warmth, color, drama, and suffering – a sensual religion which emphasized not the cold virtues of self-denial but the sensual delights of confession and repentance.'

Of course Desbarats did not deny that Montreal was also a twentieth-century city, a burgeoning city of ramrod glass and steel skyscrapers, sprawling suburbs, street hockey, and up-market cafés, a city increasingly acclaimed 'a "grand dame" of international society.' But, according to Desbarats, if Montreal was a 'grand dame' she was not a Victorian prude. She had an earthiness about her and enjoyed both earthy pleasures and playing the role of tart. 'Beneath the mink stole, she still cherishes the old bawdy.' Nor was this bawdiness reserved to Catholic Montreal. Desbarats suggested this same bawdiness explains something of what he regarded as the characteristically gritty quality in Montreal Jewish life.

There might even be a relationship between this Catholicism and the creativity of the Jewish community in Montreal. This is the only Canadian city where European Jews, particularly those from eastern Europe, were surrounded by a familiar European Catholicism complete, at rare times, with an element of conscious anti-Semitism. Is this why the Jewish writers, poets and artists of Montreal are among the best in Canada, because their fathers did *not* celebrate Brotherhood Week at the local Rotary Club?[1]

Did Desbarats capture something of the inner essence of Montreal and Montreal's Jewish community? Maybe. Certainly, in the absence of any notion of integration into what was still a French Catholic–dominated Montreal, the Montreal Jewish community of the early 1960s, cast back on itself, pulsed with a vibrant cultural and intellectual life of its own. What is more, as the Quiet Revolution seized the province, many Jews in Montreal continued to see themselves as a people apart. How could it be otherwise? In a Quebec where talk of 'two solitudes,' one English speaking the other French, increasingly defined public debate, the majority of Montreal Jews, English speaking though they might be, regarded themselves a 'third solitude.' Certainly, life in Montreal dictated that Jews would engage with French Canadians. After all, they shared the same civil space and there were important if often low-key efforts at opening avenues to dialogue between Jews and French Canadians.[2] But, for the most part, Jews in Quebec and French Canadians continued to view one another from opposite sides of a wall built of historical, linguistic, religious, and institutional difference. Nor was this the only wall that divided Montreal Jews from others. Montreal Jews also felt cordoned off from an economically dominant, English-speaking and Protestant establishment widely regarded as tainted by deep-seated antipathy to Jews, which was returned in kind. Thus, Montreal Jews understood themselves as forming a separate estate not just from French Canadians but from other English-speaking Montrealers, an estate Mordecai Richler described as 'an almost self contained world. Outside of business there was minimal contact with Gentiles.'[3] The intuited lines of demarcation, boundaries that separated Montreal's Jews from other English speakers, were as clearly fixed in the Montreal Jewish mind of the early 1960s as they had been for decades. They might just as well have been chalked in the street. And in some ways they were. In 1969 Mordecai Richler published *The Street*, an ode to Saint Laurent Boulevard, or 'the Main' as it was commonly known, the central artery of Montreal's Jewish immigrant-receiving neighbourhood through the post-war years. But the Main was more than a street. According to Richler, it was also a boundary separating the Montreal Jewish world from the world of others.

> If the Main was a poor man's street, it was also a dividing line. Below, the French Canadians. Above, some distance above, the dreaded WASP. On the Main itself there were some Italians, Yugoslavs and Ukrainians, but they did not count as true gentiles. Even the French Canadians, who were our enemies, were not entirely unloved. Like us, they were poor and coarse with large families and spoke English badly.[4]

But Montreal Jews were not so isolated as to be immune to the political, economic, and social main event then unfolding around them. The death of Duplessis in 1959 unleashed powerful convulsions in the long rivalry between the French Catholic and English Protestant communities in Quebec and Montreal in particular. The Quiet Revolution would also shake the Jewish community of Montreal, and as the then centre of Canadian Jewish gravity, what impacted the Montreal Jewish community reverberated through the entire Canadian Jewish community. In 1959, when Duplessis died, the Montreal Jewish community was home to approximately 100,000 Jews, the largest such community in Canada. The community had a strong and active institutional infrastructure supported in part through the generosity of a wealthy Jewish 'family compact' dominated in the post-war years by Sam Bronfman.[5] Nobody else in the Montreal Jewish community could come close to Bronfman in wealth or, some might argue, ego and yearning for respectability. But while Richler might argue otherwise, even as an aging Bronfman continued to tower over the community through the early 1960s, much of the energetically 'coarse' – *grob* – character of life on the Main that Richler portrayed was sliding into history, as more and more Jews moved out of the immigrant, working-class inner city to green-lawned and middle-class Montreal suburbs.

Moving off the Main, however, did not necessarily erase the boundaries that separated Jews from the other two solitudes. Jews moved but the boundaries persisted.[6] Nor were these boundaries exclusively those of neighbourhood, faith, or language. Jews knew full well they were also subject to boundaries, formal and informal, denying them access to much of Montreal's and Quebec's educational, political, and corporate sectors. Rare was the Montreal Jew, no matter how wealthy, educated, or culturally accomplished, who did not know exactly where he or she was welcome and where not. McGill University, an institutional crown jewel in English-speaking Montreal, had only recently done away with restrictive quotas limiting the number of Jewish admissions. It was widely speculated that this was less out of a desire to ensure that McGill grant access to the best possible students than out of a desire to attract deep-pocketed Jewish donors. All the while elite social clubs still routinely barred Jewish membership – encouraging moneyed Jews to establish their own thick-carpeted variations. Broad sectors of Montreal's and Quebec's corporate world and government administration were also understood to still be no-go zones for Jews. Everyone knew it. That's the way it had been and that's the way it was. As former McGill professor Ruth Wisse put it, Montreal's social context was so religiously and linguistically polarized that 'Jews were forced back on one another.' Assimilation was not an issue in Montreal because, as Wisse noted, 'there was no place to assimilate to.'[7] Richler made much the same point in reverse. With regard to relations with the other solitudes, he noted, 'as long as the English and French were going at each other they left us alone.'[8]

Making a virtue of separation, Montreal Jews demonstrated a remarkable aptitude for community building and economic engagement. The Second World War and the boom which marked the post-war era afforded ample economic elbow room for those with entrepreneurial skills or professional training. Often working in niche Jewish economic sectors such as clothing manufacture or relying on a Jewish client base as a platform on which to build, many individuals did well. According to Manny Batshaw, a long-time senior Jewish community official, as the Depression faded into memory, Montreal Jews successfully constructed a socially and culturally self-contained, 'cohesive and committed' Jewish community.[9] Sociologist Morton Weinfeld agrees. If necessity dictated that Montreal Jews be a third solitude, that solitude was vibrant and warmly embracing. There might be some who felt it was too embracing, even smothering, but for most Montreal Jews, Weinfeld contends, there was a reassuring sense of belonging, a sense of being at home, a sense that if left to do its own thing, the Jewish community would do fine.[10]

Much as the Montreal Jewish community might be pridefully self-contained, it was certainly not internally monolithic. In the early 1960s the community was characterized by a rich diversity of social, religious, and political expression. Right, left, centre. Zionist, non-Zionist. Observant, not so observant, and secular. Uptown, downtown. Yiddish speaking, English speaking, and with the arrival of North African Jews, Arabic and French speaking. They were all there and so were organizational structures that paralleled this diversity. So too were community-wide organizations and social agencies. Montreal's Jewish Public Library was one of the better libraries in the city. The YMHA was a hub of social and athletic activity. Montreal's full-service Jewish General Hospital, modern seniors' facility, and Jewish day school system compared favourably with any in North America.[11]

Montreal's Jewish community in the early 1960s was also unique in North America in its intake of thousands of Sephardic immigrants, Jews from North Africa and the Arab Middle East. Through the previous decade, the gradual crumbling of French imperial dreams in North Africa set off a trickling outflow of Jews from French-administered territories. The initial destination of preference for most of these Jews was either France or Israel. But Moroccan independence in 1956 and a violent insurrection against French rule in Algeria caused a more panicked outflow of Jews. The organized Canadian Jewish community successfully negotiated with Ottawa for the admission of Jews from former French North Africa. In 1957 the first of an estimated 11,000 French-speaking North African Jews, mostly from Morocco, began arriving in Montreal. During the next few years, still more Sephardic Jews arrived in Montreal from North Africa, Iraq, and elsewhere in the Middle East.

Jewish social service agencies in Montreal reached out to the new arrivals, but the integration and settlement of Sephardic newcomers did not always go smoothly, not in the view of the immigrants or of Montreal's mainstream Jewish leadership. Certainly, in the early stages of the Sephardic inflow, the prevailing view within the established Jewish community was that newly arrived Moroccan Jews would be best served by quickly integrating themselves into the larger Montreal English-speaking Jewish context. But many early arrivals, disproportionately young and single Moroccan Jewish men, found little place for themselves in the predominantly middle-class, English-speaking, and European-origin Montreal Jewish community. More than that, many of the early-arrived North African Jewish single men felt the Jewish mainstream looked down on them, devaluing their traditions and culture as 'primitive' and best discarded. An early sign of distance between the newly arrived Jews and the Jewish majority was that many of these young men sought out the company of French-speaking Montrealers rather than their English-speaking co-religionists. Considering they were often detached from family, ill at ease among English-speaking

Montreal Jews, and without Sephardic organizational connections or rabbinic oversight, the results might have been predicted. There was a spike in intermarriages between Sephardic Jewish men and French Canadian women, much to the shock of many in a Montreal Jewish community where intermarriage was still uncommon. Thus, in the first years after the new immigration began, social contact between immigrants and the larger Jewish community was minimal. It wasn't that the two groups were talking past one another. It was that they were barely talking at all.[12]

As more Sephardic women and family units began arriving in Montreal, not only did the Sephardic community grow stronger; so too did its commitment to its religious, familial, communal, and linguistic heritage. Rather than integrate into the mainstream Jewish community, the newly arrived French-speaking Sephardic Jews tended to cleave to one another. And if new arrivals might turn to established Jewish social agencies for social and economic assistance, they otherwise kept their distance from the community mainstream. And the more Jewish officials attempted to guide the Sephardim towards the community mainstream – to make 'them' into 'us' – the more the Sephardim began to organize their own institutional structures.[13]

Some established Jewish leaders quietly grumbled that North Africans were all take and no give. They were over-represented as clients of Jewish social service agencies, but under-represented when it came to contributing to mainstream Jewish communal activities and fundraising efforts. Some Jewish leaders even worried that a Sephardic 'we-are-different' attitude smacked of French separatism. If push came to shove, some wondered, where would these French-speaking North African Jewish arrivals line up in the French-English debate then heating up in Quebec?

For all the unease, miscues, feelings of distance, and mutual mistrust between the mainstream English-speaking Jewish community and the new arrivals, a strong Sephardic community gradually took root in Montreal. What is more, it finally dawned on leaders of the established Jewish community that the immigrant integration process that had well served post-war European Jewish immigration to Montreal was not necessarily adaptable to the North Africans and other Sephardic immigrants. A new model was needed. That model was parallelism. With cooperation and financial assistance from a mainstream Jewish community ready to try something new, a resourceful Sephardic leadership cohort began to emerge and, where appropriate, a parallel Sephardic

institutional infrastructure took shape. Jewish social agencies restruc-
tured their programs so as to better complement the cultural needs and
sensitivities of the growing Sephardic community. And as that community developed a strengthened sense of communal place and identity in
Montreal, so too did Sephardim begin inching their way into a more active role in shaping the larger Jewish communal agenda. If intra-Jewish
relations were seldom without strain, there was little doubt that growth
of a strong Sephardic presence in Montreal provided a shot in the arm
to Jewish numbers and gave the Montreal Jewish community a distinctive Sephardic flavour unknown in the rest of Canada.[14]

As Jewish leaders knew only too well, assisting in the settlement of
immigrants, maintaining the extensive Jewish institutional and social
service infrastructure, including educational and welfare agencies, as
well as assisting overseas Jews in distress, cost money. As a result, fundraising was an omnipresent Jewish community enterprise. By definition, active engagement in the Jewish community meant self-taxing
in support of that community. This was especially so for the moneyed
Jewish elite. In this regard, Montreal Jews were blessed with a number
of families with imposing wealth who were deeply committed to community and ready to reach into their pockets as necessary.

The Bronfmans, the Brahman family of the Montreal and larger Canadian Jewish community, led the family compact. Head of the family
Sam Bronfman was a man of enormous wealth ready to dig into his
pocket if he was convinced it was for the good of the community. He
was also ready to lean on others to ante up. Such was Bronfman's power in the Jewish community that few dared refuse. In the early 1960s his
fingerprints were everywhere, and little of import took place in the upper reaches of the organized Jewish community in Montreal or Canada
that was not first run by Mr Sam. One long-time Jewish community
public servant described Bronfman as 'president of almost everything.'
In the Montreal Jewish community, Mr Sam and those he anointed
ruled.[15]

What was their fiefdom? Through the efforts of an engaged moneyed elite and a committed Montreal Jewish rank and file, the city's
Jewish community entered the 1960s a self-contained urban village,
remarkably complete in institutional structure. But no matter how self-
sufficient, there was no sealing off the Montreal community from
events impacting the larger Montreal, Quebec, and Canadian polities.
In the early 1960s those polities were increasingly torn by divisions
over language and, by extension, Quebec's place in Canada. But in

ways peculiar to Montreal and Quebec, language debate – debate over the respective places of French and English – was inseparable from issues of history, law, identity, and religious particularism. And just as the English and French languages had legal status in Quebec, so too did faith groups. And while individual religious practice might be a matter of choice, religious-group affiliation – Catholic, Protestant, and, for that matter, Jewish – had immediate implications in matters of law, delivery of social services, education, and, in one important area, voting rights.

Nowhere did all these pieces lock together more tightly for Jews in Montreal during the early 1960s than with regard to the hot-button issue of education. This was not new. The school question had long vexed Montreal Jewish community relations with non-Jews – so much so that no true understanding of the Montreal Jewish condition in the 1960s is possible without reference to the historical roots of the school issue. Oddly, seeds of the Jewish educational problem were sown in the absence of any significant Jewish presence. During the Confederation debates of the 1860s, agreement on the political union of separate British colonies in North America to form Canada was threatened by disagreements over education. The French Catholic leadership in what would become the province of Quebec were concerned that should education be made a responsibility of any proposed national government it would threaten French-Canadian religious, cultural, and linguistic survival in any larger Anglo-Protestant and English-speaking Canada. But if education was made an exclusive provincial responsibility, might that not erode the educational interests of Protestants in what would become Quebec? How would their religious and linguistic integrity be protected from the province's larger French-speaking Catholic majority? For that matter, what of the educational concerns of Catholics in Ontario, where Protestants were in the majority?

As part of the grand compromise necessary to ensure a positive buy-in on Confederation among Catholics and Protestants in Quebec and Ontario, article 92 of the British North America Act assigned education as an exclusive provincial responsibility. However, the deal also solidified the right of Protestants in Quebec, and Catholics in Ontario, to separate religious education. As a result, two separate and distinct confessional-based and publicly funded school systems were set up in Quebec, one Protestant, the other Catholic. Oversight of each school system was entrusted, not to a provincial educational bureaucracy, but to Quebec Catholic and Protestant authorities. The two parallel confessional systems were funded through school taxes collected from Protestant and Catholic property ratepayers and assigned to their respective school systems. As if to underscore religious control over matters of education in the province, the government of Quebec did not set up a department of education.

At the time of Confederation this grand compromise seemed reasonable enough. With responsibility for delivery of education in Quebec assigned to Catholic and Protestant groups, each system was sheltered from religious erosion at the hands of the other. Of course, not all French speakers in Quebec were Catholic or all English speakers Protestant, but the language divide closely paralleled that of faith. As a result, the Catholic school system was overwhelmingly French and the Protestant English. But because the demarcation line between the two systems was religion rather than language, the Catholic system found itself responsible for servicing the educational needs of English-speaking Catholics in Quebec, many of whom traced their roots back to the Irish-famine migration of the late 1840s and 1850s. Accordingly, where English-speaking Catholic numbers warranted, Catholic school authorities established English-language schools. This created a culturally and linguistically bifurcated Catholic system in areas of English-Catholic concentration. Ironically, just as French-speaking Catholics looked to education as a defence against the assimilative threat of a larger English-speaking Canada, so too English-speaking Catholics in Quebec guarded their educational autonomy within the Catholic educational system so as to ensure that their children would not be assimilated wholesale into French-speaking Quebec.[16]

What the Confederation compromise on religion and education had not envisioned was Jews. The arrival of large numbers of Eastern European Jews in Montreal in the several decades straddling the turn of the century created a problem. Where would Jewish children go to school? All agreed that Jewish children needed to be schooled, but since Jews by definition were neither Protestant nor Catholic, they remained outside the educational and religious compromises that underpinned the Confederation agreement. Setting up a third publicly funded school system – a Jewish system – was not in the cards. So what was to be done? Jewish children could not be left wandering the streets. They had to be assigned to one of the two existing confessionally based systems. Protestant school board officials in Montreal were not overjoyed at the prospect of a wholesale intake of Jewish children, but they were less negative about it than the Catholic school board. Thus, for lack of a workable alternative, the education of Jewish children fell to the English-language Protestant schools. In 1903 the provincial government, in a legislative sleight of hand, officially proclaimed that for purposes of education Jewish children would henceforth be considered Protestants and school taxes collected from Jews would be assigned to Protestant schools. As Jewish school-tax dollars flowed into Protestant school board coffers, Jewish children streamed into the English-language Protestant schools, cementing their future as English speakers.[17]

For both the growing immigrant Jewish community in Montreal and Montreal Protestant school administrators, slotting Jewish children into Protestant schools proved less a solution to a problem than the trading of one problem for another. The mandate of Protestant school boards was not simply to operate schools but to operate schools permeated by Protestant values. Jews were not Protestants and didn't want to be turned into Protestants. As the proportion of Jews in the Montreal Protestant schools climbed to more than 40 per cent of total board enrolment by the early 1920s, Protestant authorities felt compromised. In Montreal neighbourhoods with heavily Jewish population concentrations, the Protestant character of neighbourhood schools was not only threatened, it was obliterated. How was it possible to dispense meaningful Christian religious teaching in schools where almost all the students were Jews, where parents were derisive of all efforts at Protestant religious instruction, some petitioning that their children be exempted from these studies, and where students not exempted were happy to turn classroom religious instruction into a joke? The whole arrangement made a mockery of Protestant schools.

It was not just that Protestant school authorities, intent on ensuring the Protestant nature of their schools, faced off against Jewish parents and students intent on treating the schools as non-confessional public schools. There was also growing Jewish resentment that Protestant schools – even those with predominantly Jewish student populations – refused to hire qualified Jews as teachers. To make matters still worse, although school taxes collected from Jews were assigned to Protestant school boards, Jews were denied the right to vote in Protestant school board elections, let alone stand for election to these boards. Jews grumbled that Protestant boards regarded Jewish money as kosher but Jews not.[18]

In the 1930s, as a possible way of resolving these problems, some in the Montreal Jewish community suggested that the Quebec government might welcome the idea of setting up a separate Jewish school board in Montreal on a par with Catholic and Protestant boards. In

a single stroke this promised to eliminate friction over education between Jewish and Protestant Montrealers while affirming the centrality
of confession-based education in Quebec. On paper it was also cash
neutral. Financing the proposed Jewish board was simply a matter of
redirecting Jewish tax dollars away from the Montreal Protestant board
to the new Jewish board. The provincial government at first flirted with
the notion, but it soon ran into resistance from several different quarters. First, there was the sudden realization on the part of the Montreal
Protestant school authorities that, for all the difficulties in accommodat-
ing Jewish students in the Protestant system, the possible withdrawal
of more than one in three students from Protestant schools, along with
the Jewish tax dollars they represented, would effectively hobble the
Protestant system in Montreal. The wholesale exit of Jewish students
would leave the Protestant system with the unwelcome choice of either
paying to maintain a number of largely empty schools or closing some
schools and reassigning Protestant schoolchildren living in predominantly Jewish neighbourhoods to more distant schools, or even selling
off school properties. The board would also find itself with a pool of
excess teachers it would have to let go. Hard as it was to live with Jews
in its schools, it was going to be harder to live without them.

If Protestant school board officials were troubled at the prospect of a
parallel Jewish system, Catholic Church officials would not hear of it.
The notion that the Quebec provincial government – a government the
Church looked to as a defender of Catholic faith and values – would consider establishing a Jewish school board in parallel with existing Catholic and Protestant boards – in effect granting Judaism equivalent status
with Catholicism – was anathema to the Church hierarchy. Whether its
position was grounded in theology or entrenched Church antisemitism
or both, the Church adamantly rejected the idea of Jews and their religion being accorded state-recognized equality with Catholicism.

Nor were all Montreal Jews unanimous in support of a separate, publicly funded Jewish school board. Among 'uptown' establishment Jews
there was fear that any separate and popularly elected Montreal Jewish
board would be out of their control. Instead, it would likely become the
preserve of the more recently arrived Yiddish-speaking and often left-
leaning 'downtown' elements of the community, who were in the majority. And what would these 'downtown' Jews make of their schools?
What, some feared, would prevent them from turning these schools
into a Yiddishist, working-class educational ghetto that made a virtue
out of the very same old-world parochialism many 'uptown' Jews prid-

ed themselves on having escaped. Certainly, few if any 'uptown' Jews would gladly have their children attend such schools. And what about funding for these Jewish schools? There was an uncomfortable realization among 'uptown' Jews that if all school tax dollars collected from Montreal Jews were streamed to the proposed Jewish school board, their tax dollars would make up a disproportionate amount of the Jewish board's budget. In effect, their money would sustain a school system they would not control, would not want their children to attend, and certainly did not want to fund through their taxes.[19]

Hit by opposition from three sides, the provincial government soon lost interest in the proposition. For better or worse, Jewish children would stay in the Protestant school system and Jewish school taxes would continue to finance Protestant boards. In hopes of smoothing out points of friction, the provincial government enacted legislation establishing not an elected Jewish school board but an appointed Jewish School Commission of Montreal to advise the Protestant school board on issues of Jewish concern. To guard against renewed pressure for a separate Jewish board, the appointed commission was heavily representative of the 'uptown' Jews. And to further ensure that the commission could not itself turn into a forum for advocating a separate Jewish school board, the government 'limited its powers' to negotiating and monitoring 'contracts' with regard to the education of Jewish children in Montreal and suburban Outremont schools, which together then served the majority of the province's Jewish students.

For their part, Montreal and Outremont Protestant school board officials, also hoping to put the idea of a separate Jewish school board to rest, signed 'contracts' with the Jewish School Commission. The contracts pledged the boards would continue enrolling Jewish children within their boundaries, promising these children would not suffer from discrimination, and, at parental request, would exempt Jewish children from classroom Christian religious instruction. Moreover, Jewish children would be allowed to be absent from school without penalty on Jewish religious holidays and school officials would 'give consideration to the application of Jewish persons for teaching posts.' The contracts made no provision for Jews to vote in Protestant school board elections, let alone stand for board election. That was still forbidden. Jewish children would continue in Protestant schools, Jewish tax dollars would continue to flow to the Protestant school boards, and elected school board officials would continue to function like members of an exclusive and restricted private club.[20]

'Uptown' Jews and Protestant school board officials may have successfully squelched the proposal for a separate Jewish school system, but the contract system served only to temporarily paper over problems. In the decades which followed, Jewish resentment at their exclusion from election to board election continued to fester. In spite of pledges to 'give consideration' to hiring Jewish teachers, there were also persistent rumours that Montreal and Outremont Protestant boards knowingly discriminated against Jewish teaching candidates and that Jewish children were still subjected to ham-handed Protestant religious instruction by teachers with missionary zeal. What is more, the contracts only covered the Montreal and Outremont boards. School boards in outlying suburban municipalities undergoing an inflow of Jewish families through the 1950s and into the 1960s were not bound by contracts.

Jewish experience with suburban school boards was markedly different from that in Montreal and Outremont. Both had Protestant schools in which Jewish students were not just heavily represented, but in some cases were in the majority. As a result, the hiring of a Jewish teacher here and there was less problematic because he or she might be assigned to a school in a more Jewish neighbourhood where, with a wink and a nod, compulsory Christian religious instruction might be shelved or parallel Jewish programming offered. Schools in the suburbs were different. While there were several pockets of suburban Jewish concentration, Jews tended to be more scattered than in Montreal and Outremont. As a result, Jewish students were often in a distinct minority position within their neighbourhood Protestant school. And with little or no previous experience in dealing with Jewish students, suburban school officials were often unwilling to accommodate requests that Jewish children be exempted from compulsory religious instruction or not be penalized for their absence on Jewish holidays. There were also complaints that Jewish children were subject to proselytization, and stories circulated through the Jewish community about unpleasant exchanges between Jewish parents and this or that 'Protestant teacher, unmindful of the presence of Jewish children among his pupils.'

In turn, suburban Protestant board officials demanded that it was their assigned duty to give each and every child in their care Christian religious instruction. Jews were not exempted. Jewish children being absent on holidays or refusing to take religious instruction were disruptive, if not to the school then to the child's academic and social adjustment. Jewish parents were told the school program could not be revised to accommodate every parental whim. What is more, suburban school boards made a virtue out of rejecting Jewish parental requests for accommodation. To yield to these requests would require boards and teachers to treat Jewish children differently from non-Jewish children. To treat them differently would be discrimination, and discrimination was not to be tolerated. Of course, sameness of treatment did not extend to the hiring of Jewish teachers. That, it was argued, was expressly counter to the mandate of Protestant schools. Not completely unmoved by Jewish concerns, board officials claimed that, with good will on both sides, individual Jewish parents and local school officials might find a way to iron out this or that particular wrinkle. But all this was very ad hoc. There would be no one-size-fits-all accommodation to the needs of Jewish children that might water down the Protestant character of the school mandate or classroom.[21]

If school board officials and Jewish parents found it difficult to find common ground, Jewish children in both city and suburban elementary and secondary schools often found themselves at a distance from their non-Jewish classmates. This separation was often inherent in the culture of the school. A Jewish former student in a suburban Protestant system remembers that in secondary school he had almost no social contact with his non-Jewish classmates until he became involved in his school's hockey team. Even then, contact on the ice and in the locker room did not translate into social contact outside school. He cannot recall ever being invited home by one of his non-Jewish classmates or inviting one of them to his home. That just did not happen.[22]

What *was* happening was that post-war affluence and a continued flow of Jewish population into the Montreal suburbs gradually added weight of numbers to demands from Jewish parents that Protestant schools respect their children's Jewishness and desist from forcing them to endure compulsory religious instruction. And these parents had new allies. Protestant educational officials who dealt with Jewish parent complaints also increasingly found themselves confronting creeping secularism among their non-Jewish school population. While secular parents might not openly protest compulsory religious instruction, Protestant school boards were well aware that many nominally Protestant parents regarded compulsory religious instruction with yawning indifference. Given a choice, it is likely that many parents might even opt for its elimination. Rumour had it that some school officials were in quiet agreement. As Protestant school boards officially dug in their heels against any backsliding on the religious character of their schools, some administrators privately conceded that compulsory religious education was increasingly not worth the effort.

Whatever private doubts and internal divisions existed about the future character of Protestant schools, Protestant boards were not about to self-destruct. And if there was anything most agreed would spell the end of Protestant schools, it was not giving in to Jewish parental demands with regard to classroom accommodation for their children. Rather, it was opening Protestant school board election to Jewish voters and candidates. And it was this issue, a non-classroom issue, which more and more fuelled Jewish resentment. Jewish parents who saw Protestant school boards as unresponsive to their concerns were equally convinced this would not be the case if Jews could vote in board elections. Boards that were unready to yield one iota when it came to supporting reforms allowing Jewish parents and taxpayers to vote in board elections – let alone take a seat at the board table – were certainly not going exempt Jewish children from compulsory religious instruction or accommodate Jewish children absent on Jewish holidays or abandon anti-Jewish discrimination in the hiring of teachers. Just the opposite. In the eyes of many Jews, the boards stood fast against granting Jews voting rights as much to protect the private club-like atmosphere of the boards as to protect Protestant values. To Montreal Jews this was an old story. The Anglo elite that controlled suburban Montreal Protestant school boards through the early 1960s, and happily banked Jewish tax dollars to fund their schools, seemed cut from the same cloth as those who for decades defended restrictive covenants on the sale of land to Jews, supported a quota system at McGill University, restricted Jewish entry into professions and corporate offices, and, of course, blackballed Jews from admission to elite private clubs.

School boards, of course, were not the same as private clubs. Jews were not forced to pay taxes to maintain private clubs. They did pay taxes to Protestant school boards. What is more, while Jews could and did establish their own social and athletic clubs, they were expressly prohibited from establishing their own tax-funded school system. Protestant school boards could quote the BNA Act until they were blue in the face, but for many Jews in the early 1960s, the disallowance of Jews from participating in the school board electoral process was not only unjust, it was undemocratic and smacked of antisemitism plain and simple.[23]

In Montreal and Outremont there were Jewish parents who walked away from Protestant schools. Partly out of religious or Zionist commitment and partly out of exasperation at what they regarded as second-class treatment of Jews in Protestant schools, they enrolled their children in private Jewish day schools. Mostly located in areas of heaviest Jewish population concentration and supported by tuition fees and community financial contributions, these schools often lacked the facilities afforded to Protestant system schools and were considered by some in the Jewish community as offering children a lesser quality of education. But they were growing, and by the early 1960s private Jewish day schools were educating approximately one in four Jewish children in Montreal. That number might have been even larger had many Jews in the Montreal suburban ring not been at a distance from Jewish day schools.

Thus, into the 1960s, education remained a hot-button issue among Montreal Jews. For those who removed their children from the Protestant system, there was the financial burden of paying tuition to parochial schools on top of taxes paid to the Protestant board. For those who kept their children in the Protestant system – irrespective of what particular Protestant school board served their area – there remained ongoing issues with regard to how or whether the board in their municipality afforded appropriate accommodation for Jewish children. There was also resentment at suspected board anti-Jewish hiring practices. And to top it off, there was festering bitterness at being taxed to support Protestant school boards which denied Jews the right to vote, let alone stand for office, in school board elections.

For their part, many Protestant school board officials felt themselves in an untenable position. Even if they twisted themselves into a pretzel to accommodate Jewish children – which most were not prepared to do – officials argued that they could not escape their legal responsibility. Under the British North America Act Protestant school boards were obliged to provide children in their trust with a Protestant-based education. That, they claimed, was exactly what they were doing. To do otherwise would be in direct violation of their legal obligation.

But as the 1960s dawned, a bigger storm was brewing. Through the Duplessis years, his government kept a tight lid on the province. The premier trucked no opening to progressive change and certainly none that undermined the cozy hand-in-glove relationship his government had with the Catholic Church and the Anglo corporate elite. The Church hierarchy remained dead set against any educational reform that lessened its control of Catholic schools or their curriculum. Nonetheless, there were voices for change, especially in larger urban centres where a more secular and prosperous French Canadian middle class had taken root. Money brought with it ready access to new consumer goods – television, the automobile and ease of travel – all of which further opened Quebec to new ways of thinking. Those who had previously despaired that French Canada would forever remain a Church-ridden and anti-modern agrarian society, determined to ensure continuity from generation to generation by isolating itself from secular learning, state activism, and competitive enterprise, now sensed a growing mood for change. Even as conservatives resisted any erosion of the old ways, those who spoke out for progressive change were gaining a popular ear among French-speaking industrial workers, a growing French-speaking and educated urban middle class, and a more progressive and urban-based media.

Of course, speaking out for change was not the same as change. Old ways might be questioned and the call for reform talked up, but so long as Maurice Duplessis remained premier there was not going to be any major political, social, or economic reform. He would make sure of that. As journalist, labour and social activist Gérard Pelletier subsequently recalled, 'Quebec seemed frozen for all time in the glaciers of conservatism.'[24] In provincial election after election between 1944 and 1959 Duplessis's government courted rural voters by representing itself as the true defender of traditional Quebec Catholic values, even as it shamelessly rained patronage dollars on its friends. And it paid off. Supported by the Church, Duplessis, commonly referred to as le Chef, won election after election.

Those who challenged le Chef's control or organized to oppose his tight-fisted rule paid a price. When threatened, he was prepared to use tax dollars or the provincial police – sometimes both – to enforce his will. His friends, on the other hand, including the Catholic Church establishment, the Anglo corporate business elite, and the well-oiled and patronage-driven party machine, were amply rewarded for their loyalty. So long as Duplessis remained at the helm, few doubted that the Church would continue to reign over French-speaking Quebec's educational, health care, and welfare structure. Anglo-dominated corporations – domestic and off shore – would be assured a free hand in the resource-rich province, and the Duplessis party machine would continue to divvy up the spoils.

How were Duplessis and his party viewed by most Montreal Jews? Like pigs at a bar mitzvah. Senior Montreal Jewish leaders of the late 1950s and early 1960s had cut their teeth in the Quebec of the 1920s and

1930s. The legacy of Church-condoned if not orchestrated antisemitism in Quebec was still vivid in Jewish memory.[25] So too was Duplessis's readiness to whip up anti-Jewish sentiment if it served his political ends. In the 1936 Quebec provincial election, Duplessis, then leader of the opposition, set out to incite anti-Jewish sentiment among French Catholic voters by attacking an exemption from Sunday business closing laws granted Jewish shopkeepers who kept their businesses closed on Saturdays. Painting himself the populist champion of the poor French Canadians struggling against unscrupulous Jewish business 'interests,' leeches sucking the economic lifeblood out of hard-working and industrious people, Duplessis won ringing endorsements from the Catholic Church and the nationalist media. Although he fell just short of winning the election, his anti-Jewish crusade resonated so well with voters that the frightened Liberal government quickly moved to repeal the Sunday exemption clause.[26]

Duplessis, still leader of the opposition, again whipped up anti-Jewish sentiment in the lead-up to the 1943 mid-war Quebec provincial election. Addressing a political meeting following Sunday mass in the small Quebec community of Sainte-Claire in Dorchester Country, Duplessis delivered a barn burner of a speech. Setting the tone for the upcoming election, Duplessis accused the governing provincial Liberals of conniving with the federal Liberal government to secretly authorize the settlement of 100,000 Jewish refugees in Quebec. This deal, he charged, was a payoff to a so-called 'International Zionist Brotherhood' that, he claimed, had been covertly funnelling money into Liberal Party coffers. Ever the showman, Duplessis waved a sheet of paper in front of the crowd claiming it was a true copy of a letter detailing the Liberal settlement plot. Duplessis's charge was baseless and he knew it. It did not matter to him that there was no such entity as the 'International Zionist Brotherhood.' What mattered was that Duplessis knew the accusation would play well with voters.

A storm of denials and counter charges of political scaremongering from the government side, rather than discrediting Duplessis's accusations, only kept the charges of a secret Jewish cabal front and centre in the public eye. As the Church fanned the antisemitic brush fire, Duplessis presented himself to Quebec voters as the only one strong enough to defend French Canada against the Jews and their Liberal Party stooges. He won the election and, never hesitant to play the antisemitic card if it helped him gather votes, went on to win the four subsequent elections.[27]

Ruthless as he was, Duplessis could not escape his own mortality. In

1959 the premier died. Without *le Chef* to hold it together, the political alliance his government had forged with Church and business interests quickly came unstuck. Welled-up demand for a more progressive and reform-minded government grew. Voter support began tilting against Duplessis's party, and in the provincial election of 1960, what was previously unthinkable became reality. French-speaking industrial wage earners joined forces with a growing numbers of middle-class voters and English speakers to deliver the provincial Liberal Party, running under the banner 'Il faut que ça change' (Things must change), a narrow upset victory.

With the ascension of Liberal leader Jean Lesage to the premier's office, it was unclear, perhaps even to Lesage, where his new government would lead Quebec. But one thing was clear to everyone. The era of Duplessis was no more. A mood for change was palpable. Without a large majority in the provincial legislature, the new premier, moderate in his thinking and hardly the kind of leader who one would imagine unleashing a social and political revolution in Quebec, at first stayed true to form. He advocated a 'go-slow' approach to reform. But many of those he gathered around him and many of those who had rallied behind the Liberals in the election had a different agenda. They were committed to a progressive and government-led activism. And once the genie of reform was out of the bottle, change would not be denied.

If the Quiet Revolution had something of a sputtering start, it was not long before it swept into every nook and cranny of Quebec society. In this springtime of progressive reform, Quebec's Liberal government, buoyed by forces of urbanization and uncapped secularism and free of the now discredited Duplessis alliance with Anglo capital and Church conservatism, gradually rolled out a reform agenda that would remake Quebec. Where the previous government had abdicated active engagement in economic planning – allowing business to function as much as possible unfettered by state interference – and in social policy – ceding most responsibility to religious authorities – the new government and an empowered public service assumed a hands-on role in setting Quebec's social and economic course. There were those uneasy at the rapidity of change. Fearing the direction of government activism, they decried the decline in Church influence. Others, however, were delighted to see a new breed of educated and reform-minded French Canadian decision makers take the reins of an emerging secular Quebec state.[28]

In the Jewish corner of Quebec, it would be hard to find a *minyan* who mourned Duplessis's passing or the end of his regime. Few were upset to see the Catholic Church being elbowed out of political power. But if the church/state alliance that had so long dominated the Quebec social and political scene was in free fall, it was unclear to Jewish leaders what the new reform-minded government would mean to Jewish life in the province. The Revolution might be Quiet, but it was still a revolution, and revolutions have a way of being unpredictable. Jewish leaders could be forgiven for being uneasy at what direction reform would take or uncertain about how much hope to invest in Quebec's new rulers. Would they turn out to be different than those of the past, and be better for Quebec and for its Jews? Would this new government prove truly open, welcoming, and thoughtfully progressive or, as some suspected, gradually retreat behind the same wall of narrow and parochial nationalism that until recently had defined Quebec's political life? If the latter, Montreal Jews could come to appreciate the wisdom of the Yiddish folk tradition advising one not to invest time praying for a new Kaiser. He might end up worse than the last.

Whatever reservations Jewish leaders harboured, during the honeymoon days of early Liberal rule few if any were expressed, at least not in public. In fact, many in the tightly knit Montreal Jewish community welcomed the Liberal victory and the green light to reform it signalled. Jews had voted for the Liberals in the 1960 provincial election and would do so again in the follow-up election of 1962. They relished the prospect that a progressive government would assume more control of social welfare, health and education policy, paving the way to a more secular, progressive, and inclusive state respectful of human rights.[29] If, in the process, the old Anglo elite took a few lumps, so much the better. Wasn't this the same bunch who had been in league with Duplessis? Weren't they the gang who denied Jewish taxpayers democratic access to the publicly funded education system? Until recently didn't they treat McGill University as their private preserve, much to the detriment of Jewish applicants? Didn't they sign restrictive covenants designed to forestall the sale of property to Jews, and didn't they still restrict Jewish access to employment in major sectors of the corporate economy they still dominated? If the Quiet Revolution screwed them over, so much the better. Few Jews would complain.

But there were still reservations. Duplessis was gone and his political machine broken, perhaps beyond repair, but it was unclear how Jews and the Jewish community would fare in the emerging Quebec. It was even unclear how much of a handle Jews had on what was then going on in Quebec. Many Quebec Jews, self-contained within their insulated

English-speaking Montreal community, had only the vaguest notion of what was going on in the larger surrounding French Canada. Montreal's Jewish leadership 'never developed a comfort [level]' with the provincial government, nor did they have a sense of where the province was headed.[30] As a whole they were out of the loop. But that did not prevent speculation. Given the tight-fisted control Duplessis and his allies had maintained over Quebec, it was hard to believe that Duplessis's mix of authoritarianism and nationalism was a spent force. Some worried that the Liberals, whom Jews overwhelmingly supported election after election, could backslide into parochial nationalism – rejecting a civic nationalism embracing all those who lived in Quebec and reverting to a nationalism that trumpeted ethnic exclusivity and demanded Quebec for Quebecers.[31] If this did happen, might Jews again be labelled bogeymen of a dangerously cosmopolitan and amoral world lurking outside? Many Jews who knew the taste of discrimination were not unsympathetic to the notion of enhancing the life chances of Quebec's French-speaking majority. But again they worried that a better life for French Canadians might be bought at Jewish expense. And the issue of language was emerging as critical. Could French-language fluency become a prerequisite of civic participation, or even worse, could French lineage, in combination with French fluency, become a prerequisite for sharing equally in the new Quebec?

Certainly, language mattered. Nobody would deny it and not only were most Jews in Montreal anglophones, so too were their organizational culture and leadership. In the early 1960s few in Jewish leadership positions could comfortably string enough words together in French to form a coherent sentence nor were most prepared to try. Unilingually English, they had always functioned in English even when dealing with the government in Quebec City. As the ability to communicate in French became more and more essential, Jews felt themselves at a disadvantage. Jewish community leaders, recognizing that French-language competence was increasingly essential, were forced to rely on hired translators.[32] Some in the Jewish community were anxious about where all this was leading. In 1962 the Liberal Party in Quebec went to the polls again, this time under the slogan *maîtres chez nous* (Masters in our own home). Jews, who turned out in large numbers to vote Liberal, might quietly have asked themselves how much room there was going to be in that 'home' for them.[33]

For all their worry, the early signs were encouraging. In the 1960 election Montreal Jews had turned out at the polls to help the provincial Liberals win a surprise victory, and watched as the old order was pushed aside. The new government's watchword was *rattrapage* (catching up). As part of its *rattrapage* strategy the government served notice it was going to play a far more active role in areas of social policy planning, including education and social service delivery, than did the previous Duplessis regime. The Jewish community of Montreal, with its enviable infrastructure of social service agencies and network of private parochial schools, was at first concerned that, in the name of centralization and universal standards, the Jewish community would lose control of these community assets to the province.

Facing a new government in Quebec City and an influx of activist public servants into government ranks, Jewish leaders were at first unsure how open or sympathetic Quebec would be to maintaining the integrity of the Jewish social and educational network. Compared to Ottawa, Quebec City remained a remote and largely unknown terrain for Jews. In the past Duplessis may have been less than friendly to Jewish interests, but for the most part he and his government remained disengaged from areas of Jewish institutional concern. The new government was engaged and, something of a surprise, Jews also found it to be surprisingly receptive and positive.[34]

What about the area of education? After decades of granting responsibility for the delivery of tax-funded schooling to Catholic and Protestant authorities – in 1960 there was still no provincial ministry of education – the new government used the power of the purse to insert itself into areas of educational policy and administration. As a first step, it made new money available for educational upgrading and promised a consolidation of regional school boards, especially at the secondary school level. Also, announcing that parity of educational opportunity for all children in Quebec was a priority, the new government, much to the delight of the Jewish community, made private schools, including Jewish day schools, eligible for partial government funding. Hoping to encourage public input on the future of educational policy in Quebec, the new government also appointed a Royal Commission of Inquiry on Education in Quebec, headed by Msgr Alphonse-Marie Parent, vice-rector of Laval University. Parent's mandate was to review the state of education in the province and recommend ways in which education might be improved. The Parent commission, in turn, invited briefs from all interested stakeholders.

The Jewish community saw the Parent commission as a singularly important opportunity to make the new Liberal government aware of the anomalous position of Jewish students in Montreal's Protestant schools and of the harm done to the democratic process by the exclusion of Jews from election to school boards to which Jewish tax dollars were being directed. A Canadian Jewish Congress brief, written in large part by Louis Rosenberg, director of the CJC's Research Bureau, declared this exclusion 'an inexcusable violation of even the most basic tenets of democracy.' In an article for the *American Jewish Yearbook*, Rosenberg outlined the prescriptive thrust of the CJC's brief. The document called on the commission to recommend that Jews be accorded full political equality within the Protestant school system, even if doing so required an amendment to the British North America Act. The brief went on to argue that all Jewish children in Protestant schools should be granted an automatic, blanket exemption from religious instruction rather than individually, on the written request of a parent. The Congress brief further requested that classroom subjects such as literature, including biblical literature, be taught in a religiously neutral fashion rather than in the service of religious dogma. Finally, the CJC brief appealed for Jewish day schools to receive funding for secular studies on the same basis as tax-supported Protestant and Catholic schools. In sum, the Jewish community, speaking as a faith community on a par with Protestants and Catholics, demanded not secularization of Quebec schools, but respectful accommodation for Jewish students in Protestant schools and parity for Jewish schools within Quebec's confessional system of education.

Many of the recommendations offered up in the Congress brief rang similar to those of non-Jewish educational groups. In its brief to the commission, the Quebec Federation of Home and School Associations called on the government to extend to Jewish schools the same rights to state support enjoyed by Catholic and Protestant schools. The Protestant School Board of Greater Montreal, realizing that some kind of reform was unavoidable, tried to short-circuit any move to grant Jews the franchise in Protestant board elections by conceding that, since Jewish children constituted a large proportion of the enrolment in Protestant schools, Jewish parents should be allowed a voice in Protestant board deliberations, although not a vote. The Quebec Provincial Association of Protestant Teachers went much further. It called on the commission to recommend to government that Jews and other religious minorities be given all rights enjoyed by Protestants and Catholics, including the full and equal right to attend and teach in Protestant schools, vote in school board elections, and serve as voting members of Protestant boards – proposals that would have in effect de-Protestantized the system in all but name.

In 1961, as the Parent commission continued its deliberations, the issue of Jewish participation in school board elections came before the courts. In the town of Saint-Martin, north of Montreal, the local Protestant school disqualified a Jew who put his name forward to run in the upcoming Protestant school board election. Refusing to accept the board's rejection as the final word, he challenged its ruling in provincial court. The local court ruled in his favour, holding that as a citizen and Protestant school board taxpayer, he had every right to stand for election. What is more, the court directed his name be added to the ballot, and he was elected. Whether other courts in Quebec would have ruled the same way is an open question. But at least in this instance, the court served notice to Protestant school boards and the provincial government that egregious religious and political discrimination would no longer be tolerated in Quebec.[35]

A little less than two years later, in April 1963, the Parent commission issued its first in a series of reports on education in Quebec. This first report took as its core assumption that every student in Quebec 'must be guaranteed an education consistent with his or her interests and needs.' In a lengthy discussion of how to overhaul the structure of education in Quebec, the report rejected any notion of secularization of education. Accepting that Catholic and Protestant school boards would remain in place, the report did recommend that the provincial government establish a provincial ministry of education which would assume ultimate authority in matters of education, thus cutting into both the Catholic and the Protestant boards' monopoly in areas of educational policy and delivery. To advise the proposed ministry of education, the report also called on the government to appoint a Supreme Council on Education, with separate Catholic and Protestant committees assigned 'to make recommendations concerning religion and morals, to assure the religious character of the schools and to offer suggestions ... on religious problems which may arise when teaching certain subjects.'[36]

Jewish community leaders were not surprised that the Parent commission did not recommend dismantling denominational boards in favour of secular language-based boards. That would have been too politically and religiously divisive and, an added complication, it would have demanded an amendment to the British North America Act. None of that was seen as possible. Nor did Jewish leaders necessarily see it in the Jewish interest that there be a secularization of education in Quebec. What many wanted was for Jewish parochial schools to have funding parity with Catholic and Protestant schools. If parity was not possible, at least parochial school parents should have some kind of fiscal relief from the burden of paying both tuition to parochial schools and school taxes to their local Protestant board. With regard to the large number of Jewish children in Protestant schools, the Canadian Jewish Congress had asked the Parent Commission to recommend that the religious particularism of Jewish children be respected, not that Protestant boards be secularized. However, even as the commission accepted that school boards would continue to be faith based, it did not address major Jewish community concerns or respond to specific Jewish community recommendations, including those with regard to Jewish participation in school board elections. The silence on these matters was disconcerting. When it came to democratic reform, Parent seemed to be leaving Quebec Jews out in the cold.

When the government announced it would waste no time in introducing legislation designed to implement the commission's first batch of recommendations, the Canadian Jewish Congress requested an immediate meeting with the premier. To the surprise of those who had only known a provincial government indifferent, if not hostile, to Jewish interests, the premier agreed to a meeting, and a hastily assembled delegation rushed to Quebec City to present the premier with a brief regarding the government's proposed legislation. In what by all accounts was a positive encounter, delegates began their presentation by assuring the premier that the Jewish community welcomed the progressive tenor of the proposed legislative-reform package. However, the delegation cautioned that unless there were built-in safeguards, the proposed legislation could end up making matters far worse for Jewish children in Protestant schools. Without safeguards, there was no guarantee that Jewish children would not continue to be subject to unwelcome Protestant religious indoctrination in schools. Nor was this a small matter touching only a few children. The delegation reminded the premier that Jewish students constituted fully 25 per cent of all children in Greater Montreal's Protestant elementary schools and almost 35 per cent of the Protestant boards' secondary school stream.[37] The premier was also reminded that Jews paid a disproportionate percentage of all taxes that supported Protestant school boards in Greater Montreal.

To ensure that the interests of Jewish children in Protestant schools were protected, the Congress brief proposed that a Jew be appointed to the government's proposed Supreme Council and that Jews also be appointed to the council's Protestant committee. As the widely acknowledged and representative political voice of the Jewish community, Congress also asked that it, rather than government officials, be entrusted with selecting the appointees. The premier was also advised that Congress was not alone in pressing for these reforms. They were endorsed by a number of influential non-Jewish educational authorities, all of whom supported the Jewish proposals as consistent with the educational goals set out in the government's proposed legislation.

Much to the satisfaction of Congress, its brief found an important French Canadian supporter. Claude Ryan, influential editor of *Le Devoir*, made the case to government that, when it came to the place of Jewish children in the Protestant schools and the right of Jews to serve on Protestant school boards, more than the protection of Jewish rights in Quebec was at stake. As he saw it, Quebec's right to protect its cultural uniqueness within Canada was also at stake. In a *Le Devoir* editorial Ryan argued, 'In granting complete school equality to the Jews, who already bear heavy sacrifices to maintain their culture we [in Quebec] will show the entire country the true roots from which spring our attachment to our own cultural treasure ... We will prove that what we ask for ourselves we also want others to have.' How Jews were treated in the new Quebec, Ryan insisted, would be widely looked upon as a litmus test of the new Quebec's commitment to human rights and the building of an inclusive society.[38]

Whether the absence of protections for Jewish children in the proposed legislation was merely an oversight easily remedied, or the premier was convinced by the Canadian Jewish Congress's brief, or he was moved by the arguments Ryan put forward is unknown. Perhaps it was all three. To the surprise and delight of Jewish community leaders, much that Congress requested of the premier followed in short order. The government decided that a member of the Canadian Jewish Congress executive in Montreal should be appointed to the Superior Council and two more Jews were designated as members of the council's Protestant committee. In addition, the government extended tuition grants to parents of Jewish children in Montreal Jewish day schools. In yet another major breakthrough, the government moved to rescind the long-standing prohibition against Jews serving on Protestant school boards. Later that year the Jew previously elected to the Protestant board in Saint-Martin stood for re-election, this time not by court order but as a matter of legal right. He won again. A Jew was also elected to the Protestant school board in the largely English-speaking Montreal area municipality of Westmount.[39]

The Greater Montreal School Board, hoping to forestall the impact of government authorization of Jews running in its school board elections – perhaps fearing a number of long-serving board members would go down to defeat in Jewish neighbourhoods – offered a compromise. Reminding the government that by law the Quebec educational system was still confessional based, the board argued that giving Jews the vote in Protestant board elections would not turn Jews into Protestants, but could make it impossible for the Montreal Protestant school board to function as a truly Protestant board. Rather than giving Jews voting rights, thereby diluting the Protestant nature of the board, the board declared its readiness to grant several Jews non-voting status so they might sit at the board's table and advise on issues related to Jewish children in Protestant schools.

As far as the Canadian Jewish Congress was concerned, the Protestant board just didn't get it. If the Protestant school board was going to bank Jewish tax dollars, it was going to have to make room for Jews at the board table. Congress rejected the proposed compromise as insultingly too little too late. However, there was some room for compromise. As if to reassure the Protestant board it need not fear a Jewish takeover, Congress accepted the board's suggestion that the notion of Jews being appointed to the Montreal board, instead of battling it out in elections, had merit, especially if Congress had a hand in selecting the appointees. Following several months of tough negotiations between Congress and the Protestant School Board of Greater Montreal, an agreement was hammered out. Jews would become voting members of the board – but, at least for the time being, not by election. The previously all-Protestant eighteen-member board was expanded to twenty-five, five of whom would henceforth be Jews appointed with full voting rights. One of these Jews was also to sit as a member of the board's executive committee. Elsewhere in Quebec Jews could stand for election the same as any Protestant whose taxes were directed to a Protestant school board. A bill incorporating this compromise agreement was unanimously passed by the Quebec legislature.

Acknowledging that the day was long overdue that Jews could sit as voting members of Protestant school boards, the new minister of education expressed regret that 'numerous obstacles had in the past prevented those of the Jewish faith from having complete freedom for the education of Jewish children.' Removal of barriers to Jewish participation on Protestant school boards was, he said, a clear signal of Quebec's wish 'to assure the existence of schools where the minority groups can educate their children, and also allow them to administer their schools.'[40]

It was hard for some to believe. Five years after the death of Duplessis, the provincial educational system was being reformed in ways unimaginable while *le Chef* was still alive. Jews and Protestants sat together on school boards. But even as one issue was resolved another was heating up. Differences over the place of the English and French languages in Quebec would more and more come to dominate public debate and, to a large degree, the agenda of the Montreal Jewish community. What was at stake for Montreal Jews, the vast majority of whom were English speaking, was more than just the institutional integrity of their community. It was the place the next generation of Montreal Jews would have in an increasingly francophone Quebec. Recognizing which way the wind was blowing, in 1966 Sam Bronfman, who knew very little French, authorized publication of a short article over his signature advising that the Jewish future in Quebec demanded that the next generation of Montreal Jewish children be fluent in both English and French.

Every country has its problems. In Canada we have language and cultural problems; we have two founding peoples trying to find a way to retain identities and yet create an important Canadian nation. We have a task of building a unified country, though there are the serious cultural and language difficulties. French Canada does not want to be a backwater province, subject to the economic exploitation of others. It insists that it has suffered this for 200 years. It also is fighting for its national survival.

In this the Jewish population has a great stake, of course. Quebec represents over 40 per cent of the Jewish population of Canada, and Montreal is by far the largest and most important Jewish centre. It is the capital of Canadian Jewry. The Jews are by nature and history sympathetic. However, our cultural and educational affinities have, as a result of historic occurrences, been largely with our Anglo-Saxon co-citizens.

In the past this did not work too badly but we must recognize the wave of the future and the priority of French in a province where 85 per cent of the population is French speaking. Our schools must create a bilingualism to a greater extent than ever before and our [full-day] Jewish schools, which educate 25 per cent of the [Jewish] children of Montreal, must not lag in this enterprise. If the future generations are to be part and parcel of the new Quebec, these things must be done and become our first priority.[41]

Bronfman's message – Quebec was changing and to be part of that Quebec Jews needed to change with it – was easy to say. It was not so easy to do. Some worried that Jews would never change enough to be fully accepted as part of that new Quebec. Speaking French and being French, they insisted, are not one and the same thing. In this regard, might those calling for the supremacy of the French language in Quebec be speaking in code? Was their real goal defending the French language or advancing a parochial nationalism based on lineage and firm in its advocacy of Quebec's separation from Canada?

As Jews in Quebec wrestled with the new political and language reality unfolding around them, so too did the federal government. As the Quiet Revolution took a violent turn in 1963 with the organization of the nationalist Front de libération du Québec (Quebec Liberation Front), commonly known as the FLQ, Ottawa was increasingly concerned that the existing paradigm for English–French relations was unravelling and nobody seemed sure what should be done. In part to explore options and in part to buy time, Prime Minister Lester B. Pearson appointed the Royal Commission on Bilingualism and Biculturalism, jointly chaired by Montreal *Le Devoir* editor André Laurendeau and Davidson Dunton, president of Carleton University in Ottawa. The B&B Commission, as it was popularly known, was charged with inquiring and reporting upon 'the existing state of bilingualism and biculturalism in Canada and to recommend what steps should be taken to develop the Canadian Confederation on the basis of an equal partnership between two founding races,' British and French. Almost as an afterthought the federal government gave a politic nod in the direction of Canadian ethnic groups. It charged the commission with taking 'into account the cultural contribution made by the other ethnic groups to the cultural enrichment of Canada and the measures that should be taken to safeguard that contribution.'[42]

In public sessions held in Quebec and across Canada the B&B commissioners were taken aback by presentations by spokespersons from some of Canada's older and more established Euro-ethnic communities. Rather than enter into the debate on the English-French linguistic divide, ethnic spokesperson after ethnic spokesperson insisted their constituents felt demeaned by the very notion of biculturalism, a vision of Canada as a binational state in which 'two founding races' had a proprietary monopoly on public-policy debate. Pointing out that those of non-English and non-French descent formed fully one-third of Canada's population, a so-called third force, they demanded recognition as full cultural partners in Canada. Images of the illiterate Slavic peasant tilling marginal lands of the Canadian northwest, of Jews hunched over sewing machines in the factories of the garment industry, or of southern European and Asian labourers swinging picks as they laid railway track or worked the mines and forests of the Canadian interior may have been true in the past. Ethnic spokespersons insisted, however, that these images were now no more reflective of Canada's new reality than the image of the happy, pipe-smoking, *tuque*-wearing, French Canadian *habitant* or the musket-toting Anglo-Canadian Loyalist wrapped in the Union Jack. Of course, the past should not be forgotten. Commission members were reminded that in the past immigrants and their parents had endured the Great Depression side by side with other Canadians; they had sacrificed sons and daughters to the national war effort and their industry now helped ensure Canada's economic strength. Articulate, politically astute, economically resourceful, increasingly middle class, educated, and impassioned, the ethnic spokespersons declared, their communities were not one iota less Canadian or deserving of cultural affirmation and support than those of the English or French charter groups. What is more, these spokespersons offered themselves as proof positive that the assimilationist passion of an earlier generation of gatekeepers had not worked, at least not in their case. They and their children were Canadians, proudly so and not about to take second place in the national identity debate. Arguing that a new national identity model was overdue, they proposed not an exclusionary biculturalism but an inclusive partnership of all cultures represented in Canada.

It cannot be denied that some ethnic leaders harboured a group-based agenda. When the commission heard from the spokespersons for Eastern European groups, especially Ukrainian Canadians, what they heard was a pained sense of cultural dispossession in the face of the 'Russification' of their homeland. For many committed Ukrainian Canadians, ensuring the survival of their heritage in Canada was not just a familial or folk priority. It was a cultural imperative. Seeing their religious, linguistic, and cultural heritage under attack in Ukraine, they were concerned that if the Ukrainian culture was going to survive at all, it would survive in part sheltered within a Ukrainian diaspora committed to making it happen. This would not be easy. It was even unclear how committed the Canadian-born generation would remain to

Ukrainian cultural survival. What was needed, some felt, was for the Canadian government to put its weight behind this survivalist agenda by assigning virtue and capital to the cause of ethnic retention in Canada.

To bolster their cause, ethnic-community spokespersons pressed an alternative vision to that of biculturalism – a blueprint for Canadian identity based on public acceptance and support of cultural pluralism. Again and again they argued that ethnicity and cultural pluralism were the essence of the Canadian reality. And rejecting the notion that cultural pluralism was somehow un-Canadian, they argued it was the essential Canadian reality, a Canadian phenomenon shaped and reshaped by the encounter with Canada. Ethnicity, they insisted, does not run counter to the flowering of a distinct Canadian identity. It *was* Canadian identity. Accordingly, ethnic spokespersons pressed that the ethno-cultural mosaic be officially recognized as both the source and expression of Canadian culture. In effect, they demanded public endorsement of ethnic diversity as the essence of Canadian identity. They demanded Multiculturalism.[43]

Where was the organized Canadian Jewish community in this unfolding debate? Divided. Some, especially in the Jewish labour movement and those in more multi-ethnic urban Ontario and western Canada, felt that Jews would do well to weigh in on the national identity debate on the side of ethnic pluralism. It would, they argued, add value to Jewish cultural expression and help cement positive ties with other ethnic communities.

Jewish leaders in Montreal were of a very different mind. They cautioned against anything that would designate Jews as an ethnic group as opposed to a faith community. In his address to the opening session of the 1965 Plenary of the Canadian Jewish Congress meeting in Montreal, Saul Hayes, Congress executive director, expressly cautioned against the organized Jewish community endorsing any campaign that might designate Canada a multi-ethnic state. The idea of cultural pluralism, he reminded delegates from across Canada, was regarded with especially deep suspicion in French-speaking Quebec as an effort to dismiss Quebec's aspirations as simply one of many ethnic awakenings. Any Jewish endorsement of multiculturalism, Hayes warned, could well put Jews on a collision course with French Canada.

There is ... a complete acceptance [as] part of the mores of this country that one has not simply the right to pursue one's own religious and social life alone and in a water-tight compartment and uninterruptedly but there is almost an obligation to do so. The exclusion from social groups merely gives further evidence and solidifies the existing situation. This is part of the game and these are the ground rules of the game.

I must here introduce the jarring note that in Canada we are even a [*sic*] retrogressing and if ever there was evidence of how these cadres must exist you will find it reflected in State documents, in government thinking and almost no one to denounce the order-in-council [setting up the B&B Commission] stating once and for all and no nonsense about it, that Canada is a partnership of two founding races. In the words of [Quebec] Premier Lesage, 'first and foremost the Constitution is a treaty between the English and French Canadian nations which gives them an advantage over neo-Canadian minorities.' I do not interpret, I do not gloss, I quote.[44]

Hayes contended that the governments of Canada and Quebec were not in dispute about Canada being a 'partnership of two founding races.' Their differences were over how that partnership should be organized and run. In this regard, Jews in Montreal had to walk a political tightrope. For the most part English speakers, Montreal Jews had a vital stake in the unfolding debate, especially as it related to the status of the English language. At the same time, to successfully safeguard Jewish interests – including language interests – in Quebec it was imperative that Jews not allow the government of Quebec to relegate them to being just one of many English-speaking 'neo-Canadian minorities.' The Jewish street might be an ethnic street, but when it came to representing Jewish interests, Hayes demanded, Congress, as the political voice of the Jewish community, should stick to the strategy that underscored the 1959 bicentennial of Jewish settlement in Canada. That is, Jews must present themselves to government not as one of many ethnic groups but as one of Canada's three senior founding faith communities, on an equal footing with Protestants and Catholics.

In a 1963 talk to Jewish leaders from across Canada, Hayes had claimed that whatever success Jews had in lobbying government was a matter of simple arithmetic. The Hart celebration aside, the reality was that there were only two entrenched charter groups in Canada – English and French. That was not about to change. Of course there were also a large number of ethnic groups, some of which were bigger than the Canadian Jewish community, including, he noted, 'German, Italian and Polish or Ukrainian origin Canadians.' Should the Canadian Jewish community become primarily identified as an ethnic group,

Hayes warned, it would not just be one of many, it would not even be a particularly significant one of many. Overshadowed by larger groups, the Jewish voice might not be heard above the crowd. However, as a religious group, Jews were one of three – Catholic, Protestant, and Jew. 'In political life, this is of some importance.' As far as Hayes was concerned, all those jokes that began 'There was a priest, a minister, and a rabbi' had critical political meaning, especially when it came to protecting Jewish interests, and especially in Quebec.[45]

Hayes was well aware that Canadian Jews straddled the religious-ethnic divide. Ethnic community. Faith community. Jews were both. If that made Jews anomalous, it was and is an anomaly acknowledged in the Canadian census. On Canadian census forms there are questions with regard to both heritage and religious identity. Jews are listed under both headings. But as far as Quebec was concerned, no matter the census or the reality of the Jewish street, Hayes insisted, it was essential for the organized Jewish community to hold fast to the religious designation. The added value of that strategy was that in the Quebec of the Quiet Revolution, even with its increasingly more secular-minded state leadership, the organization of social service and health care delivery remained largely structured and funded along faith lines. During the Duplessis years the state was largely hands off with regard to the setting of social policy, preferring to leave it to faith-based charitable organizations. As in the case of education, faith communities charted their own course. Post-Duplessis Quebec governments increasingly assumed a leading role in social policy planning and coordination, including in education, but they did not dismantle the existing faith-based infrastructure. They worked with and through religious groups – including the Jewish community.

So long as the Quebec government allowed faith-based groups to continue to deliver educational and social services, Jewish leaders were insistent that the Jewish community hold tight to its religious designation. Let the government set high standards. Let it hold agencies accountable for the quality and universality of service. Let it be a partner in funding. All that was to be wished. But to ensure that the Montreal Jewish community retain a high level of social services and, as much as possible, the autonomy and financial integrity of its educational, social, and health network, it had to protect its claim to equal status with Catholics and Protestants.[46]

Reaching the provincial government with this message was critical and had very practical community implications. Interacting with the government and doing so in French became a Jewish priority. What is more, as Jewish community leaders acknowledged, post-Duplessis governments in Quebec might still be largely ignorant of the Jewish community but, unlike during the Duplessis regime, they sensed no inherent hostility to Jews.[47] Dealings with the Quebec government on education afforded something of a case in point. The government's channelling of funds to Jewish day schools and its readiness to act on long-standing Jewish grievances with regard to the Protestant school system indicated a stunning sea change in government–Jewish relations. Still, Hayes insisted, this change remained predicated on the provincial government continuing to deal with the Jewish community as a faith, rather than an ethnic, community. If some Jewish leaders outside of Quebec found merit in Canadian Jews supporting the call for a multi-ethnic vision of Canada, Hayes warned, this was a perilous political proposition for Quebec Jews and could well undermine their future status in Quebec.

The issue landed four-square on the Congress agenda when in 1965 the Royal Commission on Bilingualism and Biculturalism invited briefs from community-based organizations. Viewing the royal commission's mandate as a minefield of problems Congress would do well to avoid, Hayes huddled with Congress officials on whether they should submit a brief on behalf of the Canadian Jewish community and, if so, what it might contain. Hayes, who preferred that Congress, as the key Canadian Jewish umbrella organization, not submit a brief, urged that if it was decided Congress should do so, it emphasize the centrality of the Jewish religious identity:

> Shall we point out that within the context of biculturalism there ought to be special recognition for the religious element, which is generally recognized as one of the main, if not the main, basis for cultural identification? It is in this context that the Jewish community has a right to put forth a claim beyond its numerical strength. The Jewish faith is practically universally accepted as one of the three major religions within the Western civilization.[48]

While Congress weighed the pros and cons of submitting a brief, Hayes was asked by the commission to recommend someone who might write an essay about the Canadian Jewish contribution to Canadian society – one of ten commissioned works. He suggested Ruth Wisse, who had worked as Congress's press officer in Montreal for several years.

She left in 1959 to do a doctorate in Yiddish Literature at Columbia University, returning in 1962 to Montreal and a faculty appointment at McGill University. Wisse agreed to write the essay and was invited to Ottawa along with other commissioned essay writers for a meeting with commission officials. Wisse recalls that nobody at the meeting, not the officials or the essayists, came away with a clear notion of what the commission wanted. She was on her own. In the end, after discussion with Hayes, Wisse wrote a piece that did not ignore the notion of ethnicity or 'enclave groups, intent on maintaining in unadulterated form their traditional mode of living.' The major focus of her essay, however, was the richness of Jewish contributions to Canadian society, and rather than joining the chorus of those demanding government recognition of multiculturalism, she spoke to the value of Jewish religious particularism in the context of a Canada welcoming faith as much as ethnic diversity.[49]

While Wisse was still working on her essay, the Canadian Jewish Congress held its 1965 national plenary meetings in Montreal. Among the many sessions was a panel discussion entitled 'The Canadian Jewish Community in a Rapidly Changing Society,' which focused on how the Canadian Jewish Congress might best respond to the royal commission's invitation to submit a brief, which it was assumed Congress would do in the end. The panel disagreed on whether the Congress brief should 'deal with matters of direct concern to the Jews, or should rather speak up on matters of general concern for the welfare of all Canada.' But all did agree that any brief should stress the need for a national human rights strategy. With regard to official recognition of ethnic pluralism, the panelists, echoing Hayes, were against Congress climbing onto any ethnic bandwagon. One speaker warned that 'to take the multi-cultural approach [being advocated by some ethnic-group spokespersons appearing before the commission] ... would place all ethnic groups on the same basis as the English and French groups in Canada [and] would ... open a Pandora's box of unknown dangers.'[50]

Unknown dangers? Not as far as Hayes was concerned. Anything that undermined the claim of Montreal and Quebec Jews to parity with Catholics and Protestants was a danger, and any labelling of Jews as an ethnic group akin to Italians or Ukrainians, Hayes warned, would do exactly that. Accordingly, as historian Richard Menkis points out, to avoid getting dragged into the ethnic-pluralism debate, Congress finally opted out of submitting a brief to the royal commission and made no formal presentation. Individual Jews and local Jewish organizations across Canada might do so, but as the representative voice of Canadian Jews, it was decided that Congress would do best to give the multiculturalism debate a wide berth. If Jews in Quebec were to remain a 'third solitude,' it was essential that they be a third religious solitude.[51]

The priority given to Jews presenting themselves as a religious rather than an ethnic community even shaped Canadian Jewish participation in the 1967 Centennial celebrations. In 1960 Canadian officials began preliminary consultations with various stakeholder groups in anticipation of a year-long national celebration of Canadian confederation. In a very preliminary effort to feel out religious communities on how they might participate in the celebrations, officials invited the Canadian Jewish Congress to meet and review ideas for centennial involvement with representatives of other faith groups 'in an atmosphere of receptivity.' Congress readily accepted.[52]

Internal Congress discussions about joining the centennial celebration did not begin until a few years later. At a 1963 Congress-organized meeting in Montreal with representatives from a number of national Jewish organizations called to discuss coordinated Jewish involvement in the upcoming celebrations, one of the first things delegates agreed upon was that under no circumstances should the Jewish community allow itself to become involved in any combined ethnic celebration. Banging a familiar drum, Saul Hayes warned, 'Our dilemma in this regard is a serious one,' particularly in Quebec. Talk of ethnic pluralism, he cautioned delegates, did not play well in Quebec. He recalled how remarks by a western Canadian spokesperson from the Ukrainian community caused consternation in Quebec when he 'stated he was a great believer in bilingualism and biculturalism but he believed that the second language [of Canada] should be Ukrainian.'[53]

It sometimes took diplomacy to avoid what Hayes regarded as an ethnic trap. In 1965 federal senator Paul Yuzyk, active in the Ukrainian effort to secure federal support for multiculturalism, organized a meeting in Ottawa of ethnic-group leaders from across Canada to discuss the very thing Congress wanted to avoid – coordinated ethnic group participation in the national centennial celebrations. He invited the Canadian Jewish Congress to be represented. Determined to steer clear of anything that might officially lump Jews in with ethnic groups, but not wanting to insult Yuzyk by turning down his invitation, Congress reluctantly agreed to send not a delegate but an observer. The Congress 'observer' avoided entering into most of the discussion except to explain that the Jewish community had yet to consider its options with regard to its participation in the centennial.

Congress might be at pains to finesse its way out of joining in multiethnic coordinated centennial events, but it was pleased to take a high-profile role in coordinating faith-group involvement in the celebration. Even as it gave Senator Yuzyk's efforts a pass, Congress became a charter member of the Canadian Interfaith Conference, established in 1965 by the federal government's centennial commission charged with encouraging centennial celebrations across Canada. The Interfaith Conference was assigned the task of promoting cross-Canada celebrations by faith communities. Lavy Becker, a Montreal business executive, former chair of Congress's National Bicentenary Committee and a national vice-president of Congress, was asked to chair the conference, a feather in the Jewish community cap.[54]

There is arguably no better example of the Montreal Jewish community's insistence on presenting itself as a faith community than its participation in Expo 67, the world's fair held in Montreal in 1967. Oddly, the Montreal fair was something of an accident. Canada had originally applied to the International Bureau of Expositions to host the 1967 fair as part of national celebrations of one hundred years of confederation, but lost out to a bid by the Soviet Union. The Soviets intended to mount the fair in Moscow as a showcase event honouring the fiftieth anniversary of the Bolshevik Revolution. Two years later, in 1962, they decided against staging the world's fair, and the prize reverted to Canada.

With two years of preparation time lost, the scramble was on to find a Canadian venue for the fair and get facilities built. After a little jostling between major Canadian cities, the fair was awarded to Montreal. Some doubted there was time to pull together a world-class event by the 1967 launch date. Certainly, it was a monumental and expensive undertaking. Just creating the fair site was an engineering feat of staggering proportions. Using landfill, an artificial island with a magnificent view of the Montreal skyline was created in the St Lawrence River and a rapid transit system, the Metro, was constructed to connect the fair site to the rest of the city.

The fair's content also took shape. Expo 67 adopted 'Man and His World' as its central theme and invited the world to participate. Five interrelated theme pavilions were constructed to represent 'man' the creator, explorer, producer, provider, and man and community. With a few notable exceptions – China, Brazil, Poland, Spain, Portugal, Pakistan, Turkey, and Argentina – countries around the world lined up to build national pavilions. Private industry and the not-for-profit sectors were also invited to participate. The United Nations Association built a pavilion and seven different Christian denominations set aside theological differences so they might build a joint pavilion. Their tent, however, was not big enough. Conservative evangelicals built their own pavilion.

What about Jewish participation? With two Christian pavilions announced, Rabbi Wilfred Shuchat of Montreal's Conservative Shaar Hashomayim Synagogue felt that Judaism also needed a presence at the Montreal fair. His first thought was that a functioning synagogue should be incorporated into the Israel pavilion planned for the Expo 67 site. After preliminary discussions, the Israelis vetoed the idea. They argued that while Israel was homeland to the Jewish people, it was also holy to three great world religions. The Israel pavilion was meant to showcase the land's significance to all three faiths, not just Jews. It was therefore inappropriate for it to house a functioning synagogue.

Rather than give up on the idea of locating a synagogue within the grounds of Expo 67, Rabbi Shuchat took the liberty of having plans for a small on-site synagogue drawn up and, accompanied by fellow rabbis from Montreal's Orthodox and Reform streams, approached Sam Bronfman to gain his support for the synagogue project. Bronfman was taken with the idea of a synagogue at Expo 67, so long as it operated under the auspices of the Canadian Jewish Congress and Allied Jewish Community Services in Montreal. He also pledged financial backing for the project, but declined a hands-on leadership role. With still more money needed, Montreal grocery store magnate Sam Steinberg agreed to head a foundation that would fundraise on behalf of the project, oversee construction, and help with programming, but only after he was assured of two conditions: first, the project must have the unqualified support of all religious streams within the Montreal Jewish community and, second, all must agree that the project be expanded in its vision from a small on-site synagogue to a Pavilion of Judaism 'proclaiming the wonder of Jewish survival and the meaning of Judaism to man and his world.' All agreed the synagogue would be open for daily prayer services – except on Saturday and Jewish religious holidays – and the larger pavilion would offer fairgoers a comprehensive program of exhibitions, lectures, and cultural activities exploring Jewish religious and communal themes.[55] A press release outlining the final plans – not for a 'Jewish' pavilion but for a Pavilion of Judaism – stressed the unifying motif for the pavilion would be the Torah.

> In front of the pavilion there is a sculpture by Elbert Weinberg called 'The Procession' which consists of a group of life-sized figures in bronze carrying the Torah.
>
> In the upper area of the pavilion a series of continuous thematically staged, and artistically designed exhibits will reflect the theme 'Man and His World' in the light of Judaism as a religious philosophy of life.
>
> Programming in the pavilion will be based on six principles of Judaism
>
> Torah – learning, education and law
> Avodah – love of God, worship
> Gemilat Hasodim – love of man, charity
> Emit – the quest for truth
> Din – the quest for justice
> Sholom – the quest for peace
>
> These fundamental ideals and their present-day implications will be illustrated through monumental works of Jewish thought and creativity: Masterpieces of art, paintings, sculpture, graphic pageants, ceremonial art objects of Jewish festivals and tradition, Torah Scrolls and Ark Curtains from different periods and lands, rare manuscripts, historic documents and Hebrew incunabula.

Special care was taken to ensure there was no overt overlap between the Pavilion of Judaism and the Israel pavilion. The Pavilion of Judaism was to be self-consciously devoted to exploring issues of Jewish faith with special emphasis on its Canadian context. In addition to the synagogue there would be one exhibit honouring great Jewish theologians, philosophers, and social theorists and another exploring the history of Jews and Judaism in Canada. On a larger canvas, it was intended that the Pavilion of Judaism impress visitors with Judaism's 'contribution to the universal ideals of mankind.'[56]

The Zionist narrative and proclamations of Jewish peoplehood, of Jewish connection to homeland, and of the bonds tying Jew to Jew around the world were left to the Israelis. A short press release issued by the Israeli consulate in Montreal about the Israel Pavilion emphasized this point. It explained: 'Israel has a dramatic story to tell. What both architecture and exhibits will try to express is the dramatic rebirth of the nation which, after 1900 years of adversity, has recovered and restored its homeland.'[57]

When Expo 67 opened in the spring of 1967 to a chorus of rave reviews, Montreal's Jewish elite could take well-deserved pride in their successful construction of a pavilion that spoke eloquently of Judaism's place in the world even as it underscored their desired vision of Canadian Jews as a partner faith community in Canada. The small glass-walled synagogue held only about twenty-five worshippers, and on many evenings an overflow crowd of worshippers spilled into the pavilion courtyard. What the pavilion organizers did not expect was that within weeks of its opening, their concern to present Jews as a faith community within Canada, avoiding issues of Jewish peoplehood or national destiny, would suddenly be overtaken by events unfolding half a world away. As war clouds gathered in the Middle East during the spring of 1967, Jews in Montreal and across Canada were suddenly convulsed by fears for the survival of Israel and their own place in the world. With a passion of purpose that no one could have predicted, Canadian Jews, fearful for their survival as a people, rushed to embrace *amcha*.

CHAPTER THREE

Second City

In the spring of 1967 Jews in Toronto, like those in Montreal, were gripped by fear for Israel and the Jewish people. But if the degree of passion was the same, the context was not. Most obviously, Jews in Toronto were at a distance from the social, economic, and political upheaval brought on by the Quiet Revolution in Quebec. Unlike Jews in Montreal, Jews in what was then Canada's second city had no concerns about the displacement of the English language or the status erosion of English speakers or the rebirth of a populist nationalism that might be tinged with antisemitism. Former Torontonian, and for many years rabbi at Montreal's Congregation Beth El, Allan Langner, observed that through the 1960s 'Jews in Toronto did not appreciate what Jews in Montreal were going through.'[1] The same can also be said in reverse. Montreal Jews had little idea about the world of Jews in Toronto. How could they? The discourse of intergroup relations was so different in Toronto, including that which related to the place of religion in the public square and in the tax-funded school system. And different as Toronto was from Montreal, so too were the issues which engaged Toronto Jews and the way that Jews, individually and collectively, dealt with them through the 1960s.

Jewish Toronto might be different from Jewish Montreal, but for the leadership of the Toronto Jewish community, as elsewhere in Canada, there was no ignoring Quebec. Donald Carr, a respected lawyer and power in the Toronto Jewish leadership group, recalls: 'It wasn't in the purview of the rest of us [Jews in Toronto] that they [Jews in Montreal] lived in a different world.' Yet when it came to setting the Canadian Jewish Congress's national policy agenda, one issue dominated. How would it play in Quebec? 'On countless, countless, countless occasions when decisions on a national basis had to be made on approaches to government,' Carr notes, 'they were not carried forward because they would have a deleterious effect on their [Montreal Jewish] relationship with French Canada and French Canadians.'[2]

The willingness of Congress leaders across Canada to grant Montreal Jewish officials veto power over any program or policy initiative that might negatively impact Jews in Montreal – as in not presenting a brief to the federal B&B Commission – was more than just an acknowledgment of how volatile were issues related to Quebec and French Canada. It also reflected deference to Montreal as Canada's then premier Jewish community and the corporate headquarters of the Canadian Jewish community.

While organizationally differential to Montreal, by the early 1960s Toronto was emerging as a Jewish metropolis in its own right. Five hours' drive west of Montreal along Highway 401, Toronto had a Jewish population of approximately 90,000, slightly smaller than Montreal's. There is no denying, however, that the Toronto Jewish community had a very different feel about it. Even today, trying to pinpoint the differences between the Montreal and Toronto Jewish communities is something of a Canadian Jewish parlour game. Much can be made of differences in immigrant origin. In the early 1960s Yiddish-speaking Eastern European immigrants and their Canadian-born children made up the majority of both communities, but there was lots of room for tongue-in-cheek joshing about the respective old-country roots of the two communities. During the peak period of Jewish immigration to Canada from the 1890s through the 1920s, immigration into Montreal was dominated by Jews from Russia and Roumania who were reputed to pride themselves on being more urban, educated, and culturally sophisticated than the more small-town and dirt-poor Polish and Galician Jews who gravitated to Toronto. The reply from Toronto was incredulous. How dare Russian Jews talk about sophistication? They put pepper rather than sugar into gefilte fish and declare themselves sophisticated. And Roumanians? Do you know the recipe for Roumanian chicken soup? First, you steal a chicken. And, of course, there are the bagel wars. Connoisseurs of Toronto's heavy-as-lead bagels hail them as infinitely superior to the gummy, shrivelled-up bagels Montrealers claim as their own. Not to be outdone, devotees of Montreal smoked meat contemptuously trash Toronto corned beef as much like something one might expect to scrape off the bottom of their shoe.

Joking aside, there were core differences between Canada's two largest Jewish communities shaped by the different historical encounters each community had had with the surrounding world. This is no surprise. Jewish communities everywhere tend to take the shape of the pan they are baked in. In the case of Montreal, it might be argued, as did Peter Desbarats, that while the Jewish community there might see itself as a third solitude sandwiched between larger Anglo and French Canadian communities and welcomed by neither, it was also a community which absorbed much of Montreal's more sensual, free-spirited, and creatively exuberant European-style elan.[3] At the same time, wedged in by boundaries of geography, language, and acceptance, McGill sociologist Morton Weinfeld argues, Montreal Jews successfully created an internally spirited community, a community characterized by 'warmth' and welcome. How, according to Weinfeld, did that compare with Toronto?

> Traits like 'warmth' are obviously hard to quantify, and as a Montrealer I should resist the temptation to disparage Toronto. On a per capita basis, Montreal outperforms Toronto in terms of Jewish philanthropy and – in my view – the variety of vibrancy of its Jewish institutions. But there are other subtle differences in the character of the two communities. Montreal Jews seem to have a more comfortable, core confident sense of Jewish identity. In the world of Gershon Hundert, a native Torontonian teaching at McGill, 'The difference has to do with the "Orangeness" of Toronto. Toronto Jews seemed to act with a certain discretion about their Jewishness, which is not the case in Montreal. In Montreal, Jews have their place in the social landscape.' In Toronto it is a short hop from insecurity to smugness, to compensate for Jewish underachievement. In Montreal's place in the social landscape – a 'third solitude' – could lead to greater self-confidence. Whatever the case, the Montreal Jewish community for a long time set the standard for Jewish cultural creativity and communal leadership. In the world of historian Frank Bialystok, Toronto's Jews are chronic underachievers, '180,000 people sitting on their ass.' Toronto Jewry has more people, power, and money, all of recent vintage. For whatever reason, Montreal, a declining community, has more *ta'am* (good taste) and *savoir faire*.[4]

Weinfeld is not alone in placing the blame for what he regards as Toronto's lack of '*ta'am*' at the foot of a dispiriting and repressive municipal Orangeness, a crust of Anglo-Protestant values that defined Toronto society in the years before and just after the Second World War and held the Toronto Jewish community in its grasp. Measured against their own community, many Montreal Jews regarded the Toronto Jewish community, like Toronto itself, as narrow, uncultured and bland – like matzah, flat, dry and tasteless.

During the course of an oral interview, historian of the Montreal Jewish community David Rome was once asked what the Toronto Jewish community was like during the 1940s when he was English language editor of the *Toronto Hebrew Journal*. He thought for a moment then asked the interviewer a seemingly unrelated question. Did the interviewer know anything about *muktza*? No. Rome then explained that *muktza* was the term used for those things an observant Jew would not touch or carry on the sabbath, or *shabbat*. There were, according to Rome, three categories of *muktza*. Because *shabbat* is the day of rest, his first category included all those things that had to do with the work-a-day week – a sewing machine, a hammer, money. Because *shabbat* is the day of life, the second category of items one did not touch involved all those things that had to do with death – a shroud, a tombstone, a coffin. And because *shabbat* is the day of beauty, Rome continued, the third category forbid Jews to touch those things that struck the eye as vile and ugly, those things so esthetically unappealing that their very existence seems to defile the beauty of the *shabbat*. The Toronto Jewish community, he laughed, fit in that third category.[5]

If the Toronto Jewish community might be regarded as *muktza*, it was, Rome insisted, because at their core Toronto Jews were Torontonians, and as a community Toronto Jews simply mirrored Toronto's well-deserved reputation for enforced insipidness. If life was a symphony Torontonians were tone-deaf, or so it seemed to Rome. And there is no denying the Toronto of the past was very different from the tony and trendy multicultural metropolis of today. Just before the outbreak of the Second World War, Toronto was a city of about 650,000, the vast majority prideful of their British roots and traditions. The dominant community imagination was so overwhelmingly Anglo-centric that Toronto was commonly regarded the 'Ulster of the North,' a municipal bulwark of imposed Anglo-Protestant Victorian restraint where the Orange Lodge, draconian liquor legislation, and tight-assed Sunday blue laws held sway. Pre-war Toronto had changed little since 1923, when Ernest Hemingway was working as a reporter for the *Toronto Star*. At the time Hemingway enjoyed an active correspondence with Ezra Pound. In a letter Pound asked for Hemingway's impression of Toronto. Hemingway, seldom at a loss for words, replied, 'It can't be worse. You can't imagine it. I'm not going to describe it.'[6] Others were less hesitant. Shortly after the outbreak of the Second World War, visiting English author Wyndham Lewis dismissed Toronto as no more than 'a mournful Scottish version of an American city' and the rest of English Canada as 'a sanctimonious icebox.'[7]

What of Toronto's Jews? Was it true, as Montrealers might joke, that a generation of displaced Jews from south central Poland somehow stumbled upon a 'mournful Scottish version of an American city,' and morphed into a spiritless band of tight-sphinctered Anglo-Protestant wannabes? No. While there is no denying that Toronto's former blue-stocking conservatism and ordered public reserve gave the city a very different tone and texture from that of Montreal in the post-war years, by the 1960s this characterization of Toronto was wearing thin. Toronto of the early 1960s was not the snore it once was. Of course there were those who held tenaciously to the past and dug in their heels against any slackening of the blue laws that had long clogged Toronto's cultural arteries. But the larger municipal mood of the early 1960s was one of expectant change as this once sleepy and self-satisfied backwash of Empire witnessed unprecedented economic expansion fed by a massive intake of immigrants from southern and eastern Europe. In this era of new money and new immigration, Toronto's Jews found themselves in a very different city and with different rules of engagement than their parents knew.

If Montreal Jews continued to define their community as a 'third solitude,' Jews in Toronto sensed a crumbling of barriers, a lessening of restrictions that previously denied Jews access to the public square. This did not mean that barriers had simply collapsed. Far from it. But, like storm fronts on a weather map, the lines separating Jew from non-Jew in Toronto were slowly shifting. Of course, looking back there is no denying antisemitism was as much a part of the Toronto Jewish experience as it was Montreal's. In a talk to the Toronto Jewish Historical Society in 1972, Toronto-born Ben Kayfetz, soft-spoken executive director of the Canadian Jewish Congress in Toronto, listed example after example of how antisemitism had narrowed the life chances of Jews in Toronto well into the post-war years, including, no doubt, many of those who sat listening to Kayfetz. 'I know,' said Kayfetz, drawing in his audience, 'each one of you could multiply the cases I've mentioned and supplement episodes and incidents from other callings and professions unmentioned by me.' Even as many nodded in agreement, Kayfetz continued.

The question that occurs to me is: why was our community so silent in those days? Why did we endure so patiently the kind of treatment we wouldn't tolerate for a moment today?

Well, for one thing we were not the same kind of community that we are today. We were predominantly an immigrant community, our parents were then in charge and who were they? Men and women from Russia, Poland and Roumania, not fully integrated into the society, certainly not acculturated, not yet secure in their identity and still adjusting, however imperfectly, to an unfamiliar Canadian society.

And what's more important, it was all very relative. They had come in the main from a Czarist society where Jews were regarded as an alien element, were barred from secondary (even primary) and advanced education, where to train themselves for a profession they had to cross countless hurdles including study abroad, where they were forbidden even to live in the main urban centres. In contrast to what they had been exposed to, the open society of Canada where their sons and daughters at least had a 'fighting chance' at entering a college, embarking on a professional career – was so far in advance of what they knew that they were willing to put up with the discrimination obstacles which to them were challenges to be overcome.[8]

But that was then and now was now. Kayfetz, who served for many years as the Canadian Jewish Congress point person battling anti-semitism in Toronto, was adamant that compared to that earlier day, the years following the end of the Second World War produced dramatic changes for the better both in Toronto and in the place of Jews in Toronto. Once confined to the social and economic margins, Jews had become players in a bourgeoning and exuberant city – a far cry from the world that was. If Toronto Jews were not yet regarded as fully *white*, few would deny there was a lot of *whitening* going on.

Of course, Kayfetz would not deny that antisemitism was still a force in early 1960s Toronto. However, it was different than in the past. Raw, in-your-face antisemitism in housing, employment, and education was more and more a thing of the past. What remained seemed somehow muted and genteel if no less pernicious. What is more, unlike Montreal, in Toronto there was no linguistic impediment to Jews accessing the mainstream. Also, unlike Montreal, where ethnic, linguistic, and religious boundaries tended to silo groups – a Jew was a Jew, an Anglo an Anglo, and the French were French – Toronto of the 1960s was somehow more fluid. Yes, Toronto was home to a geographically close and organizationally active Jewish community. And, yes, that community afforded a narrowly sheltered Jewish life to those who sought it. But Toronto also afforded increasing opportunities for Jews to access the mainstream and to do so as Jews, if they were not too Jewish or too visibly so. This could involve some juggling. How much Jewishness for how much access? How Jewish could one appear to be and expect to have entree to a still Anglo Protestant–dominated public square?[9] Maybe one need not anglicize his or her name, but it might be wise to quietly park other obvious Jewishness at home. For others the maxim might be 'dress British but think Yiddish.' Jews who wanted to be 'players' might do well to master the codes of the surrounding Anglo world, even if they thought of themselves as relying on their *Yiddishe kop*, Jewish head, or innate Jewish instincts, to navigate that world. Thus, unlike in Montreal, individual Toronto Jews might sense they had Jewish wiggle room in which to work out personal terms of engagement with the larger mainstream. And as the borderland between the Jewish and non-Jewish worlds in Toronto became more fluid, the list of Toronto Jews who emerged prominent in business, education, politics, and arts and entertainment grew in influence and number. But again, the issue was not just *if* Jewish but *how much* Jewish. In some cases the answer might be 'not very.' This inspired one wag to quip that among the powerful in Toronto 'even the Jews are Anglos.'[10]

It might be argued this fluidity was the promise of 1960s Toronto. Since the turn of the century, when large numbers of Eastern European Jews began arriving in Canada, English-speaking gatekeepers held out the hope of admission to the mainstream to those Jews who would but debone themselves of their 'foreignness.' Forget later talk of multiculturalism, respect for pluralism of cultural expression, or social traditions. Canada's embrace of the mosaic was still decades in the future. In Toronto, as in the rest of English-speaking Canada, social workers, police, Protestant clergy, and public school teachers all preached a theology of assimilation. Jews, together with Catholic Irish, were a 'foreign' element requiring special concern, especially when it came to public education. As the cutting edge of efforts to assimilate immigrant children, the school's message was simple. Canadian society was open to those who would embrace Canada, cast off old-world ways, and enter the mainstream as quickly as possible.

In practice what did this mean to Jews? Was it supposed that Jews would somehow strip themselves of any hint of Jewishness or was there some way in which Jewish religious or cultural identity was compatible

with being Canadian? On this gatekeepers were divided among themselves. While there was general agreement that immigrants and their
children needed to Canadianize by adopting the English language and
mainstream values, some argued that this did not mean that the Jewish
faith was by definition inconsistent with the 'Canadian way.' For them
the issue was not so much that Jews were Jews, but rather that there
were those Jews who used their Jewishness to wall themselves off from
Canada. Of most concern were those, mostly immigrant Jews, who did
not know or care to know the 'Canadian way' and sought to prevent
their Canadian-born children from adapting the Canadian way. But the
welcome mat was out for those Jews who were prepared to accommodate to Canadian values and worked to ensure their synagogues and
homes reflected those Canadian values. Accordingly, these assimilators
saw it as their task not so much to de-Jew the Jew as to Canadianize the
Jew, to rebrand Jewish immigrants into Jewish Canadians.

Other gatekeepers disagreed. Echoing an earlier assimilationist article of faith, they held that being Jewish and being a *real* Canadian were
mutually incompatible. Canada was a Christian dominion from sea to
sea. Being Canadian was synonymous with being Christian and, better still, Protestant. The goal must be to turn the Jewish them into the
Protestant us.[11]

In spite of this divide between gatekeepers, most agreed that for
Canada the end of the assimilation process must not be the creation of
some hybrid national stew into which every generation of immigrants
added their own unique flavour. That was an American melting-pot
vision. No. The Canadian assimilationist model was what historians
have come to call Anglo-conformity. Rather than welcome immigrants
to contribute to and thereby change the collective national identity – a
sure way to debase the Canadian coin – across English-speaking Canada the goal was for immigrants to recast themselves so as to be, in
behaviour and mode of thought, Anglo-Canadian or, in the language
of the day, English.[12]

The lure of assimilation has been a running theme in Canadian immigration literature. In John Marlyn's classic tale of an immigrant child
growing up in pre–Second World War Winnipeg, for example, the
young protagonist, grabbing for the assimilationist brass ring, wanted
nothing so much as to be able to peel off his immigrant skin and disappear into the Anglo mainstream. Even as a schoolboy feeling trapped in
a working-class ethnic home, he dreamed of squeezing himself through
the Anglo keyhole and entering the promised world of mainstream ac-

ceptance. He pleadingly attempted to explain to his old-world father why becoming a 'real' Canadian was so critical and, equally important, why to be a 'real' Canadian one must be English. "'The English,'" he whispered. "Pa, the only people who count are the English. Their fathers get the best jobs. They're the ones nobody ever calls foreigners. Nobody ever makes fun of their names or calls them 'bologna-eaters' or laughs at the way they dress or talk. Nobody." He concluded bitterly, "'cause when you're English it's the same as bein' Canadian.'"[13] Even as a young boy, he understood that the term 'English' referred not so much to a language or to those who came from England, but to an ideal to which one should aspire. English was the other side of the lace curtains. English was the promise of access and acceptance and success. To be English was to cross the line from immigrant to Canadian, to cast off difference and escape to the sheltering invisibility of sameness. Well into the 1960s, many Toronto Jews used the world 'English' as an adjective to differentiate what was inherently 'theirs' from what was inherently 'ours.' The soft, white sliced bread sold in cellophane bags and bearing little resemblance to the hard-crusted rye or black breads sold in Jewish bakeries was English bread; public school was commonly referred to as English school, light years different from the often airless and undisciplined *cheder* that occupied many Jewish children in the late afternoon; English holidays were those statutory holidays – whether Christian or civic and patriotic – that passed largely uncelebrated in Jewish homes; English friends were those with whom one might share recess play but little if anything else once school was out.

Adjectival use of the word 'English' persisted among Jews in Toronto even as 'English' Toronto, the Toronto of the Orange Lodge, Sunday business and entertainment closures, and separate male and female entrances to drinking establishments gave way to a new and more open cosmopolitan spirit. The roots of this changing spirit run back into the war years. The war and the orgy of public spending that it precipitated sparked massive urban industrial development and full employment. Economic planners worried, however, that an allied victory would bring a return of bad economic times. Without war-related government pump priming, industrial production would decline, unemployment would grow, and markets for goods and services would suffer. These worries proved misplaced. In the post-war years the Canadian economy boomed. This boom was fed in part by pent-up domestic consumer demand for goods and services in short supply, not just since the beginning of the war but during the Great Depression which preceded it, and, in part, by offshore demand for Canadian manufactured goods, extractive resources, and agricultural production. As the demand for goods and services grew, so too did demand for labour. The result was a looming labour shortfall that threatened to douse economic growth. To ensure an adequate labour pool, labour-intensive industries joined in calling on the government to lift long-standing restrictive barriers to immigration. At first reluctantly, then as a matter of state priority, Canada reopened its doors to European immigration, including the immigration of Jews. Much of that immigration flowed into Toronto, which quickly became the country's major immigrant-receiving centre.[14]

The opening of Canada's doors to Jewish immigrants was not the only impact of economic growth on the Jewish community. During the war, the organized Jewish community, battling against talk of Jewish slackers and black-market profiteering, put its full effort into mobilizing Canadian Jews behind the war effort. Special priority was given to encouraging Jewish enlistment into the Canadian military. Meanwhile, on the home front, economic depression gave way to full employment. In the war's prosperity, a number of economic sectors thick with Jews – scrap dealing, the clothing and fashion industry, retail sales, food processing and marketing, entertainment, real-estate development and property management, and white-collar professions – became not just profitable but, in some cases, critical to the war effort. In the post-war years the organized Jewish community led by the Canadian Jewish Congress, redoubled its efforts against still legally sanctioned antisemitism in employment, housing, and provision of services, including education, especially as it impacted the integration of new immigrants, including many Holocaust survivors. At the same time, Jews, Canadian-born and immigrant alike, were swept along in a tide of expanding possibilities. If few could ever hope to match the wealth of the Bronfmans in Montreal, there was a sense among many Toronto Jews that they were entering on a trajectory of upward mobility. As they prospered, Jews might not find themselves invited to break bread with Toronto's old-moneyed economic and business elite, but even as new players in town they would have *shlep*.[15]

As Jews reached for the greasy pole, a continuing influx of immigrants was changing the demographic face of Toronto. The Ulster of the North was gradually being buried under the weight of tens of thousands of arrivals from southern and eastern Europe. By 1961 the Canadian census revealed that more than 40 per cent of all Toronto residents were born outside of Canada, and almost 30 per cent of those who lived in Toronto had come to Canada since the end of the Second World War. Together, the foreign-born and their first-generation Canadian-born children made up the majority of the city's population. More and more, the bulwark of Anglo-Victorian values and its Anglo-conformist spin-off that had so long characterized Toronto into the post-war years proved out of step with the changed urban reality. The drift towards respectful pluralism had started. More than that, the provincial government, pressed to enact human rights legislation, responded to the new post-war demographic reality and its economic and political impacts by passing legislation prohibiting discrimination in housing and employment.[16]

As the larger Toronto community changed, so too did Jewish interaction with that community. By the early 1960s, for example, many Toronto Jewish-affiliated community agencies were incorporated under the larger United Way umbrella. This effectively eased some agency costs from the shoulders of the organized Jewish community, while opening the participant agency client base to include the larger Toronto community.[17]

All the while, individual Toronto Jews emerged in prominent areas of business, science, medicine, the arts, and the media that were previously a Jewish no-go zone. Jews also successfully entered the larger political arena, not just as Jewish candidates in a Jewish area, but as the 'people's' choice. It was especially telling that in 1955 mayoralty candidate Nathan Phillips defeated the incumbent mayor and broke generations of Orange Order control of Toronto city hall. During the election the incumbent, appealing to sectarian prejudice, called on a then still-predominantly Protestant electorate to reject a Jew as mayor. The anti-Jewish campaign failed. Phillips won, an event journalist Pierre Berton declared a watershed moment in the conversion of a backwater town of 'smug, satisfied Anglo-Saxons' into a modern multicultural metropolis.[18] Unthinkable though it might be in Montreal that a Jew would be elected mayor, Phillips was re-elected to a second and third term. After a one-term hiatus, another Jew, Philip Givens, fluently Yiddish-speaking and prominent on the Toronto Zionist scene, was elected mayor. If the election of two Jewish mayors almost back to back was groundbreaking in Toronto, equally important is the fact that after Phillips's success the Jewishness of a politician in Toronto barely merited comment. Voter response seemed to be: 'So he's Jewish. So what?' And that is the point. As one study of ethnic integration in Toronto recently concluded, 'The election of Jewish mayors reflects not only the social mobility of Jews in Toronto over the twentieth century, but the extent to which massive multicultural migration to the city since 1950 has transformed assumptions of who is fit to play a lead role in the city's affairs.' By the early 1960s there could be little doubt but that litmus test of belonging that had previously denied Jewish access to the mainstream was no longer politically operative.[19]

This is not to argue that this accessibility came without struggle by the organized Jewish community or that individual Jews did not feel pressured to 'tone down' their Jewishness as the price of admission. Nor does it deny that entrenched pockets of exclusion persisted. What it indicates is that antisemitism, if not a spent force in Toronto, was in decline through the late 1950s and into the early 1960s, although much more grudgingly in some areas than in others. As if to underscore the simultaneous decline of antisemitism in the public square and its tenacious hold on important areas of the private sphere, one need only note that the breakthrough election of a Jewish mayor in Toronto took place even as many of Toronto's elite clubs, private schools, and corporate boardrooms remained off-limits to Jews. For the organized Jewish community the issue was how to beat back social antisemitism that hid behind a veil of voluntary association. Many Jewish leaders remained convinced that the best way to chip away at social antisemitism was to educate the public out of the negative stereotypes that fed anti-Jewish sentiment. This was the underlying intent of the 1959 year-long bicentenary of Canadian Jewry. Similarly, community leaders approved the building of a Pavilion of Judaism at Expo 67 to showcase the richness of Jewish religious and cultural contributions to Canada within the frame of a shared Judaeo-Christian tradition. And to forestall accusations that Jews were dangerous radicals, disruptive of Canadian social and political norms, community leaders took pains to ensure that Jewish approaches to government – even on issues of immediate community concern – remained respectful and low key. No noisy, fist-in-the-air, placard-waving public protest demonstrations. And, publicly challenging any notion that Jews were selfishly only out for themselves, the organized Jewish community made common cause with organized labour, liberal churches, the media, and other minorities, the same coalition that had previously joined with the Jewish community in successfully lobbying for legislated human rights protections, in extending that human rights blanket to cover others as well.

And with an optimism born of economic expansion and a continued immigration inflow, Jewish community leaders could point to improve-

ments in the status of Jews since the end of the war. Especially important, quota systems and other systemic discrimination at Canadian
universities, including professional schools, were largely a thing of the
past. Toronto Jewish folklore held that one of the prime reasons for the
1923 founding of Mount Sinai Hospital – originally a thirty-three-bed
maternity and convalescent facility – was to provide a practice facility
for graduate Jewish doctors in Toronto, denied internships or residency
positions in other Toronto hospitals because they were Jews. And one
of the worst-kept secrets in the Faculty of Medicine at the University of
Toronto was that into the post-war period it conspired to limit Jewish
admissions. Underscoring the degree to which Toronto changed, and
dramatically in the years following the war, in 1962 Mount Sinai, by
then a respected and large modern multi-service facility on University
Avenue's hospital row, became a teaching hospital affiliated with the
University of Toronto's Faculty of Medicine.[20]

   The end of discrimination in medical education and service delivery did not necessarily translate to other professions, including law.
Arthur Drache knew this first hand. Originally from Winnipeg, in 1955
Drache was a third-year student in the Faculty of Law at the University
of Toronto. He was starting to look for an articling position with a local
law firm when one of his professors invited Drache to his office for a
talk. Bora Laskin, later appointed chief justice of the Supreme Court of
Canada, had some friendly advice for his student. Offering Drache a
chair, Laskin proceeded to explain the facts of Jewish life with regard to
the legal profession in Toronto. The man who would eventually go on
to lead Canada's highest court cautioned Drache not to waste time or
energy applying to local law firms that would under no circumstance
consider hiring a Jewish law student, no matter his or her academic
qualifications. As if to reinforce his point, Laskin, who spoke from bitter personal experience, proceeded to list the prominent local law firms
that he knew discriminated against Jews.[21]

   Laskin need not have bothered. Drache and his fellow Jewish students were well aware of how antisemitism was played out in the legal fraternity. They had heard the snickering antisemitic one-liners that
passed among lawyers – 'Every litigator knows that when a Jew puts
on a skullcap to testify, he is about to hear lies.' The Jewish student
pipeline was also up to date on which law firms would never consider
hiring a Jewish articling student and which just might consider taking
on an exceptional Jewish student who did not present himself or herself

as 'too Jewish.' The students also knew which local law firms were reputed to hire articling students – Jewish and non-Jewish – on the basis of merit. And, of course, the students were acquainted with the city's 'Jewish' law firms – firms where the principals were themselves Jewish and where Jewish students knew they would be well received – if only they could get hired.[22]

Drache's experience turned out to be a little different from that of other Jews in his graduating class, in which he graduated fifth. He found an articling position with a then-expanding legal firm, and worked under the firm's senior tax lawyer, who, as it happened, was also the firm's only Jewish lawyer. Drache did well but among all the students articling with the firm, at the end of the year, he recalled, he alone was not asked to stay on with the firm. The reason was not secret. Drache was taken aside and quietly informed that, although his work had been exceptional, some of the firm's senior partners would feel 'uncomfortable having two Jewish tax lawyers.' It was suggested Drache would be 'happier' at a Jewish law firm. Angry, but not really surprised, Drache went off to do an advanced law degree at Harvard.

Reflecting on his articling experience, Drache argues that, even though he was given his walking papers, law firms that had previously blackballed Jews, and others judged unable to fit into the firms' club-like corporate culture, were even then beginning to have second thoughts. However, Drache contends this was not a result of goodwill but self-interest. The corporate cold shoulder experienced by many Jews began to give way because formerly Jew-free law firms began to fear that discrimination could run both ways and adversely impact their respective bottom lines. How so? A firm reputed to blackball Jews could well find itself blackballed by Jews, moneyed Jews increasingly prominent in the city's economic and professional life. And there was also another issue to consider. At a time when a Jew could be elected mayor of Toronto or appointed to the provincial cabinet, might not the firm's reputation for antisemitism in hiring negatively affect its prospects of landing lucrative legal work with the city or province or with those hoping to do business with government? According to Drache, as Jews became influential in government and business, the word on Bay Street was that law firms known to be antisemitic could take a financial hit. What is more, not only might these firms cut themselves off from possible Jewish clients, they also denied themselves the services of some of the best law school graduates – graduates who could end up working for competitors. Thus, according to Drache, it was less love of Jews than love of money that influenced antisemitic holdouts in the Toronto legal fraternity to finally clean up their act.[23]

Thus, for Jews, Toronto was different from Montreal in tone and texture. Unlike Montreal of the early 1960s where, as Jewish poet Irving Layton recalled, 'dominant ethnic groups stared at one another balefully across their self-erected ghetto walls,'[24] in Toronto 'ghetto walls' seemed to be crumbling. Even as they had the comfort zone afforded by an internally complete Jewish community, individual Jewish interaction with non-Jews was ballooning. And if the organized Jewish community remained fixed on breaking down the remaining barriers, most Toronto Jews, those with multi-generational roots in Toronto, no less than recent immigrants and their children, had reason to expect those barriers would fall.[25] Nobody would deny that there was still antisemitism out there. Drache's experience was not unusual. But there was also a growing confidence that remaining pockets of social and professional discrimination would give way. If not today, then tomorrow. The next generation of Jewish children would inherit a world of boundless promise.

Buoyed by optimism about the future, Jews in Toronto were not prepared for the sight of neo-Nazis spewing antisemitic hate in the streets of Toronto and other Canadian cities. Certainly, facing off against Nazis in Toronto or elsewhere in Canada was in nobody's mind, not as the decade of the 1960s began. Of course, only a fool would deny the presence of rabid antisemites in Canada. They could be found in all countries. Why would Canada be immune? And it wasn't. But if there were Nazi-like Jew-haters in Canada, they were gratefully few in number and relegated to the outer margins of civil society. Those Jewish professionals such as Ben Kayfetz who tracked antisemitism in Canada, took these haters seriously, no matter how few, monitoring their activities in cooperation with police and other authorities. But if Jewish officials did not ignore antisemitic extremists, neither did they exaggerate their influence. With no appreciable public following for neo-Nazis, Jewish community leaders reassured their community and one another that antisemitic extremists were not a pressing problem.

In spite of repeated assurances by community leaders that homegrown Nazis posed no threat, that antisemitism was on the decline and the future for Canadian Jews was never brighter, a handful of self-proclaimed Canadian Nazis managed to tap into a deep well of Jewish anxiety and, in the process, broke the surface calm and exposed deep cleavages in the Jewish community. The result was a sharp undermining of confidence in both Congress's leadership and its non-confrontational approach to problem solving. If, in the end, Congress leaders proved right – these self-styled Nazis posed no real threat – it is important to understand that the forces they unleashed would soon force a major redefinition of what it meant to be a Jew in Canada.

The existence of a few neo-Nazis in Toronto and Canada was not new to Congress officials. What was new was the spotlight attention they suddenly attracted. This was not just true of Canada. In the early 1960s, news of a neo-Nazi revival in Europe, Latin America, and the United States, replete with affirmations of Nazi racial theories and crude antisemitism, was very much in the public view. In Germany an extreme right-wing party, the NPD, led by Adolph von Thadden, presented itself as heir to the Nazi mantle. The NPD trumpeted Aryan superiority even as it denied the Holocaust as a Jewish fabrication. In the United States, George Lincoln Rockwell, often photographed in a Nazi uniform and surrounded by a band of loyal followers, proclaimed himself the leader of a nascent American Nazi movement. From elsewhere in Europe, England, and Latin America, there were press reports of resurgent fascist and Nazi-like political parties, stained by antisemitism, goose-stepping their way into the political arena.

In retrospect, it is easy to downplay this crude right-wing eruption as no more than a momentary rash on the body politic, a flash-in-the-pan aberration that in the end gathered little support or staying power. Certainly in Canada these self-proclaimed Nazis, for all their bluster, would eventually show themselves to be no more than a motley band of disaffected malcontents. Their swastikas, straight-armed salutes, and racist rants, at first greeted with bewildering shock, were almost universally reviled as an odious affront to the community good. But unable to read the future, at the time many Canadian Jews, and Holocaust survivors in particular, regarded these latter-day Nazis as far more than a vile and ugly curiosity. They were also more than a nightmare reminder of horrors past. In the early 1960s they were a clear and present threat. If not exorcized, what guarantee was there that these Nazis would not gather strength and, with strength, power?

It had happened before. Why couldn't it happen again? Many of the more than 40,000 Holocaust survivors who came to Canada after the war, including 4500 Hungarian survivors who arrived as part of the Canadian government's post-1956 refugee resettlement program, could not be convinced otherwise.[26] Had not Nazis and their sympathizers, dismissed as posturing clowns one day, ruled the next? Those who had once suffered the Nazis were not about to dismiss the Nazi threat again. If survivors might be united in revulsion at the very idea of Nazis in Canada, they were not unified in advocating any one response. How could they be? They differed by age, national origin, education, politics, level of religious and organizational commitment, and, of course, in their pre-Holocaust and Holocaust experiences and survival strategies. With no single Holocaust narrative, they had followed different life paths in their new home. Some came to Canada with family. Some came alone – sole survivors of families and even towns. Most adjusted well. Others less well. Many were economically secure. Others less secure. Among those who settled in Toronto, the levels of active participation in Jewish community life also varied. Most made community with other Jews, or with others with whom they shared Holocaust memories. But there were also those who kept at a distance from the larger Jewish community and even from other survivors, perhaps believing that had they been at a distance from the Jewish community before the Holocaust they might have escaped the Nazi onslaught. And if *it* happened again, they did not intend to make it easy for a new breed of Nazis to find them again. For other survivors, their Holocaust experience was the cornerstone of their persona. It defined them and, feeling a disconnect from those Jews with no lived experience of the Holocaust, they found it comforting to build community among those who did. Others wanted to 'put *it* behind them,' to repress memory as if *it* never happened, and certainly keep *it* from their children. If some found it easy to enter the Jewish mainstream, for others this remained problematic. But however different were the post-Holocaust experiences of survivors, even after arrival in Canada, the disquieting awareness of a Nazi presence in Toronto and Canada could not help but give many a disquieting feeling of vulnerability. And for some this translated into a determination to confront these Nazis head on.

To many survivors, reassurances by mainstream Jewish leaders that neo-Nazis in Canada were all noise and no heat, that they posed no immediate threat to Canadian Jews, and that Jewish leaders and the police were well on top of the situation were not reassuring. Weren't the same things said about the Nazi movement in Germany when it first took to the streets? Look what happened. Maybe those who did not live through the Holocaust could believe it could not happen again, but survivors knew better. What is more, if pre-war European Jewry were ignorant of the Nazis' intent or too weak to organize against it, neither could be said of Canadian Jews. The idea that as citizens of Canada survivors of the Holocaust would silently suffer Nazis again was unthinkable.

Even if these latter-day Nazis were mostly noise, there was lots of it. Whether emboldened by a reported resurgence of Nazi activism in Europe, England, Latin America, and the United States, or as a result of heightened media attention accorded Nazi- and Holocaust-related issues since the 1961 Eichmann trial in Jerusalem, home-grown Nazis, even if few in number, made their presence known. In 1963 many in the Toronto Jewish community were shocked when scurrilously antisemitic pamphlets and fliers, often with the swastika symbol bold in black, were delivered door-to-door in Jewish and non-Jewish neighbourhoods or handed out to children arriving at local schools, including Jewish parochial schools. One pamphlet proclaimed, 'Hitler was Right – Communism is Jewish.' Another complained that Jewish control of the media was so complete that 'at present we [Nazis] have no means of bringing the truth to the people, except our leaflets, etc. To expose ourselves now would be suicide.'[27]

Perhaps wanting to give what seemed a world-wide Nazi revival a local spin or perhaps hoping that local Nazis, like sex maniacs and serial killers, would sell newspapers, the Toronto press gave homegrown Nazis extensive coverage, sometimes interviewing Nazi spokespersons and quoting from their publications. That the Canadian press would grant these self-proclaimed Nazis publicity, Jewish community leaders feared, would only encourage them. To give Nazis a media platform from which to trumpet their antisemitism was an obscenity. That these Nazi ravings too often went unchallenged or, even worse, their publication defended as an exercise in press freedom was seen by many in the Jewish community as a desecration of the memory of the six million Jews murdered at the hands of the Nazis. Jewish officials also argued that by showering local Nazis with attention, the media granted antisemites a modicum of legitimacy, if not respectability, and encouraged others to support their cause.

Of course, this is not the way the press saw it. The press claimed the presence of neo-Nazis in Toronto was an important news story, and that exposing their hate-filled message was not the same as promoting it. But whether the press spotlighted local Nazis, their views, and activities because the presence of neo-Nazis in Toronto and Canada was judged newsworthy or because Nazis sold newspapers, Nazis became front-page copy. This, Jewish officials warned, is exactly what local

Nazis wanted. They fed off media attention. It made them feel validated and a force to be reckoned with. Even negative coverage served their purposes. Nazis declared it proof positive that Jews controlled the mainstream press. Canadian Jewish Congress officials urged the press to avoid being used as a soapbox from which Nazis could spread their message. If the press was truly concerned at the Nazi presence in Toronto, the press was advised, it should deny Nazis the oxygenizing coverage they craved.

Much to the unease of Canadian Jews, it was not just the broadsheet press that took an interest in the Nazis. The CBC, Canada's state-funded broadcasting network, also gave them coast-to-coast coverage, or at least far more coverage than the Jewish community thought advisable. In 1960, hard on the heels of an announcement of the establishment of a Canadian Nazi Party affiliated with George Lincoln Rockwell's American group, CBC reporter Norman Depoe filmed an interview with Rockwell in Montreal. Decked out in a Nazi uniform and flanked by several youthful followers, Rockwell proclaimed his fledgling Canadian Nazi affiliate a bulwark against the insidious scheming of Canadian Jews and their Communist co-conspirators. If that was not enough, he warned that once it assumed power in Canada, the Canadian Nazi Party would build concentration camps to house all enemies of the state. Jews, by definition, were enemies of the state.

In his study of Holocaust survivor experience in Canada, *Delayed Impact*, Franklin Bialystok details the furore set off by the Rockwell interview. Rockwell's comments were roundly condemned by the premiers of Quebec and Ontario and by the Canadian Labour Congress, which urged all Canadians to join in ensuring Nazism did not take root in Canada. The CLC also expressed solidarity with Holocaust survivors in Canada, living witnesses to the horrors of Nazism and now suffering the 'anguish' of witnessing Nazism in their new home. Survivors also took voice. Enraged by the Rockwell interview, Bialystok points out, a group of placard-carrying survivors and their supporters took to the street outside the Montreal hotel where Rockwell was staying – likely the first public demonstration ever staged by survivors in Canada. The protestors did not just direct their anger at Rockwell. They also rebuked the CBC for airing the Rockwell interview. This was not journalism. It was, they claimed, nothing less than wilful media complicity in spreading Nazi hatred of Jews.[28]

Moved by the uproar over the Rockwell interview and quietly

pressed by Congress officials, Canadian immigration officials ordered Rockwell deported back to the United States. The anti-Rockwell protesters, knowing nothing of Congress's intervention with immigration authorities, read Rockwell's expulsion as proof that their demonstration was successful in focusing government attention. Certainly, the demonstration won the attention of Canadian Jewish Congress officials. It had been organized by survivors without prior sanction or involvement of Congress, which claimed to be the authorized political voice of Canadian Jewry. Congress leaders, who prided themselves on their ability to quietly engage with those with power, insisted that was the best way to deal with Nazis. Public demonstrations were seen as counter-productive, with a potential for getting out of hand and alienating the very people Congress needed to keep on side. What is more, Jewish leaders argued, the Nazis revelled in confrontation and the spin-off media attention it generated. Instead of handing antisemites publicity, Congress advocated a 'quarantine,' denying Nazis the public exposure that is their lifeblood. Jews taking to the streets, Congress contended, served the Nazis well. It was not the Congress way. It was not the Canadian way. It should not be the Jewish way.

Congress insiders felt the best way to contain Nazi-like antisemitism and racism lay in persuading the federal government to enact a tough federal anti-hate law. Even before the CBC broadcast its Rockwell interview, Congress was quietly prodding Ottawa for legislation that would make hate speech and 'what might broadly be called hate literature' illegal under the Canadian Criminal Code.[29] Home-grown Nazis added new urgency to the Congress effort. But Congress lacked exact information on the extent of neo-Nazi activity in Canada.[30] To gather this information, Congress officials, working with police agencies in Toronto, successfully planted an informant inside the Nazi camp. In addition, community volunteers often surreptitiously attended Nazi meetings wearing a hidden recording device.[31] But if quiet lobbying in Ottawa, secret monitoring, and efforts at quarantining Nazis made strategic sense, these tactics also posed a dilemma for Congress leaders. All these activities, important though they might be, of necessity had to remain outside the public eye. As a result, except for publicly decrying the Nazi presence, to the Jewish man in the street Congress appeared inactive on the Nazi file. Concerned survivors and their sympathizers, not privy to Congress's behind-the-scenes anti-Nazi strategy, concluded that beyond mouthing toothless words of condemnation, Congress cared little about the Nazis and was doing even less. In the absence of proactive Congress leadership, some survivors concluded it fell back on them to take action. And protest worked. Hadn't the anti-Rockwell demonstration gotten the Nazi leader banished from Canada? Why wouldn't direct action work again?

Congress leaders were uneasy at the sight of placard-waving survivors, especially as the protesters claimed they were in the streets because Congress was not. But Congress insiders felt trapped. Unless Congress took a more publicly outspoken stand on the Nazis, it could be seen as uncaring or, even worse, irrelevant in the face of what many in the Jewish community, especially survivors, regarded as an imminent Nazi threat. On the other hand, stirring public outcry against these home-grown Nazis would, Congress officials feared, gift the Nazis with publicity and inflate their sense of self-importance. Trying to find a middle ground, Congress belatedly issued a public statement on the Rockwell interview. While decrying the media attention accorded Rockwell, the Congress statement suggested that his influence was exaggerated, and although he and his small band of followers were an insult to decency, they posed 'no imminent threat to Canada or its institutions.' Nevertheless, Congress demanded that, insignificant though the Nazis might be, no expression of Nazism should be tolerated in Canada. It was the duty of government, law enforcement agencies and courts, working with the Canadian Jewish Congress, to protect the public from Nazi-inspired hate whether imported or home grown. To ensure that the police and courts were sufficiently armed to this task, the Congress statement invited government to enact legislation against 'incitement to violence by fomenting racial hatred' in Canada.

Newly invigorated survivor organizations and their supporters brushed the Congress statement aside as too little, too mealy mouthed and certainly too late. As far as they were concerned, Bialystok notes, Congress was misguided if it thought the Nazi threat was overblown. And who better to judge the Nazi threat than survivors? What is more, if Congress believed public protest did not work, then Congress was wrong again. Protest had already served to alert both government and the public to the Nazi threat. As far as survivor groups were concerned, the only ones not taking the Nazis seriously were Congress officials.[32]

Wounded by survivor accusations that Congress was weak and indifferent to survivor pain, Congress leaders proved quick off the mark in early January 1963 when the organization learned that the CBC intended to broadcast a taped interview with Adrien Arcand, veteran Quebec antisemite and firebrand publisher of Nazi and antisemitic tracts in Quebec. Congress intervened with the CBC in an effort to forestall broadcast of the Arcand interview. Arguing that televised interviews with neo-Nazis such as Arcand, even if they might hope to portray Arcand and those like him as part of a lunatic fringe, still helped them disseminate their 'antidemocratic and antisemitic propaganda.' Though unintended, Congress again argued, this kind of exposure gave the Nazis a degree of public legitimacy. As a result of CBC coverage, Congress also feared some might conclude that, despicable though Nazi ideas may be, Nazis had as much right to express their views as anyone else. There were also those in the Congress camp who were unsure of where to draw the line between free speech and hate speech, between the public's right to know and its right to be sheltered from hate mongering, but few disagreed that a professed Nazi spokesman spewing antisemitism was engaging in hate speech. The CBC acceded to Congress's request, and announced that it would not broadcast the Arcand interview 'in whole or in part.'[33]

Congress officials regarded this a victory, but it was a very short-lived one. The following year Congress was not nearly so effective in preventing the CBC from televising yet another interview with George Lincoln Rockwell, this time conducted on his Arlington, Virginia, home turf. The CBC's popular television public-affairs program *This Hour Has Seven Days* prefaced the interview by explaining that, since it had begun pre-broadcast publicity about the interview, the program had received a number of protests against airing the item. Still, the decision was made to go ahead anyway. The statement explained that the segment's intent was not to offend viewers but 'to expose extremism in its monstrosity.' The CBC's preamble further argued that it would be irresponsible for the media to ignore Rockwell and his kind. By televising the interview with Rockwell, the CBC was unmasking him and his followers and the hate-filled message they delivered. This may have been the program's goal but, to the shock of many in the Jewish community, the interview allowed the American Nazi leader, again dressed in a Nazi uniform, a block of uninterrupted air time to spell out his group's program for dealing with gays, Blacks, Communists, and, most of all, Jews, whom Rockwell identified as the demonic force behind all of America's ills.

In an angry letter to the CBC, the Canadian Jewish Congress protested that there was no way to 'justify the publicity given to Rockwell personally and to his lies and invective. The CBC, in glamourizing a self-confessed follower of Hitler and preacher of genocide, is guilty of an act against the public interest.' The interview was also attacked in the House of Commons by spokespersons from all parties. In something of a case of the pot calling the kettle black, mainstream press comment also ran heavily against the CBC. The *Montreal Gazette* suggested that the CBC had yet to 'remove the suspicion that the whole thing was done for sensationalism, to create controversy and increase ratings of the show.'[34] But all this was after the fact. The interview had aired. The Nazis had again been given spotlight attention and survivor groups yet again felt let down as much by what they saw as a weak-kneed Jewish establishment as by the CBC.

In an attempt to forestall survivor criticism and further CBC broadcasts of a similar nature, Congress leaders requested an off-the-record discussion with CBC management in Toronto. The CBC, also uncomfortable with all the negative feedback the Rockwell interview had generated, agreed to meet and, in discussion, promised never again to allow Nazis uncritical access to the airwaves. But in January 1965, barely three months after the Rockwell broadcast, the CBC and *This Hour Has Seven Days* were ready with another Nazi interview. What about the agreement? Did CBC management fail to communicate its intent to production staff? Were those working in news and public affairs deliberately ignoring the CBC agreement with Congress, or was there a misunderstanding about what the agreement included? Whatever the reason, controversy exploded again when Toronto-based CBC journalist Larry Zolf, who often made reference to his Winnipeg Jewish roots, caught up with David Stanley, well known to Congress officials as an outspoken local neo-Nazi activist, as he passed out antisemitic literature on a downtown Toronto street corner. Zolf, microphone in hand, interviewed Stanley on film (for later broadcast) as passersby gathered around listening to the exchange.

News that *This Hour Has Seven Days* again was going to air an interview with a Nazi spokesperson did not sit well with many in the survivor community. Even if Zolf's intent was to hold Stanley and his followers up to public ridicule, according to the *Canadian Jewish News*, the soon-to-be broadcast Stanley segment provided yet another example of the public broadcaster's 'contempt for their employers – the Canadian people.'

Millions of Canadians who are paying the CBC for its services certainly expect it to exclude from its programs insults against any group which is part of this nation. If CBC has a role to play in this area of group relations, it unquestionably should be in a positive manner – in the direction of rapprochement among all peoples inhabiting this land; it should not dance to the tune of half-crazy agitators who openly declare that they are attempting to divide the people, to disseminate hatred and racial poison.[35]

Hoping to head off another round of CBC bashing and accusations that the public broadcaster was wilfully allowing itself to be a purveyor of Nazi propaganda, the show's producers invited Canadian Jewish Congress officials in Toronto to preview the Stanley segment and to comment on camera if they so wished. Congress leaders rejected the invitation. They feared that any on-camera comment would put Congress in the untenable position of either sanctioning the program's content or being portrayed as a censor trying to prevent Canadians from making up their own minds on the show's content.

What to do instead? With survivor groups pressing for action and CBC management apparently unable or unwilling to deliver on the agreement, the upcoming Stanley interview segment was put on the agenda of Congress' National Joint Community Relations Committee. Unsurprisingly, opinion among those seated around the table was divided. Fearing that many survivors and their supporters might take to the streets in protest and in so doing hand 'Stanley [and his followers] more of the very publicity they desired,' some committee members advocated quietly appealing to CBC management at the highest level to kill the interview. Others argued that at this point any *sha shtil* approach was ill advised. To act quietly and behind the scenes, even if effective, would again leave the Jewish street with the impression that Congress was doing nothing. Even worse, if quiet diplomacy worked, the Jewish street would be left to believe it was the threat of protest rather than Congress intervention that swayed the CBC against airing the interview. In the end, whether the CBC broadcast the Stanley interview or not, Congress would be dismissed as ineffectual, encouraging undisciplined community militants to step forward and claim that only public protest worked. To avoid this outcome, it was suggested that Congress immediately organize an orderly information picket outside the CBC's offices in Toronto. This action, it was argued, would show Congress's take-charge leadership on the Nazi issue while allowing Congress officials to work quietly behind the scenes to convince CBC management to scrap the interview.

For others on the committee the issue was not so much tactics but timing. One member insisted that with all the advance publicity surrounding the interview, Congress now had no option except to wait until after the interview was broadcast, and then, if necessary, point out a consistent pattern of CBC insensitivity to Jews, particularly Holocaust survivors. Another committee member agreed that any opportunity to forestall the interview had already passed. He lamented that Congress, in turning down the invitation to comment on camera about the segment, forfeited an opportunity to address Canadians on Jewish concerns. In the absence of an articulate on-camera Jewish voice, the viewing public would hear only a Nazi voice. Irreconcilably divided on what to do or say, the meeting resolved nothing. In a halfhearted effort at compromise, members could only agree that 'Congress and any other organization or individual who sees fit should lodge a protest but without press release.'[36]

In the absence of direction from the Joint Community Relations Committee, Congress's national president, Michael Garber, dispatched yet another sharply worded letter to the president of the CBC, protesting that it was 'a national disgrace that [the] CBC deliberately goes out of its way to give these Nazis and Fascists' a national platform for hate speech.

> On behalf of the Canadian Jewish Congress which speaks for the Jewish community, once again I come to you to protest this type of programme. Surely if there is difference of opinion in the minds of the CBC as to the values of these things you ought to take the advice of the Jewish community who are the victims of such programming and on balance decide that the questionable effects, in the name of free speech, have to be weighed against the deliberate insults and dangers which a national coverage can give to such purveyors of doctrines of racial extermination and therefore refuse to permit these, the Rockwells and Stanleys, to enjoy the facilities of the national [broadcast] system.[37]

Much to the anger of survivor groups in Toronto, Stanley got his air time. Capping an exchange of letters between Michael Garber and a CBC vice-president, Garber concluded that the CBC just didn't get it. More in frustration than in anger he wrote the CBC official: 'If you, forgetting your official position, can contemplate your having been a Canadian Jew listening to these [on-air Nazi] harangues, you will have a better answer to your letter than I can give.'[38]

If Holocaust groups were incensed with the CBC for televising the interview, they were again incensed with Congress for not stopping it. Why should a band of Canadian Nazis be allowed to spew antisemitic venom at will? Why should there be concern for the free speech of hate mongers who advocate genocide? What about the rights of Holocaust survivors to live free from intimidation and insult? Who was going to defend them and their children? Who was going to make sure that home-grown Nazis, today dismissed by Congress leaders as a ragtag band of morons, misfits, and malcontents, did not turn out to be at the vanguard of tomorrow's revitalized Nazi movement dedicated to finishing what Hitler had started? And what of Congress? Why was it more concerned with respectability than resistance?

To outraged survivors, especially in Toronto, the focal point of Canadian Nazi activity and home to one of the heaviest concentrations of Holocaust survivors outside of Israel, these questions cut close to the bone. There were Nazis in the street. These Nazis were allowed to spew their antisemitic hate on television and in the press. The Jewish establishment seemed nowhere to be found. If individual survivors may have been divided among themselves about what to do, raw memories of the Holocaust left many leery of entrusting their fate to government, the media, or Jewish community leaders who appeared indifferent if not oblivious to the Nazi threat. Maybe the world really had learned nothing from the Holocaust. Maybe the Jewish establishment had somehow slept through the Eichmann revelations. How else to explain home-grown Nazis allowed to walk the streets unchallenged? How else to explain a Jewish leadership that was all talk and no action? If concerned survivors felt abandoned by a head-in-the-sand Jewish establishment, at least activists had one another. In the absence of hands-on leadership from spineless Jewish leaders, enraged survivor groups promised to confront Nazis not with hollow words but with clenched fists should the occasion present itself. After all, who better to take on domestic Nazis and honour the memory of those who had been murdered by Hitler and his henchmen than survivors themselves?

It was bad enough that many Holocaust survivors in Toronto felt that Congress had repeatedly proved spineless in dealing with the Nazi threat and that the media appeared only too ready to give the Nazis all the publicity they could want. Still worse was the uncomfortable sense that, as a result, local Nazis were becoming more and more brazen. Bialystok notes that on 11 November, Remembrance Day, a crowd gathered in Toronto to honour Canada's fallen was showered with American Nazi Party leaflets proclaiming 'Communism Is Jewish' and 'Hitler

Was Right.' This was the first in a year-long series of Nazi provocations – public pamphleteering, swastika daubing, and even premeditated mailing of hate literature to individuals with Jewish-sounding names. In early 1964 several local Nazis handed out antisemitic fliers to fans, including many young Jews, awaiting admission to a much-anticipated Beatles concert in Toronto. Might physical attacks on Jews be next?[39]

With Nazi provocations ongoing, a growing number of survivors, 'volatile, vociferous, wanted action.' They and their supporters, feeling 'stonewalled' by what they saw as Congress's unwillingness to acknowledge, let alone confront, the Nazi menace, geared up to take matters into their own hands.[40] For their part, Congress officials refused to be stampeded into sanctioning street-level confrontation with Nazis and continued to work quietly behind the scenes monitoring Nazi activities and cooperating with police and public authorities who promised to pounce if local Nazis violated any laws. Without conceding that their long-standing attempt to 'quarantine' antisemites and deny home-grown Nazis the media attention they craved had proved ineffectual, Congress officials also took the unprecedented step of publicly naming leading Canadian Nazis so the media would be forewarned about whom they were giving publicity to. Congress's single main focus remained lobbying the federal government for anti-hate legislation, which, the organization was convinced, would cut the ground out from under Canadian Nazis and Nazi-like activity in Canada. In this effort, Congress officials attempted to enlist support from the mainstream media, organized labour, liberal churches, and community groups in support of legislation criminalizing the import, publication, and dissemination of hate literature and the utterance of hate speech. Putting the issue squarely on the national agenda, two Jewish members of parliament submitted private members' bills designed to outlaw the dissemination of hate literature. If enacted, one bill would make it illegal to disseminate hate literature through the mail, while the other would make it illegal to advocate genocide. While private members' bills rarely become law, these bills did have the effect of focusing government and media attention on how to control hate speech and hate literature without running roughshod over freedom of expression.

To push its case for anti-hate legislation, a Canadian Jewish Congress delegation headed by Saul Hayes, national executive vice-president of Congress, and Maxwell Cohen, dean of McGill Law School, met with federal justice minister Guy Favreau in Ottawa. The delegation presented the minister with a formal brief calling for changes to the criminal code that would protect Canadians from hate literature and hate speech. As a first step in that direction, the delegation proposed that the minister appoint an extra-parliamentary committee to study the problem of hate propaganda in Canada and recommend appropriate legal remedies to deal with those who promoted hatred.

The minister, perhaps hoping for guidance on what avenues for legal redress were available to government in handling the ballooning problem of hate propaganda, or hoping to buy time for government deliberation, agreed to appoint a special committee on hate propaganda, which Maxwell Cohen was asked to chair. Also appointed to the committee was Saul Hayes. But the government did not want the committee to be seen as a tool of the Canadian Jewish Congress. Far from it. With issues of free speech and freedom of the press at stake, the government appointed two prominent law professors to the committee – Mark MacGuigan of the University of Toronto and Pierre Elliott Trudeau, then teaching law at the University of Montreal.[41] The committee chair promised to give the hate propaganda issue a full airing.[42]

Congress hailed the establishment of the Special Committee on Hate Propaganda in Canada as proof the government was finally committing to pressing ahead on the anti-hate file. However, committee deliberations were barely under way before they were overshadowed by events on the ground. In the spring of 1965 self-proclaimed Toronto Nazi leader John Beattie called a press conference. Flanked by several young supporters, Beattie made a show of removing his trench coat to reveal a black and red Nazi armband. After several 'sieg heil' salutes, Beattie announced yet another incarnation of the Canadian Nazi Party and then took questions from reporters. His answers were mini-lectures on Nazi racial theory and the scourge of the Jew. He ended the press conference by announcing he and his followers were planning to hold a Sunday afternoon public rally in a public park in a down-on-the-heels downtown Toronto neighbourhood.[43]

The press gave Beattie and the announcement of his new Nazi Party extensive coverage. Congress officials, unable to stem the tide of Nazi news stories, denounced the new Canadian Nazi Party and declared the group ample justification for quick passage of anti-hate legislation.[44] For their part, survivor groups demanded to know how the organized Jewish community was going to respond to the new Nazi menace, especially to the 'gross provocation' of the announced Nazi rally in Allan Gardens. Congress appeared stymied. Try as it might, all its efforts to 'quarantine' Beattie and those like him had not worked.

While Congress denounced the proposed rally and pleaded for calm as the federally appointed special committee moved ahead with its deliberations, Congress offered no game plan to combat the Nazis, or at least none that increasingly anxious Jewish community members could see. As the rally loomed closer, notes Bialystok, Congress simply warned community members against being baited into a public confrontation that could only lavish the Nazis with still more media attention, pleading with the community to leave Beattie and his band of followers to Congress officials and the police.

Unbeknownst to the larger Jewish community, Congress and police officials were working behind the scenes on a plan to short-circuit the announced Nazi rally. After checking with municipal officials, it was discovered that Beattie had not secured the requisite permit to hold a meeting in a public park. If he and his Nazi followers attempted to hold their rally, they would be in violation of city ordinances and Beattie subject to arrest. The police promised to be ready.[45]

For Congress leaders there remained a problem of optics. For their plan to work, it had to be kept secret not just from Beattie and his followers but from an increasing number of Jewish activists. Publicly, Congress was seen to be doing little more than blowing smoke. Survivor groups, decrying a vacuum of moral courage at the top, again dismissed Congress as impotent, its leaders more concerned with containing Jewish anger than confronting Nazis. Even as Congress leadership called for restraint, militant voices declared restraint not the kind of response that in-your-face Nazi provocation demanded or Nazis understood. The very notion that local Nazis felt confident enough to hold a public rally in a downtown Toronto park was reason enough for Jews to organize in their own defence. Nazis needed to be taught that Toronto in 1965 was not the Berlin of 1935. And there were those determined to teach that lesson. Activist survivor groups, together with a newly organized Toronto Jewish self-defence group, N3, named for Newton's Third Law – for every action there is an equal and opposite reaction – called on Jews to stand tall and fight back against those who dared organize in Hitler's name. Labelled a 'vigilante group' by a Congress informant who attended N3's organizational meetings, the group reportedly was 'toying with the idea of some counter-action against the neo-Nazis.'[46]

With tempers already frayed, an ugly incident further rattled the Jewish community. Two weeks before the announced rally, about twenty-five young members of a local synagogue youth group were enjoying a day of picnicking and baseball in a local park. Without provocation, they were set upon by a gang of about forty 'wielding baseball bats, chains and rubber hoses.' Several Jewish youth were injured. The attack reportedly began when the Jews were mistaken for another group of young people with whom the attackers had previously had some sort of dispute. The synagogue's rabbi, who was not present during the incident, lashed out. Yet to be fully briefed on what had taken place in the park, he declared the attack racially inspired. 'I think,' he told reporters, 'that the time has come that there should be immediate action to show the antisemites that they cannot insult, harass, threaten or molest Jews in this country.'[47]

Outraged by the attack and compelled by an urgent sense of purpose, N3 publicly rejected Congress's caution that Jews stay away from the Nazi rally and allow local authorities to handle the Nazis. Defying Congress, the self-defence group issued a call for all Toronto Jews, and Jewish youth in particular, to turn out at the Allan Gardens rally, announced for 2:00 p.m. on the afternoon of 30 May. This, N3 declared, would prove once and for all that Jews in Toronto would not be intimidated.[48]

At noon on 30 May a crowd began to gather in Allan Gardens. By 2:00 p.m. estimates of its size varied widely at somewhere between 1500 and 5000. Many were young men. There were also a large number of Holocaust survivors. Reasons for being there likely varied from individual to individual. Some may have felt duty-bound to stand side by side in solidarity with other Jews in defiance of Nazi provocation. Others may have hoped to do some Nazi bashing. Still others may have come out of curiosity or because others they knew were going to be there. With no script for the event, people just milled about and chatted as they waited for something to happen. Also waiting to see what would happen were about fifty uniformed police officers, a number of plain-clothes officers, an expectant group of local reporters, Toronto's Jewish mayor, another Jewish member of city council, and several Canadian Jewish Congress staff members quietly hoping that the event would somehow pass without incident.

What followed had many elements of low comedy – exaggeration, mistaken identity, and even slapstick – but it was anything but funny. As Bialystok clocks the event, at about 2:00 p.m., the time pre-announced for the Nazi rally to begin, half a dozen young men, innocent members of an out-of-town motorcycle club, one wearing a black leather jacket, approached the park curious about the large crowd. As they neared the park police stopped and questioned them, but they were soon allowed to proceed. No sooner did the young men step into the park than they were mistaken for Beattie supporters and set upon. As police tried to rescue the innocent men in one corner of the park, Beattie, a Nazi armband in his pocket, arrived at another corner without any of his supporters visibly in tow. Even as a Jewish city councillor at one end of the park shouted into a bullhorn that the men being chased down and beaten were not Nazis and that there were no Nazis in the park, the crowd at the other end of the park surged towards Beattie. Before anyone could reach him, the police surrounded the Nazi leader, bundled him into a waiting police van, and whisked him away.

Most in the park did not participate in either of the two separate eruptions, but word that fighting had erupted spread through the crowd like wildfire. Without knowing exactly what was happening or where, those distant from the violence began pushing first this way and then that, some perhaps hoping to get in on the action, others equally intent on getting out of harm's way. But soon there was nothing to get in on or out of. Thanks to quick police action it was all over in a few minutes. Uncertain about what had happened or what might yet happen, the crowd milled about for a time before it began slowly to disperse.[49]

As Bialystok points out, Congress observers found small consolation in the fact that events could have been worse. From Congress's point of view, the whole event was wrong headed. What militant hotheads who called Jews out to demonstrate in Allan Gardens ended up demonstrating was their dangerously sorry lack of organizational skills. Individual protesters may have thought they were standing up for Jewish pride, but according to Congress officials, they instead precipitated violence and, in so doing, presented the Nazis with yet another bonanza of media attention. They even allowed Beattie to cast himself as a victim of Jewish violence. And nobody should have been surprised that there was violence. Those who showed up in Allan Gardens knew they were not going to a Sunday school picnic. They were going to a Nazi rally. With such an unorganized and undisciplined crowd, some of whom were apparently spoiling for action, it was no surprise that innocent onlookers were accosted. As far as Congress officials were concerned, those who roughed up the innocent men gave the whole Jewish community a black eye.

The legal fallout from the Allan Gardens 'riot' proved minimal. Before the crowd finally dispersed, eight Jewish demonstrators were arrested on various charges. In addition, Beattie, who turned up without a permit, was arrested for unlawful assembly. All but one of the Jews were eventually acquitted. So too was Beattie, who, the court ruled, could not be found guilty of unlawful assembly since, as Bialystok observes, 'there were no other persons assembled to act in concert with him.'[50]

Fallout from the Allan Gardens 'riot' inside the Jewish community was not so easily dismissed. Most mainstream community leaders were conspicuous in their absence from the event, but they were shaken by its aftermath. As an article of faith, they rejected the politics of confrontation. Street-level protest was to be avoided unless meticulously choreographed so as to further community interests. But public violence? Never. That was thuggery and would inevitably give the Jewish community a bad name. Instead, Jewish leaders preached a self-disciplined and restrained response to provocation, a response that prudently deferred to well-placed *shtatlonim*, intermediaries, who could respectfully advocate for the Jewish community within the corridors of power. And what had the Allan Gardans episode accomplished? While protesters did little to rein in the Nazis, leaders feared they did damage to the carefully cultivated Canadian image of Jews as law-abiding citizens, not an out-of-control mob – people of the book not the fist.

N3, survivor groups, and others who stood ready to confront the Nazis in Allan Gardens saw things very differently. Rather than being contrite, many were energized by a sense of 'we-showed-them' pride. After all, it was they, not the Jewish establishment, who proved themselves ready to stand up to the Nazis, just as rank-and-file Toronto Jews did in 1933 when they slugged it out at Christie Pits with a gang of swastika-carrying youth.[51] Then, Toronto Jewish leaders, not knowing what the Nazis would eventually do to European Jewry, might be forgiven for not being in the thick of the Christie Pits dust-up. But what excuse was there for Jewish leaders in 1965, knowing what the Nazis had done and what they would do again if given the chance, not standing shoulder to shoulder with those in Allan Gardens? None. So, who should be ashamed? Not those who defended Jewish honour.

With survivor groups defiantly unrepentant and promising more of the same, Congress officials in Toronto shifted into damage-control mode. The issue was no longer just about dealing with a small band of self-proclaimed Nazis, it was also about who should speak for the Jewish community, who should set the communal agenda. The reputation of the Jewish community as respectful and law-abiding seemed to hang in the balance. Media response to the Allan Gardens affair left

Congress insiders upset. While certainly not endorsing the Nazis' right to hold their rally, the press condemned the violence. Understanding the outrage felt by many Jews at the notion of Nazis parading in Toronto parks, one Toronto daily was equally uneasy at the existence of a 'secret' group of 'anti-Nazi vigilantes' in the Jewish community. What might they do next?[52]

Congress insiders asked themselves the same question. Determined to reassert Congress authority while reassuring the community that the Nazi problem was in hand, Toronto-based Congress officials drafted a follow-up, four-page 'Report on Neo-Nazism and Hate Literature,' to be delivered to approximately twenty thousand Jewish homes in Toronto. Unfortunately for its drafters, a copy of the report was inadvertently delivered to the press before it was mailed out to the community. The press jumped on the report or, more accurately, picked out juicy tidbits from it. The parts given most media attention were controversial and, taken out of context, appeared even more so. Taking deliberate aim at the protesters, one section of the report assigned blame for the Allan Gardens violence and the spate of bad publicity which followed on 'these [dissident] persons and groups for irresponsibly creating a tense and inflamed situation which involuntarily was bound to erupt into violence and which unfortunately did so; let's face it – the consequences of the riot could have been more ugly, even tragic.' The report reaffirmed Congress's determination to eschew violence, work with responsible authorities to quietly monitor and quarantine antisemites, and court 'support from all elements in Canadian society ... Our firm and aggressive policies both in opposition to neo-Nazism and in support of [anti-hate] legislation will continue. We must above all exercise the restraints and self discipline that is absolutely indispensable if we are to avoid the climate of terror, mob-rule and intimidation which can only serve the purposes of the neo-Nazis.'[53] Congress was not just upset by the negative light the Allan Gardens affair cast on the Toronto Jewish community or the defiance of Congress's time-honoured quarantine and *sha shtil* approach to dealing with publicity-seeking antisemites. What was unstated in the report was that Congress insiders regarded the Allan Gardens affair as a brazen attempt by loose cannons in the community to usurp authority reserved to Congress. How dare upstarts who had not earned any leadership position attempt to override responsible Jewish officials and, in the process, offer themselves up as the voice of community. And to what end? To spread anxiety among survivors and others in the Jewish community with wildly exaggerated tales of a Nazi threat in Canada? To demonstrate that Jews in Toronto had as much testosterone as anyone else? To gift Beattie and his small band of followers with a bumper crop of publicity, maybe even sympathy?

If Congress leaders expected demonstration organizers to be contrite, they were disappointed. The Jewish establishment's view of the Allan Gardens incident and its anger with those involved did not sit well with many survivors and Jewish self-defence advocates such as N3 and its supporters. Congress could write all the reports it wanted, but to many who were there, Allan Gardens held a very different meaning. Yes, perhaps in retrospect, the gathering was not as carefully planned as one might have wished. Perhaps things got a little out of hand. Certainly it was regrettable that innocent individuals were attacked. Regrettable yes, but given Nazi provocation and the way Nazis were coddled by the media, also understandable. And there was something else as well. What of the pride and self-respect felt by those who stood ready to confront the Nazis? What about the importance of serving notice to local Nazis and their sympathizers that the day was past when they could strut about with impunity, waving their swastikas and advocating genocide without consequence? Let court Jews, heads bent, go cap in hand begging authorities to protect Jews against home-grown Nazis and their friends. But sometimes pleading is not enough. There are times when, like Samson, Jews had to show they are ready and willing to fight back, even if it embarrasses or inconveniences a do-nothing Toronto Jewish establishment. Those who stood boldly, shoulder to shoulder with one another in Allan Gardens declared for all to hear that those who were, as one, ready to square off with the Nazis and deal with them again as the occasion might warrant deserved thanks not condemnation. What is more, if Jewish self-defence was not possible in 1930s and 1940s Germany and Poland, Hungary or Holland, France or Lithuania, it was possible in Canada in 1965. Since it was possible, Jews doing anything less than standing up in their own defence against the current crop of Nazis was reprehensible. Of course, Canada was not Germany and 1965 was not 1935. Nobody said they were. But if history does not always repeat itself, who was to say in this instance that it couldn't? The episode in Allan Gardens showed latter-day Nazis who hoped to finish what Hitler had started that they had better watch their step. Jews were no longer going to cower in the shadows. Nazis would never again go unopposed by those they sought to murder.

And who dared say Jews had no right to stand together in their own defence? Toronto's Canadian Jewish Congress leaders? Who were they anyway? Were they in the park ready to go nose to nose with the Nazis? No. They were off holding meetings. Passing resolutions. Writing reports. If hot air was a weapon, the Nazis would be trembling in their jackboots. Sure, the Toronto Jewish establishment talked a good game about protecting the community. When it came to action, however, they wrung their hands and presented one another with fancy plaques at conventions and black-tie dinners. What did they actually have to show for all their talk about dealing with the Nazi scourge infesting Canada? Another Ottawa committee? Just more talk. How then did establishment leaders have the temerity to write a report censuring those who were ready to look Nazis in the eye and say, 'Never Again'?

A week after Congress's report was delivered to Toronto Jewish homes, the Association of Former Concentration Camp Inmates and Survivors of Nazi Oppression issued its own 'Open Letter to the Jewish Community of Canada.' A lengthy and scathing attack on both the Congress report and those who drafted it, the letter offered an alternative narrative of events leading up to and immediately following the Allan Gardens rally. It recalled years of Nazi provocations which created 'a dangerous climate of tension' in Toronto even before the announced founding of a Nazi Party of Canada and the Allan Gardens confrontation. Where was Congress through all this? According to the 'Open Letter,' Toronto Congress leadership had proved two-faced in response to the Nazis. On the one hand, Congress officials tried to play down the Nazi threat, but when it came to the announcement of a Nazi rally in Allan Gardens, Congress warned that the proposed Nazi rally was a deliberate and dangerous 'provocation.' How could the Nazis not be a threat but their rally be a provocation? What is more, the letter challenged the Congress view that the battle of Allan Gardens had given the Toronto Jewish community a black eye. Not so. If anything, media coverage of the confrontation was declared to be far more understanding of Jewish protesters than was Toronto's Congress leadership. Cutting to the heart of the matter, the letter accused Congress leaders of being ingenuous in telling the Jewish community that the Nazi threat was in hand, that all was well, that community leaders were working closely with local police and the federal government on anti-hate legislation. Not only was the federal government not yet on side about passing anti-hate legislation, but, the letter argued, some prominent Congress leaders were themselves opposed to anti-hate legislation as an unwarranted restriction on freedom of speech. Following the events in Allan

Gardens, these same Congress leaders dared call for community unity while 'a large segment of Canadian Jewry has been smeared in a public Congress statement.' The 'Open Letter' from the survivors group demanded that these Congress leaders found to have deliberately misled the Jewish public and acted in contempt of the popular Jewish will should be 'removed from their functions in Congress' and Congress be reformed 'for the benefit of the entire Jewish community.'[54]

The dissidents had their allies. An editorial in the English-language *Canadian Jewish Chronicle* castigated Toronto Congress leaders for first dropping the ball when it came to the Nazi threat, then, to cover their shame, lashing out at those in the Toronto Jewish community who shared memories of the Nazi horrors – Holocaust survivors. Claiming that the Congress report on the events in Allan Gardens could only mean that 'someone in the Toronto leadership of the Canadian Jewish Congress panicked,' the newspaper 'doubted that Congress as a whole is behind the statement.' No one of goodwill could endorse the report. In fact, the editorial argued, the report was not only an overreaction; it was also a mean-spirited assault on the very Holocaust survivors Congress should be protecting. Bad enough that Nazis attacked Jews. Worse still that Congress added to survivor pain by attacking those who dared stand up to the Nazis. No doubt the anti-Nazi demonstration was ill planned and undisciplined. Nobody denied that. But for Congress officials to blame the Jewish demonstrators for the riot rather than the Nazis and their 'provocations' was cruelly to blame the victim.

> If the victims turned on their tormentors and drove them from their midst, would it be sound judgment on the part of the leaders of these victims if they came out with a public statement placing the blame for the violence on their own people? ... Let nobody be surprised if Jewish tempers flare up when neo-Nazis publicly advocate the destruction of Jews. We [Jews] are no different from French-Canadians, or Ukrainians, or Greeks, or Italians or even WASPS. The remedy is not to denounce any action or non-action by Jews – but to put a stop to the shameful baiting, the open incitement to hatred, the naked preaching of murder.[55]

A week after the 'Open Letter' was released, the Toronto Jewish establishment confronted a second challenge. Two hundred and fifty delegates from forty different community organizations, almost all of them constituent Congress organizations, assembled in the main hall of the Labour Zionist building in Toronto. Billing themselves as the Conference of Jewish Folk Organizations and Survivors of Concentration Camps, the delegates, in the main European-born and Yiddish-speaking, tripped over one another in expressing outrage at the Congress report and, in the end, unanimously voted non-confidence in Congress's leadership for remaining more concerned with its public image than with the Nazi threat.

> The Conference of Jewish Folk Organizations and Survivors of Concentration Camps, attended by two hundred and fifty delegates representing forty organizations, held Tuesday, June 22nd, 1965, at Viewmount Ave., Toronto, Ont. – which is affiliated with the Canadian Jewish Congress and which recognized the Congress as the official spokesman and unifying force of Canadian Jewry – expresses its shock and resentment at the public statement regarding the Allan Garden events, recently issued by the leadership of the Central Region of the Canadian Jewish Congress.
>
> This statement which was directed in the main against the victims of Nazism than against the Neo-Nazis, was proof of the fact that those who issued it fail to understand the whole problem of the revival of Nazism and of the dangers facing the Jewish people. The statement deliberately minimized the Toronto Nazi group and disregarded entirely the philosophy of Nazism which this group represents – a philosophy that caused the greatest holocaust in Jewish history and the loss of six million of our people and untold millions of others.
>
> The reference to those who demonstrated in Allan Gardens as a mob led by rabble-rousers is an insult to the feelings of thousands of Jewish people in our city.
>
> This conference demands:
> (1) That Congress should publicly withdraw and renounce the above-mentioned statement.
> (2) The resignation of the responsible parties.[56]

The line was drawn. Congress, controlled at the top by an older, entrenched, and moneyed Toronto Jewish elite, long preoccupied with opening the public square to Jews, faced a grassroots revolt. Its large immigrant and Yiddish-speaking constituency was in rebellion. There had always been dissenting voices in the Toronto Jewish community. How could it be otherwise? Jews are a fractious lot. But never before in Toronto had there been such a publicly loud and angry denunciation of leadership by many of those Congress claimed to represent. Something needed to be done and done quickly or the rift might well undermine Congress's ability to continue as the representative voice of the Toronto Jewish community. And what if the revolt spread to Montreal and Winnipeg?

As Congress leaders huddled in discussion, the organization's own Joint Community Relations Committee called an emergency meeting to assess the crisis. If Congress officials hoped committee members would line up behind the leaders, they would be disappointed. In a rare act of unity, committee members added their voices to the growing chorus of anger and disappointment at the Congress report. One long-time committee member accused Congress leaders of being 'not at all attuned to the community.' Rather than take the position that they were 'beyond reproach' with respect to the report and the hurt it has caused, he asserted, the Congress 'establishment' owed the community an apology. A prominent and outspoken Toronto Reform rabbi concurred. The report, he warned, drove a wedge between 'newcomers and old timers,' between Yiddish-speakers, including Holocaust survivors, and more establishment Jews. It also did 'a grave disservice to the [entire] community and deeply wounded the dignity of all.' What needed to be done? He and others demanded that Congress leaders call a meeting of 'representatives of every organization involved [in the Allan Garden affair] and every Jewish organization that has something to say about the letter' so all might 'speak their mind and submit briefs.' The alternative was to court a falling away of support from Congress in Toronto, which in the end would leave a vacuum in community leadership just when it was particularly needed.[57]

Boxed in by criticism of the report, Congress insiders did not want to be told they needed to turn down the heat before it did irrevocable damage to the organization. But how? In a post-mortem on the report, Ben Kayfetz, Congress executive director in Toronto, concluded the organization's leaders had fallen short in keeping the community plugged in, thereby leaving the impression that Congress had lost touch with the community grassroots. If it was to mend fences, Congress had to quickly figure out

> how to convey to the Jewish community [Congress's] policies and actions and keep it abreast of what is going on. This has been a particular problem in the matter of neo-Nazism where a segment of the community feels that because there have been no marches to Ottawa and picket protest that Congress is not doing anything or not doing enough and where perhaps another segment feels that too much is being made of the matter and it is being given too much attention and publicity.[58]

Even as Kayfetz proposed that Congress look to better and more openly communicate with the larger community, others called on Congress
leadership to hear out those offended by the report and then publicly eat
crow by apologizing for any and all hurt the report had caused. There
were also those who insisted that the only way to make Congress's
problems go away was to open up the organization's decision-making
process to those who felt themselves dispossessed of voice – especially
the Yiddish-speaking and survivor groups. It was feared that without
institutional reform, Congress would continue to lose credibility, perhaps to the point of irrelevance.

Dealing with the fallout from the Allan Gardens episode was felt to
be all the more urgent because there was no indication that local Nazis
were about to hang up their armbands and call it a day. Most agreed a
strong and representative voice of community was an asset. So, rather
than reinvent Congress, why not reform it? Rather than pull down the
Congress tent, how about enlarging it? Using this approach as an opening, Congress sought discussion with dissidents. As one concerned
Congress insider explained, 'In the future we are going to have to work
with these people. There are going to be other incidents. Rather than
condemn these people, we will have to try to bring them within the
scope of this Congress. We must bring the entire Jewish community
together – and work within the law of this country.' Certainly, it was in
nobody's interest – except the Nazis – to see a rupture in Jewish community unity.[59]

While it was important to become or appear to become more inclusive, as far as Congress insiders were concerned it was also important
to ensure the continuity of responsible leadership – by which, of course,
they meant their own. Their backs against the wall, they devised a plan
they hoped would bring peace to the Congress house and return survivor groups and 'folk organizations' to the fold without ceding their
control. As a first step Congress officials announced a 'Community
Conference' that, carefully choreographed, they hoped would dissipate
anger over the offending report and, instead, redirect energy into support for a Congress that would more effectively confront the common
enemy of all Jews – the Nazis. To avoid the conference devolving into
a communal gripe session, they prearranged that no sooner would the
meeting begin than a 'spontaneous' motion would come forward from
the floor calling on the local Congress to establish a body specifically
mandated to deal with the Nazi threat and, by extension, all Holocaust-
related issues in Toronto, including remembrance and education. When

the resolution was approved, leaders expected survivor groups and 'folk organizations' to claim they had successfully tamed the Congress beast and forced Congress to assume a more vigorous public profile in combating Nazism in Toronto. But, assuming the responsibilities and composition of the committee, once voted into existence, would be left to Congress officials, it might be possible to channel survivor passion to less confrontational activities and even engage the positive involvement of outspoken dissidents. As one Congress insider suggested, with any luck,

> the community meeting [would endorse] a militant program of action against Nazism, to be led by a special, widely representative committee; that there should be no raising of the issue of the circular letter at the community meeting; [and] that the position to be taken regarding a further Nazi rally or appearance at Allan Gardens would be that there be no 'demonstration' or mass attendance by members of the Jewish community and in this connection the leaders of the folk organizations would get up at the community meeting to so call upon their members and anybody else.

And the meeting went very much according to plan. While it was billed as a 'Community Conference,' a hand-picked 'register' of individuals was invited, ostensibly to guarantee representation from all organizational segments of the community, especially survivors and Yiddish speakers. Approximately 350 people showed up at Toronto's Holy Blossom Temple, including some 'guests' not on the 'register.' Among them were three members of N3 who, after first being denied access to the meeting, were permitted to participate. 'None of them took part in the discussion,' however.

With Holy Blossom's Rabbi Plaut in the chair, the meeting began with several brief comments on the need for community-wide unity and for Jews 'not to fight Jews but to fight Nazis.'[60] In hopes of forestalling acrimonious discussion of the Congress report and its aftermath, as planned, a motion was immediately introduced from the floor calling on Congress to establish a special committee to implement 'an active and vigorous anti-Nazi program in the Toronto area.' While some 'queried the lines of responsibility and authority of such a special committee,' the meeting voted unanimously to endorse establishing an anti-Nazi committee. Instead of rancour, the mood in the 'Community Conference' was suddenly upbeat. The unanimous passage of the motion, coming as it did from the floor, created an instant sense of empowerment in the room. While a few delegates still wanted to punish Congress leaders for their report, much of the anger that had brought many out to the meeting drained away. Of course, discussion of the report could not be entirely avoided. A motion was moved from the floor condemning it as 'irresponsible and having caused perhaps irreparable damage to the good name of the Jewish community of Canada' and demanding it be retracted and its authors removed from Congress. Amendment after amendment watered the resolution down until the report was simply dismissed as somehow 'ill advised and could therefore be considered as not representing the spirit or attitude of Congress toward the struggle against Nazism.'[61]

The meeting adjourned late in the night with another call to unity – 'to speak of the one community and no longer to speak of the division' – and a promise from Plaut that the anti-Nazi committee would be up and running as soon as possible. Plaut added one last note of caution. Nobody, he advised, should expect the new committee, no matter how representative of the community or how well intentioned, 'to do miracles. I don't think we can eliminate Nazism by wishing for it. But one thing I know this special committee will help the community to do ... It will help to set it on a special path of action. It will be active and it will keep you informed and I hope from time to time we may come together as we did tonight and exchange opinions.'[62]

It took several weeks of discussion over the committee's size, membership, and responsibilities before the newly minted Community Anti-Nazi Committee finally came together for its first meeting.[63] This initial organizational meeting did not go any smoother than any meeting of Jews might be expected to go. Differences among appointees over adding new members and lines of authority threatened to scuttle the committee before it could turn to discussion of how best to deal with the Nazi threat. But rather than see a committee that appointees had hoped would spearhead a community-wide campaign against the Nazis end up stillborn, in a spirit of compromise it was agreed to set aside contentious issues for later resolution. Discussion finally turned to how to deal with the problem of Nazism.[64]

Committee members, in the main hand-picked survivors, soon learned it was easier to set up an anti-Nazi committee than devise a workable plan to deal with the Nazis. As a first point the committee agreed fist-in-the-face confrontation might have its place, but it was not the best answer to Nazi provocations. But what was? The committee did not have an answer, or at least not one that was in any meaningful way different from what Congress was already doing – including calling on government to enact anti-hate legislation, supporting public education on the Nazi threat, and working in cooperation with the police. It did demand that Congress be more high profile in its anti-Nazi activities and less reticent about well-planned public demonstrations, but this hardly qualified as new thinking on how to deal with the Nazi threat.

A cynic might argue that bringing former dissident voices into the Congress fold was more cosmetic than real – designed to paper over community divisions while firming up the authority of the existing Congress leadership cohort. And the cynic might not be far off the mark. But this view also ignores the larger context. Congress officials may have artfully defused community revolt, but after the Allan Gardens 'riot' there could be no return to business as usual in the affairs of the organized Jewish community in Toronto. A corner had been turned. Much as establishment Jewish leaders at first tried to contain, then bottle up, the activist spirit that the Nazi episode unleashed, there was no putting the activist genie back in the bottle. Congress in Toronto, long focused on opening doors to Jewish entrée into the larger community mainstream, was uncomfortable with aggressive assertions of Jewish particularism. But that particularism could no longer be denied. What is more, while the governing clique of the Jewish community in Toronto had not been dethroned, its leadership was now going to be more and more judged by how well it served an awakened sense of Jewishness. Yes, breaking down social barriers and challenging other discrimination would remain a priority. But as the establishment would soon learn, Nazi threat or not, the Jewish rank and file was possessed by issues, often emotive ones, close to the Jewish heart, issues that spoke to Jewish cohesion, to the interdependent nature of Jewish peoplehood, and to the rescue of oppressed Jews around the world. Nothing so clearly demonstrated this awakened passion for Jewish bonding than the Toronto and Canadian Jewish response to the 1967 Six Day War.

CHAPTER FOUR

The Last Torah in the Fire

In February 1967 the American Jewish Committee issued its annual *Report from Israel*. Compiled by an 'Israeli observer of affairs in that country,' the report reassured readers that, while Israel had any number of pressing concerns, the threat of war was not among them. Israel, the report continued, was 'more beset by internal problems than by external dangers ... Three months ago there was real danger of war in the Middle East. This has passed, at least for the moment. American officials, after looking thoroughly into the situation with the detachment which only distance can give, are convinced that war is not likely either now or in the foreseeable future.'[1] The American officials were wrong. Less than four months after the report was published, Israel was at war.

The *Report from Israel* was not alone in misreading the Middle East tea leaves. The war seemed to come out of nowhere. Scholars looking back to the late spring of 1967 still argue about when and why storm clouds began to gather, but most agree that 15 May 1967 was a critical date. After an escalation of tension along Israel's border with Syria, including several aerial dogfights that did not go well for Syria, the Soviet Union brought pressure on Egypt to rally behind Syria. On 15 May Egyptian president Gamal Abdul Nasser ordered the mobilization of Egypt's military forces.[2] Two days later Nasser demanded the United Nations remove its peacekeepers, including Canadians, from the Sinai, where they had been stationed since the Sinai War more than ten years earlier. Canada, which had been instrumental in initiating the UN's peacekeeping operation, petitioned the United Nations Secretary General to intercede with Nasser, requesting he rescind his withdrawal order.

It was too late. Other countries contributing peacekeepers to the Sinai force had already announced their intention to pull out. And so it was. The United Nations, according to the *Montreal Gazette*, 'packed up and left with barely a word.'[3] Within a week Egyptian troops, equipped by the Soviet Union, moved into position along Egypt's border with Israel. Most provocatively, Egyptian artillery batteries were installed along the narrow Straits of Tiran, the essential gateway to Israel's southern port of Eilat. Training their guns over the waterway, they effectively closed the Straits to all shipping to and from Israel.

In a rare show of solidarity, neighbouring Arab states rallied behind Egypt and put their military forces on alert. As Jews in Canada and around the world looked on, Syria, Jordan, and other Arab governments pledged support for an all-out struggle with Israel. Israel in turn declared that its right to free passage through the Straits of Tiran was guaranteed by international agreement. It branded the armed Egyptian blockade an act of aggression and declared that any interference with Israeli shipping 'would be considered by Israel as an attack entitling it to exercise its right of self defense.' As Israel mobilized its military and called up the reserves, war jitters grew.[4]

But were President Nasser and his allies really hell-bent on a military confrontation with Israel? Even today the answer is unclear. According to the *Toronto Star*, Nasser, who appeared 'willing to risk all in a gamble for Arab glory as the "liberator" of Palestine,' may have actually had a more modest goal. Perhaps he assumed a firm show of Arab unity and military might would be enough to force casualty-shy Israel into making concessions as the price of avoiding conflict. If that was Nasser's strategy, the *Toronto Telegram* suggested, many Israelis believed that Nasser had calculated correctly. Under the headline 'Gloom in Israel' the paper claimed that 'Israelis are now convinced the Mid-East crisis is worsening by the hour and even if outright war is averted, Nasser will emerge as the only "victor."' And what concessions from Israel might be enough to satisfy Nasser? Perhaps knuckling under to Egypt's blockade of Eilat or backing off from border confrontations with Syria? In fact, anything that would be seen in the Arab world as a concession by Israel would bolster Nasser's and Egypt's claim to leadership in the Middle East and all without firing a shot. Given the prize, Nasser may have judged a toe-to-toe standoff with Israel worth the risk.[5]

The Middle East, however, is a tinderbox. What if Israel did not back off? What if war broke out? Middle East watchers painted a bleak picture. Pundits not only warned of heavy Israeli casualties, but also without foreign military assistance some regarded Israeli defeat on the battlefield a distinct possibility. And Israel could forget about assistance. The Soviet bloc lined up in support of the Arab cause. The West remained officially neutral. Some countries, sensing Israeli weakness, courted Arab favour. As war clouds loomed and Israel mobilized its forces, France, a major arms supplier to Israel, officially imposed a military embargo on the Middle East and cautioned Israel against any precipitous military action.[6]

Canada, unlike the major world powers, had only a limited profile in the Middle East. As a small player in the region, Canada under Prime Minister Lester Pearson positioned itself as 'even handed' in the ongoing Arab-Israel dispute. If Canada saw any special role for itself in the mounting crisis it was in the context of Pearson's vision of Canada as a staunch supporter of the United Nations peacekeeping efforts and as a possible 'honest broker' helping where it could to mediate international conflicts. Canada, then a member of the United Nations Security Council, pressed the council to take up the crisis and guide the disputing parties to the negotiating table. It was not to be. Canadian efforts to have the Security Council tackle the issue were frustrated by the major powers, especially the Soviet Union, which was actively backing both Egypt and Syria with supplies and logistical advice. And Canada's efforts at balance went unappreciated in the region. Official Canadian statements that any framework for peaceful resolution of the Middle East crisis must guarantee Israel's survival even as it resolved outstanding Arab grievances were denounced by Egypt as pro-Israel. There could be no guarantee of Israel's legitimacy or sovereignty. Rejecting Canada's claim to be an honest broker, Nasser dismissed Canada as one-sidedly anti-Egyptian.[7]

What of the United States? With its forces bogged down in Vietnam, the Johnson administration was concerned with growing Soviet influence in the Middle East, but remained determined not to get drawn into any Middle East conflict. Hoping to avert war, a war that might suck in the major powers, the American administration appealed to the Israelis for restraint as it sought a peaceful solution that would dismantle the Egyptian blockade of Eilat. First the Americans tried marshalling support for an international flotilla that might challenge the Egyptian blockade. The idea went nowhere when only Holland and Canada showed even guarded interest.[8] American diplomatic pressure on Nasser to pull back also went nowhere. After its previous cancellation of funding for the Egyptian Aswan Dam mega-project, the Americans had lost virtually all leverage with Egypt. And why should Egypt pull back? If, as some suspected, Nasser was looking not so much for armed conflict with Israel as for Israeli concessions as the price for avoiding war, he may have concluded that time was on his side. The Egyptian military was well supplied and he was buoyed by popular backing across the Arab world and from the Soviet bloc. There appeared to be nothing to gain from cooperating with an American-brokered peace initiative. Just the opposite. It might well be interpreted as a sign of weakness. If Nasser played his cards right, if he was patient, if he did not lose his nerve, Israel would eventually have to bend.

If that was Nasser's game plan, it was a dangerous one. The *Toronto Telegram* reported that Nasser had pledged not to precipitate war by sending his troops into Israel. However, the newspaper speculated that Nasser was now convinced that, should push come to shove, his forces were in a good position to defeat Israel on the battlefield. Whether a realistic assessment or not, if Nasser subscribed to this view, it would only stiffen his resolve to stand bold in the face of American mediation attempts. In any event, with his troops creating new facts on the ground by closing off the Straits of Tiran, Nasser appeared ready to bide his time.[9]

For its part Israel officially welcomed the American peace initiative, but historians have since suggested that Israeli government insiders were secretly concerned that talk of compromise was diplomatic code for coupling an Egyptian pull-back with Munich-like concessions by Israel. What concessions could Israel make that would not weaken its security, compromise its sovereignty, and lead to demands for still more concessions? Certainly there could be no compromise on the blockade of Eilat. And for Israel time was running out. The longer Israel waited to respond to Egyptian provocations, the more the Egyptian blockade took on an air of permanence. What is more, with so much of Israel's human capital on a war footing, the Israeli economy was grinding down. Something had to change. When the American peace initiative turned up sum zero, the Israelis secretly sent emissaries to feel out the Americans on a pre-emptive Israeli strike against Egypt. The American response was not to give the Israelis a green light, but it is safe to say that, if the Johnson administration did not condone an Israeli go-it-alone military initiative, it signalled that it had effectively retired to the sidelines. Israel was left to decide what was in its own best interests.[10]

Israel's leadership community was not of one mind on how to handle the crisis, but there was agreement that Israel could not indefinitely endure a blockade of its southern port without compromising its security and sovereignty and inviting further Arab initiatives. This could not happen. Eventually convinced that diplomacy, short of selling out Israel, would not convince Nasser to pull back, Israel increasingly saw military action as the only option. As the world held its breath, media pundits debated whether or not superior military training gave Israel any kind of edge over the far larger Arab troop numbers and stores of Soviet-supplied equipment. But they did agree on one thing. Any war between Israel and its neighbours would be protracted and costly in human life.[11] Israel, experts warned, did not have enough depth in territory, supplies, or troop numbers to fight a lengthy war. Even if Israel won, which many believed was far from guaranteed, the body count and damage to the Israeli state infrastructure would be horrific. And what if Israel did not win?[12]

As the experts debated, what they, the media, and the larger public did not know was that Israeli military strategists were confident that Israel's military was more than a match for Egypt and its allies – especially if war began with a pre-emptive Israeli air strike.[13] Jews in Canada, in Israel, and around the world knew nothing of this confidence. Instead, many feared the worst. They were convinced that Israel stood in great peril, being goaded into a war that might be its last. As the crisis deepened, Canadian Jews, like Jews across the Western world, fearing the abyss, rallied behind Israel. Never before or since was Canadian Jewish consciousness so simultaneously traumatized and galvanized.

Why this happened still remains to be fully explained. Undoubtedly, the various forms diaspora Jewish support for Israel took were shaped by each community's particular circumstances. In the West, unlike in the Soviet bloc and the Arab world, Jews felt free to express public support for Israel, lobby on Israel's behalf, and send Israel what aid they could muster. And they did.[14]

Canadian Jews were no exception. If few Canadian Jewish leaders foresaw the crisis, fewer still could have imagined that so many Canadian Jews of every stripe would instantly and unreservedly rally behind Israel. More than that. Few could have imagined that Canadian Jews would draw a direct line between the threat to Israel and the Canadian Jewish future, between Israel's survival and their own. In retrospect, however, just below the surface calm that Canadian Jewish leaders extolled as a community virtue was a rising tide of anxiety, a barely bottled up sense of foreboding that the threat of war in the Middle East accentuated. In part, this 'pall of desperation' reflected an emergent Holocaust consciousness percolating in the Jewish mind since the trial of Adolf Eichmann, a consciousness reinforced by the coming of age of Holocaust survivors as a force in the Canadian Jewish community and by fears of a growing neo-Nazi revival in both Europe and North America.[15] The Allan Gardens episode and its aftermath underscored how an issue so viscerally felt could ignite street-level activism, even in defiance of a Jewish establishment committed to projecting an image of Canadian Jews as a compliant, respectful, and dignified religious community. And in Montreal, then Canada's largest Jewish centre, there was the added uncertainty about the place of Jews in the new Quebec. Would the promise of liberal democratic reform in the end prove empty as Quebec retreated into a narrowly parochial nationalism reminiscent of the 1930s and 1940s? The clear and present threat to Israel served to intensify the anxiety of Canadian Jews already unsettled at home.

No corner of the Canadian Jewish community seemed untouched. Even Jews with no previous attachment to Israel, including many previous anti-Zionists, were drawn to Israel's side. They were not alone. Surprising themselves, many who prided themselves on their emancipation from what they regarded as the narrow strictures of Jewish parochialism were suddenly and inexplicably compelled by pro-Israel stirrings they could not explain even to themselves. Speaking of Jews who felt they had transcended their Jewishness, Vancouver psychiatrist Robert Krell speculated that some may have suddenly become uneasy at the notion that assimilation was no guarantee against those who would do Israel and Jews harm. They may have felt Israel's secure existence was somehow a precondition for their own security. 'If Israel can't hold them [Jew haters] off,' suggested Krell, 'they were next no matter how well disguised.'[16] Thus, they too found themselves heartsick at what they saw unfolding in the Middle East in the late weeks of May 1967. Like other Jews, they too were gripped by fear that for the second time in a generation the survival of all Jews, and not just those in Israel, hung by a thread. And nobody but other Jews seemed to care. If a modern, democratic Israel might be laid waste as an uncaring world stood by, what reason was there to hope that Jews anywhere, even in the West, even in Canada, would be secure? The Holocaust was still a living memory. Now it might happen again to the very state which was widely seen as having risen, Phoenix-like, out of the ashes of the Holocaust.[17]

Indeed, it is hard to exaggerate the depth of Jewish distress in Canada and around the world, a mass anxiety attack Lucy Dawidowicz described as a 'reliving of the Holocaust.'[18] Even before 1967 the Holocaust had ceased being a private preserve of Holocaust survivors and their children. In the wake of the Eichmann revelations, the Holocaust increasingly took hold as a cornerstone of shared Jewish memory, as did the realization that, but for Hitler's defeat, all Jews everywhere would have been consigned to a common fate. And it seemed so again. As they listened to the news out of the Middle East, many feared another Holocaust was in the making. So why wasn't the civilized world screaming out in protest? Wasn't one Auschwitz enough? Why was the world so ready to eulogize dead Jews rather than support living ones? On 2 June a *Canadian Jewish News* article entitled 'People on the Brink' lamented that a Middle East war would be another chapter in the never-ending saga of a hostile world's determination to eradicate the Jewish people – an unbroken line of suffering that threads from Haman and the Dispersion, through the Crusades and Inquisition, to the pogroms of Khmelnytsky and Petlura, and on to Hitler and finally to Nasser. The stage and actors might change, but the script remained the same. Nasser, abetted by his Arab allies and Soviet sponsors, was but the latest act in this bitter drama.

> For many Israelis this was a familiar situation. They had fought for survival before – in Belsen, Treblinka, Auschwitz and other death camps. They had withstood the combined onslaught of the Arab armies in 1948. They had participated in the successful Sinai battles in 1956.
> And now they were again ready to fight to the death if necessary, even if the Russians supported Nasser. For they were accustomed to fighting for their lives against the might of a Super-power. Previously it was Nazi Germany that had sought their extermination. Now they would stand up to Moscow as they had against Hitler. This was the mood of Israel as they stood on the brink.[19]

The mood among Rabbi Wilfred Solomon's Vancouver congregants was no different. They too were gripped by Holocaust-like fears. A disaster of Holocaust proportions was edging ever closer. It was, he recalls, 'as if we were being held by the throat ... It was as if someone was about to throw the last Torah in the fire.'[20] Montreal Jews, claimed Rabbi Allan Langner, felt this was the last moment 'before a second Holocaust.'[21] Holocaust-like fears created Holocaust-like rumours. Reminiscent of the Kindertransport rescue mission which brought nearly 10,000 predominantly Jewish children from Nazi Germany and the occupied territories of Austria, Czechoslovakia, and the Free City of Danzig to

Britain in the nine months before the outbreak of the Second World War, distraught western Jewish leaders were rumoured to have secretly approached Israeli officials with a plan for the mass evacuation of Israeli children to Europe and North America. The Israelis, it was said, rejected the plan, even as Tel Aviv's seafront hotels were being secretly refitted as emergency hospitals and thousands of graves were being dug in anticipation of the worst.

In this moment of impending cataclysm, Ruth Wisse, then teaching at McGill University, recalls, Jews 'couldn't translate what they felt to others.' Feeling 'estranged from fellow citizens,' they were instinctively drawn to the only ones they were sure would understand. They were drawn to one another.[22] If difficult to calculate, the urgency of Jewish bonding with Israel and other Jews, a bonding driven by gut certainty that one's own fate was inseparable from that of Israel and the Jewish people, was nonetheless real. In fact, by the late spring of 1967 many Canadian Jews seemed no longer able to distinguish where they left off as individuals and where their embrace of Israel and other Jews began. This passion for Israel instantly cemented links between Israel and Jews around the world, including Canada. Canadian Jewish leaders who had previously promoted the notion that Jews must present themselves as a Canadian faith community, the same as Catholics and Protestants, suddenly found their efforts undone by grassroots Jewish assertions of peoplehood.

Even as Israel's very existence seemed to hang by the most slender of threads, a World Jewish Congress meeting in Milan issued 'An Appeal to the Conscience of the World':

IN THIS FATEFUL HOUR, when the existence of the State of Israel is threatened, the Jewish People throughout the world stands steadfast, shoulder to shoulder with their brothers and sisters in Israel, and pledges its unwavering support in defence of Israel's freedom and independence.

We cannot believe that the Great Powers, which took the historic decision, some 20 years ago, to recognize the right of the Jewish people to live in freedom in the land of its ancestors, will deny Israel the right to and means of defending itself against forces that threaten its destruction and imperil the peace of the world.

We call upon the Great Powers and the United Nations, which was established to preserve peace and to safeguard the right of all nations, great and small, to live in peace and maintain their independence, as well as on the maritime states of the world, to uphold the right, enshrined by international law and custom, of a member state of the United Nations, to enjoy unrestricted freedom of access to the oceans of the world, so vital to its livelihood and very existence.

We appeal to men and women of good will, irrespective of race or creed, in all countries and continents, who cherish justice to rally to the defence of Israel and save the peace of Jerusalem and of the world.[23]

The same day the World Jewish Congress issued its appeal, a young Canadian Jew living in Israel sent his own letter of appeal to the Canadian Jewish Congress office in Toronto.

As a Canadian citizen, now working and living and hoping to remain in Israel, I write to you in the hope that I may endorse or emphasize what you already understand.

The very existence of the State of Israel is in peril and likewise the lives of another two million Jews. Nasser's policy statement that any war with Israel would be a war to crush her completely – never to rise again, is not to be regarded as mere rhetoric.

Likewise, the ever-growing daily broadcasts, put out in radio broadcasts from all the Arab countries and broadcast in all the principal languages, are not simply propaganda.

I write without a feeling of exaggeration, that the 'hate' programmes that I have heard this week, are full of the ingredients that were in daily usage in Nazi Germany and the anti Israel, Zionist and Imperialist chant now includes the anti Israel one.

Only in one direction are the Arabs united – and in only one, that of their desire to exterminate Israel and in this they are profound.

As an individual and as a Jew, I have the utmost confidence in the people of Israel and in the Jewish people throughout the world … but without the powers fulfilling their promises – we will be lost. Please, please, exert *all* your energies to this end.[24]

These appeals struck a responsive chord. Fearing Israel's annihilation was a looming possibility, the organized Jewish community, the Zionists and Canadian Jewish Congress in the lead, cranked up their lobbying of Ottawa on Israel's behalf. This was not entirely new lobbying terrain for Jewish leaders. Canadian Zionists had long petitioned on Israel's behalf, but it would be wrong to think of their lobbying as particularly well organized or unified in voice. It wasn't. In spite of efforts to forge a unified Zionist community in Canada, Zionists and other pro-Israel partisans remained a divisive lot, internally split over policy and ideology. Certainly they dared not claim to speak on behalf of the entire Jewish community. In the past, many in the Jewish community, if not indifferent to Israel, would certainly not have self-identified as Zionists. In the spring of 1967 the lines separating different ideological streams of the Zionist movement and Zionists from non-Zionists disappeared as fear for Israel's survival became a singular Jewish community concern.

As fear for Israel grew, the Canadian Jewish Congress took the reins of pro-Israel lobbying. Congress leaders well understood that Canada had only limited influence in the Middle East. Nevertheless, they believed Canada might still be instrumental in forestalling war, a war that threatened to grind Israel to dust. And what might Canada do? During the spring of 1967 Canada remained a member the United Nations Security Council and was widely regarded as influential with the neutral and non-aligned bloc. What is more, Canada was publicly on record as endorsing Israel's right to exist – it had voted in favour of the United Nations 1947 Partition resolution which led to the declaration of the Israeli state in 1948. Canada had also endorsed Israel's right to free navigation through the Straits of Tiran. With war in the Middle East regarded as potentially catastrophic for Israel, and with Arab states supported by the Soviet bloc seemingly hell-bent on Israel's eradication, Canadian Jewish leaders were desperate that Canada, the international peacekeeper, use its moral suasion at the United Nations to help find a peaceful resolution of the crisis without sacrificing Israeli security.

Encouraged by Congress, Jewish organizations and their members showered Ottawa with telegrams thanking the government for its steadfast support of Israel's right to free navigation while, at the same time, encouraging Canada to pull out all the diplomatic stops in an effort to avert war. As the crisis worsened, an aging Sam Bronfman went to Ottawa to plead with the external affairs minister and his officials to intervene on Israel's behalf wherever it might prove useful.[25]

To shore up support for Israel in the larger Canadian community, the organized Jewish community also reached out to long-time allies in the human rights struggle – the press, progressive politicians, organized labour, and liberal churches – asking that they publicly affirm solidarity with Israel and the Canadian Jewish community in this moment of crisis. The response was mixed. Across Canada the mainstream press tended to be sympathetic to Israel. Often painting Israel as an encircled David facing a war-like Arab Goliath, editorials called for peace, for an end to Egypt's violation of Israel's right to free navigation of the Straits of Tiran, and for Canada to speak out boldly on behalf of Israel's right to exist within secure borders. Across Canada, local politicians attended pro-Israel peace rallies where they offered 'greetings' and expressed hopes for peace. But efforts to find respected non-Jews who would go public with their support for Israel netted uneven results. At the end of May, Jewish leaders in Toronto were pleased when a group of local 'Christian religious leaders, including clerical and academic representatives, issued a rather good statement in defense of Israel's right to exist and warning of the dangers of the Arab threat to destroy Israel.' The group, which included University of Toronto professor Marshall McLuhan and a number of other eminent scholars and religious leaders, invoked memories of the Holocaust in a plea to world religious and political leaders to help save Israel from annihilation.

> Once before in this century the leader of a nation proclaimed the aim of destroying Jews. The world did not believe him. The world stood by. Again the leader of a nation has proclaimed the aim of destroying Jews – this time the State of Israel. Let us not believe that the unbelievable cannot happen again. This time let us not stand by. The undersigned speak as Christians who remember with anguish the Nazi holocaust and are filled with deep apprehension about the survival of Israel.[26]

This unreservedly pro-Israel appeal to conscience proved more the exception than the rule. In the main, the Canadian Christian community seemed not to comprehend the depth of Jewish fear for Israel's survival, let alone share in it. The prevailing view of mainstream religious leaders was that an unfortunate political drama was unfolding in the Middle East which the Christian community regretted and prayed would be resolved in peace, but it was not one in which it should take sides. In late May, the Anglican primate for western Canada was invited to send a representative to a pro-Israel peace rally in Winnipeg. In a letter to a local Zionist leader, the primate explained there could be no official Anglican represented 'at a meeting which was sponsored by a group closely associated with one of the sides in the Middle East troubles.' It was imperative, the primate explained, that the Anglican Church be seen to remain neutral. 'I realize that the time for a neutral stand may speedily come to an end, but my judgment is that at this moment we should still strive to keep open the ways to negotiation.' Instead, he hoped to issue a call for peace together with 'leaders of other Christian communions in this country.'[27]

Winnipeg Jewish leaders who had long worked with the local Anglican leadership on issues of human rights were taken aback by the primate's assertion of neutrality. How, they asked, was it possible for people of good will, especially religious leaders, to remain neutral when the very survival of Israel and the Jewish people was in doubt? The promised Anglican statement, co-signed by Roman Catholic and United Church authorities, offered no solace. It called for peace, but did not mention the right of Israel to exist as an independent state.[28] It appeared that in the name of even-handedness religious leaders were prepared to abandon Israel and the Jews to their fate – a stance that dredged up, for the Jewish community, still unresolved memories of church abandonment and the betrayal of Jews during the Holocaust, and raised doubts about the value of years of bridge-building between Canadian Jewish and non-Jewish communities. As the Middle East crisis deepened, the litmus test of relations with non-Jews would increasingly become 'Where do they stand on Israel?' Hearing that American evangelist Billy Graham refused to speak out on the Middle East crisis, a Winnipeg rabbi lashed out, 'Ministers will make statements of concern about Vietnam, but here the Jewish state is facing extinction and no one is willing to say a thing about it.' Billy Graham failed the test.[29]

Jews might be disheartened by what at best could be described as indifference to the plight of Israel and at worst out-and-out hostility to Israel by some of their fellow citizens. But in truth, whatever Jews might have felt, for most Canadians the Middle East crisis just did not arouse anything near the same degree of passion. Why should it? For most Canadians, the Middle East was hardly a major area of focus in the spring of 1967. Interest? Perhaps. Gut-wrenching concern? No. To the degree that the larger Canadian public gave the Middle East crisis thought, they may have been more disposed towards Israel's position than that of Egypt, but the Middle East was just too distant and too complicated to get excited about. The public mind was on the end of the school year, approaching summer vacations, Canada's centennial celebration, and Expo 67. That is not to say that Canada of the day was devoid of political issues. Not at all. The press was full of speculation about when the current prime minister, Lester Pearson – twice handed minority governments by the voters – would step down and who would join the race to replace him. On the international scene it was not the threat of war in the Middle East that topped the Canadian list of concerns. It was American engagement in Vietnam. Few Canadians would disagree that their government should use its good offices to prevent the outbreak of a Middle East war, but few were losing sleep over the crisis. For as long as anyone could remember, Israelis and the Arabs had been at each other's throats – unfortunate but nothing Canada did or did not do was likely to change that reality. If Canada could help keep the two sides from killing each other, that was all to the good. If not, it was best that Canada not be drawn into what was widely regarded as but the latest in a seemingly endless string of confrontations between these Middle East adversaries.[30]

Unlike their compatriots, Canadian Jews *were* losing sleep as the Middle East crisis increasingly crowded out almost every other concern. Fear for Israel's fate spread like the common cold. Community rallies and lobbying were the public face of a community in which anxiety at the possibility of war and its nightmare-like consequences ran deep. No one seemed immune, not even the young. The march to war in the Middle East erupted just as Canadian university students were beginning their vacations or summer jobs. Out of nowhere, a rumour began to circulate that Israel was in desperate need of volunteers. Perhaps surprising themselves, many Jewish students put their summer plans on hold. Across Canada young men and women lined up at local Zionist offices offering to go to Israel. Admittedly, their passion for Israel may have been matched by a desire for adventure or the possibility of escaping parental authority for a while. There may even have been a few who naively thought a hard-pressed Israel would put a gun in their hands or harboured romantic dreams of reinventing themselves as *halutzim*, pioneers, in Israel. 'Please,' wrote one young Jewish man to the Congress office in Montreal, 'send me all … the information and detail on how I can go to Isreal [sic]. I heard on the C.B.C. News last night that 300 people from Toronto are going to work in the factories. I would like to offer my services. I am Jewish and am very proud of our State of Isreal. After this affair is settled soon with G-d's help, I would like to work on a Keputz [sic] where I can get some sort of education and start a new life.'[31] The majority of those who lined up to volunteer, however, wanted only to be useful to Israel in its moment of need, to be put to work on farms, or to fill in for a workforce thinned by the call-up of so many to military duty.

This grassroots outpouring of youthful concern for Israel took Canadian Jewish leaders by surprise. That there had been no Israeli appeal for volunteers from the diaspora did not matter. Talk that volunteers were needed brought more and more people – including some who no longer qualified as young except perhaps in spirit – to the offices of Zionist organizations asking to be sent to Israel, some saying they would gladly pay their own travel costs. The symbolic importance of so many young Jewish men and women stepping forward to volunteer for Israel was not lost on the organized Jewish community leadership. The spontaneity with which volunteers stepped forward was a gratifying sign that support of Israel was not limited to any one generation. Jewish officials in Canada, as elsewhere in the West, at first taken aback by the sudden influx of volunteers, soon applauded the volunteers' commitment.

The question, however, was what to do with the volunteers? Israel had not asked for volunteers and there was neither a Canadian Jewish organizational framework in place to process applications nor an organized infrastructure in Israel to oversee placement of the volunteers should they arrive in large numbers. It was also unclear whether at that moment of crisis Israel would or should welcome an influx of young volunteers. The offers of help were gratifying, but with war threatening, was it responsible, useful, or even morally justifiable to send young people into what might soon be a war zone? And even if it was decided that Israel could organize to deal with all the volunteers, who would cover all the costs and how, for that matter, would they get to Israel? Transportation was at a premium. As the crisis deepened, international air carriers began cutting back or cancelling flights into the Middle East, including those into Israel. There was talk of some Western countries imposing a moratorium on travel bound for the Middle East. Some governments issued travel advisories and cautioned their nationals in the region to leave. El Al, Israel's national airline, continued to fly, but was giving priority seating to Israeli reservists abroad returning home to serve in their military units.

In spite of all the ethical questions involved in sending volunteers into a likely war zone and unresolved organizational issues around the processing, transportation, and placement of volunteers into meaningful work in Israel, there was no denying Israel needed workers, and here were thousands of young people volunteering to do whatever was needed. Maybe the idea of sending volunteers to Israel, which only a few days earlier was on no one's radar, had merit. Even as Israeli and diaspora officials debated on whether and how to send volunteers to Israel, there were questions about what to do with the parade of volunteers who lined up at Zionist offices. Pending agreement on what to do with them, nobody wanted to dampen their enthusiasm, let alone turn them away cold. Perhaps the best thing to do was to accept applications in the hope that, should Israel agree to take volunteers and logistical challenges get ironed out, there would be a ready pool of people on hand and ready to go. Across Canada the Zionists cobbled together a makeshift procedure for assessing applications.

In Montreal and Toronto during the last weeks of May and the first few days of June those who arrived at offices of the Canadian Zionist Organization to volunteer were first asked if they were prepared to commit to a minimum three-month stay after they arrived in Israel. If so, they were given an application form. The form included questions about their educational background, language facility, skills, and work experience. All were told that applications would be sorted by skill set. Louis Greenspan, long active in Young Judaea and in 1967 a newly minted philosophy instructor in Toronto, lined up to volunteer. Asked about any special interests he had, Greenspan replied he was a philosopher. That brought a dismissive 'We already have two million of them.'[32] Greenspan made it two million and one. If philosophers were not sought after, who was? Rabbi Plaut explained to the press that Israel was most in 'need of surgeons, anaesthetists, registered nurses, truck, bus and ambulance drivers and train conductors.'

In addition to listing their interests and skills, all applicants under the age of twenty-one were required to provide proof of parental consent. As word spread that parental permission was required, parents began accompanying their children to Zionist offices so they could sign permission waivers on the spot. All applicants also had to pass a medical examination administered by a local volunteer doctor. Applicants who did not have a valid passport were told to get one. Completed forms were then filed and volunteers, their lives suddenly on hold, were advised to be ready to leave at a moment's notice.[33]

Under the best of circumstances, the crush of those turning up to volunteer would have overtaxed the capacity of hard-pressed community officials to process applications systematically. And the last week of May and first few days of June hardly afforded the best of circumstances. Even when Israeli authorities finally indicated they would welcome a carefully controlled inflow of appropriately skilled volunteers, there seemed no way of booking any large block of airline tickets to Israel. With luck, reservations were secured for a first group of forty Toronto student volunteers in the last week of May. Another three hundred who had been carefully selected from among the growing pool of applicants were promised that they would be sent as soon as airline seats became available. In the meantime they were asked to be patient. For how long was anybody's guess. All the while the number of young volunteers kept growing. Already swamped by applications and phone inquiries, Zionist offices received an estimated 1000 volunteers in the last few days of May. Those responsible for filing the backlog of applications simply lost count.[34]

While community leaders appreciated the commitment and generosity of spirit demonstrated by the volunteers, insiders knew that with transportation shortages and bare-bones on-the-ground organization in Israel, there was little likelihood of sending any large contingent of volunteers to Israel in the immediate future. What is more, the processing of applications from volunteers was eating up time that overworked organizational staff might productively devote to more urgent matters. Thus, while Jewish leaders continued to sing the volunteers' praises, staff quietly began assigning the processing of volunteer applications a lesser priority. Applications gradually started to pile up, unfiled. In some cases, those arriving to sign up were thanked and told to wait at home until there was a general call for volunteers. A notable exception was the maintenance of a roster of volunteer doctors, nurses, and others deemed to have essential skills who, in an emergency, could be dispatched to Israel at a moment's notice.[35]

Some young people, sidestepping the application process, headed out on their own. A few managed to wangle last-minute reservations on Israel-bound flights. Among them were three young men and a young woman from Vancouver, all in their early twenties. The local Jewish press recorded the scene at the airport as they left.

> They departed to the calls of good luck and 'Godspeed' uttered by some 50 family and friends gathered at the [Vancouver] airport to bid them 'Shalom.' A few rounding bars of 'Am Yisroel Chai' – 'Israel still lives,' were heard as the youngsters boarded their plane. The atmosphere remained light and cheerful until the final moment of farewell, when sobriety suddenly took over and, in one or two cases, those remaining here found it impossible to keep their emotions in check.

According to the *Western Canadian Bulletin*, they joined 'hundreds and hundreds of other American and Canadian volunteers in New York whence they will travel by El Al Israel Airlines.'[36] But those who somehow managed to secure flights to Israel were few. Others, also unwilling to wait for their applications to be processed, packed a knapsack and set out on their own without an Israel flight booking. Hoping somehow to piece together their own circuitous route to Israel, they flew to London, Paris, Amsterdam, Rome, and Athens or, for those on a tight budget, to Luxembourg on Icelandic Airlines – wherever they could camp out at an airport and, with a little luck, score a seat on an Israel-bound flight. Some succeeded. With no flight to Israel taking off with an empty seat, every 'no show' passenger was a seat filled by a volunteer. While there are no accurate figures on the number who arrived in Israel in the shadow of war – most simply had their passports stamped as tourists – estimates run to several thousand, including several hundred Canadians.

Although most volunteers who made it to Israel were young and enthusiastic, the few overworked Israeli officials assigned to deal with volunteers were at first unsure of what to do with them. With a state of emergency in Israel, there were few on-site resources available to sort volunteers into work slots appropriate to their individual skills. Just making sure every volunteer had a bed and a roof over his or her head meant that even highly skilled individuals were sometimes posted to menial jobs or agricultural work, usually in kibbutzim which proved best equipped to accommodate large numbers of the volunteers. Eventually some were independently able to secure alternative placements, while others, wanting only to contribute in any way they could, accepted whatever work was assigned them in good grace. Still others, totally unprepared for physically demanding manual labour or unhappy with the spartan kibbutz lifestyle, walked away from their placements and set off on their own to backpack around an Israel soon to be at war. Still, even if the volunteer labour was not always used to best advantage, there is no doubt that the arrival of young diaspora Jews, including Canadians, was a morale boost to Israelis. In an Israel then making 'morbid preparations' for war, the presence of these young volunteers from abroad, 'in numbers greater than Israel could absorb,' was a singular bright spot.[37]

If taxed Israeli officials had no accurate count of the volunteers who arrived before the war, Jewish officials in Canada, more surprisingly, were equally unsure of the number of Canadian volunteers who stood ready to leave for Israel at a moment's notice. In what would eventually prove to be the week before the outbreak of war, some fifty volunteers in Winnipeg, including several non-Jews, attended a meeting to discuss last-minute preparations in advance of getting the green light to travel they all expected momentarily. Even as the fifty kept their bags at the ready, Zionist leaders in Winnipeg confessed they had completely lost count of how many more volunteers had been processed and stood ready to leave. Nor did they know how many more applications were still piled up, waiting to be processed. As a Congress staff member explained to the local press, 'No exact figures were available from Winnipeg, but it was indicated that the final total would substantially exceed the figure of fifty who had volunteered for service in defense of Israel in 1948.' He was right. During the weekend before war broke out, the Zionist office in Winnipeg reported more than a hundred calls from individuals wishing to volunteer. An even larger number simply walked in off the street to fill out applications. Lest anyone think that once in Israel these Canadian volunteers were going to be handed a rifle and sent into battle, the Winnipeg official was at pains to reassure the press that this was not the case. 'They are not experienced military men, but they are willing to work in the fields if necessary to relieve reservists who may be needed in the armed forces.'[38]

As the young lined up to go to Israel, their parents lined up to give to Israel. By mid-May, the annual United Jewish Appeal/United Israel Appeal campaigns in local communities across Canada were just closing their books, donations already earmarked to support Jewish social service, educational, and communal needs in Canada and Israel. The capital target for Toronto, a modest increase over 1966, had been set at $3 million. As was often the case, it had taken a last-minute push by fundraisers to put the Toronto campaign over the top. But in mid-May, after six months of effort, the 1967 target was within grasp. The campaign chairman happily proclaimed, 'Success is near at hand; it is within fingertip reach,' and an end-of-the-month party for fundraisers was planned to celebrate the closing of the 1967 campaign.[39]

But the Toronto Jewish community was hardly in a party mood. What is more, across Canada Jewish fundraising was about to change forever. Even as the annual fundraising campaigns were wrapping up, Canadian Jews, driven by fears for Israel, for the future of Jews around the world, and for themselves, proclaimed solidarity with Israel and reached into their pockets. An urgent appeal to Canadian Jewry from the world chairman of the Keren Hayesod – United Israel Appeal in Jerusalem stressing Israel's urgent need for money was hardly necessary. Canadian Jews already knew it. As if money could yet buy Israel a shelter from the impending storm, Canadian Jews dug deep. Unlike the just ended annual UJA campaign, which was carefully budgeted and planned out in detail, this spontaneous explosion in crisis-driven giving caught fundraisers and Jewish community leaders by surprise. While many donors directed their funds to UJA offices, others were unsure where to direct their money. As the crisis in the Middle East worsened, many pounded on whatever Jewish organizational door was at hand and pressed contributions on staff. The only instruction was to make sure the money went to Israel. Without any central coordination, synagogues, Jewish fraternal organizations, women's groups, and professional, business, and labour groups, sometimes tripping over one another, announced community-wide fundraising gatherings or smaller parlour meetings where all who attended knew the ground rules. You come. You give.

And give they did. While much of the money collected was often handed over to local UJA officials, it proved impossible to keep track of where all the money ended up. This eruption of giving was true not only of Montreal and Toronto, but also of smaller communities across Canada. Regina, the capital of Saskatchewan, had a Jewish community of about two hundred families dominated by a small group of shopkeepers, businessmen, and white-collar professionals.[40] Nobody would mistake Regina for Jerusalem. As one former community member recalled, 'The rabbi's job was to be a Jew.' Otherwise the community was comfortably low key. The Jewish calendar was observed and life-cycle events quietly shared. Jewish social and organizational spheres were inseparable from Jewish family life. Much of the community's activity focused around the single synagogue, but there was also a flourishing Hadassah-WIZO chapter, a local Young Judaea youth group, and a modest annual UJA campaign. While some might elect to remain at the margins of community, the committed Jewish community was close, many convinced they knew what was cooking in the other's pot.

Regina was far from Montreal and Toronto, and even further from Israel, but the distance seemed as nothing in the spring of 1967. Even in their corner of Saskatchewan, Jews felt the earth shaking beneath their feet. Overwhelmed by a nightmare vision of Israel's impending destruction, many lived hour to hour, newscast to newscast. Every conversation seemed to begin with, 'Have you heard anything new?'

A year earlier George Promislow, then in his early thirties and of modest means, chaired Regina's 1966 annual UJA campaign. 'Nobody else,' he recalled, 'wanted to do it.' As the Middle East crisis darkened in late May 1967, Promislow joined discussions on reopening community fundraising only recently closed down with the end of the annual campaign. As a first step, it was decided to sort through the list of 1967 UJA contributors in Regina and identify those individuals who might be counted upon to come up with at least another $1000. Fifteen likely donors were invited to a noon meeting the next day. None was under any illusion as to what was expected. Israel needed money and needed it quickly. And all were told to forget about pledges. Meeting organizers made it clear they expected everyone to pony up cash or a cheque.

When the meeting convened in a private downtown office, more people showed up than had been invited – some angered that they had been left off the list or, even worse, passed over because organizers thought they could not be counted on for at least $1000. The meeting was delayed as more chairs were squeezed into the room. When the meeting finally began there were no introductions. There was no need. They all knew one another. There was also no opening pitch. Again there was no need. The Middle East crisis had turned everyone into a news junky. Nobody in the room had to be told that things looked bleak. With no fanfare the meeting chairman simply began by personally putting a cheque for $25,000 on the table. He then went around the room gathering everyone else's contributions. Promislow, who had previously arranged with his bank manager to cover a large overdraft, gave three times the amount his family had just finished paying to Regina's 1967 UJA campaign. When the meeting ended, Promislow remembers, there was $150,000 on the table. The Regina UJA campaign just ended had raised about $40,000.

The next evening the entire community gathered in the local synagogue. The sanctuary was full. The crowd 'included people who hadn't been in synagogue for years.' Community members sat quietly as a respected member began the meeting by explaining to the information-hungry crowd that he had only just hung up the phone after talking with Jewish officials in Toronto. He passed on what information he had been given on the situation in Israel as of that hour. No sooner had he finished than the crowd erupted. Demonstrating no patience for any of the other fundraising speeches the organizers had planned, those in attendance surged forward to hand in envelopes filled with cash. In a community where most people felt they knew what each family could afford to contribute, generosity far exceeded expectations. Two brothers, local scrap dealers, rewrote their cheque twice during the evening. One man nobody previously knew to be Jewish handed over a cheque for $10,000. Counting went on well into the night.[41]

Regina was not alone. In Vancouver, with a community of approximately 9000 Jews, a key community fundraiser explained, 'In this hour of grave danger, Israel must turn for tangible help to her only true ally in the world – the Jews of the West.' Given Israel's 'tangible' need for money, he was convinced Vancouver Jews would open their wallets 'and give to this emergency appeal as never before.'[42] He did not have to wait long. A group of about forty wealthy community leaders met privately and set a $1 million local fundraising target. Almost a quarter of that amount was raised then and there.[43]

Several days later, on 28 May, an overflow crowd of more than 2000 turned out at the Orthodox Schara Tzedeck Synagogue in what was billed as 'a demonstration in favor of peace in the Middle East.' A standing-room crowd of 1600 jammed into the synagogue's sanctuary and loudspeakers were hastily installed on the synagogue roof so the overflow crowd standing outside in a heavy rain could hear the proceedings. The event opened with the singing of both 'O Canada' and 'Hatikvah,' followed by a prayer for the State of Israel. Several speakers addressed the crowd, including a local Liberal member of parliament and a spokesperson from the Zionist Organization of Canada. Then, before the appeal for funds, a stand-up vote 'unanimously endorsed a resolution commending the Canadian government for upholding UN principles and expressing unfaltering solidarity with Israel.'[44]

As he looked out from the *bimah*, Wilfred Solomon, rabbi at the neighbouring Conservative congregation, was struck not by how virtually every committed Jew in Vancouver had come together under one roof. That did not surprise him. What surprised the rabbi was seeing outspoken anti-Zionists and others who, he was sure, had likely never stepped inside a synagogue before, including a few who had never previously identified themselves as Jews, at least not publicly. How was this possible? Vancouver's Jewish community was not as small as that of Regina, but it was not as large as that of Montreal, Toronto, or Winnipeg either. Would not most local Jews, committed or not, be known to Jewish leaders? No. Rabbi Solomon explained that Vancouver afforded something of a haven for those who wished to closet their Jewish selves. More than most other Canadian cities, Vancouver was a city where almost every adult Jew seemed to be from somewhere else. No one had history. It was easy for a Jew arriving in Vancouver to refashion identity, step outside his or her Jewish skin, and live beyond the reach of the local Jewish community. Some Jews might even have come to Vancouver to vanish from Jewish community contact. One observer noted that intermarried

Montreal or Toronto couples might move to Vancouver where no family meant no pain.

But there seemed no hiding from fears for Israel, not even for the most assimilated of Jews. As Rabbi Solomon remembered it, all Vancouver Jews, all Jews everywhere, were suddenly and inexplicably drawn together by a singular overarching fear for the future of Israel, the Jewish people, and themselves. And what could they do? They gathered. They sought what comfort they could in being with others who understood and shared their fears. And they joined Jews across Canada in giving as never before. The amount of money donated that evening in Vancouver exceeded the organizers' expectations several times over. Rabbi Solomon recalled one Vancouver family mortgaging their home so as to give just that much more to Israel. Others gave with a Jewish heart for the first time in their lives. In one case, a wealthy Vancouver businessman who, as far as Rabbi Solomon knew, had previously never given a penny to a Jewish cause, stunned local Jewish leaders with the generosity of his contribution. One of those who attended the meeting was a local Catholic priest who was a regular at a weekly poker game with a group of Jewish cronies. He contributed $1000.[45]

In Winnipeg, as war loomed, more than 1300 people, secular and religious, Zionist and non-Zionist, turned out at Rosh Pina Synagogue for a mass meeting 'called in support of Canada's peacekeeping efforts and as a demonstration of solidarity with Israel.' As in Vancouver, a stand-up vote unanimously endorsed a resolution praising Canada's support of Israel's navigation rights and efforts to seek a peaceful resolution of the crisis. Local rabbis announced they were sending a joint telegram to Prime Minister Pearson calling on his government's continued support of Israel and peace in the Middle East. 'We extend our prayers and bless your continuing efforts in the United Nations and among our allies to avert hostilities and to achieve a just and peaceful resolution of the crisis so fraught with catastrophe for all mankind. May the Almighty strengthen your hands.'[46]

The rabbis might call on the Almighty to strengthen the prime minister's hands, but it fell on local Jewish leaders to strengthen their own hands in fundraising on Israel's behalf. The evening after the Rosh Pina meeting a group of community leaders gathered at the Shaarey Zedek Synagogue to pick eight delegates to attend a Montreal meeting called by Sam Bronfman for 4 June to iron out details of a national coordinated Israel emergency campaign. Working on advance information that the target to be assigned Winnipeg was $1 million, the chair of the Winnipeg gathering got the contribution ball rolling with a generous personal donation. As others in the room followed suit, contributions soon topped $500,000. A fundraiser the next night for deep-pocketed community members who could not make the previous night's meeting added another $100,000 to the total. With the expected Winnipeg target already more than half in the bag and the larger Jewish community not yet even officially asked to contribute, Jewish leaders were confident that Winnipeg Jews could more than double Bronfman's expected target for them and perhaps do even better than that.

Bronfman knew none of this. What he knew was that money for Israel was flowing in from across Canada and there was no national coordinated oversight for the giving. Gratifying as was this spontaneous outpouring of generosity on Israel's behalf, he and other national Jewish leaders were intent on imposing order on the fundraising process so as to avoid duplication of effort, ensure that Canadian laws, especially tax laws with respect to charitable giving, were observed, and take care that all the money was properly accounted for, receipted, and streamed to where it could do the most good. To this end, Sam Bronfman called his meeting of about a hundred Jewish leaders from across Canada for Montreal for 4 June. The group assembled that Sunday morning at Montreal's Jewish elite Montefiore Club knew they were there to ratify Bronfman's plan for a centrally administered emergency campaign. Bronfman intended that all ad hoc local fundraising end. In its stead the UJA would be reactivated so as to oversee a coordinated across-Canada community fundraising campaign for Israel. And in the Canadian Jewish world, Bronfman, 'Jewish royalty,' usually got what he wanted.[47]

When the assembled delegates were called to order, nobody in the room had any doubt who was in charge. A Winnipeg delegate recalls that Bronfman was in the head chair, with several trusted Montreal Jewish community officials flanking him. Bronfman began by addressing the gathering. He applauded the fundraising efforts already well under way, but insisted that centralized coordination was essential. He won quick approval for his plan to launch a UJA-administered Israel emergency campaign. Bronfman then went on to propose that the emergency campaign announce a national target of $10 million, well in excess of any past Canadian Jewish fundraising effort.[48] Montreal and Toronto, he expected, would each be able to raise $4 million, Winnipeg $1 million, and the rest of Canada $1 million. To get the ball rolling, Bronfman announced a personal contribution to the emergency campaign of triple his already-generous donation to the recently completed

1967 community UJA campaign, an announcement greeted with a loud round of applause. Everyone in the room knew that Bronfman was setting a personal bar for them as well. They would be expected to at least triple their contributions to the annual campaign and push others to do the same. But Bronfman was not finished yet. As the applause died down, he cautioned the gathering that the emergency campaign, critical as it was to Israel's survival, had to be conducted without further exacerbating the high level of anxiety that then existed within the Jewish community. Bronfman urged the assembled Canadian Jewish leaders that they must demonstrate calm and remain businesslike. This, he insisted, would reassure the Jewish community that 'everything was business as usual.' With that Bronfman sat down and the floor was opened to discussion.

If Bronfman expected the usual ringing endorsement of his remarks, he was sorely disappointed. Unaccustomed to being challenged, Bronfman was taken aback when an incensed Sydney Spivak, then a provincial cabinet minister in Manitoba and a lifelong Zionist, demanded to speak. He applauded Bronfman's initiative in pulling together a much-needed and centralized Canada-wide emergency fundraising campaign. Nevertheless, Spivak totally rejected the notion that the larger Jewish community was going to be reassured by its leaders pretending that everything was 'business as usual' when everyone knew it wasn't. Even worse, Spivak protested, Canadian Jews would not appreciate their leaders acting cool and businesslike when Israel and the world Jewish community were engaged in a life or death struggle. Canadian Jews wanted and needed their leaders to demonstrate the same passion for Israel that they felt. In that spirit of passion for Israel and the Jewish people in their hour of need, Spivak declared that Bronfman's $10 million campaign target for the Israel emergency campaign did not cut it. Looking around the room, Spivak demanded the target must be twice that, if not more. And forget about the $1 million target for Winnipeg. Knowing that Winnipeg already had far more than $1 million in hand, Spivak insisted that Winnipeg could raise $3 million.

The room erupted. Not only had Bronfman been challenged, the Winnipeg delegation had raised the fundraising ante beyond anything those in the room had ever dreamed could be raised by the Canadian Jewish community. As delegates shouted over one another demanding the floor, Bronfman, sensing he was losing control of the meeting, called a break. He asked delegates to grab a bite to eat and caucus among themselves on how to proceed. Delegates from Toronto, who had chartered a plane to come to the meeting, had originally hoped the meeting would be short enough for them to squeeze in a visit to Expo 67. That was not to be. Instead, they spent the next hour huddling over the numbers. How much could the Toronto Jewish community raise? Few doubted that Toronto could raise more than the $4 million assigned by Bronfman, but how much more? Unable to agree among themselves, the Toronto delegation opted to suggest that the emergency campaign not set a goal. It should be left open ended.

When the meeting reconvened with Bronfman back in the chair, most delegates were in agreement that the original target of $10 million was too low. The Toronto suggestion for an open-ended campaign was rejected on the grounds that the Jewish community needed to have a target to aim for, one that reflected the gravity of the situation then facing Israel and the world Jewish community. In the end, Bronfman's originally proposed $10 million emergency campaign target was more than doubled to a previously unimaginable figure of $25 million, which some felt was still too low. When the meeting finally adjourned, the Middle East was only hours away from the outbreak of war.[49]

As they headed home, some of the delegates may have feared that the gathering, swept away by emotion, had overreached. Twenty-five million dollars was a king's ransom. Could it be raised? Yes. And Bronfman calling for 'business as usual' ran counter to every instinct of a community convinced that Israel was facing annihilation. There was a distinct possibility that nothing would ever be 'business as usual' again – not for Israel and not for Jews around the world. With Jewish survival hanging in the balance, there might be no second chance to offer up every support, and Canadian Jews dared not be found wanting. Rabbis might lead the community in beseeching God's mercy, but when it came to *tuchas offen tisch*, laying it out on the table, there was only one thing that most individual Canadian Jews could do. They could reach into their pockets. Official emergency campaign or no official emergency campaign, faced with looming catastrophe in Israel, Jews gave as never before, and then gave again. Nor was it only individuals who dug deep. The Synagogue Council of Greater Montreal called on member congregations to give 'to the maximum ... even if synagogue buildings had to be mortgaged' to do so.[50] Many institutions and organizations stripped their budgets to the bone to contribute the maximum.

Across Canada it was much the same. Bronfman's meeting was called not to initiate fundraising but to impose order on fundraising already under way. In Winnipeg, for example, six simultaneous fundraising meetings at the six largest synagogues were already planned for the evening after the Bronfman meeting. Lest anyone misunderstand the importance placed on giving to Israel at that moment, a local rabbi broke with tradition and used his regular *shabbat* sermon to talk not about matters of spirit but about money, Israel's critical need for money, and what he expected of his congregants. This, he told them, was no time to nickel and dime Israel. More than ever before, the need 'was for substantial support, not token gifts of $100 or $150.' And there was no time to waste. 'The grim truth was that if adequate financial support ... was not invested today, there might not be a second chance to make good the default.'[51]

In advance of Bronfman's Montreal meeting, fundraisers in Toronto met to plan the local launch of a 'unified, coordinated total community effort to mobilize instantaneous and unprecedented support to match the sacrifices of our brothers in Israel.' Directing the Toronto efforts was a hurriedly assembled Coordinating Committee for Emergency Aid to Israel, made up of staff representatives from the UJA, the Canadian Jewish Congress, and the Zionists. As elsewhere in Canada, in Toronto the problem was not convincing people to give. It was dealing with the money and support for Israel already pouring in so fast that it sometimes outstripped the ability of officials to keep track of all that was going on. 'Every synagogue and club, every trade and profession, every organized group and society, rich and poor, large and small, was calling meetings of its entire membership. The aim: to ensure that every man who recognizes himself as a son of the Covenant has been approached and apprised of the dire circumstances which the tiny band of million souls [in Israel] now face, albeit in triumphant victory.'[52] Prominent names in the community were enlisted to act as spokespersons on Israel's behalf. After addressing one community meeting, Rabbi Plaut found himself talking informally with several people when a woman he did not know came up behind him. Preferring not to interrupt the rabbi's conversation, she simply reached over and stuffed a thick wad of cash into his pocket and hurried away before he could even get her name.[53] A Toronto woman tells the story of her Yiddish-speaking mother walking into the house and proclaiming she had concrete evidence that the *Mashiach* was on his way. She had just attended an Israel fundraising event called by the previously anti-Zionist Jewish Labor Bund.[54]

With all the fundraising meetings going on, just gathering all the donations in one place was complicated. A long-time Toronto community fundraiser remembers spending the last week of May and first few days of June driving from community event to community event collecting donations and stuffing them into the trunk of his car. With his trunk full of cash and cheques, he headed back to the UJA office, unloaded and returned to the road.[55]

In Ottawa, as the crisis loomed, the local Jewish community, 'a seamless cloth' as compared to any of the larger Jewish centres in Canada, poured into a fundraising event at the large downtown Beth Shalom Synagogue. The wall between the main sanctuary and an adjacent assembly hall, previously opened only on the High Holy Days to accommodate the crowd of worshippers, was opened for the fundraiser. It was still not enough. The throng spilled out into the street. Bernie Farber stood next to his father as they listened to a speaker from the Israeli embassy. It was the only time Bernie ever remembers seeing his father cry.[56]

In Hamilton, with about 1300 Jewish families, a number of prominent individuals offered their homes for fundraising parlour meetings. The weather was warm enough that many of the meetings were moved into backyards. The mood, however, was anything but spring-like. A local Orthodox rabbi who made the rounds addressing these fundraising gatherings wasted little time delivering any kind of soft, subtle pitch. Speaking in Yiddish he looked into the crowd and simply said, 'Z'geest Yiddish blit' (Jewish blood is spilling). The annual UJA campaign in Hamilton in 1967 was set at $180,000. The Emergency Campaign quickly surpassed $500,000. This included a donation from a man in nearby Burlington who phoned the Jewish Community Centre in Hamilton and asked the executive director if he would be kind enough to drive to Burlington and pick up a cheque. A 'non-Jewish Jew' who had never before publicly identified himself as a Jew, or contributed to any Jewish cause, handed over $5000.[57]

Like the Burlington man, there were others who shied away from attending fundraising events. Cutting out the middleman, they too either asked for someone to come pick up their donation or went straight to whatever Jewish organizational door they found open and handed over all they could. After business hours on 4 June, just hours before the war erupted, an elderly woman walked into the Zionist Centre in Toronto carrying a paper shopping bag and looking a little lost. Finding only one office door open, she asked the lone man still at his desk if this was where she might make a donation to Israel. She was advised that everything was closed to the public for the day. Could she please come back tomorrow. Intent on her mission, she paid no attention and

Governor General Georges Vanier (seated) and Samuel Bronfman (standing) at
celebration of 1959 Bicentenary of Canadian Jewry.

Window of downtown Toronto store with display honouring 1959 Bicentenary of Canadian Jewry.

Arrival of Moroccan family at Dorval Airport in Montreal.

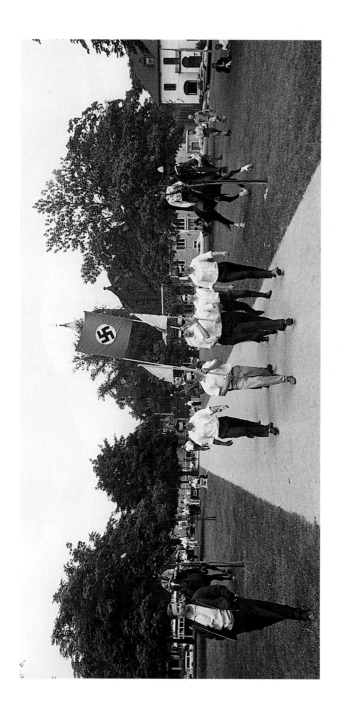

Nazis parading in Allan Gardens, Toronto, 24 July 1965.

Swastika daubing at Shomrai Shabos Synagogue, Toronto, 4 May 1963.

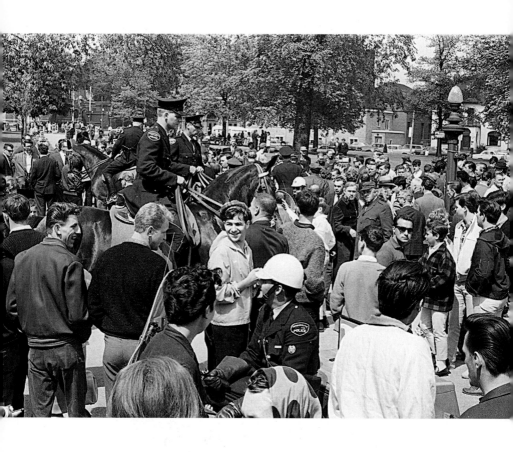

Crowd gathered to protest Nazi rally in Allan Gardens, Toronto, 30 May 1965.

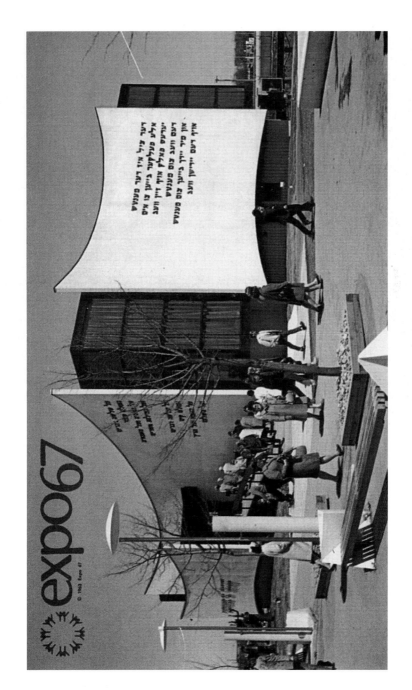

Pavilion of Judaism at Expo 67, Montreal.

Cardinal Paul-Émile Léger visiting the replica of the Second Temple in Jerusalem on display in the Pavilion of Judaism at Expo 67, Montreal.

Israel emergency meeting at Beth Tzedec Synagogue, Toronto, 7 June 1967.

"STATE OF ISRAEL EMERGENCY FUND"

Heeding the need and responding to the urgent call for help from our fellow Jews in Israel, Harry Chaimberg of St. Louis Hardware is marking Tuesday, June 20, as "Israel Emergency Fund Day".

WE WILL HAND OVER the <u>TOTAL GROSS RECEIPTS</u> OF THIS DAY TO THE EMERGENCY FUND

We invite one and all to join us in this worthy effort. Help us make this day a grand and total success . . . remember it all goes to Israel.

Rabbi Sydney Shoham of Beth Zion Synagogue has fully endorsed our endeavor and has accepted the responsibility of handing over the money to the Directors of the Fund.

We also strongly urge our fellow businessmen both of Cote St. Luc and Greater Montreal to take this lead and follow up with "Days" of their own — "For Israel".

Harry Chaimberg
ST. LOUIS HARDWARE
Cote St. Luc Shopping Centre

'Israel Emergency Fund Day,' *Montreal Star*, 7 June, 1967.

A.C. Forrest.

United Church of Canada Moderator Robert B. McClure addressing Toronto Zionist Council. Rabbi W. Gunther Plaut seated on the right, 15 January 1969.

Public hangings in Baghdad, Iraq, 27 January 1969.

Meeting between Canadian and Soviet political leaders in the Kremlin, June 1971. From left to right – Pierre Elliott Trudeau, Barney Danson, interpreter, Alexsei Kosygin, Andrei Gromyko.

Twenty-four-hour Soviet Jewry vigil for the 'Leningrad Nine,' City Hall Plaza, Winnipeg, 17 May 1971.

Sign left at Soviet Embassy in Ottawa during Kosygin visit to Canada, 19 October 1971.

Soviet Jewry rally in front of Canadian Supreme Court, Ottawa,
19 October 1971.

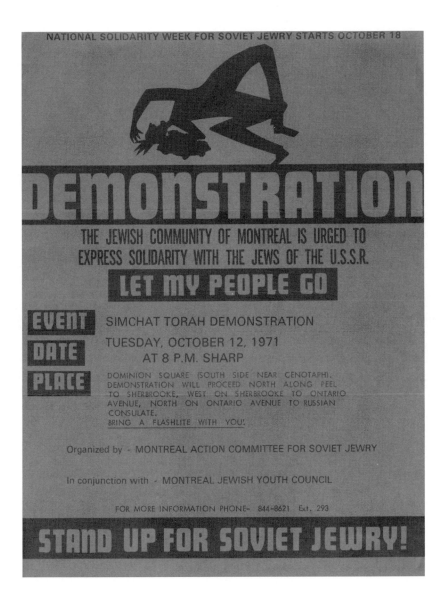

Montreal Action Committee for Soviet Jewry flyer during Kosygin visit to Canada, October 1971.

KOSYGIN VISIT

TORONTO

24 HOUR VIGIL

SUNDAY, OCT. 24
6 p.m. to
MONDAY, OCT. 25
6 p.m.

INN ON THE PARK
(LESLIE & EGLINTON)

MASS RALLY AND MARCH

MONDAY, OCT. 25
6:45 p.m.

Assemble INN ON THE PARK
followed by march to ONTARIO
SCIENCE CENTRE for mass protest

PROTEST Persecution of Soviet Jews!
Let My People Go!

Sponsored by Student Council for Soviet Jews
The Actions Committee for Soviet Jewry   Canadian Jewish Congress
For information call 635-3647 or 363-7190

Actions Committee for Soviet Jewry, Canadian Jewish Congress, Central
Region flyer during Kosygin visit to Canada, October 1971.

Elie Wiesel addressing Toronto Soviet Jewry demonstration during Kosygin visit to Canada, 25 October 1971.

Electric illuminated Star of David across from the Inn on the Park, Toronto, during the visit of Kosygin to Canada, 25 October 1971.

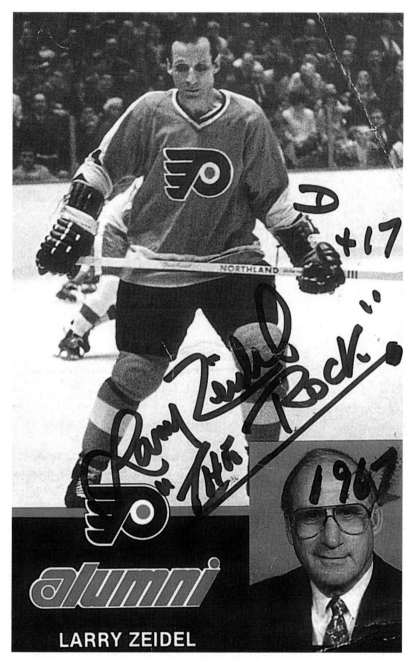

Larry 'The Rock' Zeidel in Philadelphia Fliers uniform, 1967.

T. Millar Chase, Granite Club President, and Isadore Sharp, President of Four Seasons, turning the sod for a new Granite Club facility on Bayview Avenue in Toronto, 9 November 1970.

Golda Meir during visit to Toronto, 1 November 1970.

Students dancing around Torah during Simchat Torah rally in Nathan Phillips Square, Toronto, 12 October 1968.

simply emptied her bag onto the young man's desk – a small amount of cash, silver *shabbat* candlesticks, a wedding ring, and a few other pieces of jewellery. Israel, she insisted, needed it all more than she did.

As she turned to leave, the young man behind the desk, unsure what to do with the items on his desk, had the presence of mind to request the elderly woman's name and address. He explained that a receipt would need to be issued to her before anything of hers could be sold and the money sent to Israel. The next morning he arranged to have her personal effects returned to her with a letter of thanks explaining that much as Israel needed money, it also needed the light which glowed bright from her candlesticks every Friday evening. She reluctantly took back all her personal items except the cash. The cash, she demanded, must go to Israel. It did.[58]

Montreal was no different. One Montreal Jewish official remembers elderly, ashen-faced Jews, many of them Holocaust survivors, arriving at the UJA office on Sherbrooke Street West, donating all they could afford, sometimes more than they could afford. Children arrived with their parents to empty out piggy banks on the office counter. One man insisted on signing over the deed to his home. The flood of cash in Montreal was so great that the mechanics of handling it all became a problem. Staff were kept so busy collecting and counting money that regular trips to the bank to deposit the money proved impossible. As a result, most days cash was simply stuffed into big bags and dragged into the UJA's old walk-in safe. A team of about a dozen volunteer accountants was marshalled to count donations, often through the night. When there was no more space in the safe to store cheques, cash, and negotiable bonds, a trip to the bank was organized. Another Jewish official was only exaggerating slightly when he joked that all his office 'did for weeks was deal with money.'[59]

But the money donated, important as it was in its own right, had importance beyond the goods and services it could buy. Donors knew their financial gifts could not buy what they wanted most – a guarantee of Israel's survival. That in the end was going to be up to Israel and Israelis. But each contribution, no matter how small, made the donor a stakeholder in the fate of both Israel and the Jewish people. And in that darkest of moments, thousands of Canadian Jews, shaken to their very core by a desperate fear for Israel, became stakeholders. They gave because they could not do more and dared not do less.

In late May 1967, even as Israel and its Arab neighbours edged ever closer to war, Israeli president Zalman Shazar was in Montreal on an official state visit to Canada in honour of Canada's centenary and, in particular, to attend Israel Independence Day ceremonies at the Israel Pavilion at Expo 67 in Montreal. Recalled to Israel, Shazar cut short his Montreal visit and cancelled a planned trip to Toronto. Yet even as he prepared to head for the airport, Shazar made time to meet with a group of prominent local Zionist leaders. Asked what more they could do beyond donating money in support of Israel, Shazar called on them to organize mass demonstrations to 'reaffirm unshakeable support and solidarity.' Israelis, he lamented, felt isolated from the world. They needed to know that the diaspora stood with them as one.

The Montrealers took Shazar at his word. With only a few days of planning, the largest of many Canadian 'peace rallies' was held in the ballroom of Montreal's Sheraton Mount Royal Hotel in the city centre. Not even a bomb threat kept people away. An estimated 14,000 Montreal Jews, well beyond the expectations of the rally's organizers, local Zionist organizations, and the Canadian Jewish Congress, turned out. The crowd would likely have been much larger still if all those headed to the rally had not snarled traffic heading into the city core for several hours. The crowd that made it to the rally 'was so huge that it spilled out of the ninth floor [ballroom], down through the lobby and out into the street.' As speaker after speaker praised Canada's support for Israel and efforts on behalf of peace, police outside desperately attempted to cordon off the surrounding area from traffic as the thousands jamming the street outside the hotel organized their own spontaneous demonstration. Inside, though organizers took comfort in the turnout, the mood remained grim. A prominent local rabbi addressing the ballroom crowd captured the mood well when he asked, 'How long is the crucifixion of Israel going to last? Must we continue to be the whipping boy of blundering governments? We categorically reject this role and with faith in our destiny, ourselves and our God, we shall carry on.' An unspoken fear that Jews might soon have to carry on without Israel was implicit in his remarks.[60]

The day of the Montreal rally, the day after the elderly woman in Toronto handed over her precious personal effects, the day after the community fundraising rally in Vancouver, and the day after Bronfman met with Jewish leaders, Israel was at war. At 7:10 a.m. on the morning of 5 June 1967, jet fighters began taking off from military airfields across Israel. Within twenty minutes some two hundred Israeli jets were in the sky. The launch of an Israeli air armada was detected by Jordanian radar and a coded message dispatched to Cairo warning the Egyptians that an air attack was imminent. To the disbelief of Israeli military leaders who anticipated heavy resistance to their attack, confusion in decoding the Jordanian message meant the Egyptians were still in the dark about the attack when the first Israeli jets swooped down on Egyptian air force installations at 7:30 a.m. Sortie after sortie successfully hit their targets. By 8:15 a.m. the Israeli military high command knew the Egyptian air force had ceased to function as a fighting unit. At that same moment, Israel's land forces attacked into Gaza and the Sinai.

When Canadian Jews woke up on 5 June to news of war, they had no clue that Israel had already secured unchallenged air supremacy. Israeli officials had clamped a cone of secrecy over the conflict. The American and Soviet intelligence-gathering capability ensured that both superpowers were generally up to speed as events unfolded, but through the first day of the Israeli news blackout, the world media and even the Israeli public remained in the dark about what was happening. Rumour, conjecture, the if-this and if-that pronouncements of pundits, and a barrage of 'official' Egyptian media reports of sweeping battle successes filled the information vacuum from Israel. As Jews across Canada huddled around radios and televisions, Canadian broadcast media interrupted regular programming with war bulletins. The first reports Canadians heard from the battle zone were the claims from Cairo and other Arab capitals of Arab victory in repulsing the Israeli air attack and reports of triumphant advances by Egyptian ground forces into Israel. As Israel enforced its news blackout, Western correspondents stationed in Arab capitals spoke of celebration in the Arab street at reports of victories and martial music dominated the local airwaves. Even as it cast doubt on the reliability of the early Arab reports of resounding victory, a *Toronto Star* editorial entitled 'The Fear of Civilian Atrocities' warned that the battle for Israel's survival was promising to be bloody.

Even if Israel is militarily capable of handling the Arab nations, as most Western experts think, she is vulnerable to heavy civilian losses and suffering in the current war.

The population centres of the tiny country are all within quick reach of enemy air attack and several of them are within Arab artillery range.

The Israeli government also has cause to be apprehensive of poison gas attacks on civilians ... There is nothing in the official indoctrination of the Arab armies or peoples which would incline them to show mercy to any

Israelis who fall within their power. They have been unceasingly taught
that to remedy an historical injustice to the Arabs of Palestine, it is their
honorable duty to exterminate Israel.[61]

Glued to radios and televisions through that first day of war, Canadian Jews were racked with anguish. It was as if all their worst night-
mares were coming true. As the West sat by, Israel was being crushed,
suffering huge numbers of casualties, military and civilian. Later, writing about the first few hours of the war, Rabbi Plaut recalled, '[Canadi-
an] Jews did not know what would happen: they only knew their fears
and their anxieties and their total involvement. I saw many tough men
cry on that day.'[62] In Winnipeg telephones in Jewish homes started ringing as word spread that Israel was desperately short of whole blood.
The Canadian Red Cross, it was said, was sending all it could. Meanwhile, the local Canadian Red Cross blood donor clinic was besieged
by callers wanting to know where they could contribute on Israel's behalf. Jewish leaders were forced to issue a statement to the press that
'contrary to previous reports there has been no request for donations of
blood at this time.'[63] Nevertheless, in Toronto a blood drive was hastily
organized in cooperation with the Red Cross. A press advertisement
announced that all blood donated would be 'for all the injured – Jew
and Arab alike.' And soon word was circulating that a desperate Israel
needed more than blood. As fears for Israel's losses gripped Canadian
Jews, across Canada Jewish community centres and synagogues were
hastily converted into drop-off points for clothing, bedding, medicine,
and just about anything else that anyone imagined a besieged Israel
– or its survivors – might require. Unsure what would eventually be
needed, volunteers sorted the goods as best they could and made efforts to find places to store what came in until it could be sent to Israel.[64]

  With war engaged and the mood grim, contributions of money
spiked, although in the early hours of the war donors were heartsick
at the prospect that there might not be an Israel to accept their donations and instead the funds would go to helping survivors. Israel was at
war. So too, they felt, were Canadian Jews. UJA organizers in Winnipeg
dispatched a telegram to smaller Jewish communities across the west
mirroring the grim mood and pressing for a redoubling of fundraising efforts. 'Emergency campaign United Israel Appeal underway in all
communities for largest amounts ever raised. Sacrificial cash donations
being made many times exceeding all previous give levels. Urge Lake-
head follow example of Winnipeg and Vancouver, etc. These funds ear-

marked for food, clothing, medical and other welfare needs in Israel.' In Toronto two hundred Jews, dreading the worst, assembled for a previously scheduled noontime fundraising meeting in the Empress Room of the downtown Park Plaza Hotel. Just as a guest speaker was about to start his talk, a power failure blanketed the hotel in darkness. Finding prophetic meaning in the mishap, a rabbi at the back of the room shouted out, 'The Jews have sat in darkness before ... They that sit in darkness shall see the light.' As hotel staff scrambled to find candles, organizers decided to scrap the talk. Without working microphones, they simply shouted out that those wishing to contribute should line up. The line was long. When the meeting adjourned ninety minutes after it began, the room was still in darkness and hotel staff carrying candles guided people down the stairwells to the street.[65]

Early that same evening, the first day of the war, Winnipeg Jews gathered in the city's six major synagogues to attend pre-planned pro-Israel fundraising rallies. After a long day glued to radios, many were disconsolate at the reports of catastrophic Israeli losses. As evening approached they might well have wondered if Israel would have many more days, and whether the feared second Holocaust had begun. Their mood was about to change. At 1:00 a.m. Israeli time, 5:00 p.m. in Winnipeg, Yitzhak Rabin, commander of the Israeli armed forces, went on Israeli radio to lift the veil of official secrecy that had denied both Israelis and the larger world an accurate picture of how the war was progressing. As Israelis huddled around their radios, Rabin described the situation. Israel was at war and the military had incurred casualties. There would be more. The Israeli military, however, was then advancing on all fronts. The Israeli air force had total dominion over the skies. There was no doubt that Israel would be victorious.

No sooner had Rabin finished reading his statement to the nation than restrictions on the international press were lifted. The BBC special correspondent in Jerusalem went on air to London reporting 'Israel has already won this war in 15 hours.' The BBC announcer in London cautioned his listeners that the report had 'not yet been confirmed from any source.' Even as they reported on Rabin's statement, Canadian news media were unsure just how much of Rabin's statement to accept. A special late edition of the *Toronto Telegram* carried the headline 'Israeli Army Claims Gaza "Breakthrough."' Even as Winnipeg Jews assembled, local radio broke the news of Rabin's statement. Although his statement had yet to be verified, a stone was lifted off the Jewish heart. As word of the statement circulated through the six synagogue sanctuaries, Winnipeg Jews gathering as if for a funeral suddenly found themselves celebrating as if at a wedding.

As the second day of battle dawned in Israel the morning *Globe and Mail* remained cautious. The lead editorial explained that, with all the conflicting claims of military victories, there remained an air of uncertainty about what was happening on the ground. 'Exactly what had happened yesterday was far from clear. There were extravagant claims of aerial victories from both sides. Israeli tank forces were engaged with Arab armor in the [Israeli] Negev desert. Artillery fire was exchanged between Israeli and Jordanian sectors of Jerusalem. The Syrians claim to have set fire to a large oil refinery at Haifa.' All that could be known for sure, according to the editorial, was that after twenty-four hours both sides remained in pitched battle.[66]

By the end of the second day of battle, however, there could no longer be any doubt – not in the Canadian press and not in the Canadian Jewish community – as to how the war was going, only how long it might last. Even as Jordan and then Syria entered the battle, the results on the Egyptian front were now clear. As day three began, Arab radio continued to broadcast martial music and report fictitious Arab victories, but reports from Western capitals and from correspondents in Israel verified that Israeli forces had taken the entire Sinai Peninsula and had reached the Suez Canal. The Soviet Union, witnessing the collapse of its Arab clients, threatened punitive action if Israel did not agree to a ceasefire. Undeterred, Israel pressed on and after another three days it had occupied East Jerusalem and the west bank of the Jordan River, formerly under Jordanian control, and wrested the Golan Heights from Syria. Israel's military triumph was startling.[67]

Canadian Jews were transfixed by the news out of Israel. Like emotional whiplash, dread that Israel's destruction was at hand was replaced by joy at her deliverance and that of their own. For observant Jews this was a moment to *bench gomel*, to offer thanks to God for deliverance from mortal danger. For all those who had dug so deep, for the thousands who stepped forward to volunteer, for those who endured sleepless nights out of fear for Israel and the Jewish future, there was a sense of having been spared the horror of a another Holocaust. There was also a personal sense of being invested in Israel, in a secure Jewish future, and in shared responsibility for alleviating the plight of embattled Jews and those who remained at risk wherever they might be.

Without skipping a beat, Canadian Jews who had given to Israel out of fear during the days of despair leading to the outbreak of war, gave with renewed passion as the news of Israel's triumphs on the battlefield were confirmed. Sam Bronfman received a telegram from Nova Scotia. 'Jewish community of Bathurst, Campbellton, Dalhousie comprising ten families join Canadian Jewry in wholehearted support of Israel in heroic struggle for survival and honourable peace. Remitted today five thousand seven hundred dollars for emergency appeal to Halifax. *Techzakna Yedeichem* [to be strong in unity].'[68] In Winnipeg a woman 'presented a cheque which represented a loan which she made against her insurance policy' and a young lawyer recently admitted to the bar made 'a contribution beyond his immediate financial capacity' by taking out a bank loan to cover a series of personal postdated cheques.[69] In Montreal Harry Chaimberg, owner of a local hardware store, placed a notice in the *Montreal Star* announcing an 'Israel Emergency Fund Day' at his store. He pledged to donate the total gross receipts for the day to Israel and urged other 'businessmen both in Cote St. Luc and Greater Montreal to follow his with "Days" of their own – "For Israel."'[70]

Across Canada many non-Jews were also moved by Israel's unexpected military triumph. Winnipeg was no exception. 'At one of the [six simultaneous] synagogue meetings ... a street cleaner of Polish descent walked in to say that he had helped save Jewish lives in Poland as an underground fighter in World War II. He made a cash contribution because, as he commented: "I don't want Jews to be killed again."'[71] The mail brought more contributions from non-Jews. A non-Jewish lawyer in Winnipeg wrote that since he was too old to personally volunteer for Israel, he was 'reduced to demonstrating both my indignation and support through the wholly inadequate method of financial contribution.' He allowed that after 2500 years of history, the Jewish people and the young state of Israel may not 'require' his support, but non-Jews such as himself 'will be lesser men & the world poorer if we permit the destruction of this symbol of man's dedication & determination to exist.'[72] He was not alone. Another Winnipeg man wrote:

I am not in a position to know the rights and wrongs of the war in the Middle East, but I see that Israel must need help desperately because I see my Jewish friends making substantial contributions at some sacrifice to themselves.

I do not want to contribute to financing a war, but I know there will be much hardship as a result of it, and I would like to help out by making a contribution for non-military purposes.

Therefore I enclose my cheque for $1000.00.[73]

In Vancouver, Moe Steinberg, then the only Jewish faculty member in the English Department at the University of British Columbia, was working late when he heard a shuffling sound at his door. He called out, 'Come in,' but nobody entered. Steinberg went to the door and found an envelope with $100 for Israel from his departmental chair and a note saying only that he wished he could do more.[74]

Donations to the emergency campaign poured in so fast during the week-long war that many communities met or even surpassed their assigned Israel Emergency Campaign targets well before the shooting ended. On 8 June, only four days after Calgary's target was reset at $450,000 and three days after the war's outbreak, the Calgary campaign director remitted the full $450,000 to the national campaign headquarters in Montreal. As additional contributions are processed, he promised, 'we will make further remittances.'[75]

Money was one thing. What about all those who had signed up to go to Israel as volunteers? All was on hold. There could be no sending Canadians into an active war zone. What is more, the task of securing seats on those few flights still going to Israel was an even greater challenge than before the war began, and, with the war emergency, the infrastructure necessary to place volunteers into meaningful work situations just was not there. But if war derailed any organized Jewish hope of somehow getting volunteers to Israel, it encouraged some to light out for Israel on their own. Canadian Robert Krell was among them. In the spring of 1967 Krell, a child survivor and graduate of the University of British Columbia medical school, was doing a psychiatric residency at Temple University Hospital in Philadelphia. He recalls his workload as 'all consuming,' leaving him little time for anything else. But there was no locking out the escalating tensions in the Middle East. Krell identified deeply with Israel. As he put it, 'I didn't need the label Zionist to know that my being was tied up to Israel.'

In a rare break from hospital routine, he and a friend, also a doctor and child survivor, drove to an Israel peace rally in Washington, DC. On their return to Philadelphia Krell resigned his residency. He felt he was needed somewhere else. Krell had previously served a two-year internship in an inner-city hospital. He had a wealth of emergency-room and trauma experience. Convinced that Israel was in need of doctors with his training, Krell grabbed the first flight he could to Europe, Icelandic Airlines to Luxemburg, intending to somehow connect to Israel. While he was en route the war broke out. With few carriers except El Al taking off for Israel, and all El Al flights packed, Krell was stranded. Try as he might, he could not get a flight to Israel. Even when the war ended, airlines had to work through a huge backlog of passengers awaiting flights. If it was unclear when he might get to Israel, it was increasingly clear that his particular medical skills were no longer an Israeli priority. His money running low, Krell finally turned around and went back to Philadelphia, where he was gratefully allowed to resume his residency.[76]

Krell was not the only doctor who put his life on hold in order to assist Israel. On the second day of the war, the Zionist Organization in Montreal received an emergency call from the Jewish Agency in Israel. The Agency, a non-governmental body which works to coordinate links between overseas Jewish communities and Israel, reported that Israel was desperately short of doctors. While news from the battlefront spoke of Israeli military successes, these had been hard won. Israel had suffered severe casualties. Nobody knew how many more there would yet be. The Jewish Agency described Israeli doctors as overextended and fearful that as the war continued they would not be able to tend to all the wounded. Medical specialists were especially in short supply. Was it possible, the Jewish Agency representative asked Jewish officials in Montreal, to immediately send a group of anesthesiologists, orthopedic surgeons, and other essential specialized medical personnel to Israel?

Without hesitation Montreal promised the doctors. In a masterpiece of organization, word went out to Jewish communities across North America that specialists were needed. Local lists of volunteer doctors were quickly scoured for specialists. Within hours volunteer doctors were packing, arranging for colleagues to fill in while they were gone and, with no clear idea of how long they would be gone or what dangers they might face, and heading for local airports. Overnight, a group of more than twenty medical specialists from across North America assembled in Montreal.

Myer Bick, the young director of the Student Zionist Organization in Montreal, was assigned to shepherd the doctors to Israel. The doctors flew Sabina Airlines out of Montreal for Brussels, unsure of what awaited them. In Brussels, after resting up for a few hours at an airport hotel, they were assigned priority seating on an El Al flight dispatched to bring Israelis in Europe home to join their military units.

Landing in Israel, Bick recalls the airport in Tel Aviv was a *balligan* – a scene of total confusion. With priority given to the nation's war needs, many of the administrative, service, and professional staff who normally operated the civil airport were in uniform. As a result, the airport was understaffed. In any event, except for some El Al flights, there were few international flights entering or leaving Israel. Customs and immigration procedures were observed in the breach. In the departure terminal, flight cancellations had left many out-bound travellers stranded. Some of those waiting for flights stood guard over piled up luggage while relatives, friends, or fellow stranded passengers scurried about seeking information about if and when cancelled flights would be rescheduled. Nobody seemed to know what was happening.

Meanwhile, in the arrivals area the doctors gathered their luggage and waited for whoever was supposed to meet them and take them to their medical posts. Nobody came and, as it turned out, nobody had been assigned to come. Somewhere between the initial Jewish Agency call to Montreal that set off the scramble for doctors, and their arrival in Israel, communication and planning had broken down. Not only was nobody assigned to meet the group, but in light of Israel's military successes, the emergency call for doctors had also been withdrawn. Neither Montreal nor the doctors had been informed. A group of bone-weary North American medical specialists gathered around their luggage in a corner of the airport, with no place to go and no way to get there.

Tired and frustrated, Bick repeatedly phoned his contact at the Jewish Agency in Jerusalem who, he hoped, could sort things out. It took a while before Bick got through. After explaining the situation, instead of being offered assistance, Bick found himself being lectured. Didn't he know there was a war on? Didn't he know that within blocks of the Jewish Agency Building in Jerusalem fighting had only just ended? Israeli troops were still securing former Jordanian-controlled East Jerusalem. Did he expect everything to stop so his little problem could be resolved? The number of Israeli casualties and the severity of their injuries were turning out to be less than originally feared. The Israeli medical community had everything in hand. The North American doctors were not needed. Go home.

Bick was taken aback, but had no choice except to be firm. The group had travelled too far and too long simply to be told to forget it. Certainly, in a county still at war, meaningful medical assignments could be found for the doctors. His contact, after letting off steam, became a little more conciliatory in tone and promised to do what he could. In the meantime, Bick was told to get the doctors into cabs and to a hotel in Tel Aviv for the night – no mean trick in itself. Bick eventually rounded up transportation and found rooms for the group in a small Tel Aviv hotel, slightly past its prime.

By the next morning, Bick's contact at the Jewish Agency had things arranged. Bick and the doctors were shuttled to Jerusalem, about an hour and a half's drive from Tel Aviv. Here they were divided into several teams and assigned to care for wounded prisoners of war at hospitals in Jerusalem, Haifa, and Beersheva. Now free of his charges, Bick connected with several friends from Montreal who had been in Israel when the war erupted. Together they joined the first throngs of Israelis permitted into the old city of Jerusalem after its capture from Jordanian control – the first unrestricted Jewish entries into East Jerusalem and its holy places in almost twenty years.[77]

The personal commitment that individual Canadian Jews such as Bick felt for Israel – volunteering to go there, contributing money, blood, and material goods to Israel – came from the heart, but it was channelled through the offices of the organized Jewish community in Canada. And as Israel more and more became a Canadian Jewish priority, so too did Israel advocacy by the organized Jewish community and its leadership. Indeed, making it clear that henceforth the larger organized Jewish community and not just the Zionists would be vigorous in lobbying on Israel's behalf, in the lead-up to the war the Canadian Jewish Congress assumed a formal leadership role in organizing Canadian public, government, and media support for Israel. Canadian Jewish leaders had already concluded that 'externally, that is outside the Jewish community, there is need to do a major job of convincing public opinion of the justice of Israel's cause, and of the position the Jewish community is taking vis-à-vis Canadian government action.' Like fundraising, this required coordination from the centre. And with fundraising assigned to the UJA/UIA and coordination of volunteers assigned to Zionist organizations, the Congress head office in Montreal folded primary responsibility for Israel advocacy in Canada under its wing, overshadowing the Zionists, with whom Congress pledged to continue working in 'close liaison.'[78]

To ensure that local Jewish leaders who might be called upon to speak on Israel's behalf were kept 'on message,' Congress's public relations director in Montreal pulled together a guide sheet on how local community spokespersons should be framing public comment on the Middle East crisis.

Instead of referring in statements to 'the Arabs,' 'Arab countries' etc. (i.e. as opposed to a 'Jewish country'), try using such phrases as 'Communist-backed,' 'Russian-subsidized,' 'Soviet sphere of influence' etc. etc. I realize that these can be improved on, but you get the idea. This could be a matter of policy, that is, not just phraseology for news releases but incorporated in statements by your officials, worked into answers in interviews and so forth.

Hopefully this could have two results – make people equate Israel political posture more withour [sic] own; make it difficult for groups like the Syrian Businessmen's Association or whatever to take a political stand for at least the present regimes of certain countries.

This approach might generate more support than one which essentially is a plea for aid and understanding of a *Jewish* cause. The appeal would be to self interest rather than sympathy.[79]

Two days after the war began, several Congress leaders and officials in Toronto met to review options for firming up local support for Israel while, at the same time, boosting the community's fundraising efforts. Among the ideas considered were organizing a series of radio spots 'on a public service basis if possible,' placing pro-Israel advertisements in the mainstream press, collecting supportive 'statements of conscience' from prominent industry, labour, and religious leaders, and organizing a speakers bureau that would be available to address non-Jewish groups.[80]

Compared to today's professionally run public relations campaigns, this in-house organized pro-Israel lobbying might appear a seat-of-the-pants effort. But even if amateur by today's standards, it represented a sea change for the organized Canadian Jewish community. By making Israel a central concern, the larger organized Jewish community, and not just the Zionists, was affirming that which Canadian Jews had internalized during the lead-up to war in the Middle East and during the war itself – Canadian Jews were indivisibly bound up with Israel. For Canadian Jews, Israel had become as close as their breath. At a rally on behalf of Israel, a Toronto Jewish leader spoke from the heart when he declared, 'We are here for the sake of our children who will live as free men when this [war] is over and Israel is free to pursue its existence in peace.'[81]

On 7 June, as Israeli troops rolled across the Sinai and consolidated their control of East Jerusalem and much of the west bank of the Jordan river, Arab states supported by the Soviet bloc demanded the UN force Israel to halt its advance and retire to its pre–5 June positions. That same day Sam Bronfman again led a delegation to Ottawa to meet with Prime Minister Pearson, his external affairs minister, Mitchell Sharp, and opposition leaders. What Bronfman hoped was to firm up Canadian support at the UN for an Israel then at war. While a sudden bout of illness on arriving in Ottawa prevented Bronfman from participating in the discussions, the Jewish delegates nonetheless were warmly received. Even so, their pro-Israel message met with a mixed response. In spite of hostile Arab rejection of Canada's pre-war efforts to broker a settlement, the Pearson government remained determined to follow an 'even handed' approach to the Middle East crisis. Though Canadians were generally supportive of Israel, the government was not about to tilt in Israel's favour. When the war ended, now almost certainly with an Israeli victory in the field, Canada expected there would be a need for architects of mediation. Pearson hoped to be one of them. Opposition leaders, however, were more outspoken in support of Israel. After meeting with delegates, John Diefenbaker, leader of the opposition, proclaimed in the House of Commons, 'There can be no neutrality by Canada with regard to those who have the specific objective and purpose of destroying the Hebrew race.'[82]

If the delegation's pro-Israel message received a guarded response, all those who met with the Jewish group could have no doubt that, at that moment, Canadian Jews, normally a fractious lot, were at one with Israel.[83] What is more, in the wake of the Middle East crisis, whether or not politicians, or for that matter the Congress delegates themselves, recognized it, the Canadian Jewish community was a much changed one. While the full measure of that change had yet to be taken, there could be no denying that during the Six Day War crisis the Canadian Jewish community underwent something akin to an emotional meltdown. Israel, the Holocaust, and the historical chain of Jewish being were welded together into a seamless mass. Debate over whether Jews should present themselves to non-Jews as a faith group – akin to Protestants and Catholics – or as an ethnic group with a sense of shared past and common destiny might matter to those, especially to Jewish leaders in Quebec, who represented Jews to government and the larger society. But all that was beside the point to most Jews. In the heat of crisis, Canadian Jews felt themselves inextricably bound up with a larger Jewish people and its fate. Yes, Canadian Jews lived in an increasingly welcoming Canada, and as Canadians they demanded equality of status with all other Canadians. But this did not lessen their gut-level bond with Israel and Jews around the world. There was a new centre of Canadian Jewish gravity.

The Six Day War proved a shot of adrenaline for the organized Jewish community. It emerged from the war united in its commitment to

Israel and the security of dispossessed Jews everywhere. Simply stated, the Six Day War was a rebranding experience, locking past to present. The many who grew up understanding their Jewishness as a familial artefact handed down from generation to generation, an inheritance that came with a package of time-honoured traditions and rituals that many observed in the breach, woke up from the Six Day War to find their Jewish point of reference shifted from the past to the present, from remembering to being. Yes, there were still rituals that came with a storied Jewish past. But all of a sudden there was a consciousness of obligations and responsibilities that came with being Jewish. For many, being Jewish suddenly meant doing Jewish. And while those who rekindled bonds to Jewishness in that turbulent spring of 1967 might have found their rediscovered Jewishness an uncomfortable fit, now that they were outed as Jews, slipping back to the Jewish margins was not always the easiest option. In-your-face Jewishness was the new normal. Any attempt to turn the Canadian Jewish mindset back to the way it was before the Middle East crisis would have been like trying to unscramble an egg. It couldn't be done. And for both the organized Jewish community and the growing community of committed Jews in Canada, the Six Day War coloured their responses to the rush of events that would follow through the decade in motion.

CHAPTER FIVE

Prestige Pride

The Six Day War was a turning point in Canadian Jewish history. But did it write *fini* to the old order? Many thought so. Writing about the fallout from the war, McGill political scientist Harold Waller contends that Israel emerged a singular driving force compelling Jewish activism. 'The Six-Day War,' he concluded, 'challenged Canadian Jewry's historic passivity and stimulated the creation of a politicized community that had no choice but to respond to the Middle East events that have occurred since 1967.' In a similar vein, historian Gerald Tulchinsky argues the Six Day War not only turned Israel into 'an overriding focus for a majority of Canadian Jews,' it sparked an uptake of things Jewish. Canadian Jews embraced their Jewish selves. According to Rabbi Plaut, 'Proud identification with the valor and courage of the Israelis gave the [Canadian] Jews a new image, not the least in their own eyes.' Saul Hayes, executive director of the Canadian Jewish Congress, concluded that the Six Day War provided Canadian Jews with something that was previously missing in their lives. Before the war there was a sense of 'Jewish emptiness in the lives of many of the present generation,' which, he felt, threatened 'the Jewish psyche.' That emptiness 'is being filled,' claimed Hayes, 'but not by a return to customs and practices with which other generations were familiar. "La recherche du temps perdu" is not for the new breed. Large segments of the Jewish people are finding in Israel a real substitute for their former identification. It is a concept or belief. It requires only the effort to be touched by the regeneration of a nation.' Rabbi Stuart Rosenberg of Toronto's Conservative Beth Tzedec Synagogue, writing a few years after the war, cautioned that swelling Canadian Jewish pride in identification with Israel was not without its disquieting aspects, particularly for younger members of the community. 'Growing up among Canadian Jewish youth, as with Jewish youth everywhere,' he suggested, 'is an accelerating awareness of the world's double political standard toward the Jews, and their own concomitant need to find the resources necessary to survive as Jews. All seem to agree that these are primarily to be found within the Jewish people itself.' Feeling Jewish spurred Jewish communal attachment and Jewish communal attachment spurred a desire to 'do Jewish.'[1]

Bernard Avishai, Montreal-born author of several books on Israel and Zionism, was eighteen and a student at McGill University when the Middle East erupted into crisis. Glued to Montreal talk radio, he remembers hearing the voices of Jews possessed by fear 'of an impending Holocaust.' Imagining Israel as a 'big Camp Massad,' Avishai lined up with many other young Jewish Montrealers to volunteer for Israel. The war broke out before he could get to Israel, but no sooner did the fighting end than Avishai was Israel-bound. He found a country in 'celebration.'

Four decades later Avishai reflected on the impact the Six Day War had on Canadian Jews. Yes, the lead-up to war evoked horrific images of an impending Holocaust. Yes, Jews galvanized behind Israel. Yes, the war crisis energized Canadian Jewish pro-Israelism, fundraising, and institutional growth. But the war did more than that. Avishai believes the events of 1967 reset the Jewish clock. According to him, before the Six Day War the Canadian Jewish community understood itself as 'derived from a people of the past' and was inclined to look backward rather than forward in constructing both a communal identity and a communal agenda. Even as Jews deepened their attachment to Canada, Avishai contends, they tended to regard their Jewishness as largely commemorative, a historical bequest hollow of future purpose. As a result, he asserts, Canadian Jews had neither a framework for assigning Jewish meaning to current experience nor 'active ingredients' for envisioning a vibrant Jewish tomorrow.

The 1967 war changed all that. According to Avishai, it did not so much uncouple the Jewish present from the Jewish past as energize the unfolding of 'active Jewish identification as important to our own [Jewish] daily lives.' Canadian Jews, in effect, reset their mental clocks forward. Being Jewish was no longer an inherited shadow of what *was*. Rather, it was valued as a life commitment shaping what one *is* and what one *will be*. Accordingly, being Jewish mattered because what happens today matters, and so does what will happen tomorrow. And for Canadian Jews in the late spring of 1967, the key reference point of their transformed identity was Israel, the living symbol of the Jewish present and the hope for a secure Jewish future. Just as Canadian Jews joined as one in support of Israel in its hour of distress, they suddenly felt themselves 'equal participants' in defining a new Jewish tomorrow that the Israeli victory promised them. According to Avishai, Israel gave Canadian Jews a 'prestige pride in being Jewish.' And with 'prestige pride,' what it meant to be a Jew shifted for many from bequest to catalyst, from remembering to doing.[2]

If the Six Day War produced an awakened or intensified sense of Jewishness, the seeds of that awakening were sown in the several years before the war. They are found in growing Jewish unease at how the Quiet Revolution might unfold and impact Jewish life in Quebec. They are found in the smouldering discontent of what many Toronto Jews regarded as the local Jewish community establishment's spineless betrayal on the neo-Nazi issue. But, if there was an unaccustomed edginess in Canadian Jewish community ranks before the war, it was the lead-up to the war that reset the course of Canadian Jewish history. For Canadian Jews the realization that, barely twenty years after the Holocaust, a Jewish state could suffer annihilation as an indifferent world stood by had a galvanizing impact. In their fear Canadian Jews rallied behind Israel and, with Israel's victory they were filled with a spillover pride at being Jewish and at one with Israel. And for Canadian Jews, Israel was not just a country among countries. It became a source of Jewish inspiration, a haven for the Jewish oppressed, and an ancestral homeland where barely any Canadian Jews had ever set foot. The oneness that Canadian Jews felt with Israel in the wake of victory was so close it changed common speech. Before the Six Day War, Canadian Jews were likely to speak to one another about Israel in the third person. The war crisis and Israel's triumph shifted third person to first person – 'Israel did' to 'we did', 'Israel's struggle' to 'our struggle,' 'Israel's victory' to 'our victory,' 'Israel's future' to 'our future.'

Given the intense bonding with Israel, one might ask why more Canadian Jews did not pack their bags and make *aliya*, move to Israel? This is one question Allan Pakes did not have to ask himself. Born in 1941, Pakes grew up within Edmonton's small and tight Jewish community. He attended the Edmonton Talmud Torah and was active in Young Judaea. A good student, Pakes studied law at the University of Alberta. But his heart was elsewhere. In the summer of 1963 Pakes visited Israel. Taken with the land and people, he made up his mind that Israel was where he would live. The following spring, three days after he was awarded his law degree, Pakes moved to Israel. Entering Israel on a tourist visa, he lived on the cheap in Jerusalem while he learned Hebrew. He also found a job working with English-speaking Zionist youth visiting Israel and changed his legal status from tourist to *oleh*, immigrant, which granted him Israeli citizenship. He married and relocated from Jerusalem to Tel Aviv.

In 1967 the war crisis broke. Pakes had not yet been called to compulsory military service. But unwilling to sit on his hands while Israel mobilized around him, he volunteered to work wherever it was felt his particular skill set could be put to best use. An English-speaking law graduate with proven people skills, he was handed a shovel and assigned to dig trenches along one of Israel's borders. When the war ended, Pakes put down his shovel and took a job with the Association of Americans and Canadians in Israel assisting the young volunteers flooding into Israel from North America find housing and work. Most of the Canadian and American volunteers with whom Pakes had contact were secular or religiously indifferent and not particularly well educated Jewishly. Few, he recalled, had any knowledge of Hebrew – unless one counted a few Hebrew prayers committed to memory years earlier. Asked why they came to Israel, most told Pakes they just wanted to help. Asked why help Israel rather than volunteer to work with the needy at home, the response was often a shrug. According to Pakes, it was difficult for North American volunteers to wrap words around what was at its core a visceral response to the 1967 crisis. Many, he contends, were caught off guard by the sudden fear for Israel's survival that gripped them in the lead-up to war. In the aftermath of Israel's victory they simply wanted to be 'part of the drama' that was Israel.

When they arrived in Israel, few if any volunteers had a clear notion of what they would encounter. Some harboured Sunday school images of biblical Israel or *Exodus*-inspired visions of pioneer soldiers guarding a desert turned green by Jewish sweat. Others did not even have that. And hardly any in the rush of volunteers who arrived in the months following the war had any notion of what they were going to do in Israel. Perhaps, as in the words of a classic Zionist melody, they felt that in Israel they would build and be built. Imagining Israel as some sort of Jewish Peace Corps, they intended to make a 'useful' contribution to the country and, in the process, find meaning in the 'spirit of Israel.'

But young Canadian and American volunteers did not always find Israel an easy fit. Not only did few have a working knowledge of Hebrew, most were light on marketable work skills. As a result, many were streamed into labour-intensive agricultural work that often involved more heavy lifting than many volunteers were prepared for. And without Hebrew some found it hard to connect to Israelis. Still, Pakes contends, Israel proved an eye-opener. Many young, eager, and impressionable volunteers became caught up in an Israel that seemed both immediate and purposeful. Israel presented them with a Jewishness palpably different from that of Sunday school classes, high holy day services, lox and bagels, and parental pressure to get good grades and date Jewish. Different, too, than a Jewishness of remembered smells from a *bubbie*'s kitchen, the odd Yiddish word or phrase slipped into conversation, the mandatory *hora* that begins every bar mitzvah party, or the sneak away from the sedar table every Passover for a quick peek at the Stanley Cup playoffs. Israel presented a Jewishness of the moment, a wrap-around Jewishness that pulsed with pride and nation building.

But much as Israel might excite feelings of Jewish pride and attachment, it was not home, and the vast majority of volunteers went home. Many, Pakes suggests, boarded flights in Tel Aviv promising themselves they would come back soon and come back to live. Most didn't, or at least didn't come back to live. Life got in the way. But even if they did not return to live in Israel, Pakes is convinced that Israel left its mark on most North American volunteers. At a minimum, it solidified their attachment to Israel and pride in identifying as Jews.[3]

Even as volunteers returned home to Canada, there were those Canadian and American Jews who did start new lives in Israel. Mordechai Bar-On, appointed director of the Youth and Chalutziut Department of the Jewish Agency in 1968, explained that in the first few years following the Six Day War approximately twenty thousand Canadian and American Jews came to Israel to live. Some estimates put the number much higher, and according to Bar-On, whose department was responsible for promoting *aliyah* from around the world, that number could have been higher still. There was, Bar-On contends, an untapped pool of *aliyah*-ready Canadians and Americans who would have immigrated if Israel had more aggressively encouraged it. Why then did Israel not do more to promote *aliyah* among North American Jews? In Bar-On's opinion, Israel's North American priorities shifted dramatically after the 1967 war. In an effort to solidify the North American Jewish community's financial and lobbying support, Israel began to downplay the Zionist point of creed that a Jew can only truly live as a Jew, a whole Jew, in Israel. Instead, the new mantra of Israel's relationship to North

American Jews was that of an Israel-diaspora partnership, one in which both Israel and North American Jews would take strength from one another. As a result, active Israeli promotion of *aliyah* from North America, if not abandoned, was not pursued nearly as strongly as Bar-On argues it might have been and, in retrospect, should have been.[4] In fact, there was a North American market for the *aliyah* message. According to Bar-On, in the first few years after the war there was a pool of North American Jews weighing the possibility of *aliyah*. With a little more active encouragement from Israel, he feels, many might well have reached the tipping point of commitment and packed their bags.

Whatever Israel's failings in actively promoting *aliyah* from North America, there were those North Americans who did move to Israel, and they were gladly welcomed. Allan Pakes, who moved on to work at the Jewish Agency's North American desk under Bar-On, agrees that there might have been far more North American *olim* had Israel promoted *aliyah* more energetically. But Pakes still regards the few years immediately following the Six Day War as the 'golden age' of North American immigration to Israel. Those who made *aliyah*, Pakes explains, were generally older, more mature, and had more marketable skills than the youthful North American volunteers who came to Israel for short stints following the war. Most *olim* were also married, secular, highly educated – if not always Jewishly so – often new to Zionism, and, in many cases, new to active Jewish engagement. If anything, many came to Israel to put Jewish meat on their newly found Jewish bones.[5]

Barbara Promislow was among them. As a Winnipeg teenager her Jewish involvement was largely confined to the B'nai Brith Youth Organization – 'boys had jackets, girls had sweaters.' Once married, she and her husband first lived in Regina before moving to Edmonton, where they became active in the local Jewish community. Active as they were, *aliyah* was nowhere on their radar until after the Six Day War. Swept up with passion for Israel, Barbara recalls first toying with the idea of *aliyah*, but, unsure how her husband might respond, she was very reluctant to broach the subject. When she cautiously raised the idea of *aliyah*, to her surprise and delight, her husband was enthusiastic. Still, there was an air of unreality to their move. Even as she and her husband prepared to decamp for Israel, Israel remained for them 'more an idea than a place.' Their notion was that Israel would 'Jew them.' It did.[6]

The experience of being made to feel more fully Jewish, Israel-style, was not without difficulty. Canadian *olim* might come to Israel hoping to live more fulfilling Jewish lives, but many of them were white-collar professionals and business people for whom the move to Israel involved an economic step down. The drop in standard of living, coupled with the demands of learning a new language, social and cultural adjustments, and frustration with the tangle of Israeli bureaucracy made worse by homesickness for family and friends left behind, caused some to re-pack their bags. Others, including Barbara Promislow, her husband, and children, gradually built a home for themselves. And as much as many *olim* credit Israel for permitting them to fulfil themselves as Jews, Pakes contends, the impact on Israel from North American *olim* was as great as the impact of Israel on the *olim*. Pakes credits the small wave of post-1967 'Anglo Saxon' *olim* with being a shaping force in the development of Israel's successful finance, science, education, and hi-tech industrial sectors.[7]

The Promislows were exceptions. For the vast majority of Canadian Jews, passion for Israel did not translate into *aliyah*. But passion for Israel did pave the way for many to become more Jewishly engaged. This could mean different things, but there is no doubt that many young Canadian Jews expressed excitement at attachment to their Jewishness. On Canadian campuses, previously regarded by many in the Jewish community as something of a black hole when it came to Jewish content, many young people built on their newfound connection with Israel and concern for Jewish belonging. Even those with limited Jewish education, little or no exposure to traditional religious practice, and no familial connection to either Zionism or *Yiddishkeit* proved open to connecting Jewishly. For them the campus emerged as a place where they could 'do Jewish' outside of home and synagogue, and many did. Whether advocating for Israel on campus, supporting the Soviet Jewry campaign, or attaching Jewish meaning to anti–Vietnam War activism, one Montreal Jewish official remembers, in the aftermath of the Six Day War 'the best and brightest became enmeshed in Jewish life.'[8]

Few would deny that there was a new and palpable energy in the community both for individuals and for the organized Jewish community. According to historian Jonathan Sarna, the Six Day War acted like a tank of 'high test gasoline in infusing energy to North American Jewish life.'[9] Among other things, it jump-started increased Jewish communal participation, including a huge increase in Jewish day school attendance. It also set off a wave of ethno-tourism to Israel, fuelled Jewish student demand for university-level Jewish studies courses and programs, and deepened commitment to campaigns to ease the plight of Soviet Jewry and Jews in Arab lands. It also spurred the building of a full-time, professionally organized Canadian Jewish lobby effort on behalf of Israel and issues of Jewish concern and precipitated a papering over of long-festering rifts in the Jewish community so as to give the outward appearance of unity.[10]

In order to pay for all the bricks and mortar, personnel, institutional infrastructure, and program expansion, fundraising was cranked up. Stories of Jewish fundraising remain the stuff of legend. It has been said that, like Moses, professional Jewish fundraisers can produce water from a stone. But professional fundraisers also know the truth of the Yiddish saying that holds the longest distance is into your pocket. But not in the aftermath of the Six Day War. Nobody had ever experienced anything like the level of voluntary giving that took place during the war crisis and its immediate aftermath. At first giving was as disorganized as it was spontaneous, leaving community leaders scrambling to impose order on the flood of money that poured into Jewish organizational hands. In Toronto the 1967 UJA campaign target, reached just before the Middle East crisis erupted, was only met through the generosity of several of the community's wealthier members, who came through at the last minute to put the campaign over the top. They gave again and more to the Israel Emergency Campaign. So did others. People lined up to give, some donating to a Jewish charity for the first time ever. According to one report, the average per capita Canadian Jewish contribution was $110, well beyond anything Jewish fundraisers had ever previously dreamed possible. Given this new benchmark, in Toronto there would be no return to the $3 million UJA target. That was yesterday's number. There was a new bar. The 1968 Toronto UJA target was bumped up almost threefold to $8 million, to be divided between local and Israel-based needs. Of course, setting a target was not the same as meeting it. That would take work. But fundraisers felt assured the money was there. Many in Toronto were doing well. According to Donald Carr, what the 1967 war did was pry open their wallets as never before.[11] And knowing the hold Israel now had on the Jewish heart, Jewish fundraisers who had previously emphasized giving to meet local community needs refocused on the needs of Israel and the plight of oppressed Jews in Arab lands and behind the Iron Curtain. A formula apportioned UJA contributions between local and Canadian needs and those of Israel, but the threefold increase in the total dollars collected in Toronto, and similar increases elsewhere, meant not just more money for charity work in Israel. It also meant a greatly enlarged pool of funds to cover local Jewish community needs.[12]

It should be noted that the UJA did not have a monopoly on Jewish fundraising. Far from it. Other Israel-centric fundraising efforts also upped their campaign goals. The annual State of Israel Bond Drive doubled its target.[13] Canadian charities gathering donations on behalf of this or that Israeli university, this or that Israeli hospital, social service agency, or religious institution also raised their funding targets. So too did fundraising efforts on behalf of local Canadian Jewish religious, educational, social service, and healthcare institutions.

It hardly mattered whether the increased availability of funding sparked increased activity or vice versa. What mattered was new energy in the Jewish community. This was especially true of Jewish education. Through the mid-1960s, synagogue-based Sunday or late afternoon schools, supplemental to the public school system, dominated. But the years after 1967 saw a dramatic upswing in day school enrolment to a point where day schools gradually supplanted supplementary schools as the preferred Jewish school option. In the large communities of Montreal, Ottawa, Toronto, Winnipeg, Calgary, and Vancouver, the number of day school students not only challenged supplementary school students, a phenomenon which distinguishes Canadian communities from those in the United States. They also deflected a growing percentage of the school-age Jewish population away from the mainstream public system, especially at the elementary school level. What is more, if in the past the Jewish day school population was disproportionately children of the more Jewishly active and religiously committed, much of the post-1967 growth in day school population came from among those newly invested in Jewish identity – many secular and non-affiliated. In Montreal and Toronto, instead of a one-size-fits-all day school system, parents had a number of religiously or ideologically based school options from which to choose. In Toronto a smaller and secular Labour Zionist day school suddenly found itself bursting at the seams, while local Reform congregations, in a break with long-standing North American Reform tradition of support for public schooling, joined in organizing a Reform Jewish day school.

While Quebec made public funds available to Jewish day schools, in Ontario Jewish day schools received none. In Ontario, Jewish day schools charged tuition but, committed to the notion that no Jewish child should be denied a Jewish education on account of financial need, communal Jewish funding was made available to families that could not afford to pay all or, in some cases, any tuition. As enrolment in the day schools grew dramatically, so too did the amount of money the UJA had to earmark for tuition assistance, to a point where, in Ontario, education became the single largest Jewish communal expenditure. All the while, the curricular balance in Jewish schools was shifting. Jewish history, Hebrew language and religious instruction, and holiday celebration remained core, but Jewish schools increasingly infused Israel and Holocaust studies into their programs.[14]

The explosion in Jewish communal and organizational activity was bound up with Israel. The war may only have lasted one hundred and thirty-two hours, but from the early dawn of 5 June 1967, when Israeli aircraft first swooped down on Egyptian airfields, to the moment when the United Nations–brokered ceasefire came into effect at 6:30 p.m. on 10 June, the Canadian Jewish community was remade and Israel became front and centre. As one Toronto Jewish leader put it, 'After 1967 those for whom Israel had previously been an afterthought, Israel became their centrepiece.'[15]

Of course, the Israel and larger Middle East that emerged from six days of battle were not the Israel and Middle East of just a week earlier. Without rolling back history, it is impossible to imagine how different the Jewish world would be today if the Six Day War had not happened or if it had unfolded differently. But intriguing as it is to play with the 'ifs' of history, there can be no rolling back time. The war was as it was, and in its aftermath Israel found itself occupying 42,000 square miles of territory captured in battle, a land mass more than three times the size of Israel itself. The occupied territories included the west bank of the Jordan River, formerly controlled by Jordan. Israeli troops were also dug in on the eastern bank of the Suez Canal and held the vast Sinai Peninsula and Gaza Strip, reinstating Israel's unrestricted access to the Straits of Tiran and the Red Sea. Israel also sat atop the Golan Heights, where Israeli troops stationed along the new armistice line with Syria could see the night glow of Damascus to the east. And, emotionally significant to Israelis and Jews around the world, Israel captured east Jerusalem, previously under Jordanian control, and declared it sovereign Israeli territory, an integral part of Israel's national capital.

Israel occupied not only a vast swath of real estate, it also found itself in the unfamiliar role of unwelcome military occupier responsible for administering Arab populations in the various occupied territories, including approximately 1.2 million Palestinians. Much as Golda Meir, who became prime minister of Israel on the death of Levi Eshkol, might negate the notion that there was such a people as the Palestinians, in the shifting sands of the Middle East, the 1967 war that gave Israelis and Jews around the world a momentary sense of triumphal pride also provided fertile ground for the ethno-genesis of a Palestinian national struggle.

No sooner were the guns silent than Israel began to wrestle with the immediate issue of dealing with the occupied territories and their resident populations. But Israelis, united in war, were not nearly of one mind on what policy to follow in the occupied territories. This is understandable. Israelis regarded the 1967 war as a defensive war. It was originally hoped that Jordan and even Syria might stay out of it. Who would have believed that when the shooting stopped Israel would find itself occupying a vast territory and all its people? With little or no pre-war thought given to Israel assuming the duties of occupying power, in the war's aftermath there was no policy in place on how to administer the territories and their inhabitants. In his history of the Six Day War, Michael Oren notes that in the wake of the war Israelis – ordinary Israelis no less than their leaders – were at odds over the occupied territories. As Jews in the diaspora looked on, competing Israeli camps emerged. At one end of the political divide were those who favoured Israeli annexation of some of, if not all, the occupied territories. Some even made the irredentist argument that the territories had always been part of Israel – Israel did not occupy Arab lands, it liberated occupied Israel. Others held that the Six Day War offered proof positive that an Israel surrounded by hostile neighbours needed to hold the territories, especially the West Bank, as a strategic buffer zone in the event of another war. In opposition to occupation were some who cautioned that those who dreamed of a 'Greater Israel' would eventually wake up to a demographic nightmare. It was one thing for Israel to defend itself against aggression. It was another thing to think Israel could rule – let alone absorb – a huge and unwilling Arab population in the occupied territories. Opponents of annexation advocated that Israel extract itself from the territories as quickly as possible.

Except for declaring a united Jerusalem the indivisible capital of Israel, in the days and weeks after the end of the war it was unclear what Israel's policy was or even if it had settled on one. What was immediately clear was that the Israeli government rejected unilateral withdrawal and, except in the case of a unified Jerusalem, denied it intended any wholesale annexation of land taken in the 1967 conflict. Even for the majority of those who allowed that Israel would someday withdraw from the territory, the question was on what terms. The prevailing opinion of the day held that the occupied territories could ultimately prove to be Israel's most important bargaining chip in negotiations with its Arab neighbours. And since those neighbours wanted the land back, negotiations were inevitable. There was much speculation about when negotiations would begin and how the territorial cards would be played, but somewhere down the road a formula would ultimately be hammered out between Israel and its neighbours that exchanged land for peace or some variation thereof. It was only a matter of time. Defence minister Moshe Dayan, whom cynics said had a knack for supporting all points of view all the time, was widely quoted as saying he was only waiting for the phone to ring. As soon as Arab leaders indicated they wanted to trade 'land for peace,' serious negotiations would begin. In the meantime, Israel had no choice but to hunker down and wait.[16]

Sadly, the phone did not ring. Determined not to compound the humiliation of military defeat on the battlefield by suffering a humiliating diplomatic surrender at the negotiating table, Arab leaders assembled in Khartoum several months after the end of the Six Day War for a pan-Arab summit. Declaring a rejectionist united front, the summit made a public show of approving a 'three no's' resolution – no recognition of Israel, no negotiations with Israel, and no peace with Israel.

In a world of shadowy and secret diplomacy, historians now know that Arab unity rejecting Israel, as on other issues, often proved more apparent than real. There were wide differences in the Arab camp, as there were in the Israeli, about how to proceed. Even the Arab world's 'three no's' did not prevent some limited covert contact between Israel and its neighbours. On a public level, however, there was neither contact nor negotiation. Disappointed but not surprised, many Israelis and Jews in the diaspora hoped that the Khartoum agreement would prove to be temporary posturing. Israel's neighbours would inevitably come around and make their way, however reluctantly, to the negotiating table. This might take longer than was originally hoped, but in the meantime, even most supporters of 'land for peace' understood it was important for Israel to not give away its best bargaining chip, the territories. In this regard, it was important to avoid what happened in the aftermath of the Sinai war of 1956, when Israel bowed to American pressure to withdraw from the Sinai Peninsula in return for what ultimately proved to be hollow promises of a United Nations–monitored disengagement. Best for Israel to sit tight.[17]

This required American acquiescence to a continued Israeli occupation. To win American government favour, the Israeli government initiated a full-court-press American lobbying effort. In addition to making its case through diplomatic channels, the Israelis turned to newly energized American Jewish community leaders for help. The organized Jewish community did not need much convincing. After decades of trying to convince themselves and their neighbours that American Jews were no different than other Americans, American Jews, like their Canadian cousins, found themselves embracing Jewish particularism and a compelling attachment to Israel. And, even if the adrenalin rush of Israel's victory would gradually give way, American Jews and certainly the organized American Jewish community felt duty bound to speak out in support of Israel and its interests. That they were not necessarily privy to the nuances of Israeli policy thinking, let alone have input into shaping that policy, did not matter. American Jewish leaders did not see it as their job to decide Israeli policy. That was for the Israelis to do. The job of the organized American Jewish community was to keep the American power structure – the administration, the State Department, the media, and other influential centres – on side with Israel.[18]

For many Americans, support of Israel had much to commend itself. In the larger political arena, Israel's victory over its Arab neighbours was regarded as a major blow to Soviet strategic and military aspirations in the Middle East. And continuing Israeli strength would serve to counterbalance future Soviet adventurism in the region. On the other hand, although there was widespread sympathy for Israel in the United States following the Six Day War, there was some unease among American Jewish leaders that bedrock American administration priorities, such as the war in Vietnam, might mitigate against wholehearted support of Israel. To Israel's disadvantage, might an American administration skittish about growing domestic anti-Vietnam War sentiment be tempted 'to bracket the fates of Israel and Vietnam'?[19] Not only might the lightning-swift Israeli victory cast the administration in an embarrassingly unfavourable light given the quagmire in which the American military found itself in Southeast Asia, but also some worried that assertive Jewish lobbying on behalf of Israel could get the Johnson administration's back up, raising questions about 'selective' Jewish loyalty. As an official of the Anti-Defamation League pointed out, 'Many who are doves in the matter of Vietnam are hawks when it comes to the Middle East. It has even been claimed that American Jews as a group are guilty of this alleged double standard.'[20]

Some American Jewish lobbyists faced pointed questions about why

American Jews offered unreserved support to Israel but not to the American war effort in Vietnam. The experience of a pro-Israel delegation of Ohio Jews who visited Ohio Republican congressman Edgar Buz Lukens was not unusual. Reporting back to the American Israel Public Affairs Committee, yet to emerge as the dominant pro-Israel lobby in Washington, one delegate noted that Vietnam weighed far more heavily on the congressman's mind than did Israel. 'He voiced a complaint that his Jewish constituents, who were vocal in regards to Israel, have opposed his "hawk" attitude in regards to Vietnam. We [delegates] did point out that the Jewish community is divided on this issue as is true of the general community. His administrative assistant who was present confirmed this to Mr. Lukens, and he seemed satisfied by the explanation.' But the question of why Israel and not Vietnam hung in the air like a bad smell. Wasn't it ingenuous for American Jews, so steadfast in arguing for American support of Israel as an ally against Soviet expansionism in the Middle East, to be so vocal in opposition to American efforts to halt Soviet expansionism in Southeast Asia?[21]

The situation in Canada was notably different. Canada was not a belligerent in Vietnam and Canadian officials generally regarded the Vietnam and Middle East situations as discrete from one another. And compared to the United States, Canada was hardly a major player in either region. That is not to say that Canada was without interest in each of these problem regions. In the lead-up to the 1967 war, for example, Lester Pearson's Liberal government voiced disappointment at the United Nations' role, and especially the haste with which the United Nations bowed to Nasser's demand that international peacekeepers, including Canadians, be withdrawn from Sinai. But Pearson did not lose faith in the international body or its ability to provide 'leadership when a clash among the great powers leaves international affairs disorganized.' In the aftermath of the Six Day War, the prime minister and his foreign minister, Paul Martin, saw Canada playing the role of man-in-the-middle, an even-handed and honest broker, rather than a partisan of one side over the other.[22]

How did Canada's position on the Middle East play with an organized Canadian Jewish community that regarded Israel, like breathing, as sustaining Jewish life? Of course, Canadian Jews did not fool themselves into believing that Canada was anywhere near as critical a Middle East player as was United States. But to the organized Jewish community, Canada was important. More than just their home, Canada was touted as an important middle power, one that punched above its weight at the United Nations. Where Canada came down on Israel-related issues could well influence others. Thus, if Canada was going to be an honest broker, it was best if this honest broker tilted in favour of Israel.

Organized and effective lobbying is an art, and in 1967, when it came to Israel, it was an art the organized Canadian Jewish community had yet to master. This community had shown itself to have mastered fundraising, but it had nothing approximating the UJA when it came to a pro-Israel presence in the corridors of power, and obviously nothing to compare to the pro-Israel lobbying machine in the United States. Just the opposite. Since before the creation of the Jewish state in 1948, pro-Israel lobbying in Canada had largely been the preserve of Canadian Zionist organizations. But in the heady days leading up to the Six Day War, Canadian Zionists found themselves crowded out by others – the Canadian Jewish Congress, the B'nai Brith, the synagogues, folk organizations – all of which rallied behind Israel. It was as if Israel was suddenly too important to be left for Zionists to defend. What is more, as political scientist David Taras notes, in the immediate postwar period Canadian Zionists' lobbying track record was judged to be too 'intermittent, ad hoc and inconsistent' to adequately serve Israel's and the community's needs. Amateur hour was over. What was now demanded was exactly what the loose federation of Canadian Zionist organizations had failed to deliver – a well-funded, sophisticated, and full-time lobbying structure, more along the American lines, and one that would speak with the authority of all Canadian Jews.[23]

That the Zionists had proved inadequate to the task of marketing Israel was not news to Israeli officials either. Following the Six Day War, as Israel sought on-the-ground political and economic support, it concluded that larger mainstream Jewish organizations in the West, federation-style umbrella organizations, far outstripped local Zionists in professional organization, political access, and financial resources. One Israeli observer described the post-1967 Zionist movement in North America as 'a dead man walking,' another as a 'dead twig.'[24] Experience proved them right. Where Israel had previously seen local Zionist organizations as the most committed and best positioned to speak up for Israel, the 1967 war had shown them to be weak and ineffectual compared to the fundraising and organizational support for Israel offered by federations. No fools, the Israelis quickly leapfrogged Zionist leaders to form an alliance with the North American Jewish establishment. And federations welcomed the Israeli embrace. As sociologist

Nathan Glazer observed, after 1967 the Jewish establishment more and more shifted its focus away from issues of domestic concern to prioritize the needs of Israel and, by extension, the cause of beleaguered Jews around the world. Whether one judges this calculated eclipse of old-style Zionism as ushering in an era of bedrock pro-Israelism on the part of the larger American Jewish community or as the Jewish establishment playing catch-up ball with rank-and-file American Jews already committed to Israel is open to debate. However, there can be no debate that, as a result of the Six Day War, passion for Israel commanded the Jewish community. Support of Israel – moral, financial, and political – was a given. And leading in that effort, North American Zionists, or rather the collection of fractious Zionist organizations affiliated with different political parties in Israel, were superseded by a pro-Israelism that was as often as not distant from, if not disinterested in, the often backbiting, nitty-gritty day-to-day politics of Israel.[25]

The organized Canadian Jewish community was no less supportive of Israel than its American counterpart. The context of Canadian support was, however, different than that to the south. As in the United States, the fractious and often competing band of Zionist organizations in Canada was shuffled aside, a casualty of the Six Day War.[26] The Canadian Jewish Congress, an organization of organizations, including the Zionists, assumed oversight of pro-Israel activism. After some negotiation, in 1969 an uneasy federation of Canadian Zionists officially ceded responsibility for Israel lobbying to a tripartite partnership of the Canadian Jewish Congress, B'nai Brith, and themselves. But it was instantly dominated by Congress and supported by federation funding. Leaders set about organizing a single, effective, pro-active, professional, and full-time Canadian lobby team to advocate on behalf of Israel.[27]

There were high hopes that the new Israel advocacy group, the Canada-Israel Committee, would hit the ground running. But that did not happen. It took a little time for the fledgling group to set up business. The committee also found there were some in the Jewish leadership community who had voiced support for establishing the CIC, but were reluctant to step aside and relinquish pro-Israel advocacy to the new and untested lobby. What many in community leadership knew and were comfortable with was delegation politics and carefully choreographed meetings with federal politicians and officials. With the Six Day War just ended and the Canada-Israel Committee still on the drawing board, a Congress delegation was in Ottawa making the rounds on Israel's behalf. Mistaking access for accomplishment, delegates congratulated themselves on being granted audiences with several government leaders for what might be filed under the heading of 'a friendly exchange of views.' It all seemed carefully scripted, and in some ways it was. Just as the Zionists had done many times before them, a delegation spokesperson presented the Jewish community's take on Israel-related issues; in turn, one or another government official explained how Canada's 'even handed' approach to the Middle East was in Canada's and Israel's best interests. Lots of smiles, handshakes, and coffee, and the delegation was ushered out the door.

In separate meetings, the delegation also met with Conservative leader of the opposition John Diefenbaker and New Democratic leader T.C. Douglas. Both were welcoming, but these meetings also followed established form. Since they were not in power and were not in a position to deliver, opposition party leaders felt freer to voice support of Israel. And although the Pearson government was in a minority situation, forced to rely on support from the New Democratic Party, nobody seriously expected the New Democrats to bring the government down over its Middle East policy. What Jewish community leaders could hope was that sympathetic opposition leaders might agree to raise issues regarding Canada's Middle East policy during question period or in committees.[28]

While conceding that delegation politics had its place, the Canada-Israel Committee promised lobbying of a different order. Most important, it promised to be a constant pro-Israel voice in Ottawa. It took two years before the new Canada-Israel Committee was fully up and running, and it had its work cut out for it.[29] Canada and Canadians were certainly not as a whole hostile to Israel, but neither were they uncritical of Israeli policies. For government, acknowledging Israel's right to exist within secure borders was one thing. Endorsement of Israel's continued occupation of captured territories was another thing again, even as a bargaining chip in any future negotiations. And the idea of Israeli settlements in, or annexation of, any occupied territories? Forget it. Pearson's Liberals had staked out a role for Canada as middleman in the Middle East and was not about to be moved off that course. Canada supported United Nations Resolution 242, unanimously adopted by the UN Security Council on 22 November 1967, which called for the immediate and total withdrawal of Israeli armed forces from all territories occupied in the war, including east Jerusalem, in exchange for an end to the Arab-Israeli conflict – or as some saw it, land now for peace later. That position was not about to change.

Of course pro-Israel lobbying was more than a defence of the on-going occupation. There were many other Israel-related issues for the fledgling CIC to work on. Knowing that it was not about to dramati-cally shift government policy on the Middle East, it hoped to soften criticism and build Canada-Israel bridges, create opportunities for Ca-nadian politicians and opinion makers to have hands-on experience of Israel, encourage increased Canada-Israel economic and cultural ties, and sway media in Israel's favour.[30] This was not always easy or with-out opposition. Israel's 1967 victory may have been celebrated by Cana-dian Jews as a modern miracle and admired by many other Canadians, but support for Israel was not universal. Never mind how Israel came to occupy Arab lands, the fact of Israeli occupation quickly emerged as a bone of contention between Israel's Canadian supporters and those inside and outside government circles who regarded the occupation as both an illegal and repressive impediment to peace. Some Israel critics were less than diplomatic in tone. To many in a Canadian Jewish com-munity so recently weighted down by fear for Israel's survival, it was a shock to hear the Israel victory denounced as an expansionist land grab by a racist state. And that was coming not just from a then still tiny Arab community in Canada. It was spoken by some of those who had been long-time partners with the Jewish community in the struggle against antisemitism and for human rights in Canada, including some in the labour movement, in political circles, in the media, and, impor-tantly, in mainstream churches.

The most obvious public rupture between the organized Jewish community and a former ally in the Canadian human rights struggle was with the United Church, the largest Protestant denomination in Canada. The focal point of that dust-up centred on the Reverend A.C. Forrest, influential editor of the bi-monthly *United Church Observer*, the church's official organ.[31] According to Toronto B'nai Brith leader Lou Ronson, Forrest was a tireless crusader. When he took over the *United Church Observer*, it was a flagging enterprise. He turned it into a 'self-sustaining if not profitable' voice of the United Church, with a Canada-wide circulation of about three hundred thousand. Much to the shock of the Jewish community, Forrest also turned the paper into a voice in opposition to Israel.[32]

With the organized Jewish community lined up in support of Israel, relations with the United Church quickly deteriorated. Of course, there had always been differences between the United Church and the Jew-ish community – theological differences. But since the Second World

War these differences had not precluded close cooperation on matters of mutual interest, including the struggle for human rights. Differences over Israel were of a different order, however, and they boiled over in the critical weeks leading up to the Six Day War. As Canadian Jews were beside themselves with fear of a second Holocaust, the United Church and other mainstream North American churches neither understood the intensity of Jewish anguish nor shared in it. As Israel's very existence seemed to be in peril, churches, for whatever combination of theological, political, or historical reasons, were conspicuous in their silence. What is more, following Israel's victory, it appeared to many in the Jewish community that these same churches were intent on punishing Israel for the audacity to survive.

Why? Did Israel's victory somehow challenge Christian theology? Perhaps. It has been argued that for some Christians, liberal and conservative alike, Jewish continuity and the rebirth of a Jewish state in Israel challenged the triumphal narrative of a new and Christian covenant with God, a covenant that supplanted Jews with Christians in God's eyes. And much though Jews might be pitied for the suffering they had endured for their continued rejection of Christ, their redemptive salvation was to be found in accepting Christ not in national rebirth. Liberal Christian denominations which might have afforded compassionate support for post–Second World War national liberation struggles in former areas of Western colonization generally regarded Zionism as 'a divisive factor and opposed the Jewish state.' If that Jewish state had been stillborn or had succumbed in battle, sad as any loss of life would have been, that might be interpreted as a sign of divine displeasure with stiff-necked Jews for continuing to reject the community of Christ. But how could one explain the successful founding of a Jewish state and a now victorious Jewish state to boot? Does that not run against the grain of God's will? Certainly, offering Christian charity to the misguided and downtrodden Jewish lamb was a Christian duty. But seeing that lamb suddenly turn into a lion was something else again. And now there was a new suffering lamb – the Palestinians.[33]

Almost before the thunder of battle in the Middle East had subsided, Israel became a bone of contention between Canadian Jews, the United Church, and, to a lesser extent, other mainstream Canadian churches. Forrest, an outspoken proponent of the Arab cause, was quick off the mark, publishing articles and editorials in the *Observer* hostile to Israel and its policies. He launched a particularly biting salvo in early August 1967. In a short news item, the *Observer* reported on a speech by promi-

nent Toronto Conservative rabbi Stuart Rosenberg, in which he reportedly told a packed auditorium of his distress at the silence of Christian
leaders in the weeks leading up to the Six Day War. As the Arab world
called for the 'elimination of the Jews,' the rabbi lamented, this generation of Christian leaders proved themselves as silent in the face of evil
as an earlier generation of leaders had been as Jews faced the Holocaust. Stung by Rosenberg's criticism, the *Observer* article noted, an Interfaith Committee of Christian Concern had been struck on the Middle
East, 'which expressed simultaneous support of Israel's right to exist
and concern for Arab refugees.'[34]

In an accompanying editorial Forrest dismissed both the Interfaith
Committee and its efforts at even-handedness as wrong-minded. Forrest protested there could be no Christian even-handedness in the face
of obvious injustice, and Israel was transparently unjust in its dealings
with its neighbours and with Arab refugees in particular. Rather than
seek balance, Forrest demanded the committee call Israel to account for
its record of persecution. As for Rosenberg's reference to the historical
record of the Christian world during the Second World War, Forrest
cried foul. In his editorial 'Christians Must Be Free to Criticize Jews,'
Forrest allowed that Rosenberg might have been forgiven his outburst
if it had come 'during the June week of anguish' when Jews were pulling out all the stops on Israel's behalf. Coming as it did well after Israel's victory, the newspaper found the 'undertone' of his attack 'deeply
disturbing.' And most disturbing to the *Observer* was Rosenberg's odious comparison of those Christian leaders who did not rally behind
Israel during the lead-up to the recent war with Christian leaders who
remained silent in the face of the Holocaust. According to Forrest, tar-
ring Christian leaders with the Holocaust brush was carefully calculated to still all criticism of Israel within the Christian community by
threatening to label honest comment on Israel as akin to Nazi attacks on
Jews. According to the *Observer*, 'even more unhealthy' was the sight
of Christian leaders, fearful of being labelled antisemites, bending over
backwards 'to remind the Rabbi that they were so solidly on the side
of Israel.' Christian kowtowing to Zionist interests was not only cow-
ardly, it obscured the truth. And what was the truth as far as Forrest
was concerned? It was that 'informed and objective Christians cannot
be 100% for Israel in the Middle East struggle.' While deploring Arab
threats to destroy Israel, Forrest noted that the 'provocations and threats
were not all from one side.' And while he did not expect Canadian Jews
to be 'objective when faced with Israel's record with regard to Arab

refugees,' Forrest argued that it was the right and duty of Christians to render objective judgments without being charged with equivocation or being compared with the 'ecclesiastical hand washers of wartime Germany.'[35]

Forrest's editorial touched a raw Jewish nerve. To some in a Jewish community home to so many Holocaust survivors and their children, a community still wary of home-grown Nazis and convinced that, but for Israel's against-the-odds triumph, an indifferent world would have allowed a second Holocaust, Forrest was seen as denigrating Holocaust memory in order to legitimize Christian indifference to, if not unease with, Jewish survival. Forrest's editorial, widely reported in the Jewish press, served to reinforce the notion that, when it came to Jews, mainstream churches had changed little from the era of the Second World War. They remained ready to eulogize Jews, not support them.

As lines hardened, some individual United Church members grew uneasy at Forrest's anti-Israel position. One wrote to reassure the Jewish community that Forrest did not speak for everyone in her faith community and certainly not for her.

> If the Jews are 'paranoiac,' the Christians are 'schizophrenics' – two faced people who first extend a hand in brotherhood and then stand silently by to see if Israel will die. I have no doubt that those who are your worst critics today would have written beautiful eulogies after the death of Israel, had Israel died. Some who criticize your survival would have been the first to praise your suicide, but I say – Live Israel – live forever more – and G-d bless you! And, oh, my Jewish friends, I am not alone; all across Canada there are many in the United Church of Canada who share my feelings.[36]

How many others in the United Church shared this view is impossible to know. There was no in-house rebuke of Forrest, even as tensions between the church and the organized Jewish community spilled into the public square. Rehashing the dispute for a largely American audience, Toronto Jewish commentator Arnold Ages fired up the rhetoric. He applauded Rabbi Rosenberg for drawing a parallel between church silence in the face of Arab threats to destroy Israel and Christian silence in the face of the Nazi horrors.

> Before the end of the Six Day War in June 1967, the rabbi of the largest Conservative congregation in North America accused the Christian world

of criminal silence in the face of blood-curdling Arab threats to exterminate the population of Israel. Scarcely had the dust settled on the battle-
fields of Sinai, Syria and Jordan when a veritable chorus of Jewish voices,
both lay and rabbinical, joined with Rabbi Stuart Rosenberg in orchestrat-
ing the following theme. By refusing to condemn the intransigent Arab
rhetoric and the military encirclement of Israel which accompanied it in
May 1967, Christian leaders had acquiesced once again in consigning the
Jews to the slaughterhouse. Moreover, when the battle itself was joined,
Christian churches refused to take sides in what they claimed was a political controversy. The inertia of Christians before and during the June War
was compared to the malevolent immobility and paralysis which seized
Christendom during the Nazi holocaust. Thus, the Church had repeated
an ancient pattern in dealing with Jews – sacrificing them upon the altar
of expediency.[37]

. University of Toronto philosopher Emil Fackenheim also supported
Rosenberg. Fackenheim had previously argued that as a result of the
Holocaust a 614th commandment was added to the list of 613 com-
mandments that tradition holds God instructed the Jewish people to
observe. This 614th commandment required Jews to survive and survive as Jews. The Nazis wanted to eradicate the Jews. By surviving,
Jews deprive Hitler of a posthumous victory.

> The continued existence of the Jewish people defeats the Nazis' monstrous
> purpose. This is the ultimate question, for it transcends all politics. Moreo-
> ver, it stands between Jews and Christians even now, for when Jews ask
> why [in the spring of 1967] there was no moral Christian outcry against a
> second Auschwitz they are still widely misunderstood, as demanding of
> Christians that they side politically with Israel against the Arab states.[38]

Forrest was not about to be stilled by negative Jewish response to his
attacks on Israel. Just the opposite. He seemed to feed off the criticism,
even as relations between the United Church and the Jewish community deteriorated. In the first two years following the 1967 war, hardly an
issue of the *Observer* passed without an article or editorial attacking Zionism and Israel's supporters. Forrest, who enjoyed the limelight, also
accepted invitations to write for other publications or speak at public
gatherings and to the media, using these opportunities to hammer Israel as a bully state, playing victim while crushing the rights of the true
victims.

For speaking this 'truth' Forrest claimed he was also a victim, a victim of a Jewish community vendetta against him, his newspaper, and the United Church. In March 1970 he was the main guest at a taping of a syndicated television program, 'Under Attack,' at McMaster University in Hamilton. With the audience reportedly packed with supporters from the Arab community and their sympathizers, Forrest defended the *Observer's* coverage of the Middle East as a necessary corrective to the glaring imbalance in the coverage by the mainstream and other religious press, frightened of speaking out for fear of being attacked as antisemites. Applauded by the audience for his bravery in standing up to Jewish pressure and accusations that he was running with antisemites, Forrest, according to a B'nai Brith member who attended the taping, deliberately stirred up the crowd by proclaiming that Jewish 'charges of anti-Semitism are a new form of McCarthyism used in an attempt to discredit and destroy people like me who are anti-Zionist.'[39]

No doubt many in the Jewish community believed that Forrest not only gave comfort to antisemites, but was an antisemite. However, Jewish leaders dared not say so, at least not in public. If anything, most public Jewish comment on Forrest was purposefully restrained. In one case he was described as 'a formidable opponent because of his key editorial position.' Privately, it was a different matter. Many quietly regarded Forrest as an antisemite, who enjoyed portraying himself as the victim of a Jewish smear campaign. What is more, there was concern that Forrest's anti-Israel message was being well received within some United Church and Protestant community circles precisely because it complemented already deeply held antisemitic feelings.[40] Forrest, of course, repeatedly sloughed off any suggestion that he was an antisemite. This sort of accusation, he claimed, was nothing more than a crude attempt by Jewish community leaders to muzzle him and others, and perhaps frighten United Church leaders into silencing him. He was not an antisemite, he insisted, and he would not be deterred from speaking the truth as he saw it. He assured his readers that no amount of Jewish mud-slinging was going to silence him.

The more Forrest protested he was not an antisemite, the more many in the Jewish community were convinced that he was just that. Some worried that Forrest, a well-spoken minister and editor, unlike neo-Nazi street thugs who attempted to rehabilitate Hitler's legacy, was giving anti-Zionism and antisemitism a respectable face. But what could be done to deal with him? Some demanded that Forrest and his *Observer* assaults on Israel and the Jewish community be countered at every turn, his anti-Jewish bias exposed as such. The Israeli consul general in Toronto, for example, responding to an editorial in the Anglican Church house organ, *The Canadian Churchman*, which defended Forrest's right to speak out, free from accusations of anti-Jewish bias, asked how the newspaper could in one breath condemn 'any form of anti-Semitism,' then 'come out in defence of Rev. Forrest's new style of anti-Semitism – anti-Zionism.'

> And you say in your editorial that to be an anti-Zionist is the same as to be an anti-Communist, which does not make one anti-Russian. How can these [anti-Communism and anti-Zionism] be compared? Have you ever seen in any anti-Communist statement a call to kill the Russians? On the other hand anti-Zionism is accompanied by a call to kill the Jews.
>
> To say 'I am not anti-Semitic' is not enough to prove not being so 'in any form, at any time in history,' to use your words. Those who hold in their hands, at this time in history, the flag of anti-Zionism, and their supporters are saturated with the same ideology which caused the genocide of 6,000,000 Jews.[41]

The consul fell just short of publicly calling Forrest an antisemite. Others in the Jewish community, whatever their personal views, trod more gently. In his autobiography Rabbi Plaut discussed his role in the long-smouldering dispute with the United Church. Carefully skating around whether he personally believed Forrest's anti-Israel passion was motivated by deep-seated antisemitism or not, Plaut diplomatically suggested that in the Jewish community, 'the suspicion grew that there was more to his [Forrest's] criticism than the anti-Zionism which he began to profess.' The key question, Plaut claimed, was not whether Forrest was an antisemite but what the Jewish community should do, if anything, about his anti-Israel crusade? According to Plaut, Forrest thrived on confrontation. Any and all negative Jewish reaction played into his hands. It allowed Forrest to assume the role of brave David standing up to the Goliath Jewish community.[42] Thus, according to Plaut, going after Forrest both flattered his sense of self-importance and helped turn him into a media celebrity. Far better, Plaut recommended, to let Forrest rage away until his 'fulminations' became tedious if not embarrassing to the United Church leadership and all people of goodwill. Addressing Friday evening congregants at Holy Blossom Temple in the early spring of 1970, Plaut suggested a gradual distancing from Forrest was already happening. According to the rabbi, in Forrest's 'steadily worsening attacks on Israel and the Jewish community in general, his sense of martyrdom and his self-imagined role as a white knight in flowing turban, riding like a new Lawrence of Arabia across the desert sands – he is becoming tiresome to the Christian community. I believe he has worn out his welcome and his credibility.' Best to deny Forrest the limelight while building goodwill within the larger Christian community.[43]

Few in the Jewish community were prepared to heed Plaut's advice. Most did not regard Forrest a spent force nor did they see any readiness on the part of United Church officials to rein in Forrest's anti-Israel and anti-Jewish rhetoric. Instead, Forrest remained a burr under the saddle of relations between the Jewish community and the United Church. Few felt those relations could improve so long as Forrest's attacks on Israel and Israel's Canadian supporters continued. But if they thought things could not get much worse, they were wrong. In 1972 heated tensions boiled over as the B'nai Brith and Forrest brought suit against one another. Forrest was first off the legal block. The house organ of the Toronto Lodge of B'nai Brith, the *Digest*, published a message from the Lodge president, Alfred Green, in which he praised the courage of Donald Keating, an ordained United Church minister, for speaking out against Forrest and United Church policy on Israel. But in praising Keating, Green also took direct aim at Forrest:

> From biblical times, there has always appeared a Pharaoh, or, in plain language, an anti-semite, who attempts, for ulterior motives and by nefarious means, to besmirch and throttle the Jews. Such a character is Dr. A.C. Forrest, the Editor of the 'United Church Observer,' a paper which reaches the home of every United Church member in Canada, approx. 700,000 homes. Dr. Forrest is constantly taking advantage of his position as Editor to attack Jews and Israel.[44]

In his book about the dispute between the Jewish community and the United Church, *Family Quarrel*, Toronto rabbi Reuben Slonim notes that the *Digest*'s message greatly exaggerated the *Observer*'s circulation figures, but, more importantly, it put 'into bold print what Congress and B'nai B'rith leaders were too cautious to say.' The Jewish community could get away with calling Forrest an anti-Zionist. That was a title Forrest wore with pride. It could even claim his anti-Zionism gave comfort to antisemites. And Slonim allowed that Forrest understood anti-Zionism was regarded by many Jews as in the 'same family of ideas' as antisemitism. But to come out and publicly label him an antisemite plain and simple crossed the line. Not prepared to overlook the accusation, Forrest served notice of libel action against the Lodge president, the *Digest*, and, by extension, B'nai Brith.[45]

A counter lawsuit followed as night follows day. At 'the worst point in the dispute,' with Forrest's lawsuit still fresh, the *United Church Observer* reprinted an article entitled 'How the Zionists Manipulate Your News' by John Nicholls Booth, a former Canadian, graduate of McMaster University, and Unitarian-Universalist minister in Gainesville, Florida. The article previously appeared in the *American Mercury*, widely read by the American Christian right. The publication regularly attacked Zionism along with the graduated income tax, the NAACP, the United Nations, NATO, and the American Civil Liberties Union.[46] The fact that the *Observer* would reprint any *American Mercury* article, and especially one by Booth, set off alarm bells among Jewish authorities. Booth was well known. Previous articles of his had appeared in both the *American Mercury* and *The Cross and the Flag*, edited by veteran American antisemitic crusader Gerald K. Smith and described by one Canadian Jewish official as 'the most vicious antisemitic publication in existence.'[47]

As far as Jewish leaders were concerned, the Booth article reprinted in the *Observer* was unashamedly antisemitic. It accused Israel and American Jewish organizations, especially the Anti-Defamation League of the B'nai Brith, of conspiratorially attempting to undermine and control the American administration, American universities, and the media. This was not difficult for Jews because, according to Booth, Jews already controlled the American press and media. And how did Jews use their control? To advance Israel's interests at American expense. In so doing, Booth charged, the B'nai Brith and other American Jewish Zionist organizations were not just willing tools of Israel but also treasonously disloyal to their home country.

> It can be seen what enormous resources, grim determination and sometimes unethical means Zionists have been willing to further the interest of Israel at the expense of the rights, security and welfare of other people and nations. Without counter-balancing sources of information, millions of us have unconsciously absorbed an incomplete and biased understanding of the Middle Eastern problem. No amount of plaques, fellowship dinners and ecumenical dialogue should be allowed to purchase our support for injustices, once we have learned the truth.

Booth contended that only the brave dared speak out against the Zionist conspiracy. He accused the B'nai Brith and other Zionists of using 'economic reprisals' and 'character assassination' to intimidate opinion makers and the media into towing a pro-Israel line and underreporting the truth. According to Booth, the most effective weapon Jews employed to crush the freedom of speech of those who dared speak out in opposition to Israel, its policies, or actions was to label them antisemites. Nor were non-Jews the only victims of the antisemitic smears. Booth accused Zionists of whipping up fear of antisemitism in order to manipulate and control Jews as well. Misreading Jean-Paul Sartre, whom he erroneously describes as a 'French Jewish philosopher,' Booth argued that Sartre shared his view that antisemitism was encouraged by Zionists as a way of 'holding Jews together. Where there is no actual anti-Semitism,' Booth argued, 'it must be created.' And given the Jewish community's enormous power, who dared go toe to toe with Jews over Israel? Only the Christian press. It alone was beyond Zionist control. Standing up to Zionism was its sacred trust.[48]

The B'nai Brith sued. It charged Forrest, the *Observer*, and the United Church with libeling the B'nai Brith. With the legal fur still flying, cooler heads in both the United Church and Jewish camps began putting out discreet feelers to one another about ending the public mud-slinging that now pitted lawyer against lawyer. Accelerating this quiet outreach, in the early autumn of 1972 there was a major change in the leadership of the United Church's General Council. This new leadership quietly committed to defusing tensions. If some on the Jewish side might at first have been less interested in patching up relations with the United Church than in forcing church leaders to publicly acknowledge how deeply hurtful and destructive was Forrest's anti-Israel campaign, this view did not prevail. Most mainstream Jewish leaders saw value in reopening doors to discussion and cooperation with the leaders of Canada's largest Protestant denomination. A series of formal and informal inter-faith discussions began at various levels. Rebuilding trust was slow but marked.[49] As a positive gesture, and one designed to remove lawyers from the picture, in May 1973 B'nai Brith and the United Church agreed to drop their respective libel suits and sign a 'peace pact.'[50] An unrepentant Forrest railed against the agreement as a sellout to the Jewish establishment. But the agreement, if it did not immediately defang Forrest or usher in an era of peace between the Jewish community and the United Church, it did bring what historian Haim Genizi has called 'a stage of armistice.'[51] As Rev. N. Bruce McLeod, moderator of the United Church, who signed the agreement, explained: 'We will not agree always on problems of the Middle East, but agree to respect each others' differences.'[52]

What was the Forrest episode about? Was it just about one man's negative obsession with Israel, or did it represent a fundamental re-working of Canadian Jewish priorities? In many ways the dispute with Forrest and, by extension, the United Church was emblematic of a larg-er rupture – that between the Jewish community and others with whom the Jewish community had previously made common cause in the fight for human rights and against racism and antisemitism.[53]

This was also true in the United States, where a decades-old coali-tion between American Black leaders and the Jewish community had been a cornerstone in the American movement for civil rights and racial integration. By the late 1960s that relationship was increasingly under strain as younger and more militant Black voices preached a message of Black self-reliance and adopted the rhetoric of anti-imperialism and racial exclusivity. Many rejected integration and called for an end to cooperation with whites in favour of a Black self-realization in alliance with anti-colonial forces everywhere. And Jews were white. In major inner-city neighbourhoods, tensions flared between Blacks and Jews, no longer partners in the civil rights struggle. If local issues and turf dif-ferences exacerbated relations, Israel was easily invoked by both sides – by Jews as proof of Jewish readiness to fight back against oppression and by Blacks as a racist and imperialist oppressor. At a street level, the long-standing Black-Jewish alliance crumbled.

In New York, for example, tensions were exacerbated when a strug-gle erupted over community control of schools in the city's once-Jewish Ocean Hill–Brownsville neighbourhood, which by 1968 was largely Black and Hispanic. The struggle culminated in a teachers' strike in 1968 which pitted Black parent groups, demanding control over what was taught in local schools and by whom, against the United Federation of Teachers, with its pronounced Jewish leadership and membership. With more than one million children affected by teachers' walkouts, rhetoric soon turned shrill. While community spokespersons accused Jewish teachers of racism in deliberately keeping Blacks and Hispan-ics down, the teachers' union accused community groups of anti-white racism and antisemitism.[54]

Canada suffered nothing comparable to the racial violence that scarred American cities through the 1960s. This does not mean that racism and antisemitism were unknown. But, as in the flare-up of neo-Nazi activity in the early 1960s, Canadian Jews lay most of the blame for this racism and antisemitism at the doorstep of the political and religious right. After 1967 this changed. In the wake of the Six Day War, Jews, even those with long attachments to the liberal, left side of the political spectrum, sensed a growing chill. As with the United Church, with whom Jews and the organized Jewish community previously made common cause in the struggle for reform in the workplace, for social justice, human rights, and a more progressive social agenda, Jews more and more found antipathy for Israel as the enemy of social justice and human rights.[55]

For many Jewish youth the point of collision with the new anti-Israelism was found on campus. Canadian universities of the 1960s and 1970s were caught up by the spirit of youthful rebellion that swept across the Western world. But that activism never formed a solid block. Different issues dominated on different Canadian campuses at different times. Of course, many on campus, perhaps the majority, no matter their personal views, remained disengaged from active campus political engagement or, at most, were infrequent participants. Others did get involved, most, in the spirit of the times, on the 'anti-establishment' side of the political spectrum.

Those young Jews drawn into campus political activism found themselves entering an ideologically fractious world. But whichever of the many variants of campus-based politics might draw them in, after 1967 many carried along an attachment to Israel. Unlike an earlier generation of Jewish radicals, however, many of whom had experience of working-class poverty, much of the new generation grew up in a world of post-war prosperity. So, what provoked them to challenge the establishment? Some may have found the ideological catch basin that was campus politics something of a family tradition. Among Jewish students on campus were those previously involved with left-leaning Zionist youth movements – Habonim, Hechalutz Hatzair, Hashomer Hatzair. There were also young Jews who had grown up in tightly knit radical and anti-Zionist Jewish socialist families, communist and anti-communist. Many of these red-diaper babies felt at home with an easy mix of socialism and secular *Yiddishkeit*. For them heritage was politics. One red-diaper baby reported that the children of 1930s Jewish radicals, such as himself, 'were applying their parents' own original values. In a true historical sense they were thanking the old leftists who kept alive the sparks of the thirties in the cold, cold fifties.'[56]

There were also those from non-political Jewish homes who gravitated towards the campus left, or New Left as it was commonly called, because it seemed imbued with what many regarded as traditional Jewish values such as social justice and concern for the underprivileged.[57] Some may even have worried that these values had been forgotten or, worse, discarded by a Jewish community increasingly given over to a middle-class lifestyle. Often out of comfortable suburban homes, some may even have seen themselves battling to reassert these Jewish values into a Jewish community they saw as suffering a sclerosis brought on by rapacious materialism and spiritual hollowness. Through their political engagement they hoped to lift themselves and the Jewish community out of asphyxiating small-mindedness and engage with 'things that mattered.' As posited by McMaster University sociologist Cyril Levitt, theirs was 'a revolt of privilege against privilege.'[58] Even if they went home to eat, sleep, and pick up clean laundry, on campus they regarded themselves as part of a pulsing world of ideas, ideas that promised action. Of course, not all who flirted with the left were action-committed. There were those young Jews drawn to the left for other reasons – out of the fashion of the moment, because they were compelled by the energy of the 'scene,' or because, rumour had it, this was where it was easy to get laid.

What is more, not all who connected to campus left politics devoted equal time or energy to the project. Some were maximalists who looked to campus politics for community, for surrogate family. Others, minimalists, may have been sympathetic but restricted their involvement to dropping in now and again or, like voyeurs, sneaking an occasional peak from the margins.[59] And what about the left's agenda? The campus left, more a fractious collection of sub-groups than a unified whole, beat the drum on a broad range of issues, foreign, domestic, and university-specific: democratic reform of the university, ensuring university accessibility and responsiveness to the surrounding community, halting the 'colonization' of Canadian universities by American faculty, exploring a 'liberation' lifestyle and pressing questions of Canadian economic and social policy, the place of Quebec in Canadian society, the struggles of the developing world, the Black struggle in the United States, and, of course, Canadian complicity in the war in Vietnam.

What about Israel? Before 1967 Israel and Israel-related issues had little or no profile on Canadian campuses except among small pockets of Jewish students, especially those in Zionist youth groups who felt attached to Israel. For the majority of students, Jewish and non-Jewish, there was silence.[60] This changed, and dramatically, in 1967. Many Jewish students surprised themselves by becoming profoundly engaged with Israel in its moment of crisis. Many volunteered to go there. Even if only a handful actually made it to Israel before war broke out, the act of volunteering invested them in Israel. And whether through volunteering in Israel after the war, or as part of the many new Israel study opportunities, or as a result of expanding 'ethno-tourism' to Israel, more and more young Canadian Jews had some kind of Israel experience. With Israel important to their Jewish selves, many were caught off guard by the speed with which much of the New Left rushed to brand Israel a racist state and imperialist oppressor.

> The Jews within the ranks of the New Left were thrown into a tragic and almost dead-end conflict after the Six Day War between Israel and the Arabs in 1967. Their sympathy for the State of Israel, imbibed with their mother's milk, became a problem at the very moment when Israel, no longer weak and pitiable, began to show signs – to a remarkable extent – of a power policy emphatically refuted by the New Left. Israel had acted highly nationalistically and militaristically – in the vocabulary of the New Left, even imperialistically – inasmuch as it had taken pieces of territory from other states and was rejecting resolutions by the United Nations that it should evacuate them. As the New Left came into ever stronger opposition against American foreign policy, it began to look at Israel as a tool of American imperialism and took the side of the Third World, which included millions of anti-Israel Arabs.[61]

Suddenly conflicted within themselves, many Jews within the ranks of the New Left were forced to choose between the New Left and Israel. Many chose Israel.[62] This is not to deny there were young Jewish men and women on campus who joined the chorus of Israel-bashing. There were, and they might even claim that their anti-Zionism was a positive expression of Jewish values and that Israel's subjugation of conquered Arab populations constituted a betrayal of Jewish humanitarian teachings and a sell-out of the Jewish birthright of social justice.[63] Condemned by some in the Jewish community as self-hating Jews, these Jewish anti-Zionists, it was suggested, might siphon off other alienated Jewish students or create a climate of intolerance on campus for pro-Israel students. Angered at the increasingly anti-Israel stance of the New Left, some in the Jewish community were ready to castigate any Jews who supported positions identified with the New Left. A Second

World War veteran driving past a 1969 anti-Vietnam War protest in Toronto's City Hall Square, a stone's throw from the American consulate, was infuriated to see anti-war activist Reform rabbi Abraham Feinberg addressing the crowd. In a letter to the Canadian Jewish Congress he described the rabbi, who often sported a trademark black beret, as 'wearing a black panther beret,' as if to wilfully signal sympathy for a group which had proved itself 'anti-Jewish and pro-Arab, ... as any New York Jew can testify at the daily jew-baiting done by them, the negro panthers.' Worse still was what he took to be a large contingent of young Jews in the crowd.

> I wonder if I am going mad seeing all this, young Jews, many, acting so. Surely a re-education needs to be done, soon, to stop them supporting world Jewries enemies of today. True years ago the left politics was more for Jewry whilst right-wing wasn't so, but today it's changed. The right-wing Govts. everywhere support us, Israel. President Nixon has proven himself to be a truer friend of Israel than his predecessors, as Golda Meir said, in arms aid, etc. If Jewry acts so we will lose the friendship of the right-wing Govts then we'll be in a pickle, or Israel will, and possibly us also.[64]

In truth, however, it is impossible to know how many, or to what degree, Canadian Jewish youth parked their sympathies with the New Left, especially as it became more and more anti-Israel and, as some in the Jewish community might argue, more antisemitic. Anecdotal evidence suggests proportionately fewer Jews in Canada were in the New Left after 1967 than in the United States. Few as they might have been, however, they were a concern, or enough of a concern that in October 1969 the Canadian Jewish Congress in Toronto entertained a proposal to fund a research study of 'anti-Israel sentiment among the *Jewish* student left.' The proposal claimed: 'It is not a secret that the Student Left views Israel as an extension of Western Imperialism and as a militant expansionist power in the Middle East.' Bad enough, but according to the proposal's writers, it was still more shocking to find that 'it is often Jewish students who are the most vociferous in denouncing Israel.' Rather than dismiss these few Jewish young people as a tiny if vocal minority, the proposal cautioned that even a few Jewish firebrands denouncing Israel could grant licence to the larger non-Jewish community to do likewise and entice other non-committed Jewish youth to embrace anti-Zionism.

Farfetched though these threats might be, according to the proposal writers, Jews who gravitated to the anti-Israel left were 'highly intelligent and articulate individuals who attract the attention of the media and are able to put across their views in a dynamic and compelling manner.' What is more, since they are bright and 'excel in their university studies,' these Jewish students active 'in the Student Left may someday attain positions of prominence in Canadian universities and in the newspapers and broadcasting media of Canada.' Accordingly, whether they afford anti-Zionism a cloak of respectability, whether they prove to be pied pipers leading astray other Jewish students seeking political excitement, as leaders of tomorrow, they make anti-Zionism publicly fashionable. The proposal writers argued that the Jewish community would be well advised not to dismiss or ignore these anti-Israel Jewish student voices.[65] The proposal was seriously assessed and eventually rejected, but not because it was a bad idea. Rather, on review it was concluded that the proposed study was too large and complex to be completed on the small budget requested and in the narrow time frame promised.[66]

While they were not ready to fund the study, Congress officials in Toronto and across Canada remained concerned at the increase in campus anti-Israel activities, especially on those campuses with larger Jewish student populations. It was not unusual for a Congress observer to be in attendance at campus events which promised a forum for anti-Israel and, perhaps even overtly, anti-Jewish views. Of course, monitoring was one thing, responding was another. Here the mainstream Jewish leadership's hands were somewhat tied. Criticism, even open attacks on Israel and Zionism, might smart but was this antisemitism? Perhaps many in the mainstream Jewish community might think so, but that did not necessarily make it so in the eyes of the university, the media, or the larger civil society. Hurtful speech, no matter who uttered it, was not the same as hate speech. Furthermore, in a campus context where free speech was prized, did the Jewish community want to lay itself open to charges of fostering political censorship or muzzling open and legitimate discussion? No. But neither did it want campus attacks on Israel and Zionism to go uncountered. If they were going to be countered, it would have to be done in the marketplace of ideas, and it was best if the pro-Israel ball was carried by Jewish students themselves.

And what about Jewish students? On major Canadian campuses there were Jewish students and faculty who shared the New Left's concerns. Some may have had deep Zionist attachments or familial, social, and even religious rootedness in the Jewish community. Others might only have become attuned to their Jewishness during the 1967 crisis. But most were united in their rejection of the one-sided anti-Israel tone of the New Left, which condemned Israel as the new poster child of colonial oppression. Some who had been active in New Left campus activities felt betrayed, even exiled, by former campus friends, and retreated from activism. Others rallied behind Israel. At McGill, Sir George Williams, the University of Manitoba, the University or Toronto, and York University, all institutions with sizable Jewish student populations, many of those who supported much of the left's agenda joined in organized defence of Israel. At Carlton University in Ottawa, a 'political hotbed,' first-year Ottawa student Bernie Farber helped gather a group of like-minded Jewish students, some veterans of Zionist youth movements such as Habonim, who saw no disconnect between participating in anti–Vietnam War protests while at the same time pushing back against New Left anti-Israel propaganda on campus.[67]

In his study of 'Jewish collective consciousness' since the Second World War, historian Yosef Gorny explores the emergence of Jewish student activism in North America following the Six Day War. He notes that the core group of Jewish pro-Israel activists on any given campus may have constituted only a small minority of the larger Jewish student body. However, he argues their influence belied their numbers. Many of these Jewish students were refugees from a New Left now turned anti-Israel, and they had both demonstrated organizational skills and commitment to cause. Certainly, they expressed themselves 'frankly, bluntly and aggressively,' and were comfortable working outside 'the traditional norms acceptable' to mainstream Jewish leadership.

Leaders of the organized Jewish community, increasingly distressed by what they saw as run-away New Left anti-Zionism and antisemitism on campuses across North America, were gratified to see Jewish students stepping forward in support of Israel and Jewish-related causes. At the same time, some leaders were less than thrilled to find themselves labelled as weak-kneed sellouts by these same youthful pro-Israel activists. How so? Even as Jewish students took on the anti-Israel and anti-Zionist New Left, they snapped at community leadership for its cap-in-hand, *sha shtil* approach to Jewish distress. Mainstream Jewish leaders and the moneyed elite who funded the community, students claimed, were adept at writing cheques, throwing black-tie fundraising dinners, and presenting one another with scrolls and plaques. Jewish newspapers were filled with their 'grin and grab' photos. But they were too frightened of what the *goyim* might think to roll up their collective sleeves and get down and dirty in defence of Jews in need, whether at home or abroad. What is more, much as *balibatem* might applaud actively committed Jewish youth, they were unwilling to accord these same Jewish youth a voice in the community decision-making process. If mainstream Jewish leaders were not prepared to do more, students demanded, they should at least get out of the way of those who would.[68]

In his analysis of the emerging Jew left, Gorny identified Montreal as one of 'the four important centers' of North American Jewish student activism, along with New York, Berkeley, and Boston. Those at McGill, according to one McGill student activist quoted by Gorny, believed that building a 'truly progressive North American political movement' that was not 'seriously and consistently antagonistic to Israel' would give those who had been 'unnecessarily hurt and angered by the New Left' an alternative political home.

> The fact that the Israeli dilemma is glossed over in leftist circles does not mean that it doesn't exist. Leftists, Jewish or not, have the obligation and opportunity to break with the contradictory movement and create one of their own; to build from the bottom an ideological structure which will not admit of such gross imperfections and immoral postures as the condemnation of Israel. If a general ideal breaks down in the particular, as it does in this issue, it should be scrapped. No one can approach the realities of any situation, let alone the middle east, from an a priori position of moral superiority, and claim sanity besides.[69]

Not everyone was so hopeful about ingathering disaffected Jewish students orphaned by an increasingly anti-Israel left. Toronto filmmaker David Kaufman was at McGill for several years following the Six Day War. The child of immigrants who maintained a religiously traditional and Jewishly committed Montreal home, he first joined Hillel then drifted into a circle of more progressive and Israel-animated students. There were very few in the group, he recalls, who had previously exited the New Left after becoming disheartened by its denunciations of Israel and Zionism. Perhaps, Kaufman contends, Jews drawn to the New Left in Montreal just had weaker core Jewish links – little Jewish education or rootedness in a tradition-rich Jewish home or a network of Jewish friends. They might be Jewish enough to take offence at the shrill anti-Israel thrust of the New Left, but they did not have Jewish resources enough to slide easily from the New Left to the Jew left. And, as seen from the outside, the Jew left may have appeared just too summer camp Jewish in style and ritual, unwelcoming of those who had little or no connection to the tight Montreal Jewish social web. Whatever the reason, according to Kaufman, most alienated from the New Left and uncomfortable in the Jew left found no soft landing. They just 'floated away.'[70]

Those more comfortable in their Jewish skin, even if out of secular and non-affiliated homes, found ways to remain Jewishly engaged. Some transferred their loyalty to Zionism – often with a radical edge. Unlike the Jewish mainstream, which increasingly lined up in unquestioning support of existing Israeli policy, whatever that might be, progressive campus Zionists, much to the chagrin of some in the organized Jewish community, felt free to advocate for Israel's withdrawal from the occupied territories and negotiations with the PLO. Others students found Jewish self-expression in religious innovation and revival, debate on the hows and whys of prayer, and more participatory and gender-equal celebration of the Jewish calendar. Still others were drawn to causes such as that of Soviet Jewry. As an expression of Jewish agency, students also pressed for Jewish studies on campus, for more community funding of Jewish day schools and democratization of Jewish community life. If some community leaders welcomed student enthusiasm, others were uneasy at an often anti-establishment tone of student activism grounded in a notion that mainstream synagogue-oriented Jewish life was becoming more and more shallow, impersonal, and materialistic.[71]

As a result, the relationship of more progressive and activist Jewish campus groups, no matter how pro-Israel, with the organized Jewish community and its leadership was anything but hand in glove, although as some Jewish leaders would grumble, it was often hand in pocket – the establishment's pocket. Of course, there were differences campus to campus. On some campuses the organized Jewish community was content it was getting a good Jewish bang for its buck. At McGill, for example, while there was an engaged group of left-leaning and often vocally anti-establishment Zionist students, Hillel too remained active and outspoken in support of Israel and Jewish causes. It was not, recalled a former president of the McGill Hillel, 'just where the B'nai Brith girls went for dances.'[72]

On other campuses the story was different. Campus activists often coalesced outside of Hillel, which they regarded as the becalmed and community-funded handmaiden of the local Jewish establishment. One former student activist dismissed Hillel as 'where the nerds and religious went.' It wasn't, he argued, where the Jewish action was.[73] If these often small but active Jewish student groups took pride in their independence and distance from the organized Jewish community, mainstream Jewish leaders were left with a dilemma. Students willing to speak up for Israel on campus were often the very ones most determined to keep at arm's length from the organized Jewish community.

In Winnipeg, for example, the local office of the Canadian Jewish Congress was concerned at reports that Arab students and their sympathizers at the University of Manitoba were about to unleash a flood of 'pro-Arab and anti-Israel propaganda on campus' and that 'two Jewish new leftists ... were involved with the pro–El Fatah group.' Congress officials were relieved to learn that a 'student Zionist group was being formed on Campus in Winnipeg' under the name 'Students for Israel.' The fledgling group, however, wanted no part of the campus Hillel and refused to place itself 'under an official Zionist banner.' Convinced that the closer its ties to Hillel or the organized Jewish community the weaker would be its independence of action, the student group requested only that the organized Jewish community supply it with pro-Israel printed materials for distribution on campus. Otherwise they wanted to be left alone, to report to nobody, and to be responsible only to themselves. Grateful that there was a nascent pro-Israel student voice ready to take on the New Left on campus, the Jewish community supplied the material, along with an invitation to seek more assistance as required.

For all their efforts to forestall mainstream interference in their activities, the students soon learned that programming cost money, money they did not have. In Winnipeg, as in other centres, activist pro-Zionist campus groups eventually found themselves forced to appeal to the organized Jewish community for a cash infusion. The Jewish community was forthcoming, but, students soon learned, the funds came with strings attached – strings that sometimes tied up the giver in as many knots as the taker.[74]

The Vancouver campus scene was equally difficult for the organized community to master. According to 'living room talk' in the Vancouver Jewish community, anti-Jewish and anti-Israel activism was ripe at the University of British Columbia and still worse at Simon Fraser University, reputed to be a hotbed of New Left strength. At both schools the New Left was said to be under the thumb of a large number of American draft resisters, including Jews, in both their faculties and student bodies. Except for a very weak Hillel, there was no organized Jewish presence on either campus.

At the same time, Jewish leaders in Vancouver were unable to get their minds around the notion that one could be pro-Israel yet oppose specific Israeli policies including the continued occupation of the territory taken in the Six Day War. As a result, they dismissed the emergence of a progressive and pro-Israel campus voice, akin to those on other Canadian campuses, as a 'so-called (sarcastically) "pro-Israel-new-left" which consists of Jewish students who always preface their vicious attacks on Israel with the disclaimer that they are truly pro-Israel.' Another observer noted that some Jewish students, many of them Americans or from eastern Canada, even 'went out of their way to criticize Israel.' Unwilling to countenance any criticism of Israel and especially not from Jews, Vancouver community leaders lumped all criticism of Israel together as anti-Zionist and gave a cold shoulder to requests for assistance from these pro-Israel students and faculty, thereby hobbling their ability to challenge New Left anti-Israel activity on the two Vancouver campuses.

Trapped in a box of their own making, establishment Jewish leaders in Vancouver fretted about what they regarded as a gathering firestorm of anti-Israel campus activity. With little or no experience of the changing campus environment, they fell back on what they did best. They established two committees – a 'Tachlis' committee, called upon to tap community organizations for the funds necessary to initiate 'truly' pro-Israel programming on campus, and a 'Think' committee, 'asked to plan the best possible strategy, both on a long-term educative basis, to meet immediate situations as they arise, so that there will be a minimum dissipation of manpower and money.' Very little was achieved. Attempts to engage with Jewish students and faculty went nowhere as committee members insisted they would only engage with those who pledged to tow an uncritical pro-Israel line. As a result, committee members ended with nobody to talk with except one another.[75]

In Toronto the situation was different again. In 1969 small groups of Jewish students at both the University of Toronto and York University, most with a history of involvement in one or another Zionist youth movement, organized to combat the anti-Israel thrust of the campus New Left and its sympathizers. At the University of Toronto the group called itself Students for Israel and at York University, Progressive Students for Israel. Offering themselves up as a Jewish anti-establishment alternative to Hillel, they too ran into the problem of program money. It was either turn to Congress for money or close up shop. They asked for money. Unlike in Vancouver, however, Congress in Toronto was forth-coming, in part because even if the student group supported much of the left's agenda, its membership was a known commodity. Members were mostly Toronto born and bred and known to be Jewishly commit-ted even if regarded as a little rough around the edges.

As was often the case, however, students were chagrined to find the money came with strings attached. Rather than offering a blank cheque, Congress demanded student accountability in both spending and pro-gramming. The students reluctantly agreed, but were soon chafing at what they branded as establishment interference in their program-ming and administration. For their part, Jewish community leaders were angered by what they saw as a bite-the-hand-that-feeds attitude on the part of the students. What is more, there were complaints that while the community supported pro-Israel activism on campus, the pro-Israel student group was too involved in anti–Vietnam War and other campus-based protests that had them stand side by side with the anti-Israel New Left. If that was not bad enough, mainstream commu-nity leaders were angered when, instead of being grateful for funding, students openly attacked the organized Jewish community as out of step or, even worse, indifferent to street-level community needs. The first issue of *Masada*, York's Jewish student newspaper, subsidized by the Jewish community, set off a momentary storm in Toronto Congress circles. On the newspaper's front page was an article entitled 'Jewish Students Arise and Unite: Let's Kick the Shit Out of the Jewish Estab-lishment!' Asking why so many Jewish students remained disengaged from the organized Jewish community, the article concluded most stu-dents wanted no part of 'big, fat, influential Congress-Synagogue-B'nai B'rith-type "Jews."'

He sees every major Jewish organization supporting the 'status quo' and working its hardest to preserve capitalism. It does not matter to wealthy Jews that others do not receive a fair share in the wealth produced by society.

He sees hypocrisy, sacrilege, desecration, unbounded affluence, amidst world poverty, power, preservation of the status quo.

The situation should be 'To be Jewish is to be Radical.' Our Torah teach-es us to push for social change, to be concerned with the less fortunate. As Jews, we must return to the values of the ancient Israelites who thundered against social injustice and corrupt governments.

> If we young Jews do not start to 'kick the shit' out of the Jewish Estab-
> lishment then we are guilty of betraying our ancient heritage, and more
> important that we are guilty of betraying our basic heritage.[76]

The storm over the article subsided after *Masada*'s editorial team, their
funding on the line, promised 'improvement in both idiom and content.' But mutual mistrust persisted.[77]

On one point activist students and establishment leaders agreed.
There had to be a positive and high-profile Jewish presence on campus
and every effort should be made to engage with seemingly disinterested Jewish students – a task that Hillel, in spite of being held up as
'the central arm of the community in terms of advancing and pursuing
Jewish concerns among students on the campuses,' was failing to per-
form. So too, in spite of all their efforts, did the Jew Left, even though
it spoke boldly about 'the development of Jewish consciousness.' Quietly, those who knew the campus also conceded that, while Jewish students might be induced to turn out in support of a particular cause
– as they did during the crisis of 1967 – engaging most Jewish students
on a continuing basis was not only difficult, it was impossible. For all
the discussion of student revolt, student activism, whether Jewish or
non-Jewish, remained a minority game. Unless some compelling issue
grabbed their interest, large numbers of Jewish students would remain
disengaged. When asked in 1970 if the student 'grass roots' had input
into the decision-making process that shaped Jewish programming on
Toronto campuses, Steve Ain, newly appointed director of youth services for the Canadian Jewish Congress in Toronto, was candid. 'It is not
really a grass roots decision because the "grass roots" students couldn't
give a damn about Jewish student organizations.' Rather than throw in
the community towel, he demanded, those who were active and committed needed to be given every assistance, even if on campus the Jewish establishment did 'not have its usual veto power over anything it
doesn't like.'

According to Ain, a key to engaging wider Jewish student participation on campus was to find a cause, a Jewish cause, with which students
could identify, an Israel-linked cause that would tug at their Jewish
heart the way Israel did in the crisis weeks of 1967. What would that
cause be? For many of those young Jews who surprised Jewish leaders
and themselves by the degree to which they identified with a besieged
Israel in the spring of 1967, a victorious Israel was still besieged, and
like other committed Jews, they felt a moral obligation to speak out for

Israel and those, such as Jews in the Soviet Union, oppressed in Israel's name. If pro-Israel advocacy emerged as a first priority of the organized Jewish community, in the late 1960s the cause of Soviet Jewry was increasingly taken up by Jewish youth and, eventually, the larger Jewish community as well.[78]

Domestic concerns were also to the fore. If Israel afforded many Canadian Jews a prestige pride in attachment to their Jewishness, Israel was not alone in shaping the Canadian Jewish agenda. There remained ongoing worries about antisemitism in Canada – whether crudely enacted by home-grown Nazis masquerading as anti-Zionists, or disguised as a more genteel social exclusion festering under the radar of human rights legislation – about the place of Jews in a changing Quebec, and about the plight of Jews elsewhere who suffered under the heel of anti-Israel and anti-Jewish regimes. All these concerns would be dramatically impacted by the election of a new Canadian prime minister, Pierre Elliott Trudeau.

CHAPTER SIX

'The Maddest and Most Passionate Fling'

Pierre Elliott Trudeau died in Montreal on 28 September 2000. The death and state funeral of a man who had served as Canada's prime minister for all but one year between 1968 and 1984 evoked an unprecedented outpouring of public grief. Thousands stood quietly outside Notre-Dame Basilica during Trudeau's state funeral or wept openly as the funeral cortège made its way through the streets of Montreal towards Trudeau's burial place. Prominent among the mourners were many Canadians of non-English and non-French descent who regarded Trudeau as their champion, a man who both fought to preserve the Canadian state and took concrete steps to ensure that all Canadians, regardless of origin, were treated equally and justly within that state.

Jews had particular reason to reflect on their relationship with Trudeau. It was a relationship at once close and prickly. In retrospect, it was also a relationship as complicated as the man himself. Trudeau likely never gave much thought to his shaping influence on the Canadian Jewish community of the 1960s and early 1970s – it would have been dramatically out of character for him to do so. Yet, his vision for Canada and for Canada in the world, his political imperatives, and his institutional legacy had a massive impact on Canadian Jewish life, both on the life chances of individual Jews and on the corporate life of the organized Jewish community. Nor did that impact all run one way. Jews influenced Trudeau's thinking, the unfolding of his political career, and the organization of his government and its policy initiatives.

While Trudeau dominated the Canadian political landscape for almost twenty years, surprisingly little has been written about his impact on and relationship with Canadian Jews. A singular exception is a chapter entitled 'Meltdown in the Melting Pot' in Larry Zolf's short 1984 volume *Just Watch Me: Remembering Pierre Trudeau*. With much tongue in cheek, Zolf, a journalist and social satirist, describes Trudeau's relationship with Jews as a full-blown love affair. 'Indeed,' writes Zolf, 'Trudeau's love affair with Jews is probably the maddest and most passionate fling that Trudeau ever flung; of this love affair Lenny Bruce could only have observed that Canada may be goyish but Trudeau is certainly Jewish.'[1]

We may doubt whether Lenny Bruce's 'fudge-is-goyish-chocolate-is-Jewish' division of the world can be fruitfully employed to distinguish the essential Canada from the essential Trudeau, but it is true that many Canadian Jews found in Trudeau a political leader who, without intending it, shared many of their fears and reflected many of their hopes. This was especially true for the Jews in Montreal. When Trudeau assumed the prime minister's office in 1968, one of his central concerns was assuring the place of Quebec within Canada. For Jews in Montreal, uneasy at growing nationalist and separatist sentiment in Quebec, at threats to the status of the English language, and at the seeming inability of Lester Pearson's Ottawa to comprehend, let alone get a handle on, what was going on in Quebec, Trudeau's progressive image, his bilingualism, and especially his determined federalism were reassuring. Jews elsewhere in Canada may not have been as possessed by the upheaval in Quebec, but many were drawn by Trudeau's promise of a new, more open and enlightened Canada.[2]

With so much Jewish hope riding on Trudeau, could he deliver? As a determined federalist, Trudeau had no problem with the parallel notions of inclusive civic nationalism and sovereignty of the state. Canada, he believed, was a melding of both. He would truck no compromise with a nationalism grounded in ethnic, racial, or religious exclusivity, a nationalism rooted in lineage and appeals to the emotions, a nationalism that gives proprietary and preferential citizenship to one group, suffering the presence of others in some lesser citizenship status. This was anathema to Trudeau, a small-l liberal who prided himself on being a champion of rationalism and progressive social values, the rights of the individual, respect for pluralism, and the removal of barriers to citizen participation in society. Inasmuch as his aversion to nationalism grounded in ethnic exclusivity made Trudeau a staunch federalist and proponent of equal rights for all, he made common cause with the vast majority of the Canadian Jewish community.

If many of Trudeau's social and political views resonated well in the Jewish community, there was something else that also drew Jews to

Trudeau and Trudeau to many individual Jews. Career diplomat Allan Gotlieb, one of Trudeau's closest Ottawa advisers, jokingly described Trudeau as a 'rootless cosmopolitan.' By this he meant that Trudeau, more than any Canadian prime minister before or arguably since, had a worldly sophistication about him, an appreciation of urban and urbane tastes. He enjoyed debating ideas. He liked theatre and music. He appreciated architecture and fine food. He was as much at home exploring New York, London, and Paris as he was in his own Montreal. All this, Gotlieb argues, brought Trudeau into more contact with Jews than was typical of most francophone Quebeckers. What is more, his professional world, political interests, and human rights advocacy in Quebec and Montreal crossed linguistic lines and, as a result, amplified his contact with Jews. This must not be misunderstood. It was not that Trudeau sought out Jews. Rather, Jews were just well represented in the English-language social, cultural, and political milieus to which Trudeau gravitated. As a result, according to Gotlieb, Trudeau developed a high comfort level with Jews, although he might not have thought of it in those terms. It followed that by the time he entered the prime minister's office, Trudeau had a wide circle of individual Jewish contacts. Without likely giving conscious thought to who was or was not a Jew, he freely tapped into this talent pool to advance his government's agenda. As a result, Trudeau's administration became open to the participation of Jews at the highest policy level and in numbers that would have been unimaginable only a few years earlier.[3]

All this begs the question of what shaped Trudeau's values and ultimately his openness to Jews? Until recently the widely accepted narrative of Trudeau's formative years portrayed him as the product of an unconventional home in a rigidly static Quebec society. In an early biography that set out the popularly received story, George Radwanski notes that Trudeau was born into a wealthy Montreal family and, in the Quebec terms of the day, was the child of a mixed marriage. His father, Charles-Émile Trudeau, was a successful and wealthy French Canadian businessman whose enterprises included a chain of gasoline service stations across Quebec. Though Trudeau's father was financially well to do, Radwanski contends, he was also something of an outsider to Quebec's French Canadian social elite. His choice of a marriage partner only underscored his outsider status. In a Quebec where the English-French divide remained wide, he married a woman of Scottish heritage. The Elliott in Trudeau's name was his mother Grace's family name. Although she spoke both English and French, Trudeau's mother insisted her three children all speak to her in English.

Moneyed but not at home within either the French or English Canadian social elites in Montreal, according to Radwanski, the Trudeau family lived in a comfortable, linguistically and ethnically mixed neighbourhood. Equally at ease speaking French or English, Trudeau had among his first friends the Jewish children who lived next door. He was sent to Collège Jean-de-Brébeuf, a prestigious private Jesuit-run French-speaking school in Montreal. Somewhat shy and slight of build, again according to Radwanski, Trudeau, like his father, felt himself something of an outsider. Even as he did well in the classical studies that were at the centre of the school's curriculum, he is described as having to sometimes defend himself against the taunts of classmates who were openly derisive of his mixed parentage. Out of this experience, it is suggested, Trudeau may have first developed his disdain for, if not outright hostility to, narrow and parochial nationalism. What is more, refusing to be bullied ethnically, intellectually, or physically, Trudeau is said to have developed an appreciation for the value of robust intellectual and physical conditioning. The more he stood his ground, the more confidently comfortable he became with himself. Trudeau also absorbed a Jesuit-like respect for the value of logic and reason over emotion. Priding himself on being something of a non-conformist, according to Radwanski, he delighted in tweaking the nose of authority and demonstrating his independence of mind by showing no fear of being odd man out.

Perhaps it was his insistence that new and different ideas had to be entertained and debated as part of a rational and orderly decision-making process that eventually drew Trudeau to study law at the University of Montreal. He graduated with honours and was called to the Quebec bar in 1944; but he was still not ready to settle down. Naturally curious about the larger world, perhaps feeling stifled in Quebec, and needing to test himself on a larger terrain, Radwanski argues, Trudeau packed off to study at Harvard, then at the École des Sciences Politiques in Paris, and finally at the London School of Economics, where he studied under Fabian socialist Harold Laski. Curiosity about the world and a yen for adventure also sent him backpacking through eastern Europe, Asia, Africa, and the Middle East, long before adventure travel became fashionable. His off-shore education and extensive travels, often deliberately steering himself into world hot spots, according to Radwanski, broadened his world view and appreciation for difference. All this experience stood him in good stead when he entered the political arena.[4]

This received narrative of Trudeau's early years has not gone unchallenged. A recent book on Trudeau's early years paints a very different and much more challenging portrait of the man who would eventually be Canada's prime minister. In *Young Trudeau: 1919–1944: Son of Quebec, Father of Canada*, Max and Monique Nemni argue that during his formative period Trudeau was anything but the youthful rebel, adventurer, and uneasy outsider that many previously believed. Search as you might, they argue, you would find little of the liberal thinker and champion of a united Canada whom Canadian voters would elect prime minister in 1968. Instead of the battling outsider, Trudeau is described, from his early days at Collège Jean-de-Brébeuf, as a much-admired student, active in student affairs and comfortable rubbing shoulders with the children of the French Canadian elite among whom he felt he belonged. Through the late 1930s and early 1940s in Quebec, Trudeau found social and political inspiration in an authoritarian and nationalist Catholic Church that he saw as battling back against Quebec's dispossession by bourgeoning English-speaking capital and its political allies. He much admired iron-fisted Catholic dictators such as Salazar in Portugal, Franco in Spain, Mussolini in Italy, and especially Vichy France's Henri-Philippe Pétain, who was later sentenced to life imprisonment for his collaboration with the Nazis.

And what of Trudeau's vision of Quebec? Young Trudeau was a nationalist, one who dismissed liberalism, democracy, and individual rights as tools of Quebec's English overseers, who used them to manipulate the political system so as to ensure their domination and the continued subservience of French Canadians. He supported the building of a sovereign Quebec grounded in a religious monoculture. Trudeau's Quebec had no room for 'ethnics' and certainly not for Jews, whom he saw as alien to the values of Catholic Quebec.

Where then did the other Trudeau, the liberal and federalist Trudeau, come from? Or as the Nemnis posit: 'The true mystery is how he travelled from a vision of the nation that was organic, ethnic and communitarian, to the vision of a society that is based on citizenship, that is plural and liberal – a rare and difficult transition.'[5] In answering this question the Nemni and Radwanski narratives overlap, at least in part. Both versions of the Trudeau story agree that after being admitted to the Quebec bar and deciding to leave Quebec, to study first at Harvard and then in Paris and London, Trudeau was exposed to new ideas and new people. He also came to embrace a more open, progressive, and cosmopolitan view of the world.

Rebranded, Trudeau returned to Quebec. Now on the opposite side of the ideological barricade from many of those with whom he had previously shared a common vision, Trudeau made community with those committed to building a new, open, and forward-looking society. Now an avowed civil libertarian, he was soon caught up in the critical 1949 Asbestos Strike, working pro bono to provide legal assistance to strikers battling not just their employer but Premier Duplessis's police, dispatched to do the employer's bidding. In this struggle Trudeau forged what would prove to be life-long relationships with like-minded activists, Gérard Pelletier and Jean Marchand among them. United in opposition to what they saw as a backward-looking and ethnically parochial Quebec nationalism that walled Quebec off from progressive thought and reform, the three became outspoken in their advocacy of individual rights, progressive reform, and inclusive federalism. In 1960 they campaigned for the provincial Lesage Liberals in the party's breakthrough electoral victory over the late Duplessis's faltering political machine.

While part of the anti-nationalist brain trust in Quebec and, in 1961, a newly minted professor of constitutional and human rights law at the University of Montreal and founder of *Cité Libre*, a forum for like-minded voices, Trudeau showed little or no interest in entering electoral politics. Even if Trudeau and his friends did decide to run for office, it was entirely unclear what party they would run for. Trudeau refused to publicly identify with, let alone join, any political party, federal or provincial.

In 1963 the federal Liberals under Lester Pearson were out of power and gearing up for a federal election. Desperate to attract new, younger, and, above all, electable candidates from Quebec, Pearson approached Marchand to run for the Liberals. Marchand was tempted, but refused to run unless he could bring Pelletier and Trudeau to Ottawa with him. Pearson was uncertain about the other two, but agreed to find seats for the trio. The deal fell apart when, as the election loomed, Pearson withdrew his party's opposition to stationing American nuclear arms on Canadian soil, a policy reversal the three Quebeckers denounced. More than just denounce Pearson's backsliding on nuclear arms, Trudeau and his friends supported local NDP candidates. Pearson and the Liberals barely scraped into office with a minority government.

In 1965 the Liberals again prepared to face the voters, and again Pearson reached out to Marchand, who again insisted Pelletier and Trudeau be included in any electoral deal. This time a deal fell into place. Why were the 'three wise men' ready to sign on with a party they had so recently denounced? Federalism. Trudeau and the others were increasingly alarmed at what they regarded a surging tide of separatism in Quebec and consequent erosion in federalist support. What is more, they worried that Ottawa either did not fathom the true nature and seriousness of the nationalist threat or was asleep at the switch when it came to Quebec. It didn't matter which. There was nobody in federal Liberal ranks who had any idea how to effectively counter the Quebec nationalist threat, and the three intended their election to be a wake-up call to Canadians. Trudeau later explained that he ran for office so as to alert government and Canadians to the dangers of separatism, not because he wanted a career in politics and certainly not one that would span more than two decades.

The prospect of running Trudeau for a parliamentary seat in Quebec posed something of a problem for the federal Liberals. Where could the party find a safe seat for an untested candidate, an intellectual, a bachelor with no grassroots Liberal Party support? The party reasoned a largely unknown, urbane professor of law could have trouble appealing to voters in a rural or a working-class urban French Canadian riding. But there was one Quebec seat that was urban, cosmopolitan, and bedrock Liberal enough to accept and elect an unconventional candidate such as Trudeau – Mount Royal in Montreal. This up-market, overwhelmingly English-speaking, and federalist-supporting riding had recently had its boundaries redrawn to include a large block of Jewish voters. Fully 38 per cent of the riding's population was Jewish. So too were many in the local riding association's executive. It would be hard to find a safer Liberal seat in all of Canada. Whoever won the Liberal nomination in Mount Royal was assured electoral victory.[6]

The long-time sitting member, Alan Macnaughton, a former speaker of the House of Commons and scion of Anglo Montreal's legal and business elite, held a mortgage on the seat. To get Trudeau elected in Mount Royal the party needed Macnaughton to step aside. After some backroom arm twisting, Macnaughton accepted the promise of a Senate appointment in return for giving up his seat and endorsing Trudeau once he formally entered the nomination race. However, the unexpected news that Macnaughton was not going to seek re-election encouraged several prominent Montreal Jewish Liberals, including Victor Goldbloom and Stuart Smith, both respected Montreal doctors, to immediately put their names forward in nomination. Under normal political circumstances, one of them would likely have won the nomination. There was already a quiet understanding within the largely Jewish riding executive in this most Jewish of all Canadian ridings that when Macnaughton finally stepped aside, his successor would be a Jew.

With several worthy Jewish candidates in the race for the nomination, the riding executive was none too happy about the Liberal Party national executive parachuting a non-Jewish outsider into the Mount Royal race, and at first Trudeau did little to win over the uncomfortable riding executive. For his critical first get-to-know-you meeting with Macnaughton and the Mount Royal riding executive, all of them dressed in dark business suits, Trudeau reportedly pulled up in his Mercedes sport convertible and climbed out dressed in jeans and a frayed pullover. A Liberal Party organizer intercepted Trudeau as he headed into the meeting and sent him home to change into something more appropriate.

In the end federal Liberal Party organizers got their way. The riding executive accepted Trudeau. Stuart Smith conceded the inevitable and gracefully withdrew his name from nomination. Victor Goldbloom made a race of it, but lost to Trudeau and the Liberal machine. Disappointed but good Liberal soldiers, both Smith and Goldbloom endorsed Trudeau, as did Macnaughton.[7]

The nomination secured, Trudeau's 1965 electoral campaign was a low key but well managed suit-and-tie affair that included a number of parlour meetings in Jewish homes and institutions. Cerebral and serious, Trudeau came across as a little distant but at the same time young, handsome, and flirtatiously sexy. Even if it was a foregone conclusion that Jewish voters in Mount Royal would vote for the Liberal standard bearer, some at first may have even wondered if this unconventional and little-known-to-them French Canadian academic could appreciate, let alone share, their concerns. At one parlour meeting the then president of the Mount Royal riding association recalls an elderly Jewish woman asking Trudeau if he would feel comfortable representing so Jewish a riding. Trudeau replied, 'What makes you think I can't represent Jewish causes as well as any Jew can?'[8]

The twin domestic issues that overshadowed all others for Jewish voters in Mount Royal were the language question and the closely related upsurge in nationalist and separatist activism in Quebec. Trudeau used every opportunity to make clear his uncompromising opposition to the nationalists and their agenda. He pledged that once in Ottawa he would be an outspoken champion of federalism. As expected, Trudeau handily won Canada's then most Jewish riding. He and the 'other wise men' were off to Ottawa as part of yet another Pearson-led minority government.[9]

Trudeau's rise to prominence in Ottawa was nothing short of meteoric. The three wise men quickly formed the nucleus of a federalist and reform-minded Quebec Liberal caucus and Trudeau became its intellectual voice. Trudeau also caught Pearson's eye. Shoring up his minority government, Pearson first appointed Trudeau his parliamentary secretary, then in April 1967 leapfrogged Trudeau, only sixteen months in government, over several other cabinet hopefuls and appointed the young Quebecker to his cabinet as minister of justice.

The press speculated that this would be Pearson's last government. Rumour had it that he intended to stay on through Canada's 1967 centennial celebrations, but would not lead the Liberals into the next election. While Pearson remained mum about his plans, the politics of succession soon dominated Ottawa chatter. A growing list of possible candidates to succeed Pearson was soon being bounced about. The prime minister, of course, refused comment on any possible leadership race. In retrospect, his appointment of Trudeau as his minister of justice, knowing major and deeply controversial legal reforms were in the works, including the updating of Canada's archaic divorce laws and a liberalization of laws dealing with both abortion and homosexuality, proved key in pushing Trudeau into the national limelight.[10] Arguing that 'there's no place for the state in the bedrooms of the nation,' Trudeau ably shepherded long-overdue reform in socially sensitive areas through Parliament, making him a darling of the liberal media and of a public ready for change. What is more, at a high-profile 1967 federal-provincial constitutional conference in Ottawa, the minister of justice, his trademark red rose in his lapel and a strong federalist message to deliver, stole the show.

The media quickly learned that the young, handsome, flamboyant, and fluently bilingual Trudeau made good copy. Reporters turned to him for quotable comments on various issues and he was soon in demand to address various gatherings – sometimes about his legal reform package but often about Quebec–Ottawa relations. But what about Trudeau's electoral backyard, his Mount Royal riding? Among the safest Liberal seats in Canada, it beggared the mind to think that anyone but a Liberal could win in Mount Royal. Safe seat or not, Trudeau was not much interested in the nitty gritty of riding affairs. He left most of that to his local staff. Still, he appreciated the need for a riding profile and put himself out there for his constituents to see. As time permitted, he accepted speaking engagements in the riding, including a number before Jewish groups, often arriving with the national media in tow. If the press often seemed more taken with Trudeau's flamboyant style than the substance of his talks, there was an arrogant prickliness to Trudeau that the media did not see or, such was Trudeau's growing popularity, they chose to overlook. In one instance Trudeau accepted an invitation from Hy Eiley, an early supporter in Mount Royal and up and comer among Montreal Jewish professionals, to speak to a local B'nai Brith Lodge. The minister of justice earned himself a speeding ticket on his way to the meeting. As he was about to take the podium, he cavalierly flipped Eiley the ticket and told him to 'take care of it.' The incident did not make it into the press.[11]

When Pearson finally confirmed rumours that he would step down as prime minister, a number of contenders who had been treading political water entered the race to replace him. In spite of Pearson's quiet encouragement and pressure from a number of supporters, Trudeau held back. He saw no point in replacing Pearson as head of the Liberal Party if he could not go on to carry Canada in a general election. Certainly he did not want to be left warming the opposition benches while the Conservatives carelessly mishandled the separatist file, as he feared they would. And the word was that the Conservative moment was coming. Pundits speculated that after two successive Liberal minority governments, voters were ready for the Conservatives and their new leader, Robert Stanfield, then riding high in the polls. What is more, Trudeau remained unconvinced that, if he tossed his hat into the ring to replace Pearson, the Liberals would even pick him to be their leader. Coming second in a leadership race was no prize. As a result, Trudeau held back, assessing his chances. He assumed that the majority of the Quebec Liberal caucus would be on his side if he entered the leadership race, but that was not enough. Even the Liberal Party tradition of passing the leadership back and forth between an English Canadian and French Canadian guaranteed nothing. Traditions are just that, traditions. They can be set aside. And the list of those with prime ministerial timbre already in the leadership race, some with considerable money behind them, had to be considered. With speculation building that he was testing the waters for a Liberal leadership run, Trudeau felt out a number of party insiders about his chances, including some who were not in his camp. In conversation with Jerry Grafstein, a John Turner supporter, Trudeau was blunt. 'If I run,' Grafstein recalls Trudeau asking, 'can I win?' Grafstein, equally blunt, pointed out what he regarded as Trudeau's major Achilles heel. Trudeau might be a rising star in the Quebec caucus but, Grafstein warned, 'You have to demonstrate that you can win in English Canada.'[12] Trudeau already knew that. To win the leadership and the country he needed support in Ontario and, most of all, in riding-rich Toronto. Without Toronto, home turf to several announced leadership hopefuls, any run to replace Pearson was pointless. Toronto was key.

In February 1968 a still wavering Trudeau arrived in Toronto, unfamiliar territory for him, to attend the annual meeting of the Liberal Party of Ontario. A lot hung on the meeting. Trudeau was looking for a sign that Toronto was not already locked up. Historian Ramsay Cook, who attended the gathering, was, like many there, taken with Trudeau. The still undeclared candidate was embraced by the overflow crowd, which included a who's who of younger, reform-minded Toronto business leaders, academic notables, media heavy hitters, and even several NDPers poised to bolt to Trudeau's side. Prominent in the group were a number of local Jewish Liberal players, some with very deep pockets. By the end of the evening, according to Cook, many were ready to support Trudeau as their choice for Liberal leader and prime minister.[13]

Pumped up by his Toronto reception, Trudeau plunged into the already crowded leadership race. Of all the leadership hopefuls, none was as new to the Liberal Party as Trudeau. Through the leadership campaign he gradually attracted more and more attention, not just within Liberal ranks but among the larger voting public that, like the media, seemed taken by the articulate Quebecker with shallow Liberal Party roots. Before long Trudeau became the man to beat. But would the party's old guard try to cobble together an 'anybody-but-Trudeau' crusade? Through three ballots at the Liberal leadership convention in Ottawa, Trudeau's strength grew as candidate after candidate fell away, some, including Toronto's Mitchell Sharp, tossing their support to Trudeau. On the fourth ballot the Liberals had a new leader and Canada a new prime minister. The heaviest Jewish riding in Canada also had the prime minister as its member of parliament.

To no one's surprise, after only a slight hesitation and the appointment of an interim cabinet, Trudeau went to the voters. The election campaign got off to a slow start, but soon turned into something of a media circus and a Trudeau love-in. Trudeau seemed more star than politician. The Liberals, taking advantage of his popular appeal, especially to women and younger voters, organized their campaign around maximum exposure of their leader and minimum discussion of issues, except for a few key ideas that Trudeau hammered away at again and again – assuring national unity, tackling old problems with new thinking, and creating a 'Just Society.' Swept up in a wave of Trudeaumania, many voters seemed hardly to care about issues anyway. They wanted the man. And so, Trudeau quietly went from being the one to beat to the one who could not be beaten. On election day the voters handed Trudeau and the Liberal Party a huge majority.

Among those elected to parliament in 1968 were eight Jews. Oddly, all eight, Liberals and non-Liberals alike, ran successfully in ridings where the Jewish vote was not significant or not significant enough to assure the margin of victory. Most striking was the election of a Jew as Progressive Conservative member for a Newfoundland riding known for 'cod not smoked carp.' Conversely, ridings with larger Jewish populations all elected non-Jews. Among these ridings, noted a Canadian Jewish Congress official, Eglinton in Toronto elected Mitchell Sharp, soon to be Trudeau's minister of external affairs, and, of course, Mount Royal, which elected Pierre Elliott Trudeau.

> What does this all mean? That Canadian Jewry and the Canadian electorate have matured, have come of age. It is no longer necessary for a Jewish political aspirant to be elected exclusively by Jewish voters. Canadian voters, whether they live in Windsor, Galt, or Cornerbrook, are religion-blind when it comes to elections. Back in 1917 Wilfrid Laurier set aside Cartier riding in Montreal as a 'Jewish' constituency. It was represented in turn by Sam Jacobs, Leon Crestohl, Milton Klein, until its demise in redistribution. Because French Canadians are possibly not yet ready to elect Anglo Saxons or Jews[,] Quebec is now without any Jewish M.P.s (and some feel this keenly).[14]

If the election of eight Jews from ridings with few Jewish voters was worthy of note, it was speculated there was another precedent-breaking move in the offing – a Jewish cabinet minister. No Jew had ever previously been appointed to a federal cabinet. With speculation rife, the *Canadian Jewish News* touted several cabinet hopefuls. The paper tagged Philip Givens, former mayor of Toronto, as a likely choice for a 'special government department likely to deal with modern urbanization' and suggested that a cabinet post might also await Robert Kaplan, described as a 'young lawyer and close friend of Prime Minister Trudeau.' An early member of the Toronto team backing Trudeau's campaign to replace Pearson, Kaplan was widely rumoured to have helped pull his father-in-law's considerable financial support behind the Liberal campaign. The paper also noted the election of Barney Danson in a riding just north of Toronto, but made no mention of him as likely cabinet material.[15]

The *Canadian Jewish News* guardedly hoped that Trudeau would for the first time appoint a Jew as a federal cabinet minister. It could not have imagined the reality that would unfold during Trudeau's tenure. Pearson had few senior Jewish public servants in his government and, according to Larry Zolf, 'kept his cabinet, bureaucracy and courts 99 and 44/100ths Ivory, Gentile, and Pure: there were not many notable Jewish appointments during the Pearson years.' Notable exceptions included Louis Rasminky, whom Pearson finally appointed governor of the Bank of Canada after he had previously been passed over for the post, and Simon Reisman, promoted by Pearson to deputy minister of the newly established Department of Industry.[16]

These appointments were exceptions that proved the rule – Jews faced a glass ceiling in Ottawa, and Pearson, aware of it, was not one to challenge it. Jerry Grafstein, then a member of John Turner's staff, recalls accompanying Turner to a cabinet meeting shortly after the outbreak of the Six Day War. During an informal moment, Pearson, impressed by Israel's stunning military success, put his arm around Grafstein and jokingly said, 'Too bad we don't have more of your persuasion in our government.' Not one to hold back, Grafstein replied, 'Your government wouldn't be in the shit it's in if there were more of us.' Pearson, somewhat taken aback, sheepishly mumbled, 'You're right.'[17]

Unlike Pearson, Trudeau was not Jew-shy. Nor did he feel himself beholden to the old Ottawa establishment or their traditions. In 1990 Michel Vastel, long-time Ottawa correspondent for *Le Devoir*, published a retrospective look at Trudeau's political career entitled *The Outsider: The Life of Pierre Elliott Trudeau*. It portrayed him as something of a new boy on the Ottawa block, and certainly not part of the old-guard Ottawa establishment. Trudeau did not bend over backwards to cultivate close ties with many of Ottawa's top mandarins or political heavyweights. He had only the thinnest of connections to the national Liberal Party machine when he became the Liberal leader, and demonstrated little interest in oiling its gears, at least during his first administration. Instead, he came across as distant, independent of mind, a loner who might be able to turn on the personal charm but was not much interested in fitting in with either the Ottawa or Quebec establishment. Of course, he had his political intimates – Gérard Pelletier and Jean Marchand among them – but he was also determined to take counsel from those he felt might have something important to bring to the table, including those like himself who were not Ottawa-entrenched.[18] Prominent among these were Jews. In fact, if the Pearson administrations had been averse to allowing too prominent a role for Jews, Trudeau felt no such hesitancy. Personally committed to a meritocracy, comfortable with Jews, and 'colour blind' when it came to citizen access to government, Trudeau pushed open government's doors to all Canadians with talent and ideas, without regard to heritage. The glass ceiling that previously blocked talented Jews from rising through the public service was shattered.[19]

The results were telling. Where no Jew had ever been a member of a federal cabinet, during Trudeau's tenure as prime minister four Jews served in his cabinets. He appointed a Jew, Bora Laskin, chief justice of the Supreme Court of Canada and a fistful of other Jews to federal-court positions across Canada. Maxwell Cohen, a professor of law at McGill, was appointed Canada's representative to the International Court of Justice in The Hague. Allan Gotlieb was appointed Canada's ambassador in Washington. Jews were also appointed to federal commissions and standing committees. Trudeau's personal staff was as open to Jews as were the ranks of deputy and assistant deputy ministers. Ottawa political junkies would soon become familiar with such high-profile names as H. Carl Goldenberg, Allan Gotlieb, Simon Reisman, Bernard and Sylvia Ostry, Jerry Grafstein, Mickey Cohen, and Jack Austin. Many others, less prominent but no less Jewish, found a place in government service.

It would be tempting but wrong to think that Trudeau deliberately reached out to Jews. No doubt he was at ease with individual Jews – as much as he was at ease with anyone outside his immediate circle – and he knew many Jews socially, professionally, and, if the rumour mill is to be believed, romantically as well. But he did not so much seek out Jews. Rather, in an effort to encourage the best and brightest to consider public service, he was responsible for lowering discriminatory barriers that previously had prevented talented Jews and others from accessing government jobs and political appointments.

This begs another question. Trudeau may have pushed open Ottawa's doors to Jews, but why were Jews so ready to walk through them?

Why were they attracted to government? For some it offered a good job or a stepping stone along a career path. For others, Ottawa under Trudeau seemed the place where the action was, where change was happening. Also important, a growing pool of new Jewish university graduates did not face the ethnic and religious quotas at Canadian universities that their parents had suffered. But there was still, as John Porter's *The Vertical Mosaic* made clear, social discrimination against Jews, with the result that key sectors of Canada's corporate, business, and professional world remained no-go zones for Jews. Government employment afforded a positive option.[20]

What is more, just as the door to public service in Canada was opening to Jews, another door was closing. Previously, talented Jews who found their educational or professional career paths blocked by anti-Jewish prejudice at home might have exercised the option of heading to professionally greener pastures south of the border.[21] By the late 1960s, however, the United States was far less attractive than was previously the case. American society, racked by the twin-pack problems of growing racial unrest and protest against the Vietnam War, was increasingly regarded as dangerous and divided against itself.

None of this was news to Canadian Jews, many of whom likely sympathized with the spreading antipathy to the war. In that, they mirrored the American Jewish community. A study of the impact of the war on the American Jewish community concluded: 'Shaken by the Holocaust, fearful of a nuclear war, worried about the war's effect on the country's liberal agenda, and determined to demonstrate the practical value of their faith, American Jewish religious and secular intellectuals emerged as early, vocal and effective opponents of the Vietnam War.' These 'intellectuals' were not alone. While there was also a new breed of neoconservative Jews who supported the war – most famously those who gravitated around the previously liberal *Commentary Magazine* – poll after poll indicated that the majority of American Jews were opposed to the conflict in Southeast Asia.[22]

If concern about the war was not bad enough, Canadian Jews were also well aware of the growing rupture between the American Black and Jewish communities. While most American Jews continued to be sympathetic to the civil rights movement, by the late 1960s the long-standing alliance between Blacks and Jews in the United States was crumbling. Jews watched with concern as the mainstream Black leadership, who had advocated non-violent protest and coalition building, was being supplanted by more strident Black leaders who rejected

Black-Jewish cooperation, denounced both Jews and Israel as racist, and dismissed integration and non-violence as failures. Following the 1968 murder of Martin Luther King and the New York teachers' strike, American Jews were shocked to find advocates of Black power pointing an accusing finger at Jews as a source of their communal pain.[23]

If war and racial turmoil made the United States appear less attractive, it was also less accessible to Canadians than was previously the case. As of 1965 new American immigration legislation ended virtually unfettered Canadian immigrant access to the United States. Rather than offering ease of entry, new rules assigned Canadian immigration applicants to an enlarged annual quota set aside for the Western Hemisphere. Denied privileged entry, Canadians applying for a green card were assigned to the same immigrant line as Mexicans, Chileans, Brazilians, and others in the Americas. This made the process of applying for American immigration more cumbersome and time-consuming and of less certain outcome than previously.[24]

What of Canada in the later 1960s? It basked in the afterglow of the successful 1967 centennial celebrations and Expo 67.[25] Canadians might be soft spoken in their national pride, but there is little doubt that most Canadians, even with uncertainty in Quebec, were ripe with optimism about their country and its future. The 1968 election campaign and Trudeau's victory – especially as compared to the second coming of political retread Richard Nixon that same year – seemed to confirm that, with no cities burning and no soldiers coming home in body bags, Canada was the better place to be.

It certainly seemed a better place for Canadian Jews, and the increased openness to Jews and other outsiders reflected by Trudeau's government promised still better things to come. But was this new openness to Jews really a bold step forward, or was Trudeau's insistence on a meritocracy in government simply forcing Ottawa into line with the increasing acceptance for Jews taking place in Canadian society more generally? Perhaps both. But there is no denying the rebound effect of Jews occupying key Ottawa positions. If this or that deputy minister was a Jew, the chairperson of this or that federal panel was a Jew, this or that federal judge a Jew, economic, political, and even social sectors still closed to Jews had no choice but to take notice and eventually even follow suit. Self-interest demanded it. The bottom line demanded it. Who would want to stand accused of violating the new spirit of openness in the land? Who could afford to run afoul of a newly minted Jewish assistant deputy minister or judge who might not look kindly at an old-school clubiness that barred Jews. It was quietly joked that the day a Jew was appointed deputy minister of finance was the day banks would rush to install kosher kitchens. In the late 1960s the banks might well have wondered if it was time to get the name of a good contractor.

How aware was Trudeau of the impact of opening Ottawa to Jews and other former outsiders? This is also hard to know. Once asked by a constituent why there was no Jew appointed to the Quebec Court of Appeal, Trudeau reportedly shrugged and replied that the question was silly. He selected the best individuals without reference to ethnic or religious origin. If the top ten jurists were Jews, he continued, he would appoint them all. Of course, if Trudeau was not keeping track, others were. On one occasion, when a meeting of prominent Canadian Jewish leaders was held in Ottawa, Trudeau extended an invitation for the group to join him, plus several of his ministers and officials, for a late afternoon get-together at the prime minister's residence. There was only one precondition. At Trudeau's request, the event was to remain informal. There were to be no speeches or presentations. Nevertheless, one of Trudeau's Jewish guests, moved by the sense of occasion, proposed a formal toast to the prime minister for all he had done on behalf of Canadian Jews. Trudeau protested that he had done nothing deserving of such a toast. His guest begged to differ. Just think of all the Jews recently appointed to positions of prominence, he asserted, and started to rhyme off a lengthy list of political, judicial, committee, and public service appointments. Trudeau, perhaps embarrassed, cut the speaker short with a curt 'Yes, that is a lot of Jews, isn't it?'[26]

The Trudeau who likely regarded this kind of ethnic bean counting as wrong-headed was also the Trudeau who introduced the 1971 federal multicultural policy. If some might see this as a contradiction, Trudeau did not. Without denying there was more than a little politics behind the timing of the multicultural policy statement, it is also important to note that Trudeau regarded matters of ethnicity and religion a private matter. He was certainly amenable to individual citizens and groups celebrating their identity as they pleased, or at least as long as it did not interfere with others exercising their rights and freedoms. This was at the heart of the 1971 multicultural policy statement as Trudeau understood it. But so too was the equally important assertion in the statement that there should be no barriers erected by the state against participation in the state because of religion, heritage, or identity. If some might see multiculturalism as a licence for ethnic or religious self-ghettoization, for Trudeau, multiculturalism was an affirmation of the right of every Canadian, regardless of religion, heritage, race, or national origin to participate in all aspects of society. Perhaps the simplest articulation of multiculturalism was to live and let live.[27]

Of course, ethnic communities had their own corporate interests and lobbied government with respect to those interests. Jews were no exception. Trudeau's accession to power in 1968 – a year after the Six Day War and less than a decade into the Quiet Revolution – coincided with a shift in Jewish communal interests. It was not so much that the core issues which had previously dominated the Jewish communal agenda were resolved or set aside. This was not the case. Antisemitism in all its forms and the place of Jews in the new Quebec remained very much at the fore.[28] In the past, however, mainstream Jewish leaders were possessed by the notion that the key to winning public support, especially in the Jewish community's struggle against antisemitism, was to paint a portrait of Canadian Jews as a respectable and responsible faith community no different than any other. After 1967, the Canadian Jewish embrace of Israel and the parallel priority given to support Jews under threat by repressive regimes spoke not to the sameness of Canadian Jews but to Jewish particularism and the transcendent nature of Jewish peoplehood. Yes, Canadian Jews were Canadians, entitled to equal protection under the law. But as Jews they could not and would not deny their responsibility to other Jews with whom they shared bonds of history and destiny.

How did this translate in the era of Trudeau? Domestically, the organized Jewish community remained uneasy at the growth of nationalist and separatist sentiment in Quebec and what they might portend for the future of Jewish life in the province.[29] Reassuring to Canadian Jews was Trudeau's unswerving hostility to ethnic and religiously based nationalism and his support of federalism.[30] And what of the Jewish embrace of Israel? The organized Jewish community might appreciate that Trudeau's stated position on federalism was both clear and consistent, but it was far less clear what his government's position would be on Israel or how his government might respond to the plight of Jews in distress? Immediately after Trudeau's victory, a *Canadian Jewish News* editorial described the new prime minister as 'an idealist and a man of definite opinions.' With regard to Quebec, the *Canadian Jewish News* explained, 'The new Prime Minister firmly believes in a kind of progressive Canadian nationalism, in forging one nation out of many. He sees no need to offer Quebec a special position as a cultural entity.' Beyond his commitment to federalism, the editorial confessed, there was little to indicate where Trudeau would take Canada, especially when it came to foreign-policy issues. 'We do not know exactly what his position is on NATO; on its continuation of friendship with the United States, our good neighbor; on our cultural rapport with France; last but not least, on the Middle East.'[31]

The post-election issue of the *Canadian Jewish News* also carried a front-page report that a group of prominent Jewish Liberals who had supported Trudeau 'during his successful campaign for leadership of the liberal party [*sic*]' hoped to organize a meeting with the new prime minister to discuss Middle East issues.[32] If this private meeting took place, it was just that, private and off the record. However, a little more than a month later, in mid-May, the prime minister made his first public post-election comment on the Middle East. Addressing a Jewish National Fund dinner in Montreal honouring the twentieth anniversary of Israel's founding, the prime minister affirmed Canada's support for Israel's right to exist within secure borders. 'The State of Israel was created in conformity with a decision of the United Nations and it has a right to live in peace, and all peace-loving nations must stand by Israel and protect that right.' The *Canadian Jewish News* took this to be a reaffirmation of the Pearson policy of even-handedness, of support for Israel's right to exist behind secure borders, but not for Israel's continued occupation of lands captured in 1967.[33]

What were Trudeau's private views on Israel? According to Allan Gotlieb, one of his closest foreign-policy advisers and a supporter of Israel, Trudeau was a man who 'began with first principles.' And as a first principle, Trudeau embraced the value of inclusive citizenship and, therefore, was hostile to narrow and parochially defined nationalism. He also supported the concept of national sovereignty. It followed that Israel, like Canada, had the right and duty to exercise its sovereignty within secure and recognized borders. As a sovereign state it also had the right and duty to defend itself and its citizens against aggression from sources foreign and domestic. But though Trudeau genuinely appreciated Israel's struggle to maintain its sovereignty and sympathized with Israel's proactive defence of that sovereignty from those who would destroy it, in no way can Trudeau be described as a closet Zionist. He was especially leery of a Zionism that preached ethnic exclusivity and grounded itself in parochial narrowness. But in his own way, according to Gotlieb, Trudeau also admired Israel. He saw it as a 'plucky' state that left no doubt about its readiness to defend its

national sovereignty. While Canada faced no external threats comparable to those that confronted Israel, Trudeau was convinced that Canada
could face a no less pernicious challenge to its national sovereignty,
separatism. If that threat were to become dangerous enough, Trudeau
would have no compunction about Canada defending itself with equal
determination.[34]

As to the relationship of Canadian Jews with Israel, according to Barney Danson, Trudeau's parliamentary secretary and later a member of
cabinet, the prime minister certainly understood that, given the unique
circumstances of Jewish history, Canadian Jews would take pride in Israel and offer it material and spiritual assistance. However, there were
limits. Support of Israel was fine so long as it did not blind Jews to reason or threaten Canadian or Liberal Party interests. To Danson's mind,
'Trudeau understood the roots of community [support of Israel] and its
concerns, but when it went over to nationalism he'd find it anathema
and tuned it out.'[35]

The problem for the organized Jewish community and its fledgling
Canada-Israel Committee was not knowing what that tipping point
was. Of course, Canada was hardly a heavy hitter in the Middle East,
although it did have an interest in the peaceful resolution of Middle
East tensions that eroded stability in the region.[36] Canada also had an
interest in reducing points of friction between the major powers that
might be drawn into any Middle East crisis. In this regard, according
to Mitchell Sharp, Trudeau's foreign affairs minister, Canada sought to
play the role of honest broker, trying 'to follow an evenhanded policy
toward Israel and its neighbors.' Some Israeli policy imperatives, including continuing the occupation of and beginnings of Jewish settlement on the West Bank, were regarded as impediments to stability in
the region.[37]

With the mainstream Jewish community not only committed to the
existence of a Jewish state but also supporting the policies and actions
of that state, there was an inevitable friction with the Trudeau government. And the community's pro-Israel lobbying effort, most often represented by the newly organized Canada-Israel Committee, made the
case for Israel, sometimes to positive effect, sometimes less so.[38] If the
CIC was not always as effective in advocating for Israel in Ottawa as
it might have wanted, it gradually developed the skills on how best
to reach, and it was hoped, positively influence parliamentarians and
opinion makers in Israel's favour. Much of the CIC's day-to-day energy
went into pro-Israel education of members of parliament and court-

ing media support. Of course, the CIC did not have a monopoly on pro-Israel advocacy. When a crunch issue arose – possible Canadian recognition of the PLO, PLO participation in a planned UN conference in Toronto, Canadian business collusion in the Arab economic boycott of Israel, contentious Canadian votes at the United Nations – some in the organized Jewish community were not content to sit back and allow the CIC to speak for them. They insisted on elbowing their way into debate, creating, according to Danson, more heat than light. The problem, recalls Danson, was not that the Jewish community lobbied and lobbied hard. That was expected. It was that without a clear and authoritative voice, the Jewish community message could become lost in what sometimes seemed a cacophony of badgering which tended to get officials' backs up. Even parliamentarians who were sympathetic to Israel were sometimes put off by all the unrelenting pro-Israel drumming. When cabinet dealt with Israel-related issues, Danson noted, some ministers expressed resentment at the lobbying overkill they were subjected to and the amount of cabinet time given over to Israel at the expense of other pressing legislative or administrative matters. This grumbling did not serve the pro-Israel lobby well. While some community representatives such as Saul Hayes, a consummate diplomat, were highly effective and respected for keeping 'relations on a civilized level,' others who could not even take 'yes' for an answer were regarded as a pain in the ass.[39]

As a politician, Trudeau well understood the place of lobbying in the democratic process. He also understood that there were political and constituency considerations to be factored in when responding to approaches from community-based organizations. Nevertheless, according to those who knew him, Trudeau was often put off by hard-sell or bullying tactics and was especially distrustful of those he regarded as parochially short-sighted in their advocacy of narrowly defined nationalist causes – whether from within the Jewish community, from sovereigntists in Quebec, or from others pressing their own brand of ethnic particularism. All the more so if partisans of a particular cause, no matter how frustrated by a lack of positive response from government or the larger public, resorted to political threats or, in violation of the law and the democratic process, turned to violence.

An obvious domestic case in point was Trudeau's response to the 1970 October crisis. After the kidnapping of a British diplomat and the murder of a Quebec cabinet minister by radical separatists, Trudeau invoked the War Measures Act, which granted the police sweeping emergency powers of arrest and detention. The Jewish take on the October crisis is worth noting. While many civil libertarians decried the application of the War Measures Act as an uncalled-for denial of basic rights, the move had the support of most Montreal Jews. Naomi Alboim found this out first hand. After the kidnapping of British Trade Commissioner James Cross by members of the 'Liberation Cell' of the Front de Libération du Québec (FLQ) on 5 October and before the kidnapping of Quebec vice-premier and minister of labour Pierre Laporte by members of the 'Chenier cell' of the FLQ on 10 October (his body was discovered a week later), Alboim and four friends active in Zionist activities at McGill drove down to Pennsylvania for a week-long student Zionist gathering. Cut off from news at home, she and the other Canadians knew nothing of the expanding crisis or the federal government's imposition of the War Measures Act on 16 October.

When the student meetings ended, Alboim and her friends drove back to Montreal, the car's trunk stuffed with suitcases, school books, and some Zionist pamphlets intended for distribution on Montreal campuses. The five Montreal students talked and sang the whole way home, not bothering to turn on the radio. They only realized that something was amiss after crossing the border and driving into Montreal. Streets were empty of traffic. As they were stopped at a red light, a car with two men pulled up alongside the students. Before the light could turn green, the two men donned police hats, got out of their car – an unmarked police vehicle – and began questioning the students. Who were they? Where were they going? Where had they been? The driver explained they were university students coming home from a conference in the United States. What kind of conference, demanded the police? A Zionist conference. The police appeared a little confused. Why, the police demanded, were these students violating curfew? Unaware that under the War Measures Act a curfew had been imposed on the city, the students protested they were university students, too old to have a curfew. At that the police ordered the students to open the car's trunk. Rummaging through the trunk the police found copies of a French-language pamphlet entitled 'Terrorism' with stylized blood dripping from the letters of the title. The pamphlet about Arab terrorism was being brought back from the conference to be handed out at Montreal's French-language universities. In addition, the police found several school books the students had taken with them to the conference, including several copies of FLQ founder Pierre Vallières's 1968 book *Nègres blancs d'Amérique* (translated into English as *White Niggers of America*) comparing the situation of French Canadians to that of Afro-Americans living under segregation. The book, which argued for the right to armed struggle, might have been regarded a revolutionary tract by the police, but it was assigned reading in many Canadian history and Canadian studies courses at McGill. In addition, one student in the car, a fine arts major, had with him a book about cubism – mistakenly taken by the police to be a book about Cuba.

Thinking they might have uncovered a cache of subversive material, the police escorted the five to a crowded downtown emergency detention centre. The students were refused a lawyer or permission to phone home and passed several hours before a senior police official decided that the five English-speaking Jewish students, their school books, and Zionist pamphlets did not constitute a threat to the security of Canada. They were all let go.

Alboim, angered by what she felt was an arbitrary and unjust exercise of police power, arrived home to find her parents beside themselves with worry at what might have become of their daughter. They had expected her hours earlier. Alboim explained what had happened, expecting that her parents, staunch civil libertarians, would share her indignation. They didn't. Relieved that she was safe, they were also totally supportive of Trudeau and his imposition of the War Measures Act. Their daughter's detention was but a necessary 'inconvenience.' Instead of being angry, they were reassured. The police were being vigilant in defending society against the FLQ.[40]

Alboim's parents were not alone. While Montreal Jewish Federation official Manny Weiner recalls that there were dissident civil-libertarian voices in the Jewish community outraged at Trudeau's imposition of the War Measures Act, the majority of Montreal Jews, he agrees, were 'very frightened' of the FLQ and were grateful for Trudeau's firm hand. More than that, according to Joe King, historian of Montreal Jews, Jews simply trusted Trudeau and felt 'he would never go against Jewish interests.' If Trudeau felt the War Measures Act was necessary, as far as most Montreal Jews were concerned, it was necessary and they appreciated Trudeau's firmness of action.[41]

Of course, Trudeau did not put ethnic-group lobbying in the same camp as the violently threatening actions of the FLQ. However, ethnic advocacy could and did sometimes cause political headaches for the government that could potentially have driven a wedge between the Liberal government and some 'ethnic' voters, including Jews. After 1967 Israel was not the only item on the organized Canadian Jewish community's lobbying agenda. Other issues included the need for tough national anti-hate legislation, for long overdue action against Nazi war criminals who had found haven in Canada after the Second World War, and for Canadian intervention on behalf of oppressed and beleaguered Jews behind the Iron Curtain and in Arab lands.[42]

Israel, however, was a singularly front-burner issue. And it was sometimes hard for the government or even the Jewish community to draw a fixed line between pro-Israel advocacy and other important areas of organized Jewish community concern. While agenda items seemed to overlap or run together, there was a basic difference between pro-Israel advocacy and advocacy on other issues. As Israel's occupation of Arab lands continued and the building of Jewish settlements slowly began, Israel became a harder and harder sell. What is more, the pro-Israel lobby suddenly found it did not have a monopoly on concern for Israel or Middle East–related issues. As the occupation of the West Bank continued, as opposition to the occupation increased, and as Israel began to encourage Jewish settlement on the West Bank, pro-Israel activists in Canada faced a gathering storm of anti-Israel opposition. Forrest and his *United Church Observer* may have been first off the mark, but the battle was soon joined by others opposed to Israel and its policies.[43] While these post-1967 anti-Israel voices often came across as shrill and even more disorganized than those of the pro-Israel lobby, they too were granted the government's ear.[44]

Without a monopoly voice in advocating on Canada's Middle East policy, the Canada-Israel Committee had its hands full. And even as it worked steadily to build support for Israel and improve bilateral relations between Canada and Israel, crisis issues sometimes demanded special action. Of increasing concern were the deteriorating situations of beleaguered Jews in Arab lands and behind the Iron Curtain. With the Eichmann revelations and the 1967 crisis still fresh in their minds, the organized Jewish community felt duty-bound to press the Canadian government for its assistance in easing that oppression. Two instances in the early years of Trudeau's lengthy tenure as prime minister are especially noteworthy. Exploring them in some detail reveals both how far the Canadian Jewish agenda had shifted from its pre-1967 base and how open Trudeau and his government were, not only to Jews but also to the possibility of strategic intervention to afford relief for individuals suffering egregious human rights violations. One case involved efforts by the Jewish community to engage the Trudeau government in jump-starting emigration of Jews from the Soviet Union, the other a government response to Jewish appeals on behalf of the endangered Jewish community of Iraq.

The situation of Iraqi Jews, estimated at approximately 6000 in the mid-1960s, deteriorated rapidly after Israel's victory in the Six Day War and the accession to power of the Ba'ath Party in Iraq under Hassan al-Bakr following a coup in July 1968. The Jewish community's situation reached crisis levels when, shortly after taking power, the new Ba'athist regime announced it had smashed a Zionist spy ring. A 'Revolutionary Tribunal' set up to deal with the accused spies held secret trials and found fourteen men, nine of them Jews, guilty of treason. All were sentenced to death by public hanging. International appeals for clemency, and for a public review of the trial evidence and procedures, fell on deaf ears. The hangings were marked by celebration. 'At dawn on January 27 [1969], the men were hanged, one by one, from tall wooden gallows in a macabre celebration in Liberation Square. They were dressed in red prison garb ... Baghdad Radio summoned the mob to "come and enjoy the feast." Some 500,000 men, women and children paraded and danced past the scaffolds and through the city to rhythmic chants of "Death to Israel" and "Death to All Traitors."'[45] The arrests, secret trials, and public executions did not end the terror for Iraqi Jews. Reports out of Iraq told of Jews being abducted in the streets, never to be heard from again. Jewish professionals were dismissed from jobs and Jewish businesses boycotted. Jewish children were expelled from schools. Jewish property was confiscated by the state or looted as police stood by watching. And there was no escape. Denied exit visas, Iraq became a Jewish prison.[46] Eyewitnesses later testified as to what happened to them and other Jewish men, women, and children picked up by Iraqi security police for 'questioning' about alleged Zionist connections. Only twelve years old when she was detained by Iraqi security police, one Iraqi Jewish woman recalled the brutality she and others endured while in police custody.

Beating with their hands wasn't the only thing they knew. No, they had other ways, they would tie my hands with a rope and beat me with a rubber stick and a nail all over my body (I have scars on my nape), I had long hair but it didn't last long. It was cut with a knife and then pulled out of my head. They continued beating me and then left me in a small room (dungeon). During these events I lost track of time. I do not wish to describe the cruel tormented measures that I experienced not to mention the gang rape committed with a 12-year-old Jewish girl and the joy expressed after doing so.

They put me inside a room where a man whom they had informed me I had known and would be happy to see him, but when I arrived to the room I saw a Jewish boy in his twenties and discovered that all over his body there were burn marks. He had no hair and no nails, he in fact was hardly breathing and could hardly open his eyes.[47]

Canada joined a chorus of Western nations condemning Iraq's gross violations of human rights. Gratifying as these condemnations might be, Western Jewish leaders, like Iraqi Jews, knew full well that international protest, while important, would not end anti-Jewish abuse. Few doubted that the Iraqi government would continue its systematic persecution so long as it furthered the regime's interests. And what were those interests? To the new Ba'athist regime, shaky in its control, attacking Jews served to solidify its popularity even as it afforded an object lesson to would-be opponents about what could await them if they challenged the new Iraqi rulers. And what about the Jews of Iraq? The only sure remedy to their suffering was for them somehow to leave Iraq. That seemed an impossible dream. Without the Iraqi regime's acquiescence, there could be no wholesale exodus of Iraqi Jews. And what could induce the Iraqis to allow its Jews to leave?

Enter Canada. Only a few days after the public hangings in Baghdad, Mitchell Sharp, Canadian minister of state for external affairs, and Saul Hayes, executive director of the Canadian Jewish Congress, met in Ottawa. An old and skilled hand at Ottawa politics, Hayes was well respected on Parliament Hill as a thoughtful, diplomatic, and articulate spokesperson for Jewish community interests. For his part, Sharp, whose Toronto riding was second only to Prime Minister Trudeau's Mount Royal riding in percentage of Jewish voters, prided himself on being well informed on Jewish issues. It would be a surprise if he wasn't. A prominent and committed Congress insider, Sol Kanee, was one of Sharp's fundraisers and a close political confidant. Given Kanee's close relationship with Sharp and Hayes's own reputation, it was small wonder that Hayes was granted the minister's ear.[48]

Of course, after some thirty years of lobbying in Ottawa, Hayes well knew there was a big difference between access to a minister and positive ministerial action on any particular issue. But having the minister's ear had its value, and when the two men met, with macabre images of the public hangings in Baghdad fresh in mind, the crisis of Iraqi Jews was Hayes's top priority. He hoped to convince the minister that Canada should take the lead at the United Nations in condemning Iraq and ensuring the persecution of Iraqi Jews was not brushed under the Middle East carpet. Hayes began by expressing gratitude for Canada's earlier condemnation of the Baghdad hangings. He then updated Sharp with what was known about extensive and ongoing human rights violations still being visited upon Iraqi Jews. Hayes urged that Canada take the lead in keeping the mistreatment of Iraqi Jews on the radar screen of Western states and use its good relations with developing states to bring them onside in pressuring Iraq to ease up. In something of an afterthought, Hayes mused that Canada might offer itself as a sanctuary for Iraqi Jews should Iraq ever reopen its borders to Jewish emigration. Hearing Hayes out, Sharp promised that he would consult with his officials on what more Canada could do to ease the plight of Iraqi Jews.

At most, Hayes hoped that Canada's United Nations delegation would continue to protest the mistreatment of Jews to Iraqi authorities and encourage other states to do the same. Hayes likely expected nothing to come from his suggestion that Canada offer Iraqi Jews sanctuary. It was counter-intuitive to imagine that Iraq would permit its Jews to leave, let alone agree to their wholesale resettlement in Canada. And there was nothing to indicate that Canada would consider such a resettlement project. The idea was a pipe dream, and Hayes knew it even as he suggested it.[49]

Or was it? Unbeknownst to Hayes, his sanctuary idea struck a responsive chord with Sharp. The minister knew that any positive Canadian initiative on behalf of Iraqi Jews would play well with his Jewish constituents, but that was not what first sparked his interest in the idea. More important, Iraqi persecution of its Jews was such a grievous violation of human rights that Sharp was convinced Trudeau would be onside with a bold-stroke Canadian initiative, so long as it held promise of success. Was Sharp right? On assuming power, Trudeau gave little indication of what his foreign policy direction might be. He was said to be 'sceptical about assigning the country any large international role,' and, as a result, began edging away from Pearson's active internationalism and new, high-profile peacekeeping commitments. But if Trudeau did not see Canada exercising a pre-eminent foreign affairs role, he did have broad foreign policy priorities. Uneasy at the direction of American foreign policy, Trudeau was concerned to avoid 'excessive dependence' on the United States or entanglements in American foreign policy adventures. An independent foreign policy, he hoped, would also allow Canada to promote bilateral discussions with other countries with an eye to defusing cold war tensions.

If Trudeau's foreign policy priorities were practical, they also reflected something of a romantically idealistic streak. Just as Trudeau regarded himself as a voice for rational discourse in international relations and human rights, he also held that Canada, even as it respected the sovereignty of other states, should advocate for human rights in the international arena.[50] The oppression of Iraqi Jews was nothing if not an egregious violation of human rights. Given Trudeau's human rights concerns, Sharp felt he could count on his support for a Canadian immigration initiative on behalf of the Jews of Iraq – so long as it offered realistic hope of success and did not negatively impact other areas of policy concern.[51]

There was also a timely precedent. Canada had only just finished doing well while doing good in the successful resettlement of 12,000 Czech refugees. They were part of a larger wave of refugees who escaped Czechoslovakia after Soviet troops crushed Alexander Dubček's short-lived 1967 'Prague Spring' reformist regime, snuffing out all hope of democratic liberalization. Canada also had positive experience with the admission of Jews from Muslim lands. Approximately 11,000 Moroccan Jews had resettled in Canada, most in Montreal, in the early 1960s. The organized Jewish community had been active in offering support to that immigration. There was every reason to suppose the Jewish community would offer the same assistance to any Iraqi arrivals.[52]

If Sharp had any concerns that a Canadian initiative to bring Iraqi Jews to Canada would spark political opposition in Parliament, it was soon set aside. During question period in the House of Commons, the Conservative foreign affairs critic, almost certainly briefed on Canadian Jewish concerns by Hayes, asked the external affairs minister why Jews of Iraq and other Arab lands should not be accorded the same kind of welcome that Canada gave Czech refugees? The minister, not unhappy with the question but measuring his words, replied that the government had received 'representations' on this matter and was giving them 'serious consideration.'[53]

While the minister's answer was officially non-committal, he was in fact revealing as much in public as he dared. He had quietly instructed his officials to draw up a contingency plan for Canada to offer itself as a haven for Iraqi Jews. With a green light from Sharp, officials in External

Affairs met with their counterparts in the Department of Immigration to discuss how Canada might convince Iraq to allow the immigration to Canada of all Iraqi Jews who might choose to leave. The obstacles to any successful Iraqi Jewish emigration plan were formidable and the recently completed Czech resettlement program offered no model that could be followed in this case. In the confusion of the Soviet overthrow of Dubček, thousands of Czech refugees escaped across the frontier into Austria. There international agencies pre-screened and processed the refugees for transfer to Canada and other willing refugee-receiving states. Iraqi Jews, however, were inside Iraq. No resettlement scheme, no matter how much Canada was willing to be part of it, would work if Iraq was not prepared to cooperate by allowing its Jews to leave. And what would induce the Iraqi government to allow the departure of its Jews? For that matter, how would Iraq respond to official Canadian representations on behalf of Iraqi Jewish emigration? Would the intervention be taken seriously or rejected as unwelcome meddling in Iraq's internal affairs? Would it be denounced by Iraq as the West pandering to Jewish interests or acting as a stalking horse for Israel? Even worse, in the charged political climate of Iraq, if the Iraqi regime proved negative to any Canadian initiative, as well it might, would that make the situation of Iraqi Jews more precarious? Certainly any approach to the Iraqis had to be made very carefully and discreetly. And what pretext was there for a Canadian approach to Iraq? Here again, Canada had to tread gently. It was unlikely that Iraq would approve the wholesale departure of its Jews if it would be interpreted as Iraq bending to international protest at its treatment of Jews.

Canadian external affairs officials reasoned that perhaps the first approach to Iraq regarding Jewish emigration should not even be made by Canada. Might an approach work better if made by a neutral intermediary – the Red Cross or the United Nations High Commissioner for Refugees? If a sounding on Jewish departures was not rebuffed, Canada then could enter the picture, ostensibly at the behest of the intermediary, and offer itself as a destination. In addition, if the Red Cross or the UNHCR would front for Canada, it might also make it easier to convince other sympathetic Western countries to sign on to a multilateral resettlement initiative. Canadian officials quietly flagged Holland and New Zealand as possible intake partners.

What of Israel? Would the government of Iraq allow the Jews to exit without stipulating that, if they went to Canada, they would not simply use Canada as a temporary way station en route to Israel? That could be a bit sticky. Canada of course does not refuse anyone the right to leave the country for anywhere in the world. This being the case, it was hoped that Israel would see it to be in its own interests, and those of Iraqi Jews, to forgo scoring propaganda points against Iraq should any Iraqi Jews ricochet from Canada to Israel. In this regard, would Canadian Jewish leaders intercede with Israel, asking it to withhold public comment on any Iraqi rescue program? And for that matter, what role would the Canadian Jewish community agree to play in any Iraqi resettlement program?[54]

With these questions still to be resolved, Canadian Jewish Congress leaders were invited to an off-the-record meeting with the minister of external affairs on 14 February 1969. Taking the delegation into his confidence, Sharp laid out his intention to seek cabinet approval for an as yet undefined immigration initiative on behalf of Iraqi Jews. He cautioned Jewish leaders that if anything were to come of the effort, responsibility for negotiating and organizing any resettlement program must remain with Canada. Israel could be seen to play no role, nor should it. For that matter, the Canadian Jewish community must also avoid making public comment on any departure of Jews from Iraq. According to the minster, the choice was between 'publicity and "practical results."' All communication with the press and media was to be handled by the government.

Congress leadership promised to keep all discussion of the Canadian initiative in-house. That did not mean the Jewish community could not or would not publicly protest the mistreatment of Iraqi Jews. A community protest was already in the works. Jewish tradition holds that for three weeks following the week of *shiva* – the *shloshim* or thirty days after death – mourners return to work and gradually resume normal activities and attend daily synagogue services to recite the *kaddish* prayer, but refrain from public entertainment or social activities. Jewish tradition also teaches that pain at the loss of a human life is not limited to the deceased's family alone. It is shared by the entire community. Accordingly, across Canada synagogues were asked to set aside the last Saturday in February to mark the end of the *shloshim* mourning period for the Jews publicly hanged by Iraqi authorities. Acting as a single community of mourners, congregations across Canada stood as one to recite the *kaddish*. But in accord with Sharp's call for secrecy, comment on any Canadian action on behalf of Iraqi Jews was avoided. As the executive director of the Canadian Jewish Congress office in Winnipeg quietly instructed, '*no public demonstrations* should be organized until further notice, pending a government decision on the possible [immigration] of Jews from Arab lands.'[55]

Even as the Jewish community prepared to mark the *shloshim*, Sharp updated the prime minister and cabinet on the possible removal of Iraqi Jews to Canada. Cabinet authorized Sharp to move on the Iraqi scheme as a human rights priority, but remained cautious as to process and procedure. Cabinet suggested that Iraq might prove more amenable to the departure of its Jews if during bilateral discussions Canada allowed that it was not just concerned for Jewish emigration, but was ready to engage with Iraq on enlarging possibilities for Canada-bound immigration by Iraqi Muslims, Christians, and Jews alike. If, in the end, Iraq allowed the Jews to leave, this opening could give Iraqi authorities the fig-leaf cover that the movement of Jews was neither a privileged emigration for Jews nor a retreat in the face of international pressure. It was a first step in a larger bilateral opening on immigration between Iraq and Canada.[56]

With cabinet approval, an interdepartmental working group began drawing up a final detailed action plan to be presented to cabinet for final approval. As the group began its work, the option that Canada might be able to partner with one or more sympathetic Western states was removed from the table. Canada's most likely partner, the Netherlands, informed External Affairs it had concluded that any approach to the Iraqis at that moment would be 'counter productive.'[57] Canadian officials might also have been privately concerned the Iraqis were likely to reject any approach on the emigration of Jews, but certainly it was important to try. There were still a number of bureaucratic snags to be ironed out. Immigration and external affairs officials agreed that the removal of Iraqi Jews to Canada was a humanitarian priority, but, presupposing that Iraqi cooperation was needed, there were interdepartmental differences with regard to how Canadian visa procedures should be applied in the case of Iraqi Jews. External affairs officials favoured waiving routine Canadian immigration procedures, as had been done for the Czechs, if doing so would help expedite the movement of Jews. External Affairs also suggested that Jews might 'be inhibited from applying for exit permits through fear of subsequent persecution should they fail to gain [Canadian] admittance.'

Immigration officials, by contrast, were disinclined to set aside their rules and regulations. Iraq, they argued, might be more agreeable to Jewish departures if Canada was seen to handle any Jewish exodus as a routine immigration matter, not a rescue scheme. Regular procedures need not be time-consuming or cumbersome. Immigration authorities pledged to bend over backwards to approve every application as soon as it came in. There would be no problems and no red tape.[58]

What about the initial approach to Iraq? All agreed the best bet was to enlist the cooperation of the UNHCR. As one Canadian official suggested, the UNHCR might best be able to sell the Iraqis on the notion of Canada taking off their hands 'a group of people who might be causing their government concern.' It was also affirmed that the cone of secrecy surrounding any movement of Iraqi Jews to Canada would be kept in place until the removal scheme had 'either been rejected [by the Iraqi government] or accepted and implemented.'[59]

When and if the Iraqi government agreed to the departure of Iraqi Jews, it was also understood the government would move quickly with an on-the-ground action plan. Part of that would require making it known to Iraqi Jews that they were welcome to apply to leave for Canada and could do so without fear of Iraqi reprisals. But could Canada feed this information to Iraqi Jews? Almost certainly the Iraqi government could not be counted on to publicize any Jewish emigration program, and it was unclear if the Canadian government would be welcome to do so. Here, officials believed, was a critical role for the Canadian Jewish community, which was on the receiving end of a covert communication pipeline that secreted information about the persecution of Jews out of Iraq. Surely Jewish authorities could be counted on to use that same pipeline to feed Iraqi Jews information on Canadian immigration.[60]

The plan was reviewed by the minister of external affairs and his immigration counterpart. Some last-minute back-and-forth tinkering on procedural issues was still necessary to hammer out the exact wording before an agreement could be presented to Trudeau and cabinet for approval. If Iraqi cooperation was forthcoming, the final proposal pledged Canada to deal with the 'problem of Jews in Iraq as a normal immigration movement.' Recognizing the precarious position of Iraqi Jews, all understood that immigration processing would be conducted with deliberate speed. The UNHCR would be asked to begin immediate talks with the Iraqis in the hope of ensuring their cooperation and, above all, guaranteeing the security of all Jews who might apply to go to Canada. Finally, the Jewish Immigrant Aid Society assured that it stood ready to 'provide appropriate assistance' to Iraqi Jews as they arrived in Canada and that these immigrants would be settled without major public cost. The proposal was approved by cabinet on 26 June 1969, almost six months to the day after the Baghdad hangings.[61]

Even as the Trudeau cabinet approved an unprecedented plan that might rescue the entire Jewish population of Iraq, events in Iraq overtook the Canadian initiative. The Western outcry which followed the public hangings in Baghdad at first failed to convince the new and unsteady Iraqi regime that its frontal assault on the small Iraqi Jewish community was doing the government more harm than good. The fledgling government knew its attacks on Jews were popular, shoring up its support at home while warning regime opponents of what awaited them should they challenge the new rulers.

By the late spring of 1969, however, as the Trudeau cabinet approved the Iraqi Jewish rescue plan, the Iraqi regime changed its tune. If still a little shaky in its control, it was confident it had crushed much of its opposition and began to turn to other problems. Among them was the government's need for investment capital and technology to develop the country's vast potential oil wealth. It also needed to offset a separatist threat from Kurds in the country's north and repair the damaged Iraqi image in the larger community of nations. State-managed persecution of the Jews was increasingly recognized as counter-productive to these ends, most particularly to mending international fences and encouraging Western investment.

Turning down the anti-Jewish heat, Iraqi officials quietly began issuing Jews exit visas. Distrustful that they would not be punished if they applied for an exit visa, or unwilling to wait for the paperwork on visa applications to be processed, some Iraqi Jews fled northward into the Kurdish areas of the country. Here sympathetic Kurds, rumoured to be supplied arms by Israel, could be found to smuggle Jews out of Iraq and into Turkey.[62] Other Jews slipped across Iraq's southeastern border with Iran. The Iraqi regime, perhaps content to be done with its Jewish problem, may even have turned a blind eye to the illegal departure of Jews. Once out of Iraq, most Iraqi Jews made their way to Israel. Others quietly immigrated elsewhere, some to the United States, some to Holland, and some were processed for admission to Canada.

The response of the Trudeau government to the humanitarian crisis of Iraqi Jews, while unprecedented, was also in line with the principled commitment Trudeau had made to a more action-oriented human rights agenda. But Iraq was one thing, and horrific as was the situation of Iraqi Jews, Canada was not a high stakes player in the Middle

East. The Soviet Union was something else again. One of the two major world powers, it loomed large in Canadian foreign policy planning and also engaged the Canadian Jewish community. Increasingly high on the list of the organized Jewish community's priorities was the situation of Soviet Jewry. Since the end of the Second World War there had been those demanding that community leadership address the systematic Soviet repression of Jewish religious and communal life. But many mainstream leaders feared that it was too late for Soviet Jewry. The Soviet Union, they believed, had brutally but successfully assimilated the vast majority of Jews in the Soviet Union. Soviet Jews, many believed, were lost.

During the 1960s and especially after Israel's victory in the 1967 war, this view changed, and dramatically. What few had previously imagined possible, 'The Jews of Silence,' as Elie Wiesel described Soviet Jews in 1966, began to break their silence, and some openly asserted their Jewishness and expressed a love of Zion and Israel.[63] A small number even applied for permission to immigrate to Israel. Word of a sudden awakening of Jewish peoplehood behind the Iron Curtain created excitement among Western Jews. As Soviet authorities came down hard on awakening Jewish consciousness, the organized Canadian Jewish community, pressed by student activists, united in support of Soviet Jews.[64]

At its core, the emerging Soviet Jewry campaign had but one simple message: the Soviet Union must either accord Jews full and equal protection under Soviet law and those international accords to which the Soviet Union was a signatory state, including the United Nations Charter on Human Rights, or allow Jews to emigrate if they wished to do so.[65] While the campaign built gradually after 1967, one event galvanized Canadian Jewish support for Soviet Jewry. In June 1970 a desperate group denied permission to leave the Soviet Union attempted to hijack a Soviet airliner. The attempt failed. Eleven individuals, nine of them Jews, were put on trial in Leningrad. The Leningrad trial, like the Jewish spy trial in Baghdad, was attacked by Jewish observers as an antisemitic sham and travesty of justice.

On Christmas Day 1970, the court sentenced two Jews to death and the others to long prison terms. The response from Canadian Jews came fast, and there was nothing *sha shtil* about it. In Ottawa, within hours of learning about the sentencing of the Leningrad eleven, three hundred Jews collected at the Jewish Community Centre. Bundled against the winter cold, they marched to the Soviet embassy, where a hastily prepared 'Statement of Concern' was read aloud. As no Soviet official would accept the letter, it was simply left tucked into the embassy gate. In Toronto a few days later, with the temperature well below freezing, more than five thousand people jammed into City Hall Square, where a number of prominent Jews and non-Jews spoke in condemnation of Soviet antisemitism. That same evening an equally large crowd braved Montreal's bone-numbing cold to protest outside the Soviet consulate. As the gathering ended, students announced a two-week round-the-clock vigil at the consulate on behalf of Soviet Jews. In Winnipeg, on the last night of Chanukah, the mayor adjourned a council meeting so he and others might attend a Jewish community protest.

The demonstrations were capped a few days later by another march and demonstration in Ottawa, where the local Jewish community was joined by upwards of six thousand Jews bussed in from Montreal, Toronto, and the Maritimes. Had it been possible to rent more buses, organizers were convinced, the crowd would have been larger still. The throng marched from the Ottawa Jewish Community Centre to the External Affairs Building, where it waited outside as several protesters met with the minister, Mitchell Sharp, in his office. At his insistence, the minister emerged from the building to applaud 'the spirit and purpose of the mass rally.' The crowd then moved on to the Soviet embassy, where efforts to hand deliver a cable and petition were again rebuffed as fingers in the crowd pointed to faces seen peering out from behind the embassy's closed blinds. Nobody doubted that those inside heard the blast of the shofar and the singing of Hatikvah and O Canada that closed the demonstration.[66]

Local demonstrations also took place in smaller Jewish communities from coast to coast and telegrams of protest were sent to the Soviet embassy in Ottawa and to the Kremlin. On New Year's Eve, two hundred people made their way through a snow storm to join a St Catharines protest. In Hamilton, 750 community members applauded a motion to dispatch telegrams, not just to Soviet authorities, but also to Canadian External Affairs and U Thant at the United Nations, calling on them to press the Soviet Union to rescind the sentences and allow Jews to leave. Vancouver protesters gathered in front of the downtown courthouse. Addressing the crowd, a local rabbi explained the courthouse was 'chosen as the focal point of ... protest because it symbolizes the justice which has been denied in Russia, particularly to our fellow Jews.'[67]

The Soviet Union publicly dismissed the Soviet Jewry campaign as Western and Israeli cold-war gamesmanship. But the growing assertion of communal identity and pro-Israel sentiment by Soviet Jews was not so easy to dismiss. It more and more became a problem, and not just in Soviet relations with the West. The Soviet Union was home to many restive ethnic or national minorities, many of which, Soviet authorities feared, would interpret any concession to Jews as a sign of weakness on the part of the central authorities. They too might begin asserting their own ethno-national demands, undermining central authority and enfeebling the state. Farfetched though this might seem to outsiders who viewed the Soviet Union as a monolithic superpower, to Soviet leaders the threat was all too real. Their response to the unexpected awakening of Jewish identity was to suppress unauthorized expressions of Jewish peoplehood, let alone pro-Israel sentiment. Those applying to immigrate to Israel were dealt with harshly. Of course, the optics of all this was challenging. For Western consumption, the Soviet line was simply that there was no Jewish problem in the Soviet Union. Perhaps a few criminals and malcontents may have fallen victim to Western and Israeli propaganda, but in the Soviet Union all citizens, including Jews, were treated equally. This being the case, Western meddling was not appreciated. All matters to do with Soviet citizens were an internal Soviet issue and not subject to foreign interference or bilateral discussions. Case closed.

Or maybe not so closed. In the late 1960s and early 1970s the Soviet Union, experiencing a sluggish economy, slipping behind the West's rapid technological advance and facing a breakdown in relations with China, was cautiously reaching out for better relations with the West. With talk of détente in the air, the Soviet Union sought a reduction of sabre rattling, especially on its European flank, and an increase in economic ties, scientific exchanges, and cultural contacts with the West. Progress on détente became complicated by the issue of Soviet Jews. Western nations, especially the United States, increasingly coupled the opening of better relations with an expansion of Western-style human rights within the Soviet Union, and, pressed by Western Jews, made Soviet treatment of its Jews a litmus test of Soviet commitment to those human rights. The dilemma for the Soviet Union was that simultaneously promoting détente while keeping a tight lid on the Jewish ethnic awakening was like trying to suck and blow at the same time. It couldn't be done.

As the Jewish community in Canada organized in support of Soviet Jews, it was hoped the Canadian government, which had been quietly forthcoming with regard to Iraqi Jews, would be no less positive to an appeal on behalf of Soviet Jews. That hope would soon put to the test. Shortly after assuming office, Trudeau, picking up on the spirit of détente, signalled his government's desire to thaw relations with the Soviet Union and sought to initiate positive dialogue with the Soviet government on a number of bilateral issues. As a concrete move in that direction, Trudeau announced a 1971 state visit to the Soviet Union.

The organized Canadian Jewish community saw the Trudeau visit to the Soviet Union as a possible opportunity. Might Trudeau be convinced to raise the Jewish question as part of the larger package of Canadian-Soviet discussions? Nobody expected that Trudeau would agree to act as a spokesperson for the Soviet Jewry campaign. But if he were offered a Canadian hook with regard to Soviet Jews, he just might pick up on the issue. And there was a specifically Canadian issue to address with the Soviet Union. As with Iraqi Jews, this had to do with immigration or, in the Soviet case, the state's refusal to permit Jews to emigrate. The Canadian Jewish Congress assembled a list of Soviet citizens who had been denied permission to emigrate, not to Israel, but to be reunited with family in Canada. Canadian immigration applications on behalf of all those on the Congress list had long since been filed with and approved by Canadian authorities.

In discussion with Trudeau, Saul Hayes informed the prime minister that Soviet Premier Alexei Kosygin had previously acceded to the idea of family reunification. At a press conference in Paris during a 1966 state visit to France, Kosygin was asked about Jewish immigration to Israel. He pointedly ignored any reference to immigration to Israel, but did allow that Soviet authorities would sympathetically process requests for family reunification. Kosygin proved heavy on promises but light on delivery. Soviet authorities remained anything but forthcoming with exit permits. Supplied the Canadian list of those denied permission to be reunited with sponsoring family in Canada, Trudeau agreed to request that Soviet officials facilitate their departure. In a follow-up letter to Trudeau, Saul Hayes was effusive in his thanks.

It will be no exaggeration to say that you, my dear Pierre, have already won for yourself a place in history with the new dynamic approach which you brought to your high office. I would venture to say that your role may be truly historic if you could be the instrument of Providence to help save those who are struggling against tremendous odds and which section of the community is indeed on the verge of complete attrition unless something is done to save them and done very quickly.

I want to stress once again that the issue [of immigration] is one of conscience and of humanity and it is not an attack, direct or implied, against the Soviet Union. Nothing is further from our minds that to get involved in its domestic matters. It is a deeply humanitarian problem and as such it merits, and it has, the support of much of the entire civilized world.[68]

Although Trudeau agreed to raise the family reunification issue with Soviet premier Kosygin and his officials, it was hard to read Trudeau's mind with respect to the larger Soviet Jewry campaign. Did he regard it as a legitimate Jewish community response to suppression of Jewish human rights in the Soviet Union, or an interference in the domestic affairs of another state, or a test of Soviet openness that would frame relations between the Soviet Union and both Canada and the West more generally? Interesting as it might be to know the answer to these questions, what was most important to Canadian Jewish leaders in May 1971 as Trudeau's plane set down in Moscow was that the prime minister had agreed to raise the Jewish question inside the Kremlin itself. Whether Soviet officials responded positively to Trudeau's intervention or not, they would be served notice that Canada and the West were watching.

In official diplomatic meetings, particularly with Premier Alexei Kosygin and important Soviet officials, Trudeau expressed his government's concern for the reunification of Soviet Jews with family in Canada. Once the Jewish cat was out of the diplomatic bag, Trudeau also raised other questions about human rights in the Soviet Union, including Soviet denial of the right of Jews to emigrate to Israel. Barney Danson, a member of Trudeau's entourage, recalled that the official Soviet response to any discussion of Soviet Jews was as predictable as it was unyielding. Pointedly refusing to entertain any discussion of Soviet Jews, Kosygin publicly reminded Trudeau that this was an internal Soviet matter. By attempting to raise the matter, he chided Trudeau, Canada was unacceptably interfering in the internal affairs of the Soviet Union. As a courtesy to his guest, however, Kosygin accepted the list of exit visa seekers and promised Trudeau it would be reviewed. This was interpreted by the Trudeau team as diplomatic code meaning the issue was off the table, ending official discussion of the Canadian appeal.

However, not all discussions were official or followed strict diplomatic protocol. Trudeau's Soviet visit afforded the main players downtime for informal conversation. While waiting for a meeting to begin, or during a break in scheduled proceedings, or after hours, it was not unusual for Trudeau and Kosygin, who personally got on well, to escape together, with no one except a single translator to overhear their comments. Here they spoke without attribution 'politician-to-politician and man-to-man.'[69] Trudeau later confided to Danson that the issue of Soviet Jews was among the topics the two leaders dealt with in their private discussions. But even if private, discussion was not free from political gamesmanship. Kosygin complained that a few disgruntled Jews should not be allowed to hold détente up for ransom. For his part, Trudeau explained to Kosygin that he did not want to go back to Canada without something positive to show on the Jewish issue and certainly not without something concrete on the issue of family reunification. As Kosygin well knew, Trudeau explained, this was a hot-button issue with Canadian Jewish voters, including many of Trudeau's own constituents. As a politician, Trudeau continued, Kosygin could well appreciate Trudeau's need to deliver something to this voting block. What is more, as Trudeau hinted, it would be unfortunate if disappointment over family reunification would impede progress made on other bilateral questions during the visit or scuttle the opportunity for subsequent discussion of other issues.[70]

With the issue removed from the glare of official deliberations, and couched in part as a request for a political favour and a bit of political bartering rather than a complaint about Soviet human rights violations, Kosygin could afford to be generous. According to Danson, while Kosygin was far too cagey to give away the candy store, in the months following the Trudeau visit and in preparation for a return visit by Kosygin to Canada later that same year, the Soviets began approving applications from Soviet citizens, including non-Jews, for reunification with family in Canada. In a letter to the executive vice-president of the B'nai Brith in Canada shortly after the Trudeau visit, the Canadian ambassador in Moscow noted a sudden Soviet readiness to approve the departure of those on Trudeau's list. The ambassador was guardedly optimistic about the prospects for ongoing Soviet Jewish immigration to Canada. From the list of sixty-eight names on a list supplied to Soviet authorities, three persons had already received travel documents and many more expected to receive them in short order. 'Later this autumn,' explained the Canadian ambassador, 'another list of 600 names will be presented and it is my intention to submit lists on a yearly basis. However, the procedure is too new and too fragile to permit over optimistic expectations. Nevertheless, I believe there is genuine reason for greater hope than we have had in recent history.'[71]

The ambassador's optimism was misplaced. Soviet cooperation in allowing Soviet nationals to reunify with family in Canada did not long survive Kosygin's return visit to Canada and a heating up of the cold war. However, this does not negate the fact that in both official and private conversations with Soviet officials, Trudeau gave priority to the issue of Jewish emigration. While he dared not make emigration of Jews to Canada a deal-breaker with the Soviets, he did put Canada's concern for human rights on the record with Kosygin and other Soviet leaders, much to their displeasure. And never losing sight of the immediate goal, getting the Soviets to approve the exodus of those on the list he carried with him to Moscow, of reuniting Soviet citizens with family in Canada, Trudeau cashed in some of his political chips in order to secure exit visas for those on his list.

Trudeau's personal readiness to address issues of human rights and his government's openness to individual Jews speak both to the sea change in Ottawa with respect to the place of Jews and other former 'outsiders.' It also bespeaks the shift in the organized Jewish community's priorities after 1967 – a shift marked by an embrace of Jewish peoplehood, of Israel as a defining element of Canadian Jewish identity, and of Jewish unwillingness to accept anything less than full and equal rights as Canadian citizens. Underscoring this shift was a new readiness by Jewish leaders to engage not just in professional-style lobbying of government, but in street-level protest on issues critical to the Jewish community. It remains to be seen how this new and assertive Canadian Jewish sense of self translated into the domestic arena – into battling still entrenched social discrimination and demonstrating a readiness to assert Jewish concerns at the street level.

CHAPTER SEVEN

'Let Them Have It'

Philadelphia Flyers defenceman Larry Zeidel was nicknamed 'The Rock.' No stranger to the penalty box, Montreal-born Zeidel learned early that he had to be tough to play pick-up hockey on local rinks in and around Montreal, where a Jew was best advised to think twice before stepping out onto the ice to face non-Jews with sticks. It was this same rock-hard toughness that allowed Zeidel to survive almost twenty years as a Jew in the National Hockey League. 'Hockey,' he was once quoted as saying, 'is a game of survival of the fittest. Being a Jew, I learned the ground rules for surviving earlier than most kids and it's helped me ever since.' For 'The Rock,' if surviving in the NHL meant he often had to ignore antisemitic jabs from opposition players, so be it. Name calling was just part of the game. But there were limits. When name calling gave way to intimidation, Zeidel did not to let it pass. 'I'd go for the bullies who tried to run me out of the game, and let them have it.'[1]

Zeidel 'let them have it' on 7 March 1968. That day Philadelphia and Boston faced off against each other in Toronto's Maple Leaf Gardens because Philadelphia's home rink was under repair. Halfway through the first period Larry Zeidel let Boston Bruins' Eddie Shack 'have it' in a wild stick-swinging melee that sent both players off the ice, bruised and bleeding. The fight continued off the ice. The press reported Zeidel had to be physically restrained from going after Shack again while the two players were being stitched up by a doctor. What caused the fight? Speaking to the press after the incident, Zeidel claimed that the Bruins had a history of needling him with anti-Jewish taunts. He usually shrugged it off. '"If they call you a dirty Jew, or something like that, so what?" he said. "They say the same thing about Frenchmen. It's the violent world of hockey, right? Trying to shake you up verbally to break your concentration is all part of the game."' But this time it was different. This time Ziedel felt the insults from the Boston bench were not so much directed against him as against the memory of the millions murdered at the hands of the Nazis. Zeidel explained, 'When they start saying things like: we'll carry you out on a slab and send you to the gas chamber, and there's an enforcer on the ice trying to lay you out, that's another thing.' And that other thing was that Zeidel's parents were 'from the old country.' His grandparents were murdered by the Nazis. While Zeidel later acknowledged that Shack did not personally participate in the Holocaust jeering, Shack was the Bruins' enforcer. As far as Zeidel was concerned, the reason why Shack was sent onto the ice was to put muscle behind the gas-chamber jabs. When Shack and Zeidel collided, all hell broke loose.[2]

NHL president Clarence Campbell hauled both Shack and Zeidel onto the carpet for fighting. The players were each fined $300 and suspended, Shack for three games and Zeidel for four. But the incident did not end there. The on-ice fight was not a simple dust-up in the heat of a game. It was a very public antisemitic incident. A *Toronto Star* editorial demanded the NHL purge the league of racially repugnant behaviour and name-calling. Mocking the Holocaust, the editorial protested, was 'enough to make the blood run cold ... There should be no place in civilized society for remarks of this kind.'[3]

Jewish organizations also weighed in on the incident. A *Toronto Star* news story the same day as its editorial reported that the Anti-Defamation League of the B'nai Brith in the United States and the American Jewish Congress were both planning to launch probes into antisemitism and racism in the NHL. There is no evidence that these probes ever took place, but the news report could not help but cause a chill in NHL management ranks. In Toronto a spokesperson for the Jewish Labour Committee charged that 'racist invective does not qualify as good-natured needling.' The NHL should publicly discipline anyone who condones it.[4]

Since the game took place in Toronto, local Canadian Jewish Congress officials interceded with NHL management. Hoping that a little diplomatic nudging would be all the NHL needed to come down hard against on-ice racism and antisemitism, Ben Kayfetz phoned Campbell at the NHL's headquarters in Montreal. Kayfetz assumed the NHL president of all people would be offended by anyone taunting a 'Jewish player with "putting him into the gas chambers."' During the

Second World War Campbell had served with the Canadian Army. He rose through the ranks to become a lieutenant colonel and ended the war commanding the 4th Canadian Armoured Division. Following the German surrender, Campbell, with a law degree from the University of Alberta, was appointed to the Canadian War Crimes Commission and was part of the Nuremberg trial team that found Nazi Kurt Meyer guilty of executing Canadian prisoners of war.

Campbell assured Kayfetz that there would be a thorough investigation of the Zeidel incident and, by implication, promised the NHL would take steps to root out racism and antisemitism. In a follow-up letter to Campbell, Congress reassured the NHL president that it had no argument with the fight-related fine and suspension Campbell had imposed on Zeidel and Shack. That was a matter internal to the league and not 'germane' to Congress's concern. The issue for Congress, as it should be for the NHL, was antisemitism. In this regard, Congress voiced its appreciation for Campbell's pledge to conduct a full investigation of the matter. 'We stress again that we welcome your intervention,' Congress stated, 'and urge that the investigation be an exhaustive one so that all facts may be available before the public and every step taken to see to it that such occurrences will never again happen.'[5]

The Canadian Jewish Congress was going to be disappointed. Whatever internal initiative Campbell might have quietly taken to deal with racism in the NHL, he had second thoughts about conducting an 'exhaustive' investigation that could turn into a free-for-all of bad press for the NHL. In addition to keeping the spotlight on racism in the NHL, if an investigation ended claiming racism and antisemitism were not a problem in the league or the league had the matter well in hand, there were almost certainly going to be those in the press and Jewish organizations who would claim the matter had been swept under the league carpet – bad press. If the investigation concluded there was antisemitism or racism in the NHL that needed to be addressed, that would sully the league's reputation and lead to demands for a clean-up – bad press again. Any comprehensive investigation promised a lose-lose outcome.

What the NHL needed was to put an end to bad publicity, not feed it. What the league management needed was to find a way to make the whole Zeidel affair go away, and go away fast. The problem was how to do that without making Campbell appear to be reneging on his promise to conduct a thorough investigation. The solution was artfully simple. While publicly deploring racism and antisemitism, Campbell explained that as NHL president it was his duty to deal with specific on-ice incidents, especially incidents of excessive violence in violation of the game's rules. In this case, he intended to conduct a thorough review of the single on-ice incident between Shack and Zeidel. Of course their stick-swinging violence had previously been dealt with and, as far as the NHL was concerned, dealt with firmly through fines and suspensions. The Canadian Jewish Congress had no argument with that. What remained for Campbell to deal with was the underlying cause of the fight, the thorny issue of player antisemitism. Since Zeidel had previously absolved Shack of any antisemitic utterance, Shack was personally off the hook. But there were still those antisemitic taunts, if not from Shack, then from the Bruins' bench that Campbell had promised to address. But did Campbell really want to go there? Likely not. That could rip the lid off a Pandora's box of issues to do with racism in the NHL – perhaps even expose tensions between French and English players. Better to keep a public lid on the box. But how could Campbell forestall his promised investigation?

According to the *Toronto Star*, the Philadelphia Flyers' management came to Campbell's rescue. Reportedly, while publicly affirming support for their player, decrying the kind of racial abuse Zeidel had endured at the hands of Bruins' players, and endorsing tough penalties for this kind of behaviour, Flyers' management put 'Zeidel under strict orders … to avoid further comment on the incident.' That, according to the *Star*, included discussing the matter with Campbell. The *Star*'s readers were left to conclude that Zeidel's NHL career might be in jeopardy if he continued to stir controversy. Zeidel kept silent, leaving Campbell to shrug his shoulders and claim that he was 'in a bind.' With no players talking, with the league's on-ice officials claiming that they had heard no antisemitic slurs, and without legal power to compel anyone involved to come forward with details of the incident, Campbell protested that his hands were tied. He announced, 'I can't formulate charges against any players, so it leaves me suspended in mid-air if the source isn't forthcoming.' Once again deploring bigotry of any kind, Campbell declared the investigation ended. Zeidel, his four-game suspension up, returned to his team. He retired from hockey the next season.[6]

Congress was taken aback by the NHL's now-you-see-it-now-you-don't investigation. Ben Kayfetz again phoned Campbell in hope of persuading him to pursue the matter as promised, but got nowhere. A draft letter was composed to Campbell explaining:

Our deep concern is that professional athletes who are regarded as public heroes and are adulated by youngsters should not be permitted to set a style of behaviour which is reprehensible. We cannot regard it as a matter of course, nor should any civilized human being, that people should indulge in the use of derogatory and obscene epithets in respect to race, religion or national origin. We especially refuse to believe that taunts referring to 'gas chambers' – the connotation being plainly the mass annihilation of Jews by Hitler – can be indulged in without the most severe censure.

What should that censure be? Racist behaviour should be made a 'punishable offence under the rules [of the game]. The League seeks to limit certain acts of physical violence that occur in hockey. We feel that similar sanctions should be enacted against acts, which may not use physical force, but which degrade and humiliate the individuality and dignity of all of us.'[7] But it was all for naught. The letter was never sent. If Campbell or the Flyers' management made a behind-closed-doors commitment to eliminate racism and antisemitism in the NHL, there is no indication of it found in Congress records. For Campbell and the league, the matter was closed, at least publicly. Queried about antisemitism in the NHL, a spokesperson for the Philadelphia Flyers noted, 'There's no more anti-Semitism in the league than there is in the world.' Sadly, he may have been right.[8]

Congress's quiet diplomatic approach to the NHL in the Zeidel affair fell flat. The NHL seemed more intent on dodging a public-relations bullet than on dealing with issues of on-ice racism and antisemitism, or at least was intent on not dealing with them in a publicly transparent way. If and when the league was going to clean house, it was going to do so privately, beyond media glare and without embarrassment to the organization or negative impact on its bottom line.

What about the Jewish community? Sandbagged by the NHL, Congress insiders concluded there was no point in pursuing the matter. The incident faded from memory. But the notion that quiet diplomacy of the kind applied in the Zeidel affair had its limits was not lost on a new breed of younger and more confrontation-ready Jewish activists moving to the community fore. They had their own bottom line. If quiet diplomacy did not work, perhaps there were other tactics that would.

One area that might lend itself to a more in-your-face activism was anti-Jewish discrimination in elite private clubs. The exclusive and family-oriented Granite Club in Toronto was a case in point. In a 1987 letter to a friend, Richard D. Jones, a Protestant minister in Toronto and organizer of the Canadian Council of Christians and Jews, recalled an experience he had at the Granite Club some years earlier.

> Years ago at the Christmas season, the [Granite] Club president entertained me at lunch. The dining room at the Club, then on St Clair, was decorated for Christmas and in the front had the Manger Scene with the Baby Jesus. During the luncheon conversation I asked if the Club had any Jewish members. He replied: 'Hell no, you take one and there will soon be a hundred.' I then pointed to the Baby Jesus and asked: 'How did He make it?' I do not remember the reply, but it was loaded with profanity.[9]

Of course the Granite Club was not the only private club to restrict membership. After the Second World War it was widely acknowledged that many elite private clubs across Canada denied membership to Jews. According to sociologist John Porter, this type of discrimination was an important gatekeeping device. In *The Vertical Mosaic*, Porter argued that membership in 'the clubs, exclusive and expensive as they are, [provides] an additional locus of interaction which makes for homogeneity of social type.' By restricting membership, clubs offered a closed social circle within which the privileged, who wielded social, economic, and political power, felt reassuringly surrounded by others with whom they shared a 'common outlook and common attitudes and values about the social system and place of corporate attitudes within it.'[10] Clubs were the Anglo elite's version of the union shop.

By restricting membership to all but those they regarded as their own social, ethnic, and religious kind, clubs created a comfort zone of commonality. According to sociologist Merrijoy Kelner, club 'food was terrible, but the sense of security was high.'[11] But there was more to it than that. In her study of Toronto's elite social structure, Kelner notes that 'social restrictions had the effect of containing power and prestige within a select circle,' with the goal of perpetuating itself from one generation to the next. It was in these circles that the political and economic future was written, where the daughters of the wealthy flirted with the sons of the wealthy and 'young men were selected for future leadership roles.' In the cultivated informality of these closed social circles, powerful insiders made deals that would later be formalized in corporate boardrooms or at church weddings. Those denied entry 'were at a disadvantage in their attempts to reach and maintain elitist positions.'[12]

By the late 1960s, however, some clubs, like some corporate boardrooms, were coming to the realization that exclusivity and snobbery could hobble the clubs' usefulness to members. In Toronto, for example, the wealth-generating impact of the Second World War and the economic boom it created had greatly enlarged the number of non-Anglo-Saxons who leveraged economic, political, and even social power in the community. Two Jews had even been elected mayor of Toronto. Jews and other non-WASPS were becoming political and economic powers to be reckoned with. Those private clubs which continued to hold fast to ethnic and racial exclusivity, denying membership to moneyed up-and-comers, were denying themselves the company of tomorrow's makers and shakers. In the long term, some believed, this would degrade a club's value as the power broker's home away from home and drive members to seek non-club venues to socialize with newly influential, economically resourceful and political players. To serve the needs of members, clubs would eventually have no choice but to end ethnic, racial, and religious discrimination in membership policies.[13]

Perhaps so, but 'eventually' can take a long time. Meanwhile there was resentment, certainly among Jews, and not just the moneyed elite, that entrenched social discrimination should be allowed to continue. For decades the organized Jewish community in Canada had campaigned against discrimination and for human rights in Canada. Through the 1950s and into the 1960s the Jewish community was gratified by the passage of legislation prohibiting many forms of racial and religious discrimination in the employment, accommodation, and education sectors. Most voluntary associations, professional, youth, sporting, and fraternal organizations, corporate boardrooms, and elite private clubs remained outside the scope of legislative regulation. This did not, however, make their exercise of discrimination any more acceptable to the organized Jewish community. The question was what to do about it.

In some private clubs pressure for more open membership policies came as much from club members offended by blanket rejection of Jewish membership as it did from the organized Jewish community. This was the case with the Rideau Club in Ottawa. Then located across the street from the Parliament Buildings, the Rideau Club was a watering hole for many of the capital's political, social, and business power elite. Into the 1960s it was common for Supreme Court justices to lunch in the club's dining room, often at tables separate from one another. And on any given day the justices might find themselves sharing the dining room with assorted cabinet ministers and deputy ministers. While then still a male-only bastion, the club's rules did allow members to entertain women in the dining room after seven in the evening. Women after seven. Jews never. 'The Club may have been powerful,' notes Peter C. Newman, chronicler of the Canadian elite, 'but like most of its sister institutions at the time, it was anti-semitic.' The Rideau Club's 'no-Jews' policy remained in place until 1964.[14]

The mechanism used to exclude Jews was simple – 'blackballing.' As explained by Charles Lynch in his 1990 history, *Up from the Ashes: The Rideau Club Story*, nothing in the club's rule book officially prohibited a Jew from becoming a member. Any man could be elected to membership if at least twenty-one members voted in favour of his admission. However, voting was secret and one negative vote cancelled out ten positive votes. According to the rules, any membership candidate who received fifteen negative votes was rejected, no matter what number of positive votes he received. He was eligible for nomination a second time, but once rejected a second time he was forever rejected.[15]

It was widely understood that any applicant known to be a Jew would be blackballed. This being the case, what Jew would allow his name to be put forward for membership knowing he would face the humiliation of rejection? None – unless it was not known he was a Jew. While hard to believe, Lynch notes with some amusement that both an unnamed member of parliament and Peter Newman were both granted Rideau Club membership under the 'misapprehension' that they were not Jews.[16] Membership by stealth, however, was neither possible nor acceptable to publicly known Jews. They might see the humour in Groucho Marx's self-deprecating comment that he would not want to be a member of a club that would accept him as a member, but few Jews would find anything amusing in being rejected by a club that did not want them or 'their kind' as members.

Discrimination against Jews at the Rideau Club ended in 1964, not because of pressure from Jews but as a result of a house revolt. A group of Rideau Club members, angered that membership approval for Jews was held hostage by a few antisemitic members and convinced that the majority of club members would favour a more open membership policy, challenged the blackball system. The group put forward a motion that club members elect to replace the blackball system with a nominations committee that would vet all applicants. The names of those the committee found acceptable would be posted and members invited to comment in writing. Barring any substantive reason for denying a nominee membership, club membership would be granted. And to make the reasons for their proposed change in the member-

ship process perfectly clear, the group asked four prominent Ottawa
Jews to allow their names to be put forward for membership: Ottawa
businessman, patron of the arts, philanthropist, and outspoken Zionist Lawrence Freiman; Freiman's brother-in-law Bernard Alexander, a
lawyer and businessman active in both the Ottawa Jewish community
and Ottawa cultural and charitable circles; David Golden, former pris-
oner of war in the Pacific and the first Jew appointed a federal deputy
minister; and Louis Rasminsky, economist and banking guru instrumental in the restructuring of post-war international monetary policy
at the Bretton Woods and Dumbarton Oaks conferences. After a decade
as deputy governor of the Bank of Canada, in 1961 Lester Pearson appointed Rasminsky the bank's governor. Ironically, as governor of the
Bank of Canada, Rasminsky's signature was imprinted on every dol-
lar that was spent in the Rideau Club. However, until 1964 Rasminsky,
together with the other three Jews who allowed their names to be put
forward for membership, was unwelcome to enter the club.[17] The motion passed and the four Jews were admitted as members.[18]

In welcoming Jews as members, the Rideau Club set itself off from the
anti-Jewish pack. Most elite private clubs continued to restrict membership. Speaking in the British Columbia legislature, David Barrett, the
first New Democratic Party premier of British Columbia, recalled that
when he was first elected premier in 1972 he received a card from a
downtown Vancouver club, presumably the Vancouver Club. The card
invited Barrett to become an honorary member. As a Jew he did not feel
particularly honoured.

> I phoned up the [club] secretary and said: 'Is it not true, sir, that you do not
> allow Jews in that club?' The answer was yes: 'Yes, but that policy is under
> review.' I said: 'Why did you send me the card?' 'Well, we've always had
> the Premier as an honorary member of this club.' I said, 'I'm sending you
> the card back, and when you change your policy, then I will consider be-
> ing an honorary member.'[19]

The Vancouver Club's authorized history puts something of a self-serv-
ing spin on the club's exclusion of Jews. Speaking of the club's blackball
system, the history concedes:

> The system could be abused. Despite the fact that several of the club's
> founding members [in 1889] were Jews, after the Great War there were no
> Jewish candidates proposed for membership in the Vancouver Club (and

at many other clubs across Canada for that matter) for several decades. This changed after the Second World War, but even then it was difficult for a while for a member wishing to propose a friend who was a Jew to let his name be put forward for election in case of rejection.[20]

Like Barrett, during the 1960s even the wealthiest Jews in Toronto did not need to be told where they were welcome and where not. They knew they were not welcome in the city's elite private clubs. While these clubs might claim a right to privacy and freedom of association, portraying themselves as no more than an extension of a member's living room, to Jewish leaders in the late 1960s this echoed the same racist argument that employers had previously used to deny jobs to Jews or landlords to refuse accommodation to Jews. Hard-won human rights legislation across Canada now prohibited discrimination in employment and accommodation on grounds of race, religion, or origin. Why, many asked, should private clubs be able to continue holding fast to ethnic and racial exclusivity on these same grounds?[21] As far as a new breed of Jewish community leaders was concerned, whether or not individual Jews would ever choose to become members of these clubs was not relevant. The fact that Jews could not be members just because they were Jews was the point. To accept this state of affairs, a Toronto Jewish community activist protested, was 'accepting a secondary social status for Jews as somehow "right" for the society in which we live.' If its campaign against discrimination was going to continue, the Jewish community could not accept that private clubs had the 'right' to reject Jews just because they were Jews any more than did private employers, resort owners, or the dean of the medical school at the University of Toronto.[22]

By the late 1960s the stage was set for a Jewish community punch-up over elite private clubs, and one club in particular found itself the target of dispute – Toronto's Granite Club, the city's premier family-oriented private club. While the history of desegregation differs from club to club, the Granite Club episode stands out for the symbolic importance the Granite Club held for the Toronto Jewish community. If the antisemitism of social privilege had an address in the Toronto Jewish mind, it was the Granite Club. The assault on that address began simply enough. In the 1960s, the Granite Club was much in need of new facilities. After more than forty years, the club's premises on the south side of St Clair Avenue, west of Yonge Street, were 'showing her age.' The plumbing was deteriorating and the sporting facilities were dated and in need of major repair. Retrofitting the building would prove very costly and not solve one of the club's basic problems. No amount of retrofitting would incorporate the size and kind of social and sports facilities that younger members wanted. The Granite Club needed a new building.[23]

Enter Toronto-born Sol Littman, newly appointed national director of the Anti-Defamation League of B'nai Brith Canada. Previously a constituent part of the American B'nai Brith organization, in 1964 B'nai Brith Canada separated from the American organization and began setting up a human rights advocacy program of its own. Littman was hired to lead that effort. The Canadian ADL, Littman soon discovered, was a far cry from the American ADL. The former might pay lip service to head-on confrontation with racism and antisemitism, but Littman found many local leaders 'still had a don't rock the boat, keep your head down mentality.' B'nai Brith was also a founding member with the Canadian Jewish Congress and the Zionists of the Joint Community Relations Committee mandated to deal with antisemitism. But according to Littman, the JCRC was a becalmed handmaiden of the local Canadian Jewish Congress and, like the Canadian ADL, too much given to 'quiet diplomacy' rather than head-butting combat against antisemitism. Much shaped by the experience of dealing with antisemitism in the United States, Littman rejected cap-in-hand appeals for an end to antisemitism. He was itching to see the Canadian ADL take a front-line combatant role in anti-discrimination and human rights advocacy in Canada.[24]

In October 1968, soon after taking up his new job, Littman chanced upon a *Globe and Mail* article about the Granite Club's intention to sell its property on St Clair Avenue in Toronto and construct a larger, more modern facility on Bayview Avenue in suburban North York. He felt he had found an opportune target. Sociologist John Porter did not rank the Granite Club among the top tier of Toronto's elite private clubs, but as far as Littman was concerned it had a 'wide reputation and prominence in the community.' What is more, to Toronto Jews the Granite Club, more than any other club, was widely regarded as a 'citadel of prejudice and discrimination.' Littman successfully pressed the B'nai Brith executive and the JCRC to authorize a challenge to the Granite Club's proposed move to the heavily Jewish North York.[25]

The confrontation with the Granite Club first spilled into the open at North York Municipal Council. In February 1969 the Granite Club applied to re-zone a portion of its recently acquired North York property abutting municipal park lands, a prerequisite to construction of its new facilities. Hoping to stall the re-zoning application, Littman wrote to Murray Chusid, a North York alderman, suggesting that before any re-zoning be allowed, it was appropriate for 'the municipality to make some inquiry regarding membership policy maintained by the Granite Club as it affects members of various minority groups.' Pointing to 'persistent rumours in the community' of discriminatory policies, Littman, with more than a little tongue in cheek, suggested that if the rumours 'are untrue then this information also deserves to be published.' He cautioned Chusid that the 'membership of some clubs has frequently proven difficult to evaluate.' The club might produce the name of a 'token' minority group member or feign lack of information on a member's 'religious and ethnic background' so as to 'resist inquiry.' As a way to deal with that, Littman suggested that the North York council might seek a review of the club's membership by the Ontario Human Rights Commission.[26]

Chusid took up the issue. When the lawyer for the Granite Club appeared before the municipal council in February 1969, likely anticipating little or no challenge to the club's re-zoning request, Chusid was ready. The alderman suggested that the Granite Club's allegedly restricted membership raised questions about whether it would be a 'good neighbour.' He suggested that before the municipal council approve the re-zoning, it would be best to clear the air. To this end he recommended that the Granite Club allow the Ontario Human Rights Commission to 'evaluate the matter.'

Caught off guard, the lawyer for the Granite Club promised to take the proposal back to the club's membership, but offered no hint of how the club would respond to the suggestion of an Ontario Human Rights Commission inquiry.[27] While the Granite Club pondered its options, the North York council referred the re-zoning application to the North York Parks Commission for its consideration. More bad news for the Granite Club: Chusid was a key member of the Parks Commission.

Through the spring and summer of 1969, Chusid and two other like-minded committee members stalled approval of the re-zoning pending the club's agreement to meet with the Ontario Human Rights Commission.[28] Without North York approval, the club's construction timetable and plans for renewal were disrupted. What is more, charges of discrimination and talk of involving the Ontario Human Rights Commission were becoming a public relations headache for the club. The press, knowing a meaty story when it saw it, gnawed on this one like a dog on a bone. The club's membership was not happy.[29]

A member of the club's board of directors at the time recalled that some members were 'surprised' by the accusations of discrimination. While the club may have been openly anti-Jewish in an earlier day, he insisted that to his memory the issue of Jewish membership never even came up. It is easy to understand why. It was the practice of the club that individuals proposed for membership were nominated by existing members. These nominations were then vetted by the club's board and, if acceptable, approved for membership. He could not recall a Jew ever being nominated. Since none was nominated, none was rejected. Since none was rejected, how could anyone accuse the club of anti-Jewish discrimination? If a Jew had been nominated, he was convinced, the board would have handled the nominee no differently than any other.[30]

Perhaps so, but the board's immediate problem was not how to deal with Jewish nominees, it was how to deal with its stalled re-zoning request. In late September 1969, the Granite Club finally announced it would meet with the head of the Ontario Human Rights Commission, Dr Daniel Hill.[31] When Littman learned that a delegation from the Granite Club was finally going to meet with the commission, he was optimistic. He saw it as an important precedent. An ADL official in New York agreed: 'I know of no other situation in which a private club has agreed to sit down with a government agency for the purpose of discussing its membership practices. Thus, the decision by the Granite Club to do so is ground-breaking.' The only question seemed to be how thorough and public any investigation of the Granite Club's membership practices would be.[32]

Littman's optimism proved entirely premature. The Granite Club delegation was not about to play the B'nai Brith's game. To Littman's disappointment, the club's meeting with Dr Hill in October 1969 did not go well. After all the formal introductions were finished, the Granite Club's lawyer reportedly asked Dr Hill for some clarification. Was it not the case that the commission's legal jurisdiction lay exclusively in areas of accommodation and employment? This being the case, since the Granite Club did not offer accommodation to anyone, there could be nothing to discuss in this area. But, the club's lawyer allowed that the Granite Club was an employer. He asked whether the Ontario Human Rights Commission had any issues to raise with respect to the club's employment practices. Hearing none, the lawyer declared there were no issues of substance to be addressed. The meeting, which had barely started, was over.[33]

The Granite Club advised the press that it had met with the Ontario Human Rights Commission as demanded by North York. That requirement out of the way, it now expected approval of its re-zoning application. Chusid, his hands now tied, had no choice but to agree. The re-zoning application was approved.[34]

Taken aback, the B'nai Brith was unsure of what its next move should be. Might it be possible to somehow 'intervene' with the Liquor Licence Board of Ontario to challenge the club's liquor licence? Eddie Goodman, a prominent Toronto lawyer with extensive experience in matters of administrative law, was consulted. He shot down the liquor licence idea, and suggested instead that the re-zoning application approved by North York was still vulnerable to reversal by the Ontario Municipal Board (OMB), something of a court of last resort with regard to issues of zoning and land use. The OMB would be brought into play if an official complaint was lodged against the North York re-zoning decision. Goodman suggested B'nai Brith seek leave to appear before the OMB to lodge a complaint. Goodman volunteered to act on behalf of the ADL in dealings with the OMB. Goodman cautioned, however, that while there was merit in turning to the OMB, in the end there was little likelihood of the OMB actually overturning the re-zoning. The prime value of the complaint to the OMB was that it would stall construction for a time and, if the press got wind of the story – and it was Littman's job to make sure it did – it would focus more negative and embarrassing media attention on the Granite Club's membership practices. This, Goodman suggested, was where the club was most vulnerable and that, if for no other reason, made the OMB appeal worthwhile.[35]

In late November 1969 Littman wrote the OMB, serving notice that there were issues of social discrimination to do with the Granite Club's re-zoning application on which the ADL wished to be heard. Mediation by the Ontario Human Rights Commission, Littman added, had failed when the Granite Club, as Littman explained, refused the commission leave to conduct a 'study or survey of the Club's membership policy.'[36]

With the fat in the fire, events moved quickly. Goodman filed an official complaint with the OMB charging that the Granite Club had 'a long standing reputation' for discrimination. By approving the Granite Club's re-zoning request, North York countenanced discrimination and it was in the public interest that this re-zoning approval be revoked.[37] Goodman then appeared before a preliminary OMB meeting, asking for a full public hearing on the B'nai Brith complaint. In turn, the legal counsel for the Granite Club denied any discrimination in membership – 'Admittance to the club is made by normal application by a would-be member who finds a sponsor and a seconder for his membership' – and dismissed the idea of a full public hearing. The counsel requested that the OMB affirm the re-zoning request. The board reserved judgment on the issue.[38]

During the hearing, a 'contingent of Granite Club members was present in the audience ... and heard the presentation of attorneys for both sides.'[39] So too was the press. The next day Toronto dailies carried stories about accusations of religious discrimination laid against the Granite Club. An editorial in the *Toronto Star* supported the call for a public hearing – an event almost certain to be another public black eye for the club.[40]

Among some club members there was growing discomfort with the continuing negative press coverage, 'which did not help the Club's reputation,' and fear that, even if the OMB eventually ruled in the club's favour, the B'nai Brith might have other tricks up its sleeve. Was the club ready to deal with round-the-clock picketing of its facilities on St Clair or its construction site on Bayview? What would the club do if Holocaust survivors lay down in front of earth-moving equipment? Was the club ready to call in the police? It would be a media circus. Calls for damage control grew. In the club's regularly scheduled board election, a core of reform-minded members put their names forward and were elected. They immediately set about putting an end to the matter. Beginning with the notion that when you find yourself in a hole, the first thing to do is stop digging, the board decided not just to stop digging, but to begin filling in the hole. As a first step board members wanted to begin discussions with the ADL and the Jewish community. But how best to initiate discussions?[41]

Fearing further delays and continuing bad press, and now determined to put an end to charges of discrimination, the club's new board looked for an interlocutor, someone who could facilitate discussions between the Granite Club and the Jewish community. It is an irony of the Granite Club's relocation plans that a key player in the proposed development was a prominent Jewish-owned land development corporation, Four Seasons. Four Seasons had previously contracted to design and build the Granite Club's new facilities in North York, and as soon as the club moved into its new home, Four Seasons would take ownership of the St Clair Avenue property and develop it. As it happened, James E. Kelley, a member of the Granite Club's Building Committee, was also a board member of the Koffler Group, chaired by Murray Koffler, founder of Shoppers Drug Mart and one of the principals of Four Seasons. After a regularly scheduled meeting of the Koffler Group board,

Kelley took Murray Koffler aside and asked for his help in opening dialogue with Jewish leaders in an effort to end the membership dispute. If Koffler was not personally up to speed on all the issues involved, Four Seasons was certainly aware of the club's problems. When the Granite Club encountered a delay at the hands of North York alderman Chusid, the club notified Four Seasons that construction plans were on hold until the re-zoning issue was resolved.

A business relationship was one thing. Thinking that the club would find any sympathy for its membership policy among the Four Seasons' owners was another thing. And if club members hoped Koffler would simply serve as a neutral go-between with the Jewish community, that was not in the cards either. Instead, Koffler, influential in organized Jewish community circles, made his position clear to Kelley. If the club wanted Koffler's assistance, he in turn asked for a pledge from the Granite Club board that it truly wanted to put its history of discrimination in membership behind it. The pledge delivered, he agreed to facilitate discussions.[42]

Working the phone, Koffler invited key Jewish stakeholders – the ADL, its legal team, JCRC leaders, and select Jewish community *machers*, including Ray Wolfe and Rabbi Plaut, to a luncheon meeting at the Four Seasons' Inn on the Park hotel in suburban Toronto to talk about the Granite Club membership dispute.[43] Some of those who assembled in the first week of January 1970 were a little uneasy at what Koffler was up to. There may even have been some suspicion that Koffler and Four Seasons were as much motivated by economic self-interest as the common good. After reassurance from Koffler that this was not a Four Seasons' ploy to rid itself of a barrier in its deal with the Granite Club and that the outreach by the Granite Club was genuine, the meeting got down to brass tacks. Working on the assurance that the new Granite Club board of directors was committed to resolving the membership issue, the stakeholder group agreed to face-to-face talks with Granite Club representatives, on two conditions. All discussions must be with persons fully authorized to negotiate for the Granite Club and the club must understand in advance that 'a public statement of non-discrimination would be the only valid way to conclude ... negotiations.'

Koffler called the Granite Club's point man on membership and relayed both the B'nai Brith's willingness to hold discussions and the terms set down for those discussions. They were accepted as 'reasonable and feasible.' A private meeting was scheduled for the Royal York

Hotel ten days later. For the first time since the membership dispute arose, it was agreed the press was to be kept out of the information loop, at least for the moment.[44]

On 15 January 1970 representatives of the B'nai Brith met over lunch with a number of Granite Club board members, including the club's newly elected president. If some worried the meeting would be tense or anticipated fireworks, such worries were soon put to rest. A club board member recalled the mood as positive and with 'no unpleasantness.'[45] A B'nai Brith delegate remembers that everyone was ready to deal.[46] Acting as chair, Koffler began the meeting by pointing to 'the importance of communication and the national significance of the conversation.' The Granite Club representatives then reassured the ADL that they 'received the unanimous support of their Board [for these discussions] prior to attending the meeting.' They then cut to the heart of the matter. The club wished it known that, whatever went on in the past, membership discrimination was ended. 'The Granite Club stated that there was little merit in reviewing the history of the Club and that the focus should be on the present and the future. All the representatives of the Granite Club expressed their desire to see their Club's membership open to all people. [The Club's president] suggested that it was regrettable that the Granite Club had not sought out an opportunity for such conversation previously.' The B'nai Brith representatives stated that they too 'had no wish to dwell in the past.' The meeting then shifted to suggestions for resolving outstanding issues and how to make any resolution of the dispute public. Accord came quickly. The Granite Club president agreed to immediately send a letter to Littman as national director of the ADL, stating that Granite Club membership was open to all. In return, the ADL would instruct its legal counsel to discontinue the OMB appeal. Neither the Granite Club nor the ADL would 'initiate contact with the press.' Rather, when the press asked, as they surely would, why the ADL withdrew its OMB appeal, they would be given a copy of the Granite Club letter to Littman.[47]

That very day, the Granite Club president sent the agreed letter to Littman, but the ADL did not get a chance to withdraw its appeal before the OMB. The plan was blindsided when, the day after the group met at the Royal York Hotel, the OMB issued its decision. The OMB disallowed the ADL objection and approved the North York re-zoning. It went even further. The OMB ruled that North York never had authority for delaying the re-zoning.[48]

The Granite Club now had legal permission to proceed with the construction of its new facilities, and since it no longer needed the ADL to withdraw its OMB appeal, the club could also have walked away from its agreement with the ADL. But it didn't. How could it? If it did, the Jewish community would only find other ways to keep the issue in the public eye and, wanting as much to rid itself of the taint of antisemitism as the ADL wanted to set a precedent in the struggle against social discrimination, the Granite Club signalled that it wanted to continue. The two organizations quickly conferred and decided to call a joint press conference at the Royal York to explain that, even prior to the OMB ruling, the Granite Club and ADL had agreed to 'bury the hatchet.'[49]

At the press conference, the two groups affirmed a new spirit of goodwill and understanding. The past was past and not of consequence. What was important was the club's affirmation of openness. Reporters pushed the Granite Club spokesman on the club's history and about when its 'change of policy' was approved, but the larger point was made. The Granite Club was open to membership without discrimination on account of race or religion.[50] The authorized history of the Granite Club observes simply that the two organizations pledged 'their willingness to meet again in the future in the event [they] encounter any further questions or difficulties. No further difficulties were ever encountered.'[51]

In hindsight, a senior Granite Club member allowed that he was 'glad the incident happened. It helped the Granite Club.' Given the changing character of Toronto, the Granite Club had more than a little catching up to do. Since ending its confrontation with the Jewish community it has 'devolved as a Club as society has devolved.'[52] In a summing-up memorandum, Sol Littman gave much credit for resolving the dispute to a progressive new leadership within the Granite Club. 'The unaccustomed speed with which we were able to blow down the walls of Jericho, through the activated leadership of a younger breed of prominent members within the Granite Club, proved their readiness – even eagerness – for a new liberalized membership policy.' Littman also pronounced the Granite Club episode a critical victory in the struggle against social discrimination and as a victory for in-your-face activism for which the ADL deserved the lion's share of credit. 'The fifty year problem of social discrimination on this continent has only just begun to crumble in the U.S.A., and now in Canada, largely through the efforts of the ADL.' The Granite Club episode, Littman promised, was also just a first step.[53]

Whatever the ADL's future challenges might be, the Granite Club had a challenge of its own. To demonstrate publicly that it did not discriminate, it suddenly needed Jewish members. It offered membership to the Four Seasons' principals and several moneyed B'nai Brith board members. All declined.[54] Whatever fears the Granite Club's old guard might have harboured that opening the club's doors to even one Jew would open the gates to a flood of Jewish members, the opposite was true. There was little or no interest among wealthy and prominent Jews in joining the Granite Club. No surprise. The Granite Club dispute did not erupt because there was any line-up of Jews desperate to join the club who couldn't. The dispute erupted because the club denied Jews the possibility of membership. In the late 1960s the organized Jewish community was serving notice that, as far as it was concerned, the era when social discrimination could be tolerated any more than discrimination in housing, employment, and education was over.

Of course, those in the Jewish community who took on the Granite Club in the late 1960s were under no illusion that their victory would bring on the millennium. Littman noted, 'We are grown men and we know that the millennium will not result directly from this victory. I am not sure what brings the millennium, but I do know that effective social change results from a program of graduated minor victories. I hope the [Jewish] community will be greatly encouraged.'[55]

Littman was right. Success in forcing the Granite Club to open its doors to Jews did not bring on the millennium. It was more a symbolic victory. So long associated with snobbish antisemitism in Toronto, the Granite Club might, it was jokingly suggested, now consider engaging a kosher caterer. Joking aside, only a small minority of Jews had money enough to entertain the idea of joining the Granite Club or its like elsewhere in Canada. The fight to end membership discrimination at the Granite Club was a matter of principle and that principle was that antisemitism was no longer to be tolerated.

The fight also brought into play tactics that organized Jewish community leaders had previously been shy of endorsing – pressing Jewish politicians to throw their muscle around, using legal and administrative manoeuvres to force costly construction delays, threatening public demonstrations and street-level protests, encouraging the press to weigh in against social discrimination. Only a few years earlier Jewish leaders had condemned the Allan Gardens demonstrators for using confrontational tactics that, establishment Jewish leaders warned, would lead to violence and tarnish the good name of the Jewish community. Taking on the Granite Club, community leaders, pressed by an increasingly impatient rank and file, agreed to the use of tactics that would previously have been rejected as unacceptable. In the Granite Club case, they worked. A corner had been turned.

The organized Jewish community had reason to feel satisfaction that a high-profile citadel of anti-Jewish exclusion had been forced to abandon its discriminatory policy. But whatever pleasure they took in this victory, they also knew the day-to-day impact on the lives of Canadian Jews would be minimal as compared to previously hard-won legislation banning discrimination in employment, housing, or education. In retrospect, however, the Granite Club episode was important. It was a very public episode in the larger Canadian Jewish struggle to eliminate discrimination in the private sector, the professions, corporate boardrooms, and social organizations. That the Granite Club could be cajoled into opening its membership to Jews, however hesitantly, proved that walls of social discrimination could topple, and while the time-honoured Jewish community preference for respectful and quiet diplomatic persuasion was not abandoned (witness the Larry Zeidel affair), it was paralleled by a more public and spirited activism.

Perhaps no better example of this new community activism is to be found than in the campaign for Soviet Jews. Critical as the Soviet Jewry campaign would become in the years following the Six Day War, only a few years earlier the issue was nowhere near the top of the North American Jewish community's priority list.[56] Believing that decades of state repression of Jewish religious and cultural expression had taken its toll, many Jewish leaders doubted there was any measurable Jewish presence left in the Soviet Union, let alone any hope for a Jewish future. This view was challenged in 1963 by Moshe Decter of the Jewish Minorities Research Center. In a breakthrough article in *Foreign Affairs* entitled 'The Status of Jews in the Soviet Union,' Decter argued that as much as the Soviet Union tried to repress Jewish identity, Soviet Jews not only knew they were Jews but state-sanctioned antisemitism ensured they did not forget it. Deterritorialized but not culturally deboned, Soviet Jews were caught 'in an inextricable vice. They are allowed neither to assimilate, nor to live a full Jewish life, nor to emigrate (as many would wish) to Israel or any other place where they might live fully as Jews.'[57]

The same year as Decter's article, a wake-up call to Western Jewish leaders, the plight of Soviet Jews was unexpectedly profiled in an exchange of letters between Nikita Khrushchev and British philosopher Bertrand Russell published in both the Soviet and Western press. In one letter Russell expressed dismay at the death sentences Soviet courts unjustly meted out to a number of Soviet Jews for alleged economic crimes. Khrushchev denounced the charge that Soviet courts were deliberately and systematically targeting Jews as 'a vicious slander on the Soviet people.' But the damage was done. The fact that a Soviet leader was forced to publicly defend the Soviet Union against charges of state-sanctioned antisemitism, with both the charge and the denial published in the Soviet press, further catapulted Soviet Jews into the Western public eye.[58]

The Soviet Union, much as it would like to pretend otherwise, was uneasy at rising Western Jewish concern over Soviet Jews. In January 1964 the Soviet embassy in Ottawa sent a lengthy report to Moscow dealing with anti-Soviet agitation in Canada. The report contended that 'in light of an easing of international tensions, reactionaries in the West are using the [Jewish] issue to perpetuate an atmosphere of Cold War.' In this regard the embassy had been subject to a few sporadic approaches on behalf of Soviet Jews. The report noted that several months earlier about twenty-five Jewish Labour Committee protesters had picketed outside the Soviet embassy gate. The protesters' attempt to present embassy staff with a memorandum on the treatment of Soviet Jews was refused. Protesters subsequently mailed the document to the embassy. 'The authors of the memorandum,' according to the report, 'complained that Soviet Jews are not allowed to emigrate to Israel or to maintain connections with Jews abroad and that those sentenced to economic crimes in the USSR are, for the most part, Jews.' The report cautioned Moscow that anti-Soviet agitators, using any pretext to defame the Soviet Union, had trumped up accusations of Soviet Jewish persecution in an effort to defame the Soviet Union and Soviet people. This defamation had even been voiced in the Canadian House of Commons at the behest of what the report labelled 'reactionary Jewish organizations, on direct orders of the United States.' The report to Moscow concluded on a reassuring note. 'The anti-Soviet slander campaign in Canada concerning alleged discrimination against Soviet Jews has not yet subsided. However, this campaign is not attracting wide support among the Canadian population.'[59]

The report was right in questioning the level of public interest in Soviet Jews. Twenty-five Jews picketing in front of the Soviet embassy was hardly a sign of mass public concern for the cause of Soviet Jewry, not even among Canadian Jews. Where then was the rest of the Jewish community? If there was slowly growing awareness of the Soviet Jewish question, in 1964 there was certainly no centrally organized Canadian Jewish campaign to press the cause of Soviet Jews. There was no organized Jewish community coordination, budget, or staff exclusively assigned to Soviet Jewry. Instead there were disconnected bits and pieces of activity here and there – nothing one could call an organized campaign, at least not yet. Nevertheless, as the Soviet embassy report to Moscow suggested, if the issue Soviet Jews did become a priority of North American Jewish leaders, it could be problematic, and there were signs it might.[60]

Following hard on the heels of a World Conference of Jewish Organizations' call to conscience on the plight of Soviet Jews and the Conference on the Status of Soviet Jews held in New York, in January 1964 the National Religious Affairs Committee of the Canadian Jewish Congress organized a first All-Canadian Rabbinic Conference to discuss the religious and cultural welfare of Jews in the Soviet Union. In advance of their gathering the rabbis requested a meeting with the Soviet ambassador in Ottawa to discuss the 'religious problems of the Jews in Russia.' The embassy denied the request, replying: 'The question of the religious problems of Jews in the USSR as well as of any other Soviet nationality is outside of the Embassy's competence as the church in our country is disestablished from the State.' The door was left open for a meeting with other embassy staff, presumably so the Soviet position could be explained in more detail. Undaunted, the rabbis wrote directly to the Soviet ambassador, inviting him to attend their gathering or, if that was not possible, again requesting he meet with a delegation of rabbis. An embassy spokesperson replied that the ambassador would not attend the conference nor had he changed his mind about meeting a delegation of rabbis. Without mincing words, an embassy spokesperson explained: 'Since the subject which the Conference proposes to discuss is of an artificial and obviously tendentious character, and its consideration constitutes interference in the internal affairs of the USSR, no one of our staff-members, as you can understand, will be able to attend the Conference. For the same reason there cannot be an audience for a delegation of the Conference to which you refer in your letter.'[61]

The ambassador did not attend, but more than fifty Canadian rabbis from across the religious spectrum did. They were addressed by Paul Martin, minister of external affairs. Martin assured the rabbis of 'the Government's interest in the position of Jews in the Soviet Union,' but promised no specific Canadian action on their behalf. Much to the chagrin of the Soviet embassy, the minister did, however, publicly label Soviet repression of Jews an international human rights concern. But, beyond hearing from the minister, talking among themselves, generating a few press clippings, and issuing calls for a National Day of Prayer for the Welfare of the Jews in Russia for 5 May – coinciding with the anniversary of the Soviet Union decree of the death penalty for certain economic crimes, a penalty disproportionately inflicted on Jews – little came out of the gathering. Most important, there were no steps taken towards organizing a coordinated community-wide campaign on behalf of Soviet Jews. Not yet.[62]

Three months after the rabbinic gathering in Ottawa, a delegation of rabbis finally visited the Soviet embassy, although they had to settle for a meeting with the embassy's first counsellor. The ambassador, they were told, was still 'unavailable.' For two hours the rabbis voiced concern about the mistreatment of Jews by the Soviet Union, only to be told they were misinformed about the state of Jewish life in the Soviet Union. There was no mistreatment. However, in what the rabbis took to be a sign of embassy worry that the Soviet Jewish issue could become a vexatious public relations headache, they were referred to a recent edition of the embassy's house organ *Soviet Union Today*, which contained both an article celebrating the thirty-fifth anniversary of the Moscow Synagogue and a telling piece entitled 'Soviet Jews Need No Foreign Protection.' A delegation request that a group of Canadian rabbis be allowed to visit the Soviet Union and hold meetings with Soviet rabbis was taken under advisement. The delegation took this to be a refusal. The rabbis also requested they be allowed to ship Jewish religious items into the Soviet Union. The first counsellor replied that, before a decision could be made, the rabbis should submit a list of gift items for embassy consideration. This was done.[63]

The rabbis were now dead-ended. They had met among themselves. They had heard from the Canadian minister of foreign affairs. They had sent a delegation to the Soviet embassy. But they had no next step. The door was left open to action by the same grassroots coalition of European-born and Yiddish-speaking groups, including Holocaust survivors – those one Toronto Jewish official lumped together under the heading of 'folk organizations' – who had castigated Congress leaders for their spineless response to homegrown Nazis.[64] At the 1965 Canadian Jewish Congress plenary meetings in Montreal, representatives from 'folk organizations' united with youth delegates in passing a resolution calling on Congress to organize a national conference on Soviet Jews.

Cynics might shrug their shoulders at the suggestion of yet another conference, but the conference resolution was taken by Congress leaders as something of a warning call. Still reeling from the Allan Gardens episode, leaders could ill afford to be judged indifferent to the suffering of Soviet Jews. To do so would leave the way open for others, perhaps less responsible in their tactics, to grab hold of the Soviet Jewry issue, making it their own and leaving Congress out in the cold. Accordingly, Congress officials not only began working on conference logistics, but, in an effort to give structure to passion, they also started pulling together proposals for some kind of community Soviet Jewry initiative the planned convention would want to endorse. Most programmatic strategies that suggested themselves – creating a public education campaign, courting press support of Soviet Jewry, making representations to Soviet authorities, assembling a coalition of sympathetic non-Jewish clergy, media, and political personalities to endorse the Soviet Jewish cause – fell well within the establishment's comfort zone. But for the first time Congress officials entertained a number of suggestions for public action that previously would have been dismissed as too confrontational and too populist, including a mass Jewish community 'march on Ottawa' and a hunger strike in front of the Soviet embassy.[65]

In late May 1966, three hundred delegates from across Canada convened at the Queen Elizabeth Hotel in Montreal. For several days they listened to speeches and attended workshops on the state of Soviet Jewry. In a plenary session they adopted a number of previously prepared resolutions, including one calling on the Canadian Jewish Congress to establish a special national task-force committee on Soviet Jewry made up of representatives from 'major national, central and local Jewish organizations.' The committee would 'direct itself to the matter of devising an ongoing program of action on behalf of Soviet Jews.' The committee was also instructed to publicly frame its efforts as a campaign for human rights in the Soviet Union, not a campaign to promote emigration of Jews from the Soviet Union, although freedom to migrate was understood to be a human right. Another resolution involved immigration and spoke to the need for 'Soviet Jewish families, separated as a result of the Nazi holocaust, to be re-united with their relatives abroad.' There was, however, no mistaking the larger message. The conference was endorsing a major national effort designed to pressure the Soviet Union into living up to its obligation under its own laws and to binding obligations it had assumed by entering into international treaties to protect and ensure the human rights of its Jewish citizens. If the Soviet Union chose to continue violating its own laws and treaty obligations, delegates demanded, it should permit Jews who wished to leave the Soviet Union to do so. Since none at the conference expected the Soviet Union to act voluntarily in this regard, it had to be held accountable. Delegates asserted it was the sacred trust of Canadian Jews to assist in this effort. The organized Canadian Jewish campaign on behalf of Soviet Jews took form.[66]

But what shape should that campaign take? If some of the community's old-guard leadership hoped traditional rules of engagement would apply – quiet diplomacy, top-down decision making, keeping a tight lid on the politics of confrontation and public protest – they would be disappointed. Folk organizations, still smarting from what they regarded as Congress inaction on the Nazi file, pressed for an action-oriented campaign, together with activist Jewish youth on campus, a campaign that did not shy away from taking protest to the street if necessary.[67] They were not alone. Even as Congress officials began discussing plans for a national campaign on Soviet Jews, several prominent Toronto community members, including Rabbi Stuart Rosenberg of Beth Tzedec Synagogue, Canada's largest Conservative congregation, met in mid-May 1967 to organize a Committee of Concern for Soviet Jews 'to begin at once the work of protest.' Invitations to join the committee and attend an organizing meeting two weeks later were circulated. But the timetable fell victim to events in the Middle East. A follow-up letter to interested individuals explained that the 'scheduled meeting was cancelled due to the "Six Day War." You can well appreciate the need for this postponement.' The postponement was short lived. In fact the Six Day War only served to underscore the urgency of organizing in defence of Soviet Jewry. Almost as miraculous as Israel's victory was a report that the victory was quietly celebrated by impassioned Soviet Jews who, feeling a tug to Israel, also began to secretly organize Hebrew study groups and, risking the ire of the state, even applied to emigrate to Israel.[68]

Those Soviet citizens who publicly proclaimed their Jewishness and voiced support for Israel were made to pay a steep price. In a Soviet Union that lined up in support of the Arab cause, these Jews were marked as pariahs – fired from jobs, attacked in the press, hassled by authorities, their mail intercepted and telephone calls monitored. To Canadian Jews, however, these pariahs were heroes, their expression of Jewish consciousness born of the same awakened Jewish pride that Canadian Jews felt in the wake of the Six Day War. The punishment meted out to Jewish dissidents was regarded by many as proof positive that the Soviet Union was as antisemitic at heart as the czarist regime of old.

Just as Canadian Jews cemented bonds of attachment to Israel in the spring of 1967, they also embraced the cause of those oppressed in the name of Israel. In that spirit, the new Committee of Concern for Soviet Jewry reached out to the larger Canadian Jewish community for support. 'Since June 5th,' organizers warned, 'the increase in anti-semitic propaganda, hatred, and vindictiveness in the Soviet press has reached a level and fervour of pre-pogrom intensity!' Canadian Jews, like Jews elsewhere in the West, must respond. They did.[69]

Jewish student groups were quick off the mark. Even as those with a 'paucity of acquaintance with authentic Jewish life' had rallied behind Israel as war loomed, many now rallied in support of Soviet Jews determined to live their lives as Jews.[70] While the Committee of Concern for Soviet Jewry was organizing, representatives of different Toronto Jewish campus organizations met to plan a Soviet Jewry rally on the autumn Jewish holiday of Simchat Torah, in solidarity with those Soviet Jews who braved Soviet hostility and 'once a year ... come together and express their identity as Jews by singing and dancing on Simhat Torah' outside synagogues in Moscow and other large Soviet cities. This first Canadian Simchat Torah rally took place in Nathan Phillips Square in front of the Toronto City Hall in late October 1967. In addition to several thousand university students, the crowd included younger congregants from a number of Toronto synagogues, who arrived on buses chartered especially for the event. The crowd listened to a fiery speech by New Democratic member of parliament David Lewis, followed by 'singing led by Malka and Mr. Jerry Grey of "The Travellers," and spontaneous folk dancing.' The event ended with the singing of Hatikvah and O Canada.[71]

This first Simchat Torah rally was regarded as such a success that similar rallies soon became a mainstay of the Soviet Jewry campaign in cities across Canada. In 1968 a Canadian Students' Committee for Soviet Jewry formed in Montreal invited the entire Jewish community to join a mass Simchat Torah rally, which involved marching from McGill University's Hillel House on Stanley Street, then moving along McGregor to Ontario Avenue and ending in front of the Russian consulate, where several thousand protesters listened to speakers, sang songs, and danced in the street. The second annual Simchat Torah rally in Toronto began with a torchlight procession from the University of Toronto, proceeding down University Avenue and into Nathan Phillips Square for a 'dance rally.' Upwards of 3000 young people attended the Toronto event. In Ottawa, 'calling for public attention to the plight of Jews in the Soviet Union,' local students were joined by busloads of students from Montreal and Toronto. As police and RCMP officers stood by, and with no objection from Congress leaders, who only a few years earlier would have frowned on placard-waving demonstrators, the students took their protest to the gates of the Soviet embassy.[72]

The following year the number of Simchat Torah rallies across Canada grew. Young Judaea organized a series of Simchat Torah events across the Maritimes, including a youth prayer service in Halifax. In Glace Bay on Cape Breton Island the tiny Jewish community assembled in the local synagogue to hear a guest speaker talk on the Soviet Jewish problem. After the talk 'a silent march with the Sefer Torahs was made – all children in the community participating.' CBC's International Service Russian-language news broadcasts reported on many of the Nova Scotia rallies.[73]

To the west in Winnipeg the 1969 Simchat Torah rally was held in the parking lot of Rosh Pina Synagogue, but did not go as planned. The rally was to include a few short speeches, passage of a resolution on Soviet Jewry to be telegraphed to the Soviet embassy, musical entertainment – several choirs and a local folk group – and Israeli dancing followed by light refreshments in the synagogue. A unique element was added to the Winnipeg rally – the lighting of a big bonfire contained in a specially pre-built foundation that was to serve as focal point for the evening's program. In advance of the evening event, organizers trooped from police headquarters to the offices of the Fire Department and finally to the city's Health Department in an effort to arrange a permit for the bonfire, only to be told in the end that the city did not grant permits for bonfires. According to organizers, they were quietly assured that while no permit could be issued, the community could go ahead with its bonfire so long as adequate precautions were taken to douse the fire if there was any problem.

With the crowd of more than a thousand gathered in the synagogue parking lot, fire extinguishers and a sand pile at the ready, the bonfire was lit. Flames soon crackled skyward. Unfortunately, nobody informed Rosh Pina's neighbours or the local fire hall about the bonfire. An alert neighbour looked out her window to see flames and thought the synagogue was ablaze. She raised the alarm. Within minutes fire trucks descended on the synagogue. Firemen pushed their way through the stunned crowd and unceremoniously turned their hoses on the fire. Smoke and soot filled the air. Confused and irate, members of the crowd started protesting. Frightened that his men might be set upon, the fire captain called in the police as he ordered his men onto their trucks and back to the fire station. In an effort to raise the rally out of the ashes, musicians began to play and a mass hora was hastily started. The rally, sans fire, ended with the sounding of the shofar.[74]

The Winnipeg Fire Department may have doused the communal bonfire, but not concern for the plight of Soviet Jews. In the wake of the 1967 war, support for the Soviet Jewry campaign, like support for Israel, became a Canadian and North American Jewish priority. For the Soviet Union, the escalation of protest was problematic. Facing a deterioration of relations with China and hoping to expand Western trade, the Soviet authorities needed détente. Western Jews understood this very well. Their campaign attempted to link détente to an improvement in the Soviet Union's human rights record and, most specifically, to the right of Soviet Jews to either live as Jews or emigrate. And as the Canadian Soviet Jewry campaign built up a head of steam, as more and more Jewish community energy was engaged, it expanded well beyond once-a-year Simchat Torah rallies. Often coordinating with American Jewish organizations and Israeli authorities, the campaign reached out for government and media support. To that end, the campaign sought out ways, sometimes unconventional ways, to keep the public eye on the plight of Soviet Jews and embarrass the Soviet Union. Touring Soviet cultural groups were picketed. Boycotts of Soviet goods were organized. The Kremlin was targeted with a 'Let my people go' postcard campaign. Soviet Jewish dissidents were phoned from Canada and transcripts of the conversations were released to the press in the hope that Soviet authorities would think twice about coming down hard on dissidents with Western connections. Support was solicited from prominent non-Jews. Speakers were made available to any community group – Jewish and non-Jewish – that wanted to learn about the situation of Soviet Jews. Children being bar mitzvahed in Canada were twinned with Soviet Jewish children said to be denied the opportunity to have a bar mitzvah of their own. When a Soviet freighter docked in Toronto harbour, a small group of Jewish protesters set up a film projector and, with the press on hand, screened a film about the oppression of Soviet Jews on the white hull of the ship. Canadians tourists and business people going to visit the Soviet Union – Jewish and non-Jewish – were quietly requested to take religious items for the Jewish community with them and even to meet with Jews, secretly if necessary, during their visit. Even Canadian hockey players and officials going to the Soviet Union were asked to pack religious articles along with their hockey equipment.

Of course, Canadian Soviet Jewry campaign organizers were realistic enough to know that their efforts, no matter how energetic, were something of a sideshow compared to those in the United States. But that was beside the point. Canada might not have the same level of importance for the Soviet Union as did the United States, but Canada's voice did count. It was respected in the world, as was Trudeau's effort to strike an independent Canadian posture in international relations. His raising the issue of Jewish immigration during a 1971 Soviet visit, much to the displeasure of his hosts, was regarded as a breakthrough. And later that same year, the entire world Soviet Jewry movement, the international community, and the world press would focus on Canada.

On the evening of 17 October 1971 Alexei Kosygin's plane set down in Ottawa. With all the red carpet formalities due a head of state, the Soviet premier began a state visit to Canada in return for Prime Minister Trudeau's visit to the Soviet Union six months earlier. Just as Trudeau hoped his Soviet visit would lead to an easing of Soviet–Western relations, the Jewish community hoped the Kosygin visit to Canada would be a forum for drawing world attention to Soviet abuse of the human rights of Soviet Jews. As a head of state, of course, Kosygin was entitled to every official courtesy and protection, as was his entourage. However, as Kosygin knew full well, Canada was not the Soviet Union. There was no way he could be hermetically sealed off from those who were within their rights to express public opposition to the Soviet Union and its policies. In this regard, the Jewish community felt it imperative that Kosygin and the world be made to understand that so long as Soviet Jews were not accorded equal rights and the right to emigrate, the issue of Soviet Jewry would remain a stumbling block to improved Soviet relations with the West. It was important that Kosygin hear this message at every stop on his visit, and hear it from Jews, even if at a distance.

Congress leaders asked Canadian Jews to give Kosygin a reason to remember his Canadian visit. 'In the forthcoming days the Canadian Jewish community will be gathered as one great unifying force to proclaim our Solidarity with the Jews of the Soviet Union.' Just as Soviet Jews were bravely making their statement, Congress asked Canadian Jews to raise their collective voice in solidarity. As chance would have it, Kosygin arrived in Ottawa only a few days after Simchat Torah, when thousands of Jews took to the streets around the main synagogue in Moscow and other Soviet cities. If Kosygin was sheltered from contact with the Simchat Torah protest at home, Canadian Jews were determined he would get a bellyful of Jewish protest in Canada. The organized Canadian Jewish community declared the week of Kosygin's visit to be 'National Solidarity Week for Soviet Jewry' and, forgetting about quiet diplomacy, planned a seamless program of high-profile activities and protest demonstrations.

In advance of Kosygin's arrival, Congress sent a public letter to the Soviet ambassador in Ottawa requesting that, while in Canada, Kosygin receive a delegation of Canadian Jews to discuss the situation of Jews in the Soviet Union. The letter went unanswered as community leaders suspected it would, allowing Congress to issue a press release expressing disappointment at the unwillingness of the Soviet premier to engage in dialogue.[75] Denied a meeting with Kosygin, a delegation led by Monroe Abbey, president of the Canadian Jewish Congress, met someone who *would* meet with Kosygin, external affairs minister Mitchell Sharp. Sharp was pressed to ensure Kosygin be made to understand that mistreatment of Soviet Jews was a 'complicating factor' in relations between Canada and the Soviet Union. Sharp pledged that the Soviet leader would be reminded of Canadian interest in the issue of Jewish immigration, both with regard to family reunification of Soviet citizens with family in Canada and the larger issue of Soviet refusal to act on the growing list of those who had applied to emigrate. The minister also stated Canada's intent to voice concern for the treatment of Jewish dissidents imprisoned in the Soviet Union.

As to the matter of public protest in Canada, however, the minister sounded a cautionary note. No matter how much he appreciated the Jewish community's right 'to give vent to its feelings,' any violence, he warned, 'would weaken the government's hand in making representations.' The message was well understood, at least by mainstream Jewish leaders. In encouraging its members to take to the streets in the week of Soviet Jewry events, a B'nai Brith official in Toronto warned that 'any overt demonstration which becomes disorderly and non-peaceful, tending to embarrass Mr. Kosygin,' would be counterproductive. What was desired was 'responsible demonstrations free of personal harassment and vituperation.'[76]

Just as community leaders were united in their determination to conduct loud and vigorous but peaceful demonstrations, they were equally determined to keep Jewish protest separate from an increasingly crowded field of those with an anti-Soviet axe to grind, especially Ukrainian

Canadians and others outraged by what they regarded as a deliberate Soviet policy of Russification of their homelands. Ukrainian Canadian leaders called for a dismantling of the federated Soviet state, a deconstruction of the Soviet Union into a number of separate and sovereign ethnic states. Ukrainian Canadians and others feeling dispossessed of their homelands were joined in protest by those, especially Hungarians, who demanded an end to Soviet domination of their homelands.[77]

Jews had a different interest. The organized Canadian Jewish community had no argument with the territorial integrity of the Soviet Union nor did it take a public position with regard to the Soviet Union maintaining its sphere of influence in eastern Europe. For Jews the issue was not who ruled the territory but how those who ruled treated Jews within their territory. Canadian Jews demanded that the Soviet Union accord Jews equality of citizenship or, failing that, allow those Jews who wished to emigrate to do so.[78]

Jewish demonstrators delivered this message to Kosygin at every stop on his week-long Canadian tour, starting in Ottawa. As Kosygin's plane taxied to a stop in Ottawa on the evening of 17 October, Jewish students were assembling for an overnight vigil as close to the Soviet embassy as security officials would permit. They were joined by the single largest-ever assembly of Canadian rabbis, who arrived in Ottawa from as far east as Newfoundland and as far west as British Columbia. As chance would have it, the evening Kosygin arrived in Canada was also the eve of Yom Kippur Katan, marking the imminent arrival of a new moon. Jewish tradition holds that the arrival of a new moon is, like Yom Kippur, a time of repentance and forgiveness for sins. Among the most observant, Yom Kippur Katan is observed (though not widely so today) with a day-long fast and recitation of special prayers and a Torah reading. The rabbis who assembled in Ottawa joined in Yom Kippur Katan fasting and prayer, some for the first time. The morning following the embassy vigil, as Kosygin sat down for talks with the prime minister, the rabbis convened a 'Rabbinic Conference' at the Ottawa Jewish Community Centre. Early in the afternoon the rabbis emerged wearing flowing *tallesim* (prayer shawls), and, with police keeping close watch, took to the street singing and chanting as they headed off towards the Soviet embassy. They carried a letter of petition addressed to the Soviet premier demanding religious and cultural freedom for Soviet Jews.

Unbeknown to the rabbis, earlier that afternoon, as Prime Minister Trudeau and Soviet Premier Kosygin walked from the main entrance of the Parliament Buildings to a waiting car, a Hungarian émigré and anti-Communist activist broke from behind police security lines. Shouting 'Freedom for Hungary,' he tackled the Soviet leader to the ground. It took only a second before the attacker was subdued and arrested. Kosygin, his jacket pulled from his shoulder and tie askew, was helped to his feet. He was shaken but otherwise unharmed. The Soviet premier dismissed the incident with a flick of his wrist, but the assault, televised around the world, forced an immediate tightening of security, including around the Soviet embassy.[79] By the time the rabbis neared the embassy, they confronted a reinforced line of police blocking all approaches. Rabbi Plaut, a demonstration organizer, recalled the moment:

> The marchers met with a solid cordon of no fewer than 250 Provincial and Federal police. The solid lines of uniforms (colorful, it must be admitted) presented an almost ludicrous sight. Apparently it took better than four policemen for every rabbi armed with a Prayer Book. Perhaps the precautions were directed against the two shofarot which, going by biblical precedent, could be considered dangerous weapons. In any case, the defense wall was thrown up exclusively against the Rabbis, for as soon as they left the police left also.

The rabbis, held back from the Soviet embassy gate, made a 'symbolic attempt' to cross police lines in order to deliver their letter. They were denied permission to proceed. The Ottawa chief of police volunteered to personally present the letter of petition at the embassy gate on the rabbis' behalf. As a copy of the letter was read aloud for the benefit of the press – 'Let the millions of Jews in your country be Jews in every sense of the word' – the police chief was seen attempting to hand the letter to Soviet authorities. They refused to accept it, and he returned the letter to the rabbis, who assembled mid-street to recite the afternoon Mincha prayers followed by a sounding of the shofar. They knew at least the sound of the shofar would penetrate the embassy.[80]

Rabbi Plaut regarded the rabbinic protest as a great success, but not everyone agreed. A rabbi from Laval in suburban Montreal wrote Plaut in regret that he and his colleagues had fallen short in making the kind of statement that Kosygin and beleaguered Soviet Jews needed to hear – a statement that would capture the attention of the world media. He unburdened himself to Plaut:

> I was one of those rabbis in Ottawa with you and our colleagues on Mon-

day and Tuesday [18 and 19 October 1971]. On Monday I fasted despite stomach distress having the hope of our colleagues that G-d will listen to our prayers. I have no quarrel with the spiritual element of our activities but we also came to Ottawa to create a P.R. impact as well. G-d will act in His own ways but we are not free from pursuing a course of action, which in our human capacity must reflect our compassion and willingness to sacrifice for our brethren. I must confess that here we have somehow failed. Our activities ... made page 43 of the local paper. I think we should have not asked the police inspector if he would deliver the letter which you [Rabbi Plaut] and others composed, but have gone through police lines and attempted to deliver it. Thirty rabbis arrested for this act would have made page 1. And after all don't Russian Jews risk arrest when they come to the Moscow shul [on Simchat Torah] and when they keep Hebrew books etc. They too are committing illegal acts!! ... It's too late this time. The bear has escaped. But for next time (unless G-d in His mercy redeems us!).[81]

Whatever his disappointment, the rabbi from Laval joined many of his colleagues as they marched from the embassy to the Eternal Flame on Parliament Hill, lightheartedly dubbed by the rabbis the 'National *Ner Tamid*' (the synagogue lamp which hangs above the ark containing the Torah). Earlier that day, Jewish students set up a table at the National *Ner Tamid* from which they served a 'freedom lunch' to passers-by and a group of curious members of parliament. The lunch 'consisted of 3 ozs. of acorn coffee, 4 ozs. of cabbage soup, 2½ ozs. of black bread and 1½ ozs. of herring,' said to be a typical diet for prisoners in the Soviet Gulag. As night fell, the rabbis broke their Yom Kippur Katan fast with a Gulag meal. Accompanied by other protesters, they recited evening prayers by the light of the flame and began a second overnight vigil. Wrapped in their *tallesim* and silhouetted by the Eternal Flame, the rabbis were clearly visible in the distance as Kosygin, Trudeau, and hundreds of formally dressed guests arrived on Parliament Hill for a state dinner.[82]

The following morning, more than one hundred chartered buses began arriving from Montreal and Toronto for what was billed as the National Jewish Response to Soviet Jewish Policy. Together with much of the Ottawa Jewish community and thousands more who arrived by plane and car, the crowd swelled well beyond the protest organizers' expectations. Jewish day schools in Montreal, Toronto, and Ottawa closed for the day and many adults took a day off work so families might attend together. The key event was a mass parade past the Soviet embassy. Four abreast, the crowd was estimated at well in excess of ten thousand and stretched nearly a mile, bringing downtown Ottawa traffic to a standstill. To guard against rowdiness, city police lined the parade route. Each policeman was accompanied by a Jewish parade marshal. There were no incidents. The crowd was high spirited but orderly. Rabbis carrying Torahs were scattered through the crowd, while marchers, many carrying placards, sang. As they paraded past the embassy, marchers took up the chant 'One, two, three, four, open up the iron door; five, six, seven, eight, open up the iron gate!'[83]

The parade then wound its way past Parliament Hill and past the Rideau Club, where the Soviet premier was being honoured with a luncheon. As the crowd outside roared in support of freedom for Soviet Jews, it was not lost on members of the Ottawa Jewish community that only a few years earlier not one of them would have been permitted on the Rideau Club's premises. The parade finally emptied into the park-like square in front of the Supreme Court Building. As the Supreme Court grounds filled with marchers, musicians started playing and the crowd formed a huge hora. Overhead an airplane circled pulling a banner proclaiming, 'Free Soviet Jews.' There were no speeches. None was necessary. The assembled crowd had come to make a statement not hear one. After singing Hatikvah and O Canada, and confident they had been heard, the crowd gradually dispersed.

As in Ottawa, so it was at each stop on Kosygin's week-long itinerary. Everywhere local Jewish communities turned out in large numbers to drive home the point that Soviet mistreatment of its Jews would continue to bedevil Soviet efforts to improve bilateral relations with Canada and the West more generally. If Jewish protesters often had to share the stage with others who had different anti-Soviet messages to deliver, it was the Jewish question that most dogged Kosygin's heels. Whether it was in an interview he granted the Ottawa correspondent for the *New York Times*, or in conversations with Canadian members of parliament, or in discussions with Trudeau and his officials, the question of Soviet treatment of its Jews seemed to hang over him like a grey cloud. While he repeatedly denied there was any truth to charges of discrimination against Jews in the Soviet Union and testily dismissed Jewish protesters as 'riffraff,' the Soviet premier, perhaps hoping to draw a halt to the pesky protests, again pledged that Soviet officials would look favourably at requests for family reunification of Soviet citizens with relatives in the West. Prime Minister Trudeau, answering a question on the Soviet Jewish issue in the House of Commons, explained he had been personally assured by Kosygin that any delays in approving reunification requests were a result of bureaucratic red tape not state policy.[84]

Jewish leaders read Kosygin's pledge as proof positive that their protest was having the desired impact. And sensing the Soviet government was vulnerable to Western protest, they regarded it as counter-intuitive to tone down the protests. If anything, Jewish leaders hoped to turn up the volume. In Montreal, the second stop on Kosygin's Canadian tour, Jewish protesters crowded the street outside the posh Hélène de Champlain restaurant, where the city of Montreal was hosting an official luncheon in the premier's honour. To Kosygin's displeasure, Soviet Jews turned out to be on the menu. In his welcoming speech, Montreal mayor Jean Drapeau reminded his guest that Canada was an ethnic mosaic in which many continue to feel a powerful attachment to both their ancestral homeland and those 'from whom they feel so hopelessly far yet forever close.' And, in a barely veiled reference to Jews, Drapeau continued, those who felt duty bound to speak out did so on behalf of those allowed no voice of their own. Looking at Kosygin, Drapeau assured his guest that his Canadian visit had already been 'long enough for you to hear certain messages which in their own way are cries from the heart, reaching for other hearts ... May your own heart, Mr. Chairman, be as understanding as your mind, so that in neither you keep a blemished memory of your stay in this part of the world so different from your own.'[85]

While Drapeau's remarks might have been regarded by Kosygin as undiplomatic, the Montreal Jewish community had no interest whatever in diplomacy. They were intent on making their statement loud and public. The community organized a public rally at Place Bonaventure, where actor, folksinger, and Soviet Jewry advocate Theodore Bikel spoke and sang. As the rally ended, many in the crowd made their way through the downtown towards the Queen Elizabeth Hotel, where Kosygin and his entourage were staying. The hotel was walled off by a ring of police vehicles, and as a precaution the city's riot squad was held at the ready. But that was not necessary. The crowd across the street from the hotel was spirited but peaceful. At one point, as protesters waited for Kosygin to return from a lobster dinner hosted by the Province of Quebec, an Israeli flag was run up one of the flagpoles in the nearby Place Ville Marie. After the crowd applauded and sang Hatikvah, the flag was lowered. When Kosygin's car finally arrived at the hotel, it was greeted by shouts of *svoboda*, Russian for 'freedom.'[86]

The next morning Kosygin flew off to Vancouver, where Jewish demonstrators awaited him, as they did in Edmonton two days later. In both cities the small Jewish communities were concerned to keep their protests at a distance from Ukrainian Canadians and others calling for the dismantling of the Soviet Union. In Vancouver, almost half the city's nine thousand Jews turned out for a Saturday evening rally on the grounds of the Vancouver Courthouse, across the street from the Vancouver Hotel, where Kosygin was staying. As a dozen shofars sounded simultaneously to start off the demonstration, one police officer remarked, 'Louis Armstrong they're not.' The crowd sang and listened to speakers, including local Rabbi Marvin Hier, who applauded the crowd's exuberance. 'There are no more silent Jews,' he shouted. 'Silence went out of style in 1945.' Hier then joined other local rabbis in leading protesters in a march that soon encircled the hotel.

While the marchers paraded around the hotel, a small group of Jewish students secreted themselves into the hotel lobby. As surprised security officers rushed to surround them, 'the young people formed a circle, sipped ceremonial wine, sniffed incense and sang religious songs' in a *Havdalah* service marking the end of the sabbath. Once finished their service, they exited to the street and joined other students in an overnight vigil. Off to one side, police kept watch on a lone counter-protester. The man, claiming to be president of the Canadian Friends of the Middle East, insisted that advocates of Jewish emigration from the Soviet Union were part of 'the international Zionist conspiracy.'[87]

The students' overnight vigil was just ending when Kosygin and his entourage sped out of the hotel towards the airport, where the Soviet premier boarded a flight to Edmonton for a whirlwind five-hour visit before moving on to Toronto. With so short a stop in Edmonton, the small local Jewish community had limited opportunity to impact the Kosygin visit, but it tried. Knowing that Kosygin would meet with provincial premier Peter Lougheed, Jewish community leaders held a pre-visit talk with Lougheed, during which he agreed to present Kosygin with a Jewish community petition calling on the Soviet Union to grant Jews 'the right to maintain their spiritual and cultural identities as other groups do; to release from prisons and labor camps Jews and others whose only "crime" has been a desire to emigrate.'

Kosygin's schedule also called for him to visit a nickel refining plant in Fort Saskatchewan, less than half an hour's drive northeast of Edmonton. On the day of the Kosygin visit, a group of Jewish protesters gathered in a farmer's field bordering the highway into Fort Saskatchewan. They carried signs in English and Russian demanding freedom for Soviet Jews. As the Soviet premier sped past, the Jews, monitored by RCMP officers, waved their signs accompanied by blasts from a shofar. The process was repeated as Kosygin and his entourage rushed by on their way back to Edmonton. The protesters packed up their signs, sang Hatikvah and O Canada, sounded the shofar one last time, and set off to join a rally of some five hundred Jews from Calgary and Edmonton on the lawn of a local synagogue. As the Jews sang and danced a hora, Kosygin already was at the airport boarding a flight for his last Canadian stop, Toronto.[88]

Jewish community planning for the Kosygin visit to Toronto was more problematic than for anywhere else in Canada. It was not that Jews in Toronto were any less concerned for the plight of Soviet Jews. It was that, as Rabbi Plaut acknowledged, 'Here [in Toronto] the extremes are the sharpest and here for some time opposition to the Jewish establishment has been most pronounced.'[89] That establishment had yet to fully recover from the Allen Gardens episode. Even as they pledged a more inclusive and democratic leadership style, Allen Gardens gave Jewish leaders cause to worry that undisciplined hotheads, distrustful of the establishment, might organize their own Kosygin protest events.

In hopes of bringing all factions of the testy Toronto Jewish community together, the local Congress office assigned responsibility for the Kosygin protest to a broadly based planning committee. The committee at first considered holding a number of demonstrations during Kosygin's two days in Toronto, but eventually settled on one single major community protest march and rally, to be organized for Sunday evening, 24 October, Kosygin's last night in Canada.

As the organizers would learn, sometimes all the best planning in the world is not enough. Late Sunday afternoon, an estimated twelve thousand people braved inclement weather and snarled traffic to gather in a rain-soaked field across from the Inn on the Park Hotel in suburban Toronto, where Kosygin and his party occupied the three top floors. Thousands more never made it to the protest site. Stuck for hours in long lines of traffic, they were eventually turned away by police struggling to keep roads open for emergency vehicles. Many of those who somehow made it to the assembly point were less than pleased with the logistics. As prearranged with police, the demonstration began with a half-mile candlelight march east along Eglinton Avenue to a large vacant lot to the north of the Ontario Science Centre, where the Canadian Manufacturers Association was hosting a formal dinner for Kosygin.

Led by community rabbis and escorted by police on horseback, it took more than an hour for marchers, walking through an on-and-off-again drizzle and trying to keep their candles lit, to regroup at the demonstration site.

Uncooperative weather was not the only problem. The area reserved for the Jewish demonstration left some, including Plaut, shaking their heads in disbelief. Rather than providing an open field, they found that municipal authorities had fenced in the space. Plaut was dismayed to see thousands of Jews, including many Holocaust survivors, herded into the fenced-off enclosure by Jewish parade marshals and police on horseback. Scarred by Holocaust memories, some survivors refused to enter the cordoned-off area. As organizers attempted to reassure uneasy demonstrators, the demonstration's program was delayed. Elie Wiesel, whose book *Jews of Silence* had done so much to spark interest in the plight of Soviet Jews, was scheduled to speak, but he too refused to enter the fenced-off enclosure, agreeing only to address the crowd from the back of a flatbed truck eventually rolled up to the fence. To top things off, as he began to speak, the electrical sound system failed. Even with a bullhorn, much of what Wiesel and other speakers had to say was lost.

Perhaps it was the combination of traffic, wet weather, anger over the protest-site enclosure, and failure of the sound system, or perhaps it was protest fatigue, but Plaut found the Toronto demonstration 'a distinct anti-climax' as compared to the Ottawa event earlier in the week. For all the glitches, however, the thousands who participated in the Toronto community protest were likely forgiving of the demonstration's shortfalls. They were there to make a personal statement and, even if they could not hear Wiesel, they were convinced Kosygin and the Soviet Union heard what they had to say – much though they might pretend otherwise. When the crowd, a little waterlogged, finally dispersed, many young people trooped back to the park across from Kosygin's hotel, where the march had begun several hours earlier. Here they held a soggy but spirited overnight vigil by the light of an almost twenty-foot-high electrically illuminated Star of David constructed especially for the event. They were delighted at the thought that Kosygin could not avoid seeing their Star of David lighting up the night as he looked out his hotel room window.

In their post-mortem on the community demonstration, organizers had to admit that the logistics were a bit ragged and, more important, that the effort to ensure the Jewish community spoke in one voice had failed. In fact, the main Jewish community protest was overshadowed by two others – one by Jews, inside the Ontario Science Centre, the other by non-Jews, outside. As it had done elsewhere in Canada, the organized Jewish community declined an invitation to join in a single united anti-Soviet demonstration together with Ukrainian Canadian and other anti-Soviet protesters at the Science Centre. This was fortuitous, for the problems that beset the Jewish protest were as nothing compared to the other demonstration. Its organizers, working with police, planned for a large rally to be held in an open lot immediately south of the Science Centre. An effective publicity campaign brought out thousands of demonstrators. However, the police, without informing protest organizers, reclaimed the pre-arranged protest site as part of a secure exit route for Kosygin from the Science Centre's grounds.

When demonstrators began arriving at about seven that evening, many carrying umbrellas to protect themselves from the rain, they found their assigned assembly area cordoned off by police. With no alternative location set aside for them, protesters soon filled the sidewalks, front yards, and intersections across from the Science Centre. As organizers scrambled to keep order, the growing crowd spilled off the sidewalk and into the street. Determined to keep the street clear for police and other emergency vehicles, a line of police began to push the crowd back off the road. Those on the road, caught between oncoming police and a tightly packed crowd behind, had nowhere to go. Scuffling began, and before anyone knew what was happening, police on horseback had moved into the crowd. Frightened of being trampled, demonstrators used their umbrellas to defend themselves from the horses. In came the paddy wagons. Eighteen demonstrators were arrested. A number were hurt.[90]

Meanwhile, inside the Science Centre, Toronto members of the Jewish Defence League pulled off their own protest. The League was led by firebrand American rabbi Meir Kahane, condemned by mainstream Jewish leaders on both sides of the border as a dangerous provocateur, undisciplined in rhetoric and encouraging of violence. Canadian immigration authorities denied Kahane admission to Canada during Kosygin's visit, but two of his Toronto supporters, a young man and woman, carrying an invitation passed to them by a sympathizer, infiltrated the Science Centre dinner. No sooner did Kosygin stand to address the dinner guests than the two unfurled a red banner secreted into the hall as the sash on the woman's dress. They held the banner, proclaiming *SVOBOD* [freedom], aloft and began shouting 'Freedom for Soviet Jews.' As the crowd looked on in shock, security personnel were on them in a flash. The two were quickly ushered out of the hall, but not before the incident was captured by the world media. Kosygin, standing at the microphone, was heard to ask an aide, *'Yevrei?'* ('Are they Jews?'). There was no need for an answer. He already knew.[91]

To the disappointment of mainstream Jewish leaders, the riot in front of the Science Centre and the JDL act of protest inside captured the lion's share of press coverage – much of it negative. In spite of their disappointment, there can be little doubt that when Kosygin departed Canada the next day he carried with him a message from the Canadian Jewish community – the issue of Soviet Jews was going to haunt Soviet efforts at improving relations with the West. For the Jewish community, the week of protest demonstrations also proved a measure of how much the decade of the 1960s had transformed the Canadian Jewish community. How many remembered the 'We are just like you' message of the Canadian Jewish Bicentenary celebration of a decade earlier? By the end of the 1960s there was, for many Canadian Jews, a heightened sense of Jewish particularism, a sense of being Jewish and doing Jewish. What is more, while few would deny that by the end of the 1960s Jews had achieved unprecedented access to civil society, when action was demanded and purpose was clear, Larry Zeidel took on Eddie Shack, the Granite Club ended membership discrimination and Kosygin departed for Moscow with an image of Jewish youth huddled together on a rainy night under a shining Star of David.

Conclusion

What did the 1959 delegation which presented Governor General Georges Vanier with a hand-scribed scroll in celebration of two hundred years of Jewish contribution to Canada have in common with the rain-soaked Jewish students camped out under an illuminated Star of David across the street from the Soviet premier's hotel? Obviously, both groups were Jewish and both were Canadian. Both groups were also convinced they were advancing the Jewish community's interests. But what beyond that? Did they share a common understanding of the place of Jews in Canada and the world? Did they share a common vision for the Jewish future, the Canadian Jewish future in particular? Did they even share the same Canada? No. As readers of this book have learned, the Canadian Jewish community that emerged from the decade of the 1960s was vastly different from the community that had entered the decade. So too was Canada. The falling away of an antisemitism that previously had constricted the life chances of individual Jews made Canadian Jews stakeholders in a more open and accessible Canada than their parents might have dreamed possible.

Paradoxically, even as more and more Canadian Jews stepped onto the Canadian social, political, and economic stage, Jewish communal attachment and involvement remained strong. For the organized Jewish community and its leadership, the late 1960s was characterized by institutional growth and increased budgets to pay for an explosion of community programming, including political action programming. Of course, all of this would have been for naught if there were only leaders and no followers. But there was an upswing in rank-and-file Jewish communal commitment and participation. How this decoded itself differed from individual to individual, from family to family. There were many for whom the 1960s awakened an empowering pride in Jewish self-identity and a present-tense need to 'do Jewish.' While for some 'doing Jewish' found expression in Jewish organizational participation, in volunteerism on behalf of any one of numerous Jewish causes, or in generously reaching into one's pocket in support of community, for others 'doing Jewish' had less to do with paying than praying. Perhaps first drawn by Jewish religious tradition and ritual, many sought to ground their lives through faith. But whether the issues were religious or secular, organizational membership or voluntary commitment of time and money to this or that Jewish cause, for increasing numbers of Canadian Jews being Jewish was not just what they were. It was also what they did. Being Jewish was not what they inherited from parents, it was what they wanted for their children.

Of course, it is wrong to assume that all Canadian Jews were equally or immediately compelled by their Jewishness or interpreted 'doing Jewish' in the same way. There were those for whom being Jewish did not so much shape their real-time world as give it tone and texture. Inasmuch as the decade of the 1960s opened doors to Jewish engagement in the larger society, it is no surprise that many Jews walked through those doors. But unlike an earlier generation, they no longer had to park their Jewishness at the door. Wholesale jettisoning of one's Jewishness as a prerequisite for admission into the social, political, business, or educational mainstream was increasingly a thing of the past. As a result, as much as any individual Jew might more and more centre life outside the Jewish core, pressure to detach from that Jewish core lessened. Just the opposite. As the 1960s gave way to the 1970s, in the larger urban world in which most Canadian Jews lived, heritage was increasingly being accorded value. And if it would take time for private clubs and corporate boardrooms to catch on, being ethnic was increasingly 'in.' For Jews 'out there,' it was not only acceptable, it could even be advantageous, to acknowledge and even celebrate links to their heritage. And, let it not be forgotten, there were also those, perhaps few in number but still significant, who had previously denied any Jewish connection, even to themselves. For them, any Jewish connection was like a recently purchased pair of shoes, shiny and new, but still a little uncomfortable and unsteadying. Previously, Jewishness was what their parents or grandparents had escaped rather than what they were. There were those who emerged, perhaps uncomfortably, out of the Jewish closet during the Six Day War crisis and, for the first time, acknowledged a Jewish connection. And even if they subsequently slipped

back into the Jewish shadows, theirs was also a Jewish experience of
the 1960s.

For all the changes Canadian Jews witnessed during the 1960s, for all
the expanded opportunities Canada afforded them and the increasing
comfort level many non-Jewish Canadians felt with Jews, in no way
did Canadian Jews feel themselves free of concern. There were indeed
concerns, some a legacy of generations past and some born of or exacerbated by events unfolding. There remained, of course, uncertainty over
the future place of Jews in a changing Quebec. There was concern for
the long-term well-being of Israel and for the plight of Jews oppressed
for no other reason than that they were Jews. There was also a gnawing disquiet that, while individual Canadian Jews were carving out a
place from themselves in a more open and welcoming Canada, a new
antisemitism was emerging, one not so much directed against Jews as
individuals, but against Jews as a people and against the very notion of
Israel as a Jewish national homeland.

If some problems appeared to have no solution, others seemed to
have too many solutions. Perhaps that was unavoidable in a Jewish
community which was at once diverse and committed, a community
in which fault lines of class, religious observance, geography, politics,
and generation of arrival – *gayler* versus *greener* – cut deep and in which
argument was considered an Olympic-worthy sport. No wonder the
Jewish community appeared so undisciplined, whether with regard
to issues internal to the community itself or to Jewish–non-Jewish
relations.

With so fragmented and disputatious a community, it might seem
that finding, let alone imposing, unity would be like trying to herd cats
– a waste of time. And this was often true, but not always. The Canadian Jewish community might have sometimes resembled a three-ring
circus, but there was acknowledgment, even if sometimes grudgingly,
that the umbrella-like Canadian Jewish Congress, inclusive of most elements of the community, together with local federations and their fundraising responsibilities, should take the lead in representing Jewish
interests. What is more, there was also overarching agreement on the
need to maintain a healthy, professional, and well-funded community
social-service network, to remain steadfast in rooting out antisemitism,
to be vigilant as regards events unfolding in Quebec, and, close to the
Jewish heart, to maintain steadfast support for Israel and Jews in distress. And when the stakes were sufficiently high – as in the few weeks
preceding and during the Six Day War, or during Kosygin's Canadian

visit, or during the September crisis in Quebec – most agreed, albeit temporarily, to set aside or paper over differences in the name of *shalom bayit* – peace in the Jewish house. Thus, rather than regard disharmony as a source of weakness, it should be seen as a measure of Jewish community strength. For division to exist, there had to be large numbers of Canadian Jews who cared deeply enough about issues touching the community to form opinions and who were not shy about letting their voices be heard. But, yet another measure of community strength, there were limits, self-imposed limits. When the community good was seen to demand it, the Jewish community, for all its fractiousness and grumbling, proved capable of coming together as one.

What of the future? However much Canadian Jews of the late 1960s and early 1970s felt comfortable in their Jewish skins, they could not read the tea leaves. They had no way of predicting the future. And it was partly unease about the Jewish future that brought Montreal's Jewish elite out for a black-tie dinner in the ballroom of the posh Hotel Bonaventure on the evening of 18 February 1970. The gala was in honour of Pierre Elliott Trudeau, the 1970 recipient of the Anti-Defamation League of B'nai Brith's Canadian Family of Man Award. The previous year's award had gone to Paul-Émile Cardinal Léger, archbishop of Montreal from 1960 to 1968. Cardinal Léger's Statement of Award acclaimed the prelate's groundbreaking work on the Second Vatican Council's Statement on Jews, regarded by many as a 'new beginning' in Catholic–Jewish relations.[1]

Trudeau was something else again. If relations between the Catholic Church and Jews needed mending, as much in Quebec as anywhere in Canada, relations between the vast majority of the Canadian Jewish community and Trudeau did not. Those who turned out to honour him – many of them constituents of his Mount Royal riding – had voted for the prime minister and would time and again. A Quebec Jewish community worried the Quiet Revolution could pave the way for a growth of nationalism grounded in linguistic and ethnic exclusion and even separatism, regarded Trudeau as a bulwark of federalism and a staunch advocate of an inclusive citizenship that ensured equality for all, regardless of language, religion, or heritage. Trudeau's Statement of Award lauded the prime minister

for his contribution and record of achievement in expanding the scope of human freedom: for his deep and abiding concern for the dignity and security of all people, regardless of race or creed; for his record of achievement in the fields of civil rights and social justice; for his courageous implementation of what he deemed humane regardless of the clamour of those who urged expedience; for his efforts in promoting the unity of all Canadians; for his respect for the eternal verities embodied in all religions; for his appreciation that we are all parts of the family of man.[2]

After being formally presented with the award, Trudeau addressed the gathering. In what the *Canadian Jewish News* described as his 'first "official" speech to the Jewish community since becoming head of government,'[3] Trudeau began by thanking his audience for the honour it had bestowed upon him

in the spirit of our fellowship in a common ideal. A spirit of wisdom – the spirit of the teachers of the Jewish community, custodians of the ancient wisdom of Israel; a spirit of brotherhood – the Canadian brotherhood within which the Jews form a community which is truly remarkable both for its origins and for the quality of its contribution to the Canadian way of life ... So outstanding is the Jewish contribution that it is difficult to imagine our society without it.[4]

As enviable as was the Jewish record of contribution to Canada, Trudeau continued, the Jewish community also afforded Canadians a model in miniature of what Canadian society could and should be. In a pointed swipe at Quebec nationalists, Trudeau held that Canadian Jews derive strength from their diversity of origin, mother tongue, and religious and cultural traditions. In this, Trudeau observed, 'there is a resemblance between the Jewish community ... and the structure of our country, which is both bilingual and multicultural. Indeed, the overall cohesion of the many elements of the Jewish community is indication of the degree of unity that Canadians can hope to achieve within our federation.' As Canadians built a strong, just, and pluralist federation, Trudeau continued, they would do well to bear in mind a three-fold blessing that Canadian Jews, rooted in an ancient tradition, had bequeathed to their fellow citizens: 'first the revelation of a transcendent personal God; second, the revelation of man's individual worth; finally, the revelation of the meaning of social justice.' Trudeau expressed awe that humanity should have been gifted with these revelations, the essential building blocks of Western enlightenment, by so tiny a minority within the human family.

This, Trudeau noted, was even more amazing because, as a minority,

Jews always had to struggle to survive. They also paid a heavy price for doing so. 'Jews,' Trudeau allowed, 'are destined to remain a minority amongst the peoples of the world. They are in fact the quintessence of a minority.' In spite of their gifts to humanity, as a minority they have long endured the enmity of neighbours, a murderous litany of hostility that led to the Holocaust. Decrying antisemitism as 'a problem which has afflicted our society for the past 2000 years,' Trudeau argued:

> We know of all kinds of prejudice but there is a particular persistence to anti-semitism. Some people, carrying from generation to generation a deeply rooted malevolence, still cannot forgive Israel its distinctiveness, the three-fold gift of transcendence, individual worth and justice. To walk in God's way, to love one's fellow man, and to be just in one's dealings – what unforgivable madness! For any man worthy of the name, it is anti-semitism that is unforgivable.

Declaring antisemitism incompatible with the values of state and nation that he and most Canadians desired, Trudeau insisted, 'The people of Canada condemn any defamation based on race and religion.' But, much though he might wish it otherwise, Trudeau acknowledged that antisemitism and racism had yet to be banished. Hate persisted. In an effort to shelter Jews and all victims from racial hate, he affirmed his government's commitment to passage of a bill 'that will make the dissemination of hate literature a criminal offence. We take this step with determination though not without regret that it should be necessary in our country. Let this law,' a law for which the organized Jewish community had long pressed, 'be one step towards the society we seek to build.'[5]

Trudeau then turned to address an issue uppermost in the minds of most in his Montreal Jewish audience, the future place of Jews in a rapidly changing Quebec. Deviating slightly from his prepared text, Trudeau was candid:

> I am aware that we are passing through a troubled period in this Province and that being a member of a minority can be a cause of apprehension. I know that many members of this community share this feeling and have doubts about their future in Quebec. If I speak as a member of one minority to another – stick with it! Stick with it! With all your energies and

abilities play your part in this society which you have helped to build and insist on your rights as members of it.

Then speaking past the audience, Trudeau concluded by addressing those narrow nationalists in Quebec who sought to use language, religion, and ethnic origin to withhold equal rights of citizenship from others. He brought the house to its feet in a thunderous ovation by forcefully pledging to fight this effort.[6] Trudeau was the Quebec Jewish champion of the moment. But as the applause died away, the sense of unease at where Quebec might be heading, and how Jews would fit into that Quebec, remained unresolved. Certainly Trudeau's remarks were appreciated, but they were far from entirely reassuring. Few doubted the prime minister's personal commitment to an inclusive citizenship. But no matter how well intended his comments, in pledging to battle those advocating a nationalist agenda grounded in parochial exclusivity and a call for separatism, Trudeau was acknowledging that nationalism of exclusion was not a spent force. Quite the opposite. Much as Jews supported Trudeau's aspirational vision for Canada, some in his audience might regard his call to battle in defence of their place in Quebec as proof that their future role in the province remained very much in doubt.

As the room quieted down, none in the plush banquet hall or on the Jewish street could know how events of the next several years would play out or how profoundly the Jewish sense of place in Quebec would be affected. Within months of Trudeau's address, Montreal and Quebec were jolted by the October crisis. The Jewish community of Montreal and Canada changed forever. Whatever reservations some in the Jewish community might harbour about Trudeau's invoking of the War Measures Act, with its suspension of civil rights and call-up of the army, in the main, Jews supported his actions. For many French Quebeckers, however, Trudeau's actions were decried as excessive and uncalled for. Partly as a result of pushback against the War Measures Act, support for the sovereigntist Parti Québécois, founded in 1968, began to grow. The provincial Liberal government, frightened of the nationalist surge and hoping to steal the Parti Québécois's thunder, introduced the Official Language Act of 1974 (*Loi sur la langue officielle*), also known as Bill 22. It installed French as the official language in Quebec, mandating that all public institutions address the public in French; made French the official language of contracts; and stipulated that corporations give themselves French names, advertise primarily in French as well as obtain a certificate of francization as proof the business could both function in French and address its employees in French. In education, freedom of parental choice regarding language of instruction was maintained for English-language Quebeckers, but entrance into English schools was limited to those who could prove a prior knowledge of English. Others were streamed into French-language schools.

Bill 22 was attacked by sovereigntists for not going far enough and by many anglophones, including many Jews, for going too far. In the provincial election of 1976, some of those still smarting over Bill 22 withheld support from the provincial Liberals. This helped elect the Parti Québécois, a party committed to Quebec's separation from Canada. Its election set off a tsunami of uncertainty within the Montreal Jewish community. As if in validation of their worst fears, they watched with misgiving as the new government quickly introduced Bill 101, entitled *Charte de la langue française*. Passed in the summer of 1977, this bill went well beyond Bill 22, proclaiming French as the sole official language in Quebec in virtually every aspect of provincial jurisdiction. For example, it required all advertising on billboards and most commercial signage to be in French only. All provincial government agencies were directed to employ French in all dealings with corporations and other governments in Canada. English-language schooling was further restricted to those already in English-language schools, to their siblings, to the children of those temporarily posted in Quebec and to those whose parents had received an English elementary education in Quebec.

Although Bill 101 was eventually modified so as to permit children of parents educated in English elsewhere in Canada to attend Quebec English-language public schools, for many Montreal Jews all this was just too much. For some thirty thousand Montreal Jews, Bill 101 meant Highway 401. Many younger, educated, and economically comfortable professionals packed their bags and moved out. The lion's share resettled in Toronto, thereby confirming Toronto as home to Canada's largest Jewish community.[7]

Just as those who gathered in the Hotel Bonaventure to honour and listen to Pierre Trudeau in February 1970 were not prescient when it came to events that would unfold in Quebec, the thousands who gathered in Toronto eight months later to hear from another prime minster, Golda Meir, could not have imagined how difficult Israel's path would become. In November 1971 Golda Meir attended the twenty-fifth anniversary session of the United Nations in New York, following that with a visit to Ottawa for discussions with Trudeau. En route she made a one-day whirlwind stop in Toronto to thank Canadian Jews for their unswerving commitment to Israel's security and development, and, no doubt, to encourage continued support.

She did not have to do much convincing. Memories of the dark fear that gripped Canadian Jews in the few weeks leading up to 1967 war and the exhilaration that accompanied Israeli victory on the battlefield, a victory that Canadian Jews felt as their own, were not forgotten. Thought an architect of that victory, Golda Meir – reported to have chided a colleague, 'Don't be humble. You're not that great' – was accorded a hero's welcome by the Toronto Jewish community. But the hero's welcome accorded a woman who looked more like a dowdy old librarian than a tough and seasoned politician belied a gnawing unease that was also part of the 1967 legacy. Israel may have defeated its enemies in 1967, but those enemies were not gone. Israel still confronted hostile neighbours supported by the Soviet Union. It was also threatened by terrorism at home and growing anti-Israel sentiment abroad, including in Canada.

Meir's message to Canadian Jews was simple. While it longed for peace, Israel must remain strong and resolute, both for its own defence and so it might remain a haven for all Jews in need of shelter. She delivered her message again and again during her day-long visit. The seventy-one-year-old Israeli prime minister began her day with an early morning address to a long-planned Labour Zionist Organization of Canada conference at the King Edward Hotel in downtown Toronto. Behind closed doors, well guarded by armed security officials, Meir assured more than five hundred delegates from across Canada that a vigilant Israel 'wanted to live in peace' with its neighbours, no matter how long it took to achieve that peace. 'We will never give up any opening for peace, but simultaneously – as long as there is no peace – Israel must remain strong and equipped. Only because it is our only hope for peace.'[8] Israel's hope for peace was also the theme of her second talk, this time to a United Israel Appeal luncheon at the Inn on the Park chaired by Allan Bronfman. Peace, Meir contended, required willing partners, and so far there were none. Without peace, she told the UIA gathering, Israel's defence costs were in danger of undercutting its ability to fund essential social programs and, in particular, to integrate the thousands of Jews forced to flee Arab lands following the Six Day War. Absorbing these new arrivals was a daunting task and, Meir explained, one that was best done in partnership with Western diaspora Jews. A

UIA spokesperson assured the Israeli prime minster that Canadian Jews would not fail Israel. Resettlement money would be forthcoming.

Meir received a similar pledge from more than three hundred well-to-do Jewish community members, who purchased almost $1,500,000 in Israel Bonds before sitting down to an early evening dinner with the prime minister at the fashionable Oakdale Golf and Country Club.[9] After some hurried remarks, Meir jokingly apologized for having to eat and run. And run she did. With a police escort leading the way, she and her entourage were whisked across the city to Toronto's largest synagogue, Beth Tzedec, for her final event of the day, a public speech co-sponsored by a number of the city's major Jewish organizations. Even though, according to the *Canadian Jewish News*, admission was originally supposed to be limited to 'those receiving invitations from the sponsoring organizations,' the crush of those, many without tickets, who turned up to hear Golda Meir forced anxious event organizers, working with security personnel, to seat people on a first-come, first-served basis.[10] When Meir entered the synagogue, she found more than five thousand people crowded into the sanctuary and the adjacent synagogue ballroom. An overflow crowd estimated at a further five thousand, many with invitations in hand, crowded into the spacious synagogue lobby area and out onto the surrounding grounds.

Talking without notes, Meir again stressed Israel's hopes for peace. And peace would come, she assured the gathering. The timing of that peace, however, was not in Israel's hands. It was up to Israel's neighbours. She was fond of saying, 'We will have peace with the Arabs when they love their children more than they hate us.' In the meantime, peace would not be bought with unilateral Israeli concessions in the face of Arab intransigence and terrorism. Rather than peace, concessions would only beget a demand for more concessions. Nor would peace come as a result of United Nations resolutions or big-power guarantees. They had been tried previously in the Sinai and came up empty. Peace, Meir declared, could only come through direct one-on-one negotiations between Israel and its neighbours. There could be no peace by proxy. And when those neighbours were ready to enter negotiations, she pledged, they would find Israel a receptive and responsive partner. They would also find that everything was open to negotiation bar one thing – the continued existence of a strong and independent Israel. That could not, and would never be, negotiated away.[11]

Was Meir just offering a Canadian Jewish audience a heartening message they wanted to hear or did she really believe that peace was within grasp? All that Israel's neighbours had to do was want it. In a recorded interview with journalist Barry Callaghan for the CBC's 'Weekend,' Meir asserted that Israel stood ready to relinquish control of the occupied territories as part of a comprehensive peace package – but not before. Callaghan suggested in return that, with no prospect of negotiation anywhere on the horizon, Israel's continued occupation of Arab lands and the emergence of Palestinian resistance leaders such as Yasser Arafat promised an endless Palestinian insurgency.[12] 'I don't think what we are dealing with now is the possibility of a Six Day War,' Callaghan suggested, 'but a war that might go on for twenty or even thirty years.'

Meir, using a grandmotherly tone, brushed aside Callaghan's reading of the future. There would be peace, she insisted. 'You're a young man yet. I am sure that twenty years from now people will have forgotten there ever was an Arafat. But I'm sure you and I will see peace in the Middle East. But I will see peace when my neighbours want to make peace with the State of Israel as it is – as it is means a Jewish state with a Jewish majority as we have.'[13]

Meir was wrong. For all her talk of peace, peace not only eluded Israel, but, during the next few years, Israel endured an escalating series of terrorist attacks, airplane hijackings, and in 1972 the murder of Israeli athletes at the Munich Olympics. Less than a year later, on 6 October 1973, Yom Kippur Day, Egypt and Syria launched a joint attack on Israel. In the early stages of battle, while Canadian Jews relived their worst fears of 1967, Egyptian troops overran Israeli fortifications along the Suez Canal and seemed poised to retake the Sinai and invade Israel. Syria, in turn, smashed through Israeli lines on the Golan Heights and threatened to sweep down from the Golan into the Galilee. Israel might indeed be driven into the sea. After a horrific sacrifice of men and material, and an emergency infusion of American military supplies, Israel gradually regained the momentum. Before the international community imposed a ceasefire, Israel pushed the Syrians out of the Golan and the Egyptian military back across the Suez Canal to the very gates of Cairo. Israel was victorious yet again, but it paid a very high price for that victory. And an early casualty of the war was confidence in Israel's invulnerability. While Canadian Jews never faltered in their support of Israel during and after the Yom Kippur War, Israeli voters showed their lack of support for a government that had barely skirted disaster. In the war's aftermath, Meir was forced from office and the Labor Party she led, which had governed Israel for more than twenty-five years, was defeated at the polls.

Under the new government, and in spite of Israel's statements to the contrary, the occupation took on an air of permanence and state-supported settlement construction on the West Bank expanded. In consequence, as the decade unfolded, disaffection with Israel in Canada and elsewhere in the Western world continued to grow. In Canada there were also the first hints of discord among Jews at Israel's continuing occupation and settlement policies.

Looking back over the Canadian Jewish decade of the 1960s, then, it is hard to draw hard and fast conclusions. Yes, one can trace the shaping events of the decade that dramatically altered Canadian Jewish thinking and behaviour. But concerns that percolated through those ten years – including the place of Jews in Quebec and concern for Israel – still remain unresolved. Thus, much as it might be tempting to think of the past in neatly compartmentalized decade-long slices – the roaring twenties, the dirty thirties, and on and on – lived history is not nearly that neat. The swinging sixties may have swung for some, but for many Canadian Jews the sixties was a decade of identity renewal. Catholic theologian Michael Novak might argue that, in this, Canadian Jews were not alone. In his much-discussed 1971 book *The Rise of the Unmeltable Ethnic*, Novak argued that the previous decade had seen an American and, by extension, North American flowering of 'a politics of cultural pluralism, a politics of family and neighborhood, a politics of smallness and quietness.'[14] Witness Trudeau's Multicultural Policy statement that same year. But it might also be argued that the Canadian Jewish situation was palpably different. Novak's notion of a 'politics of smallness and quietness' has faded. Multiculturalism in Canada has morphed into something Trudeau might find hard to recognize. The Jewish community, much changed in the more than forty years since the 1960s began, remains set along the course charted in that decade. Without intending to insinuate that the Canadian Jewish community was or is monolithic – far from it – one cannot doubt that events of the 1960s intensified a gut-level sense among Canadian Jews that there was no such thing as a stand-alone Jew. To be a Jew was to be part of a distinctive people. Since the 1960s the effort to veil Jewish particularism by marketing Canadian Jews as no different than other Canadians – except that Jews observe Saturday as the sabbath – has, for the most part, been missing in action. Cascading events of the 1960s not only sparked a reconfiguration of Jewish definition, but also shaped the terrain on which the next generation of Canadian Jews would walk. And that is very much the point. If the 1959 death of Duplessis and the organized bicentenary celebration of Jewish settlement in Canada provide an obvious beginning point for exploring the upheaval that was Canadian Jewish life in the 1960s – a decade that reset the course of Jewish history in Canada – there is no single event or series of events that provides closure on the decade. When Pierre Trudeau spoke in Montreal and Golda Meir spoke in Toronto, the calendar showed the decade of the 1960s was over. But the issues the two leaders addressed, issues brought into stark relief during the decade, are as unresolved now as they were then. Just as rain-soaked students protesting the plight of Soviet Jews stood under the shaded light of their home-made Star of David, Canadian Jews today continue to stand in the reflected light of the 1960s.

Notes

Chapter 1: Of Faith and Thanksgiving

1 Bernard Malamud, *The Fixer* (New York: Farrar, Straus and Giroux, 1966), 314.
2 *Debates of the House of Commons*, vol. 1 (1960), 26 January 1960, 334–5; *Winnipeg Tribune*, 14 October 1959.
3 Claude Bissell, *The Young Vincent Massey* (Toronto: University of Toronto Press, 1981), 35, 162; Claude Bissell, *The Imperial Canadian: Vincent Massey in Office* (Toronto: University of Toronto Press, 1986), 100–6, 132–5.
4 Ninette Kelley and Michael Trebilcock, *The Making of the Mosaic: A History of Canadian Immigration Policy* (Toronto: University of Toronto Press, 1998), 324–7.
5 Irving Abella and Harold Troper, *None Is Too Many: Canada and the Jews of Europe 1933–1948* (Toronto: Lester & Orpen Dennys, 1982), 48–9, 178–9, 195–6.
6 Abella and Troper, *None Is Too Many*, 101–25.
7 Georges Vanier, 'Buchenwald Concentration Camp,' CBC transcript, 1 May 1945, as quoted in Abella and Troper, *None Is Too Many*, 195; Robert Speaight, *Vanier: Soldier, Diplomat, and Governor General* (Toronto: Bungay, Collins and Harvill Press, 1970), 317.
8 James Walker, 'The "Jewish Phase" in the Movement for Racial Equality in Canada,' *Canadian Ethnic Studies* 34 (2002), 1–29; Ruth Frager and Carmela Patria, '"This Is Our Country, These Are Our Rights": Minorities and the Origins of Ontario's Human Rights Campaigns,' *Canadian Historical Review* 82 (2001), 1–35; Ross Lambertson, 'The Dresden Story: Racism, Human Rights, and the Jewish Labour Committee of Canada,' *Labour/Le Travail* 47 (2001), 43–83.

9 It would be several years before sociologist John Porter would publish his groundbreaking study of Canadian social structure, giving name to what he saw as a narrowly stratified system of Canadian ethnic and religious relations – the vertical mosaic.

10 Michael Marrus, *Mr. Sam: The Life and Times of Sam Bronfman* (Toronto: Viking, 1991), 437.

11 Sheldon J. Godfrey and Judith C. Godfrey, *Search Out the Land: The Jews and the Growth of Equality in British Colonial America, 1740–1867* (Montreal: McGill-Queen's University Press, 1995), 35–6.

12 For a discussion of Jews in pre-1790 British North America, including the Hart family, see Gerald Tulchinsky, *Taking Root: The Origins of the Canadian Jewish Community* (Toronto: Lester Publishing, 1992), 8–14; also see Godfrey and Godfrey, *Search Out the Land*, 73–126.

13 Eli Gottesman, ed., *Canadian Jewish Reference Book and Directory 1963* (Montreal: Jewish Institute for Higher Research, 1963).

14 Letter from Georges Vanier, February 1962, as quoted ibid., n.p.

15 *Edmonton Journal*, 5 September 1959; interview with Ruth Wisse, 21 October 2004, Boston (by telephone).

16 Shulamis Yellin, *The Jew in Canada: 1760–1960 – A Comprehensive Syllabus for Schools and Study Groups Covering the Role of Canadian Jewry* (Montreal: Canadian Jewish Publications, 1961); Robin Elliott and Gordon E. Smith, eds., *István Anhalt: Pathways and Memory* (Montreal: McGill-Queen's University Press, 2001), 44, 114–15.

17 *Toronto Telegram*, 9 February 1960; *Commemorative Report on National Bicentenary of Canadian Jewry* (Montreal: Canadian Jewish Congress, 1960), 27–40; Jewish Historical Committee of Calgary, M-4744-15, Mrs Eddie Cohen Papers, Program for celebration of bicentenary of Canadian Jewry, Calgary, and proclamation issued by Canadian Jewish Congress (1959).

18 Phyllis Lee Peterson, 'The Jew in Canada: Where Does He Stand Today?' *Maclean's* 72 (1959), 24 October 1959, 22–3, 62–5.

19 For a discussion of Jewish intermarriage in the early 1960s see Erich Rosenthal, 'Studies in Jewish Intermarriage in the United States,' in *American Jewish Yearbook 1964* (New York: American Jewish Committee, 1964), 3–53.

20 Sam Welles, 'The Jewish Elan,' *Fortune* 61/2, February 1960, 134–9, 160, 164, 166.

21 Milton Himmelfarb, 'The Vanishing Jew,' *Commentary* 36 (September 1963), 249, 250–1; Rosenthal, 'Studies in Jewish Intermarriage,' 3–53.

22 C. Bezalel Sherman, *The Jew within American Society: A Study in Ethnic Indi-viduality* (Detroit: Wayne State University Press, 1961), 183–9.

23 Leo S. Srole, review of Sherman, *The Jew within American Society* in *Mid-stream*, Spring 1961, 90–4.

24 Dayenu cartoon by Henry Leonard, reprinted in Erich Rosenthal, 'The Vanishing American Jew,' *Midstream* 12 (May 1966), 67–8.

25 Srole, review, *Midstream*, 90–4.

26 Robert Gordis, *Judaism in the Christian World* (New York: McGraw-Hill, 1966), 186.

27 Boris Smolar, 'Letter from America,' *Jewish Affairs* (December 1964), 23–4; Leon Jick, 'American Jewry: Flourishing or Floundering?' *American Juda-ism* 16/3 (1967), 6–7, 32. A particularly useful source for gauging Ameri-can Jewish attitudes through the 1960s is *Jewish Digest*. Modelled on *Readers' Digest*, with material excerpted from Jewish publications, Jewish-content journal articles, rabbinic sermons, and talks by communal leaders, *Jewish Digest* (hereafter *JD*) carried many articles that dealt with or related to the 'vanishing Jew' debate. The following are a sample: Isaiah Minkoff, 'Can Jews Survive in an Open Society,' *JD* 10 (October 1964), 1–9; Will Herberg, 'The Jew and America's Three-Religion Society: The Meaning of Jewish Integration,' *JD* 10 (December 1964), 29–37; C. Bezalel Sherman, 'New Patterns and Attitudes in American Jewish Life' *JD* 11 (December 1965); Manheim Shapiro, 'How Jewish Do You Want Your Children to Be?' *JD* 11 (May 1965), 19–24; 'How Widespread Is Intermarriage among Jews in the United States?' *JD* 11 (April 1966), 14–16; Jacob Marcus, 'Tomor-row's American Jew,' *JD* 12 (November 1966), 33–9; Joseph Rudavsky, 'Growing Pains of a Suburban Jewish Community,' *JD* 12 (November 1966), 21–6; Manheim S. Shapiro, 'Basic Issues Facing American Jewry,' *JD* 12 (January 1967), 1–4; Harold Weisberg, 'New Directions for the Future of American Jewry,' *JD* 12 (February 1967), 1–4. For a more scholarly review of issues to do with intermarriage during the 1960s in the United States see Arnold Schwartz, 'Intermarriage in the United States,' in Marshall Sklare ed., *The Jew in American Society* (New York: Behrman House, 1974), 303–31.

28 *Newsweek*, 7 October 1963, 97; *Time Magazine*, 17 January 1964, 45.

29 'The Vanishing American Jew,' *Look Magazine*, 5 May 1964, 42–6.

30 Library and Archives Canada (hereafter LAC), W. Gunther Plaut Papers, MG 31, F6, vol. 150, file, HBT Sermons. Rabbi W. Gunther Plaut, 'The Van-ishing Jew,' unpublished sermon, 15 May 1964.

31 Canadian Jewish Archives (hereafter CJA), CA 33, box 33, file 306: Memo-

randum of Louis Rosenberg to Saul Hayes re: Intermarriage, ca. 1961; Memorandum of Louis Rosenberg to Saul Hayes re: Intermarriage among Jews in Canada, 7 March 1966; Memorandum of Louis Rosenberg to Saul Hayes re: Montreal Jewish Population Studies, 1 November 1966.

32 Earl Berger, 'The Un-American Jew,' *Commentary* 42 (August 1966), 82.

33 For an examination of the myth of congruency between the American and Canadian diasporas see Gerald Tulchinsky, 'The Canadian Jewish Experience: A Distinct Personality Emerges,' in Ruth Klein and Frank Dimant, eds., *From Immigration to Integration: The Canadian Jewish Experience* (Toronto: Institute for International Relations, 2001), 19–30.

34 W. Gunther Plaut, 'Canadian Experience: The Dynamics of Jewish Life since 1945,' in Bernard Martin, ed., *Movements and Issues in American Judaism: An Analysis and Sourcebook on Developments since 1945* (Westport, CT: Blackwell, 1978), 285.

35 Interview with Rabbi W. Gunther Plaut, 26 June 2002, Toronto.

36 Louis Rosenberg, *A Study of the Changes in the Population Characteristics of the Jewish Community in Canada 1931–1961* (Montreal: Canadian Jewish Congress, 1965), III–VI; Joseph Yam, 'The Size and Geographic Distribution of Canada's Jewish Population' (unpublished paper, n.p, n.d.), 2–6.

37 Interview with Rabbi W. Gunther Plaut, 26 June 2002, Toronto; Rosenberg, *A Study*, vi.

38 Joseph Kage, 'The Settlement of Hungarian Refugees in Canada,' in Robert H. Keyserlingk, ed., *Breaking Ground: The 1956 Hungarian Refugee Movement to Canada* (Toronto: York Lanes Press, 1993), 100; Jean-Claude Lasry, 'A Francophone Diaspora in Quebec,' in M. Weinfeld et al., eds., *The Canadian Jewish Mosaic* (Toronto: John Wiley, 1981), 221–40; Jean-Claude Lasry, 'Sephardim and Ashkenazim in Montreal,' in Robert J. Brym et al., eds., *The Jews in Canada* (Toronto: University of Toronto Press, 1993), 395–401; Harold Troper, 'New Horizons in a New Land: Jewish Immigration to Canada,' in Klein and Dimant, eds., *From Immigration to Integration*, 3–18.

39 Ben Kayfetz, as quoted in Mindy B. Avrich-Skapinker, 'Canadian Jewish Involvement with Soviet Jewry, 1970–1990: The Toronto Case Study,' unpublished PhD thesis, University of Toronto, 1993, 42.

40 Ibid., 39–42.

41 Morton Weinfeld, 'Louis Rosenberg and the Origins of the Socio-Demographic Study of Jews in Canada,' in S. Della Pergola and J. Even, eds., *Papers in Jewish Demography, 1993* (Jerusalem: Hebrew University, 1989), 357–67.

42 Rosenberg, *A Study*, 3.

43 Kelley and Trebilcock, *The Making of the Mosaic*, 311–14.

44 Franklin Bialystok, *Delayed Impact: The Holocaust and the Canadian Jewish Community* (Montreal: McGill-Queen's, 2000), 73–4, 93.

45 Gerald Tulchinsky, *Branching Out: The Transformation of the Jewish Community* (Toronto: Stoddart, 1998), 289.

46 Yam, 'The Size and Geographic Distribution,' 14–15.

47 Ibid., 10–15.

48 For a discussion of demographic issues relating to the Jewish community in Winnipeg see Louis Rosenberg, *A Study of the Growth and Changes in the Distribution of the Jewish Community of Winnipeg 1961* (Montreal: Canadian Jewish Congress, 1965).

49 Ann Rivkin, 'The Jews of Vancouver: You've Come a Long Way, Baby,' *Chronicle Review*, June 1972, 17, 23.

50 For an introduction to Jewish community leadership organization in Canada see Harold M. Waller, 'Power in the Jewish Community,' in M. Weinfeld et al., eds., *The Canadian Jewish Mosaic* (Toronto: John Wiley, 1981), 151–69. For background on the process by which the Canadian Jewish Congress became a key force in the Toronto Jewish community and social services in Toronto were rationalized, professionalized, and centrally funded, see Yaccov Glickman, 'Organizational Indicators and Social Correlates of Collective Jewish Identity,' unpublished PhD thesis, University of Toronto, 1976, and Jack Edwin Lipinsky, 'The Progressive Wedge: The Organizational Behaviour of Toronto Jewry, 1933–1948,' unpublished PhD thesis, University of Toronto, 2003.

51 For an interesting if slightly later discussion of Jewish intermarriage in Canada, see Werner Cohn, 'Jewish Outmarriage and Anomies: A Study of the Canadian Syndrome of Polarities,' *Canadian Review of Sociology and Anthropology* 13 (1976), 90–105.

52 Jewish Historical Society of British Columbia (hereafter JHS/BC), CJC Papers, box 39, file 749. Lou Zimmerman to Saul Hayes, 12 February 1965.

53 Erich Rosenthal, 'Intermarriage among Jewry: A Function of Acculturation, Community Organization, and Family Stucture,' in Bernard Martin, ed., *Movements and Issues in American Judaism* (Westport, CT: Greenwood Press, 1978), 270–1.

54 Louis Rosenberg, 'Canada,' *American Jewish Yearbook, 1965* (New York. American Jewish Committee,1965), 322; JHS/BC, CJC Papers, box 39, file 749. Memorandum of Louis Rosenberg to Saul Hayes re: Intermarriage among Jews in Canada, January 27, 1965.

55 Simon Rawidowicz, *Israel: The Ever-Dying People* (Cranbury, NJ: Associated University Presses, 1968), 63. Rawidowicz's essay, originally published in Hebrew in 1948, was first published in English in *Judaism* 16 (1967), 423–33.

56 Samuel Bronfman, 'Canadian Jewry Today,' *World Jewry* 9/1 (January–February 1966).

Chapter 2: A Third Solitude

 1 Peter Desbarats, 'Montreal Confessions,' in *Century 1867–1967: The Canadian Saga* (Toronto: Toronto Star, 1967), 34–5.
 2 Jack Jebwab, 'The Politics of Dialogue: Rapprochement Efforts between Jews and French Canadians: 1939–1960,' in Ira Robinson and Mervin Butovsky, eds., *Renewing Our Days: Montreal Jews in the Twentieth Century* (Montreal: Vehicule Press, 1995), 42–74; also see Jacques Langlais and David Rome, *Jews and French Quebecers: Two Hundred Years of Shared History* (Waterloo, ON: Wilfrid Laurier University Press, 1991).
 3 Mordecai Richler, 'Their Canada and Mine: A Memoir,' *Commentary*, August 1961, 140.
 4 Mordecai Richler, *The Street* (Toronto: Key Porter, 1987), 184.
 5 Interview with Myer Bick, 26 March 2004, Montreal.
 6 Interview with William Shuchat, 25 March 2004, Montreal.
 7 Interview with Ruth Wisse, 21 October 2004, Boston.
 8 Richler, 'Their Canada and Mine,' 139.
 9 Interview with Manny Batshaw, 11 December 2002, Montreal.
10 Morton Weinfeld, *Like Everyone Else ... but Different* (Toronto: McClelland and Stewart, 2001), 88–9.
11 Brock University political scientist Garth Stevenson notes that Montreal was unusual in the degree to which different ethno-linguistic groups 'lived in almost completely separate worlds, with complete networks of autonomous and parallel institutions.' According to Stevenson, the Jewish network was 'less complete, less autonomous and less securely established, but quite impressive.' Garth Stevenson, *Community Besieged: The Anglophone Minority and the Politics of Quebec* (Montreal: McGill-Queen's University Press, 1999), 46. The reason why this 'institutional completeness,' a phrase coined by sociologist Raymond Breton, was 'less' than that of the 'British and French' may be that it was self-supported and did not include the structure of publicly funded education or that which might flow out from ethnically controlled municipal governments. Raymond Breton, 'The Institutional Completeness of Ethnic Communities and the Personal Relations of Immigrants,' *American Journal of Sociology* 70 (1964), 193–205.
12 Interview with Manny Weiner, 11 December 2002, Montreal.

13 For a discussion of Montreal Sephardic self-understanding see Joseph Levy and Yolande Cohen, 'Moroccan Jews and Their Adaptation to Montreal Life,' in Robinson and Butovsky, eds., *Renewing Our Days*, 95–118.

14 Jean-Claude Lasry, 'A Francophone Diaspora in Quebec,' in Morton Weinfeld et al., eds., *The Canadian Jewish Mosaic* (Toronto: John Wiley, 1981), 221–40.

15 Interview with Manny Batshaw, 11 December 2002, Montreal.

16 Alan W. Jones, 'Education for English-Speaking People until 1964,' in Gary Caldwell and Eric Waddell, eds., *The English of Quebec: From Majority to Minority Status* (Quebec: IQRC, 1982), 98–9.

17 Michael D. Behiels, 'Neo-Canadians and Schools in Montreal, 1900–1970,' *Journal of Cultural Geography* 8 (1988), 5–16; Michael Brown, 'Good Fences Do Not Necessarily Make Good Neighbors: Jews and Judaism in Canada's Schools and Universities,' *Jewish Political Studies Review* 11 (1999), 97–113.

18 Gerald Tulchinsky, *Branching Out: The Transformation of the Jewish Community* (Toronto: Stoddart, 1998), 63–86.

19 David Rome, 'Jews in Anglophone Quebec,' in Caldwell and Waddell, eds., *The English of Quebec*, 166–71.

20 Roger Magnuson, *A Brief History of Quebec Education: From New France to Parti Québécois* (Montreal: Harvest House, 1980), 84–8; *Report of the Royal Commission of Inquiry on Education in the Province of Quebec*, vol. 4 (Quebec: Government of Quebec, 1966), 66.

21 *Report of the Royal Commission of Inquiry 1966*), 214–15.

22 Interview with Michael Stein, 19 February 2004, Toronto.

23 Sheila McLeod Arnopoulos and Dominique Clift, *The English Fact in Quebec* (Montreal: McGill-Queen's University Press, 1980), 144–5.

24 Gerard Pelletier, as quoted in Jack Granatstein, *Canada 1957–1967: The Years of Uncertainty and Innovation* (Toronto: McClelland and Stewart, 1986), 12.

25 Esther Delisle, *The Traitor and the Jew: Anti-Semitism and Extreme Right-Wing Nationalism in Quebec from 1929–1939* (Montreal: Robert Davies,1993); Esther Delisle, *Myth, Memories and Lies: Quebec's Intelligentsia and the Fascist Temptation, 1939–1960* (Westmount: R. Davies Multimedia, 1998).

26 Paul La Verdure, 'Sunday in Quebec, 1907–1937,' *Canadian Catholic Historical Association Historical Studies* 62 (1996), 58–9.

27 Irving Abella and Harold Troper, *None Is Too Many: Canada and the Jews of Europe 1933–1948* (Toronto: Lester and Orpen Dennys, 1982), 162–3.

28 Reginald A. Whitaker, 'The Quebec Cauldron: A Recent Account,' in Alain G. Gagnon, ed., *Quebec: State and Society* (Toronto: Methuen, 1984), 4 –78.

29 Stevenson, *Community Besieged*, 88.

30 Interview with Myer Bick, 12 March 2003, Montreal.
31 Interview with Pierre Anctil, 13 December 2002, Montreal.
32 Interview with Joe King, 2 December 2002, Montreal.
33 A curious and largely forgotten little book, Hugh Bingham Myers's *The Quebec Revolution* (Montreal: Harvest House, 1964), explores what the author regarded as a growing spirit of nationalism in Quebec, how English-speaking Canada unwittingly fed that spirit, and why many Quebec nationalists were advocating separatism.
34 Interview with Manny Batshaw, Montreal, 11 December 2002.
35 Louis Rosenberg, 'Canada,'in *American Jewish Yearbook, 1963* (New York: American Jewish Committee, 1963), 266–7.
36 *Commission royale d'enquête sur l'enseignement dans la province de Québec. Rapport, Gouvernement de Québec* (Quebec City: Queen's Printer, 1963).
37 There was a larger percentage of Jewish children in the secondary stream than in the primary one because it was not uncommon for Jewish parents to send their children to private Jewish parochial schools for their primary education then into Protestant schools for their secondary education. Whether Jewish children went to Jewish parochial schools or not, their parents' school taxes were directed to the Protestant school board.
38 Louis Rosenberg, 'Canada,' in *American Jewish Yearbook, 1964* (New York: American Jewish Committee, 1964), 167–9.
39 Louis Rosenberg, 'Canada,' in *American Jewish Yearbook, 1965* (New York: American Jewish Committee, 1965), 325.
40 Louis Rosenberg, 'Canada,' in *American Jewish Yearbook, 1966* (New York: American Jewish Committee, 1966), 276.
41 Samuel Bronfman, 'Canadian Jewry Today,' *World Jewry* 9 (January–February 1966), 37–8.
42 Royal Commission on Bilingualism and Biculturalism, book 6, *Cultural Contribution of the Other Ethnic Groups* (Ottawa: Queen's Printer, 1970), 3.
43 Harold Troper, 'Multiculturalism,' in *The Encylopedia of Canada's Peoples* (Toronto: University of Toronto Press, 1999), 997–1006.
44 CJA, CJC Central File, CA box 33, file 306. Saul Hayes speech to CJC Plenary, Montreal, 20 May 1965; Ontario Jewish Archives (hereafter OJA), General Files, 1965, file 95, 'Look and Outlook,' summary of keynote address by Saul Hayes, QC, Montreal, 21 May 1965.
45 Saul Hayes, as quoted in Richard Menkis, 'A Case of Strategic Avoidance? The Canadian Jewish Congress and the Royal Commission on Bilingualism and Biculturalism,' paper delivered at 10th Biennial Conference on Canadian Studies, Jerusalem, 2 July 2004.

46 Interview with Manny Batshaw, December 11, 2002, Montreal.
47 Interview with Manny Weiner, 11 December 2002, Montreal; interview with Joe King, 2 December 2002, Montreal.
48 Saul Hayes, as quoted in Richard Menkis, 'A Case of Strategic Avoidance?'
49 Interview with Ruth Wisse, 21 October 2004, Boston (by telephone); R.R. Wisse, 'Jewish Participation in Canadian Culture,' an essay prepared for the Royal Commission on Bilingualism and Biculturalism, as quoted in Royal Commission on Bilingualism and Biculturalism, *The Cultural Contribution of the Other Ethnic Groups* (Ottawa: Queen's Printer, 1970), 98.
50 OJA, Canadian Jewish Congress, General Files, 1965, Press Releases, 'Canadian Jewish Community in a Rapidly Changing Society,' Montreal, May 23, 1965.
51 Menkis, 'A Case of Strategic Avoidance?'
52 CJA, CA box 77, file 767. Memorandum of Saul Hayes to M. Saalheimer re: Canada's Centenary, 26 May 1960. For a discussion of Quebec's position with regard to the 1960s and early 1970s debate over ethnic pluralism and multiculturalism see Raymond Breton, 'From a Different Perspective: French Canada and the Issue of Immigration and Multiculturalism,' *TESL Talk* 10/3 (1979), 45–56.
53 JHS/BC, CJC Papers, box 5, file 78. Minutes of meeting to discuss Canadian Centennary, Montreal, 25 November 1963; Minutes of meeting in regard of the Centennial Celebration, 12 May 1964, Montreal.
54 LAC, Lavy M. Becker Papers, MG 31 H81 Vol. 5, George E. Gauthier to Lavy M. Becker, June 8, 1965.; Gary Miedema, 'For Canada's Sake: The Centennial Celebrations of 1967, State Legitimation and the Restructuring of Canadian Public Life,' *Journal of Canadian Studies* 34 (1999), 139–160; Gary Miedema, *For Canada's Sake: Public Religion, Centennial Celebrations, and the Re-making of Canada in the 1960s* (Montreal: McGill-Queen's University Press, 2005), xii–xv, 72–3, 83.
55 Interview with Rabbi Wilfred Shuchat, 25 March 2004, Montreal; Rabbi Wilfred Shuchat, *The Gate of Heaven: The Story of Congregation Shaar Hashomayim of Montreal 1846–1996* (Montreal: McGill-Queen's University Press, 2000), 343–52; *Montreal Star*, 22 July 1966, 3; interview with Harry Stilman, 29 December 2008, Toronto.
56 CJA, ZA 1966 box 1, file 14, press release of Foundation for Judaism, re: The Pavilion of Judaism, n.d.; CJA, CA box 92, file 1079, Pavilion of Judaism Project for Expo 67: Recommendations for Programming, 16 August 1966.
57 CJA, CA box 92, file 1079, 'Israeli Pavilion, 1967 World Exposition, Montreal,' Consulate of Israel, Montreal, n.d.

Chapter 3: Second City

1 Interview with Allan Langner, 13 December 2002, Montreal.
2 Interview with Donald Carr, 29 August 2003, Toronto.
3 Peter Desbarats, 'Montreal Confessions,' in *Century 1867–1967: The Canadian Saga* (Toronto: Toronto Star, 1967), 34–5.
4 Morton Weinfeld, *Like Everyone Else … But Different: The Paradoxical Success of Canadian Jews* (Toronto: McClelland and Stewart, 2001), 87–8.
5 Interview with David Rome, 18 June 1979, Montreal.
6 Ernest Hemingway to Ezra Pound, as quoted in John Columbo, *Columbo's New Canadian Quotations* (Edmonton: Hurtig, 1987), 382.
7 Robert Fulford, *Accidental City: The Transformation of Toronto* (Toronto: Macfarlane, Walter & Ross, 1995), 2.
8 LAC, Lou R. Ronson Papers, MG 31, H 138, vol. 7, file 4. Ben Kayfetz, 'Only Yesterday,' presentation to Toronto Jewish Historical Society, May 1972.
9 Interview with Ben Kayfetz, 14 May 2001, Toronto.
10 Interview with Arthur Drache, 29 February 2004, Toronto.
11 Robert Gruneir, 'The Hebrew Mission in Toronto,' *Canadian Ethnic Studies* 9 (1977), 18–28.
12 Paul Axelrod, *The Promise of Schooling: Education in Canada 1800–1914* (Toronto: University of Toronto Press, 1997), 69–87; Robert Stamp, 'Canadian Education and the National Identity,' *Journal of Educational Thought* 5 (1971), 133–44; Keith A. McLeod, 'A Short History of the Immigrant Student as "New Canadian,"' in Aaron Wolfgang, ed., *Education of Immigrant Students* (Toronto: OISE, 1975), 19–31.
13 John Marlyn, *Under the Ribs of Death* (Toronto: New Canadian Library, 1964), 24.
14 Harold Troper, 'Becoming an Immigrant City: A History of Immigration into Toronto since the Second World War,' in Paul Anisef and Michael Lanphier, eds., *The World in a City* (Toronto: University of Toronto Press, 2003), 19–62.
15 Interview with Merrijoy Kelner, 17 June 2004, Toronto.
16 Herbert A. Sohn, 'Human Rights Legislation in Ontario: A Study in Social Action,' unpublished PhD diss., University of Toronto, 1975.
17 Interview with Donald Carr, 25 July 2003, Montreal; Troper, 'Becoming an Immigrant City.'
18 Henri Rossier and Pierre Berton, *The New City: A Prejudiced View of Toronto* (Toronto: Macmillan, 1961), 19, 52, 58.
19 Myer Siemiatycki et al., 'Integrating Community Diversity in Toronto: On

Whose Terms?' in Paul Anisef and Michael Lanphier, eds., *The World in a City* (Toronto: University of Toronto Press, 2003), 384.

20 Charles Levi, '"There is a definite limitation imposed" (Robin Ross to Claude Bissell, December 4, 1959), The Jewish Quota in the Faculty of Medicine, University of Toronto: Generational Memory Sustained by Documentation,' *Historical Studies in Education* 15 (Spring 2003), 131–8; Lesley Marrus Barsky, *From Generation to Generation: A History of Toronto's Mount Sinai Hospital* (Toronto: McClelland and Stewart, 1998), 49–53, 100–5, 116–17; Gerald Tulchinsky, *Branching Out* (Toronto: Stoddard, 1998), 275–6; Edward Shorter, *A Century of Radiology in Toronto* (Toronto: Wall and Emerson, 1995), 129; W.P.J. Millar, '"We wanted our children should have it better": Jewish Medical Students at the University of Toronto 1910–51,' *Journal of the Canadian Historical Association* 11 (2000), 109–24.

21 Interview with Arthur Drache, Toronto, 29 February 2004; Philip Girard, *Bora Laskin: Bringing Life to Law* (Toronto: Osgoode, 2005), 107, 146, 265.

22 Arthur Drache's experience was far from unique. It has been argued that the long-standing refusal of many name-brand law firms to hire Jews resulted in a disproportionate number of Jewish lawyers going into solo practice or smaller and more neighbourhood-based practice. Ronit Dinovitzer, 'Social Capital and Constraints on Legal Careers,' *Law and Society* 40 (2006), 449–52; Interview with David Greenspan, 24 November 2004, Toronto; Martin L. Friedland, *My Life in Crime and Other Academic Adventures* (Toronto: University of Toronto Press, 2007), 42–3.

23 Interview with Arthur Drache, Toronto, 29 February 2004; interview with Herb Solway, 7 April 2004, Toronto. While it is true that by the late 1960s anti-Jewish bars were coming down in the legal profession, as they were in other professions, a 1992 sociological study of ethnic elites was still tentative in declaring discrimination a thing of the past. While noting major shifts since the 1960s, the study would only go so far as to say that 'the days of domination of Canadian elites by those of British ancestry are coming to a close, and ... the original imagery of the "vertical mosaic" needs revision.' B. Ogmundsen and J. McLaughlin, 'Trends in the Ethnic Origins of Canadian Elites: The Decline of the BRITS,' *Canadian Review of Sociology and Anthropology* 29 (1992), 237.

24 Irving Layton, as cited in Ira Robinson and Mervin Butovsky, *Renewing Our Days: Montreal Jews in the Twentieth Century* (Montreal: Vehicule Press, 1995), 168.

25 Merrijoy Kelner, 'The Elite Structure or Toronto: Ethnic Composition and Patterns of Recruitment,' unpublished PhD diss., University of Toronto, 1969, 99–135.

26 Joseph Kage, 'The Settlement of Hungarian Refugees in Canada,' in Robert H. Keyserlingk, ed., *Breaking Ground: The Hungarian Refugee Movement in Canada* (Toronto: York Lanes Press, 1993), 100.

27 *Toronto Star*, 2 December 1963; David Van Praagh, 'A Message of Hate from the Rooftops,' *Globe and Mail*, 3 January 1964, 7.

28 Franklin Bialystok, *Delayed Impact: The Holocaust and the Canadian Jewish Community* (Montreal: McGill-Queens University Press, 2000), 103–4.

29 James Walker, 'Toward Equal Dignity: Canadian Jewry and the Hate Law of 1970,' paper presented to the Jerusalem Conference on Canadian Studies, 1 July 2004.

30' Interview with Ben Kayfetz, 14 May 2001, Toronto.

31 Interview with Lou Ronson, 12 November 2003, Toronto; John Garrity and Alan Edwards, 'My Sixteen Months as a Nazi,' *Maclean's*, 1 October 1966, 9–13.

32 Bialystok, *Delayed Impact*, 103–4.

33 Louis Rosenberg, 'Canada,' in *American Jewish Yearbook, 1964* (New York: American Jewish Committee, 1964), 170.

34 *IOI*, 30 October 1964; Louis Rosenberg, 'Canada,' in *American Jewish Yearbook, 1965* (New York: American Jewish Committee, 1965), 326–7; Bialystok, *Delayed Impact*, 112–13.

35 *Canadian Jewish News*, 15 January 1965.

36 Cyril Levitt Papers, Minutes of the Meeting of the National Joint Community Relations Committee, 10 January 1965.

37 Cyril Levitt Papers, Letter of Michael Garber to Alphonse Ouimet, 14 January 1965.

38 JHS/BC, CJC Papers, box 14, file 400. Letter of Michael Garber to R.C. Frazer, 10 February 1965; Cyril Levitt Papers, Jewish Community Relations Committee Bulletin, 'Position of CBC on Broadcast of Hate Literature, February 16, 1965.'

39 Bialystok, *Delayed Impact*, 111–12.

40 Interview with Donald Carr, 29 August 2003, Toronto.

41 Both MacGuigan and Trudeau would win election to Parliament under the Liberal banner in 1965. In 1980 MacGuigan was appointed minister of state for external affairs in Trudeau's government, and shifted over to become minster of justice in 1982. When Trudeau retired, MacGuigan made a failing bid to replace him. For MacGuigan's analysis of the hate law issue see Mark MacGuigan, 'Proposed Anti-hate Legislation: Bill S-5 and the Cohen Report,' *Chitty's Law Journal* 15 (1967), 302–6.

42 James Walker, 'Toward Equal Dignity: Canadian Jewry and the Hate Law of 1970,' paper presented to the Jerusalem Conference on Canadian Stud-

ies, 1 July 2004; William Kaplan, 'Maxwell Cohen and the Report of the Special Committee on Hate Propaganda,' in William Kaplan and Donald McRae, eds., *Law, Policy and International Justice* (Monteal: McGill-Queen's University Press, 1993), 243–74; Bialystok, *Delayed Impact*, 114–19, 151–5.

43 *Toronto Telegram*, 21 April 1965. Beattie announced the rally in Allan Gardens as if it was the first such event. In reality he and a small band of followers had met in the park several times but were unable to generate a crowd or much support from the few who stopped to listen to Beattie's anti-Jewish rants.

44 Cyril Levitt Papers, Minutes of the Joint Community Relations Committee, 22 April 1965; *Canadian Jewish News*, 30 April 1965, 4; *Toronto Telegram*, 22 April 1965; *Toronto Telegram*, 24 April 1965.

45 Interview with Ben Kayfetz, 14 May 2001, Toronto.

46 CJA, ZA 1965, box 6, file 57: Confidential memorandum, B.G. Kayfetz to J.S. Midanik, 1 February 1965.

47 *Toronto Telegram*, 17 May 1965, 1–2; ibid., 18 May 1965, 4.

48 CJA, ZA 1965, box 6, file 57: Confidential memorandum, Kayfetz to Midanik; Confidential memoranda re: N-3, Kayfetz to Midanik, 5 and 9 February 1965; Kayfetz to Saul Hayes, 10 February 1965; CJA, CA, box 91, file 1025A: Memorandum, Kayfetz to Hayes, 21 June 1965.

49 *Toronto Telegram*, 31 May 1965, 17; *Toronto Star*, 31 May 1965, 1; *Globe and Mail*, 31 May 1965; for a personal memoir which offers a somewhat different account of the events in Allan Gardens, see Michael Englishman, 'Neo-Nazis in Toronto,' *Canadian Jewish Studies* 4–5 (1996–7), 117–24.

50 Cyril Levitt Papers, Minutes of Special Meeting of the Joint Community Relations Committee, Central Region, 14 October 2004, Toronto; Bialystok, *Delayed Impact*, 129–34; *Canadian Jewish News*, 11 June 1965, 1.

51 Cyril H. Levitt and William Shaffir, *The Riot at Christie Pits* (Toronto: Lester and Orpen Dennys, 1987).

52 *Toronto Telegram*, 2 June 1965.

53 OJA, Canadian Jewish Congress, Joint Community Relations Committee (hereafter JCRC), MG 8/S, 1965, box 23, file 108: 'Report on Neo-Nazism and Hate Literature,' 8 June 1965; *Toronto Telegram*, 9 June 1965; *Toronto Star*, 9 June 1965; *Globe and Mail*, 9 June 1965; *Ottawa Journal*, 9 June 1965; *Montreal Star*, 9 June 1965.

54 CJA, CA, box 91, file 1025a: Association of Former Concentration Camp Inmates and Survivors of Nazi Oppression, 'Open Letter to the Jewish Community of Canada,' 17 June 1965; *Canadian Jewish Chronicle*, 18 June 1965, 1.

55 *Canadian Jewish Chronicle*, 18 June 1965.

56 CJA, CA, box 91, file 1025a: Julius Ciechanowsky and Sam Bierstone to Saul Hayes, 23 June 1965.
57 Cyril Levitt Papers, Minutes of special meeting of the Joint Community Relations Committee, Central Region, 24 June 1965, Toronto.
58 CJA, CA, box 91, file 1025a: Memorandum of B.G. Kayfetz to Saul Hayes, 21 June 1965.
59 Cyril Levitt Papers, Minutes of special meeting of JCRC, Toronto, 18 June 1965, 9.
60 OJA, JCRC, MG 8/S, 1965, box 23, file 107: Minutes of Community Meeting, 7 July 1965, Toronto, 3.
61 CJA, CA, box 91, file 1025a: Myer Gasner et al. to Friend, 2 July 1965; Memorandum of Myer Sharzer to Saul Hayes re: 'Report of "Community Conference," Toronto, Wednesday, July 7, 1965,' 9 July 1965 (and attached resolutions).
62 Cyril Levitt Papers, Minutes of Community Meeting, 7 July 1965, Toronto, 65.
63 Ibid., Memorandum, Myer Sharzer to B.G. Kayfetz re: Special Steering Committee, 3 August 1965.
64 Ibid., Minutes of the Community Anti-Nazi Committee, 21 September 1965.

Chapter 4: The Last Torah in the Fire

1 American Jewish Committee, *Report from Israel* (February 1967), 1.
2 Two essential studies of the Six Day War and the events surrounding the war are Michael Oren, *Six Days of War: June 1967 and the Making of the Modern Middle East* (New York: Oxford, 2001) and Tom Segev, *1967: Israel, the War, and the Year that Transformed the Middle East* (New York: Metropolitan Books, 2007). For discussion of the factors immediately preceding the outbreak of the Six Day War see Oren, *Six Days of War*, 61–169; Segev, *1967*, 238–337; Walter Laqueur, *The Road to War, 1967* (London: Weidenfeld and Nicolson, 1968); Donald Neff, *Warriors for Jerusalem: The Six Days That Changed the Middle East* (New York: Simon and Schuster, 1984); Elias Sam'o, ed., *The June 1967 Arab-Israel War* (Wilmette, IL: Medina University Press International, 1971); Janice Stein and Raymond Tanter, *Rational Decision Making – Israel's Security Choices, 1967* (Columbus: Ohio State University Press, 1980); and Charles W. Yost, 'The Arab Israel War: How It Began,' *Foreign Affairs* 46 (January 1968), 304–20.
3 *Montreal Gazette*, 8 June 1967.
4 *Toronto Telegram*, 23 May 1967, 1; Segev, *1967*, 228–31.

5 *Toronto Star*, 5 June 1967; *Toronto Telegram*, 27 May 1967, 2.

6 Oren, *Six Days of War*, 187.

7 *Toronto Star*, 29 May 1967, 1, 10; David Taras, 'Canada and the Arab-Israeli Conflict: A Study of the Yom Kippur War and the Domestic Political Environment,' unpublished PhD diss., University of Toronto, 1983, 34–9.

8 Oren, *Six Days of War*, 123–6.

9 *Toronto Telegram*, 27 May 1967, 1.

10 Oren, *Six Days of War*, 165–6. Several weeks after the end of the Six Day War, the *Globe and Mail*'s Report on Business discussed the economic strain imposed on Israel by the war emergency. *Globe and Mail*, 23 June 1967.

11 *Toronto Telegram*, 25 May 1967, 4.

12 For an intriguing hindsight glimpse into the different mindsets of politicians, policymakers, and military planners with regard to the Six Day War see Richard B. Parker, ed., *The Six-Day War: A Retrospective* (Gainsville: University of Florida Press, 1996).

13 For an useful outline of events in and around the Six Day War as they relate to Syria see Moshe Ma'oz, *Syria and Israel: From War to Peacemaking* (Oxford: Clarendon Press, 1995), 88–104; see also Oren, *Six Days of War*, 33–126.

14 For discussion of how the Six Day War impacted different Jewish communities around the world, see Eli Lederhendler, ed., *The Six-Day War and World Jewry* (Bethesda: University of Maryland Press, 2000).

15 Interview with Donald Carr, 25 July 2003, Toronto.

16 Interview with Dr Robert Krell, 2 November 2001, Vancouver.

17 In his controversial book *The Holocaust in American Life*, Peter Novick argues that the spring of 1967 marked an important turning point in the American Jewish 'relationship to the Holocaust.' For American Jews, Novick argues, during the crisis in the week or so before the outbreak of hostilities in the Middle East American Jewish perception of the Holocaust shifted from understanding the Holocaust as a historical event to an 'imminent and terrifying prospect.' Peter Novick, *The Holocaust in American Life* (Boston: Houghton Mifflin, 1999), 148.

18 Lucy Dawidowicz, 'American Public Opinion,' in *American Jewish Yearbook, 1968* (New York: American Jewish Committee, 1968), 203.

19 *Canadian Jewish News*, 2 June 1967, 4.

20 Interview with Rabbi Wilfred Solomon, 15 August 2001, Jerusalem.

21 Interview with Rabbi Allan Langner, 13 December 2002, Montreal.

22 Interview with Ruth Wisse, 21 October 2004, Boston (by telephone).

23 CJA, CB, box 10, file 064: World Jewish Congress, 'Israel: An Appeal to the Conscience of the World,' Milan, 28 May 1967.

24 OJA, JCRC, MG 8/S, 1967, box 31, file 77C: Max Brent to Sir, 28 May 1967.
25 OJA, CJC, Committee meetings etc., 1967, Zionist Organization of Canada: Max Goody and Dr George Liban to Friend, 30 May 1967; CJA, ZA, 1967, box 4, file 39: Submission to the Honourable Paul Martin, Secretary of State for External Affairs, 1 June 1967; Michael Marrus, *Mr. Sam: The Life and Times of Sam Bronfman* (Toronto: Viking, 1991), 447–8; Harold M. Waller, 'The Impact of the Six-Day War on the Organizational Life of Canadian Jewry,' in Lederhendler, *The Six-Day War and World Jewry*, 84–5.
26 Ben Kayfetz, 'Canada,' in *American Jewish Yearbook, 1968*, 384–5.
27 Jewish Heritage Centre of Western Canada (hereafter JHC), CJC Papers, box P3524, file 3: A.J. Harold Clark to Joseph Secter, 31 May 1967; CJA, CB, box 10, file 2064: Arnold to Harry S. Shatz, 5 June 1967.
28 JHC, CJC Papers, box P3524, file 3: 'A Statement Issued Jointly by Canadian Catholic Conference, United Church of Canada and the Anglican Church,' 31 May 1967; Memorandum of A.J. Arnold to Saul Hayes and Ben Kayfetz re: Public Relations on Israeli Situation, 1 June 1967.
29 *Winnipeg Free Press*, 29 May 1967; Haim Genizi, *The Holocaust, Israel and Canadian Protestant Churches* (Montreal: McGill-Queen's University Press, 2002), 81–3.
30 George Bain, 'The First Word,' *Globe and Mail*, 6 June 1967.
31 CJA, CB, box 10, file 2064: Joseph Jaks to Canadian Jewish Congress, 30 May 1967.
32 Interview with Louis Greenspan, 1 August 2002, Toronto.
33 *Toronto Telegram*, 6 June 1967.
34 Ibid., 5 June 1967.
35 Interview with Jerry Silver, 7 August 2004, Toronto.
36 *Western Jewish Bulletin*, 2 June 1967, 2; *Toronto Star*, 5 June 1967.
37 Interview with Mordechai Bar-On, 16 August 2001, Jerusalem. Oren, *Six Days of War*, 136.
38 *Winnipeg Free Press*, 29 May 1967; JHC, CJC Papers, box P3524, file 3: Canadian Jewish Congress, Winnipeg, press release, n.d.; ibid., file 4: CJC, Winnipeg, Statement for Release to the Local Press re Jewish Community Position on Middle East Situation, 5 June 1967.
39 *Canadian Jewish News*, 19 May 1967.
40 Joseph Yam, *The Size and Geographic Distribution of Canada's Jewish Population: Preliminary Observations* (Montreal: Canadian Jewish Congress, 1974), 12.
41 Interviews with George Promislow and with Barbara Promislow, 16 August 2001, Jerusalem.
42 *Western Jewish Bulletin*, 2 June 1967, 3.

43 JHC, CJC Papers, box P3524, file 3: Canadian Jewish Congress, Winnipeg, press release, n.d.

44 Interview with Moe Steinberg, 11 August 2003; *Western Jewish Bulletin*, 2 June 1967, 4–5, 8.

45 Interview with Rabbi Wilfred Solomon, 15 August 2001, Jerusalem; interview with Marvin Weintraub, 12 August 2003, Vancouver.

46 JHC, CJC Papers, box P3524, file 3: Memorandum to S. Lewin from Abe Arnold, re: Middle East Situation, 30 May 1967; resolution, 29 May 1967; telegram to Prime Minister Lester Pearson from Irwin E. Witty, 31 May 1967.

47 Interview with Herb Solway, 7 April 2004, Toronto.

48 *Canadian Jewish News*, 2 June 1967, 1.

49 Interview with Harold Buchwald, 1 June 2004, Winnipeg; interview with Sam Sable, 4 October 2004, Toronto; *Canadian Jewish News*, 2 June 1967, 1; Kayfetz, 'Canada,' 387; interview with Bill Stern, 9 March 2007, Toronto.

50 CJA, CB, box10, file 2064-A: Emergency Information Service, bulletin no. 2, 4, 13 June 1967.

51 JHC, CJC Papers, box P3524, file 3: Canadian Jewish Congress, Winnipeg, press release, n.d.

52 OJA, CJC, Committee meetings etc., 1967, Israel Emergency Publicity, Memorandum of Coordinating Committee for Emergency Aid to Israel to Presidents and Secretaries of Organizations and Congregations re: The Jewish Community and the Emergency, 9 June 1967.

53 Interview with Rabbi W. Gunther Plaut, 26 June 2002, Toronto.

54 Interview with Hindy Friedman, 18 July 2003, Toronto.

55 Interview with Sam Sable, 4 October 2004, Toronto; interview with Ben Kayfetz, 14 May 2001, Toronto.

56 Interview with Bernie Farber, 2 August 2002, Toronto.

57 Interview with Bill Stern, 9 March 2007, Toronto.

58 Personal experience of the author.

59 Interview with Joe King, 2 December 2002, Montreal; interview with Manny Weiner, 11 December 2002, Montreal.

60 Central Zionist Archives (hereafter CZA), box F16, file 6: Telegram, Samuel Chait to Levi Eshkol, 24 May 1967; *Montreal Gazette*, 30 May 1967, 10.

61 *Toronto Star*, 6 June 1967.

62 *Globe and Mail*, 13 June 1967, 7.

63 JHC, CJC Papers, box 3524, file 3: Press release from Emergency Campaign for Aid to Israel, 7 June 1967.

64 JHC, CJC Papers, box P3524, file 3: Memorandum, Coordinating Committee for Emergency Aid to Israel (Toronto) to Presidents and Secretaries

of Organizations and Congregations, re: The Jewish Community and the Emergency, 9 June 1967; CJA, CB, box10, file 2064C: Bulletin to Community Leaders, 13 June 1967.

65 JHC, CJC Papers, box P3526, file 10: Telegram, Federated Zionist Organization and Canadian Jewish Congress to Rabbi Bernard Hasden, 5 June 1967; *Globe and Mail*, 6 June 1967.

66 *Globe and Mail*, 7 June 1967; *Toronto Telegram*, 5 June 1967, 1; *Globe and Mail*, 6 June 1967.

67 *Globe and Mail*, 8 June 1967, 1; *Globe and Mail*, 9 June 1967, 1.

68 CJA, CB, box 10, file 2064: Telegram, Mayer Sand and William Davidson to Samuel Bronfman, 6 June 1967.

69 JHC, CJC Papers, box P3524, file 4: Human Interest Items in Connection with the Emergency Campaign for Israel, 8 June 1967.

70 *Montreal Star*, 7 June 1967.

71 JHC, CJC Papers, box P3524, file 4: Human Interest Items in Connection with the Emergency Campaign for Israel, 8 June 1967.

72 Ibid., file 3: Arthur V. Mauro to Harold Buchwald, 6 June 1967.

73 Ibid.: J.F. O'Sullivan to United Israel Appeal, 6 June 1967.

74 Interview with Moe Steinberg, 11 August 2003, Vancouver.

75 CJA, CB, box 10, file 2064: Harry S. Shatz to Sol D. Granek, 8 June 1967.

76 Interview with Dr Robert Krell, 2 November 2001, Vancouver.

77 Interview with Myer Bick, 12 March 2003, Montreal.

78 OJA, CJC, Committee meetings etc., 1967: Memo re: Community Mobilization for Israel, 6 June 1967; ibid., 1967: Israel Emergency Coordinating Committee: Minutes, Israel Emergency 'Public Relations'; Minutes, Israel Emergency Committee, Toronto, 6 June 1967.

79 CJA, CB, box 10, file 2064: Hugh E. Quetton to Sir, 6 June 1967.

80 OJA, CJC, Committee meetings etc., 1967, Israel Emergency Fund Raising: Summary of Decisions, Conclusions and Recommendations of PR Committee Meeting at Primrose Club, 7 June 1967.

81 *Canadian Jewish News*, 9 June 1967, 1.

82 *House of Commons Debates*, 8 June 1967, 1298.

83 *Emergency Information Service, no. 1*, n.d.; Oren, *Six Days of War*, 240–56; Marrus, *Mr Sam*, 448–9.

Chapter 5: Prestige Pride

1 Harold M. Waller, 'The Impact of the Six-Day War on the Organizational Life of Canadian Jewry,' in Eli Lederhendler, ed., *The Six-Day War and*

World Jewry (Bethesda: University of Maryland Press, 2000), 96; Gerald Tulchinsky, *Branching Out: The Transformation of the Canadian Jewish Community* (Toronto: Stoddart, 1998), 294; W. Gunther Plaut, 'Canadian Experience: The Dynamics of Jewish Life in Canada since 1945,' in Bernard Martin, ed., *Movements and Issues in American Judaism* (Westport, CT: Greenwood Press, 1978), 296; Saul Hayes, 'The Changing Nature of the Jewish Community,' *Viewpoints* 3 (1970), 27; Stuart E. Rosenberg, 'Canada's Jews: An Overview,' *Judaism* 20 (1971), 480.

2 Interview with Bernard Avishai, 12 May 2001, Boston.

3 Interview with Allan Pakes, 10 August 2001, Jerusalem.

4 Interview with Mordechai Bar-On, 16 August 2001, Jerusalem. Reliable figures on Canadian immigration to Israel are hard to come by, and those more available figures on immigrant arrivals from North America are open to question. However, from 1967 to 1973, the year of the Yom Kippur War, data from the Aliyah and Klita Department of the Jewish Agency for Israel give the number of immigrants as 34,291. The low was in 1967, when only 734 North Americans immigrated to Israel, with a high in 1971 of 7158 arrivals, almost a 1000 per cent increase. See http://www.jewishvirtual-library.org/jsource/Immigration/immigration_by_country2.html.

5 Interview with Allan Pakes, 10 August 2001, Jerusalem.

6 Interview with Barbara Promislow, 16 August 2001, Jerusalem.

7 Interview with Allan Pakes, 10 August 2001, Jerusalem.

8 Interview with Myer Bick, 12 March 2003, Montreal.

9 Interview with Jonathan Sarna, 14 August 2001, Jerusalem.

10 W. Gunther Plaut, 'Canadian Experience,' 296.

11 Interview with Donald Carr, 29 August 2003, Toronto.

12 *NPRC News*, 'Roundup: A Survey of the Keren Hayesod – United Israel Appeal World,' Montreal, 26 September 1967; interview with Steve Ain, 11 August 2003, Toronto; interview with Donald Carr, 25 July 2003.

13 *Canadian Jewish News*, 18 August 1967, 1.

14 United Jewish Welfare Fund of Toronto, *Study on Jewish Education* (Toronto, 1975). Interview with Donald Carr, 25 July 2003, Toronto; Michael Brown, 'Good Fences Do Not Necessarily Make Good Neighbors: Jews and Judaism in Canada's Schools and Universities,' *Jewish Political Studies Review* 11 (1999), 97–113; Stuart Schoenfeld, 'Transnational Religion, Religious Schools, and the Dilemma of Public Funding for Jewish Education: The Case of Ontario,' *Jewish Political Studies Review* 11 (1999), 115–39; Michael D. Behiels, 'Neo-Canadians and Schools in Montreal, 1900–1970,' *Journal of Cultural Geography* 8 (1988), 5–16.

15 Interview with Steve Ain, 11 August 2003, Toronto.

16 Michael Oren, *Six Days of War* (New York: Oxford, 2002), 305–27.

17 Ibid., 313–17.

18 Much has been written about the pro-Israel lobby in the United States. See, for example, Edward Tivnan, *The Lobby: Jewish Political Power and American Foreign Policy* (New York: Simon and Schuster, 1987). More recently, pro-Israel lobbying in the United States has set off a firestorm of debate. See John J. Mearsheimer and Stephen M. Walt, *The Israel Lobby and U.S. Foreign Policy* (New York: Farrar, Straus and Giroux, 2007) and Abraham H. Foxman, *The Deadliest Lies: The Israel Lobby and the Myth of Jewish Control* (New York: Palgrave Macmillan, 2007).

19 Emmet John Hughes, 'A Muddled Tale of Two Wars,' *Newsweek*, 26 June 1967, 17.

20 OJA, MG 8/S, JCRC, 1967, box 31, file 77C: Memorandum of Irwin Suall to Arnold Foster, re: Doves in Vietnam – Hawks in the Middle East? 27 June 1967. A 1966 Gallup poll exploring 'ethnic' attitudes towards the war in Vietnam indicated that 'Jews hold opinions closely comparable to the rest of the public: 41 percent of Jews approve [of the war], 41 percent disapprove and 18 percent have no opinion.' *World Journal Tribune*, 21 September 1966. For a study of how the Vietnam War played out in American Jewish and Israeli politics between 1966 and 1968 see Judith A. Klinghoffer, *Vietnam, Jews and the Middle East: Unintended Consequences* (New York: St Martin's Press, 1999).

21 Central Zionist Archives (CZA, Jerusalem), Canadian Zionist Association Papers, F39/356: Paul Flacks to I.L. Kenen, 13 June 1967. While there is little doubt that the Jewish community was divided on the Vietnam War, the nature of that division was different than it was for other faith groups. A 1970 study of the attitudes of young people of different faiths with regard to the Vietnam War concluded that those who claimed no faith were most likely to be opposed to the war, 'followed somewhat closely by Jews.' Jews were found to be far more likely to oppose the war than were Catholics or Protestants. Jerold M. Starr, 'Religious Preference, Religiosity, and Opposition to War,' *Sociological Analysis* 36 (1975), 323–34. For a discussion of the emergence of the American Israel Public Affairs Committee see Michael Oren, *Power, Faith, and Fantasy: America in the Middle East, 1776 to the Present* (New York: W.W. Norton, 2007), 336.

22 John Robinson Beal, *The Pearson Phenomenon* (Toronto: Longman, 1964), 111.

23 David Taras, 'Canada's Jewish Community and Support for Israel,' in David Taras and David H. Goldberg, eds., *The Domestic Battleground: Canada and the Arab-Israeli Conflict* (Montreal: McGill-Queen's University Press, 1989), 51–2.

24 Interview with Allan Pakes, 10 August 2001, Jerusalem; interview with Mordechai Bar-On, 16 August 2001, Jerusalem.
25 Interview with Nathan Glazer, 12 May 2001, Cambridge, MA. Interestingly, the 1972 edition of Glazer's book *American Judaism* was expanded from the original 1957 edition to include an epilogue entitled 'The Year 1967 and Its Meaning, 1952–72.' Nathan Glazer, *American Judaism*, 2nd ed. (Chicago: University of Chicago Press, 1972), 151–86.
26 For an interesting discussion of the Six Day War's impact on North American Zionism see Bernard Avishai, *The Tragedy of Zionism: Revolution and Democracy in the Land of Israel* (New York: Farrar Straus Giroux, 1985), 349–59.
27 Waller, 'Impact of the Six-Day War,' 86–90.
28 OJA, CJC, Committee meetings etc., 1967, 'Ottawa Meetings,' Emergency Information Service, no. 6, 30 June 1967.
29 Interview with Myer Bick, 12 March 2003, Montreal.
30 OJA, CJC, Committee meetings etc., 1967, 'Ottawa Meetings,' Emergency Information Service, no. 6, 30 June 1967; David Taras, 'Canada and the Arab-Israel Conflict: A Study of the Yom Kippur War and the Domestic Political Environment,' unpublished PhD diss., University of Toronto, 1983, 34–9.
31 A number of authors have previously detailed the troubled relationship between the United Church, the *Observer*, and the Jewish community. For more in-depth discussion see Reuben Slonim, *Family Quarrel: The United Church and the Jews* (Toronto: Clarke, Irwin, 1977); Gunther Plaut, *Unfinished Business: An Autobiography* (Toronto: Lester and Orpen Dennys, 1981), 278–94; David Taras, 'A Church Divided: A.C. Forrest and the United Church's Middle East Policy,' in Taras and Goldberg, eds., *The Domestic Battleground*, 86–101; Gary A. Gaudin, 'The United Church of Canada, Israel and the Palestinian Refugees Revisited,' *Studies in Religion* 24 (1995), 179–91; and Haim Genizi, *The Holocaust, Israel, and Canadian Protestant Churches* (Montreal: McGill-Queen's University Press, 2002), 109–85.
32 A similar eruption over Zionism and Israel between the Jewish community and mainstream Protestantism in the United States involved *The Christian Century*, a leading American inter-denominational newspaper. See Hertzel Fishman, *American Protestantism and the Jewish State* (Detroit: Wayne State University Press, 1973). As with the Canadian Jewish community, many in the American Jewish community were shocked and disturbed by what they saw as Christian silence in the face of the 'impending annihilation' of Israel – a point hammered home in *The Christian Century*.
33 Genizi, *The Holocaust, Israel, and Canadian Protestant Churches*, 5; Paul Charles Merkley, *Christian Attitudes towards the State of Israel* (Montreal:

McGill-Queen's University Press, 2001), 21–50, 161–94; George Giacu-
makis, 'Christian Attitudes toward Israel,' in Rogert G. Clouse et al., eds.,
The Cross and the Flag (Wheaton, IL: Creative House, 1972), 203–15.

34 *United Church Observer*, 1 August 1967, 5. While hardly a neutral account,
for a discussion of the first two years or so of the *Observer*'s articles on
Israel see Arnold Ages, 'The United Church Observer and the State of
Israel,' in *ADL Basic Documents* (Toronto: August 1969). See also A. Roy and
Alice L. Eckardt, 'Again, Silence in the Churches,' *The Christian Century* 84
(1967), 970–3, 992–5; and David Polish, 'Why American Jews Are Disillu-
sioned,' ibid., 965–7.

35 *United Church Observer*, 1 August 1967, 8.

36 LAC, Lou R. Ronson Papers, MG 31, H 138, vol. 18, file 22 (1970–1971):
R.G. Nicholls to Yehuda Noy, 23 February 1970.

37 Arnold Ages, 'Is There a Christian "Position" on the State of Israel?' *The
Reconstructionist*, 4 July 1969, 21.

38 Emil Fackenheim, 'Why I've Changed My Mind about Christians,' *Ferment
'69*, no. 3 (1969), 10.

39 OJA, MG 8/S, JCRC, 1970, box 45, file 168: Memorandum, Maria Zuker to
Sol I. Littman, re: Under Attack, 1 April 1970.

40 Ibid., 1968, box 19, file 140: Report to the Town Hall Meeting on Israel
Public Relations, 22 January 1968, Toronto.

41 Ibid., 1970, box 45, file 168: Aba Gefen to Hugh McCullum, 2 April 1970.

42 Plaut, *Unfinished Business*, 282.

43 LAC, MG 31, F 6, vol. 150: Dr W. Gunther Plaut, 'Report on the Jewish
Community,' Toronto, 13 March 1970.

44 Alfred Green, 'The President's Message,' *Digest*, January 1972, 4.

45 Slonim, *Family Quarrel*, 6–12; for insight into the B'nai Brith's initial
response to Forrest's libel action see correspondence and memoranda in
LAC, B'nai Brith Canada Papers, MG 28, series 133, vol. 11.

46 Plaut, *Unfinished Business*, 289.

47 JHS/BC, CJC Western Region Papers, Joint Community Relations Committee 1972–1973, box 13A, file 349: Canada-Israel Committee Newsletter
(confidential), 27 March 1972.

48 John Nicholls Booth, 'How the Zionists Manipulate Your News,' *United
Church Observer*, March 1972, 24–6.

49 Interview with Lou Ronson, 19 November 2003, Toronto.

50 LAC, Lou R. Ronson Papers, MG 31, series 138, vol. 15, file 8: Memorandum from J.C. Horwitz to Members of the National JCRC and National
Executive Canadian Jewish Congress, 7 May 1973.

51 Genizi, *The Holocaust, Israel, and Canadian Protestant Churches*, 160–9.

52 *Toronto Star*, 5 May 1973, 4.

53 For a discussion of how Jews and other minorities campaigned for human rights protections in Ontario see Carmela Patria and Ruth Frager, '"This Is Our Country, These Are Our Rights": Minorities and the Origins of Ontario Human Rights Campaigns,' *Canadian Historical Review* 82 (2001), 1–35; Philip Girard, *Bora Laskin: Bringing Life to Law* (Toronto: Osgoode, 2005), 247–71; and James Walker, 'The Jewish Phase in the Movement for Racial Equality in Canada,' *Canadian Ethnic Studies* 34 (2002).

54 Jonathan Kaufman, *Broken Alliance: The Turbulent Times between Jews and Blacks in America* (New York: Charles Scribner, 1988), 199–216; Jerald E. Podair, *The Strike That Changed New York: Blacks, Whites, and the Ocean Hill–Brownsville Crisis* (New Haven: Yale University Press, 2002).

55 The divide between the organized Jewish community and the left over Israel was not peculiar to Canada. For a discussion of growing tensions between the left and Western Jewish communities see David Burchell, 'The Rise and Fall of the Jewish/Left Alliance: An Historical and Political Analysis,' *Australian Journal of Politics and History* 45 (1999), 483–505.

56 Jonah Raskin, as quoted in Klaus Mehnert, *Twilight of the Young: The Radical Movements of the 1960s and Their Legacy* (New York: Holt, Rinehart and Winston, 1976), 302.

57 The term New Left was most often applied to the campus generation which came of age in the 1960s and was radicalized by social injustices, the civil rights movement, and the war in Vietnam. Detached from the left associated with labour unions, the New Left was dominated by college students, and the first major campus-linked group was Students for a Democratic Society, which was formed in Michigan in 1962. Its Port Huron Statement attacked social injustice and the values of the so-called 'Affluent Society.' The New Left expanded with the onset of the free-speech movement at the University of California at Berkeley in 1964 and gained strength as it began organizing against the Vietnam War and attacking Lyndon B. Johnson's Great Society programs for not eradicating poverty. In the early 1960s the New Left also made inroads on Canadian campuses, where, after 1967, like the American movement, it adopted a decidedly anti-Israel position. In English-speaking Canada the New Left in part grew out of the anti-nuclear-weapons campaign of the late 1950s. For alternative discussions of the New Left in Canada, its make-up, influence, and focus see Cyril Levitt, *Children of Privilege: Student Revolt in the Sixties* (Toronto: University of Toronto Press, 1984) and John W. Cleveland, 'New Left, Not New Liberal: 1960s Movements in English Canada and Quebec,' *Canadian Review of Sociology and Anthropology* 41 (2004), 67–84.

58 Levitt, *Children of Privilege*, 4.

59 For a discussion of the variations of North American Jewish youth in the period following the Six Day War and their varying agendas, with special attention accorded to Montreal, see Yosef Gorny, *The State of Israel in Jewish Public Thought* (London: Macmillan, 1994), 111–49.

60 Interview with Cyril Levitt, 12 May 2002, Toronto.

61 Mehnert, *Twilight of the Young*, 306.

62 Interview with Louis Greenspan, 1 August 2002, Toronto.

63 In the aftermath of the Six Day War, the New Left and the attraction it held for some Jewish youth were issues of some discussion in the American Jewish community. See, for example, Robert Saks, 'Jewish Youth and the New Left,' *Conservative Judaism* 21 (Summer 1967); Martin Peretz, 'The American Left and Israel,' *Commentary* 44 (November 1967), 27–34; Nathan Glazer, 'The Jewish Role in Student Activism,' *Fortune*, January 1969, 112–13, 126, 129; Nathan Glazer, 'The New Left and the Jews,' *Journal of Jewish Sociology* 11 (1969), 121–32; Seymour Martin Lipsted, 'The Socialism of Fools': The Left, the Jews and Israel* (New York: ADL, 1969); LAC, B'nai Brith Canada Papers, MG 28, V 133, vol. 99: Tom Milstein, 'The New Left: Areas of Jewish Concern,' an analysis prepared for the Jewish Labor Committee, 1969.

64 OJA, MG 8/S, JCRC, 1969, box 12, file 7: Larry Alex to Canadian Jewish Congress, 18 November 1969.

65 Ibid., box 4, file 67: Ian Sone and Associates, 'Proposal: The Problem of Anti-Zionism among the Jewish Student Left,' Toronto, 11 October 1969. Estimates run high for the number of Jews active in the New Left on American campuses. For example, from 1960 to 1970, five of the nine presidents of Students for a Democratic Society were Jews. Kirkpatrick Sales, *SDS* (New York: Random House, 1973), 663.

66 OJA, MG 8/S, JCRC, 1969, box 40, file 67: Albert Rose to Ben Kayfetz, 3 November 1969.

67 Interview with Bernie Farber, 2 August 2002, Toronto.

68 Gorny, *The State of Israel in Jewish Public Thought*, 111–32. In addition to detailing the emergence of an activist campus left in North America between 1967 and 1973, Gorny discusses both the North American *chavurah* movement and the emergence of self-defence groups such as the JDL. For contemporary alternative discussions of the New Left and Jews see Arthur Leibman, *Jews and the Left* (New York: John Wiley, 1979), 536–87; and Zvi Lamm, 'The New Left and Jewish Identity: Assimilation through Zionism,' *Patterns of Prejudice* 4 (May–June 1970), 1–8.

69 David Blustein, 'Dilemma of the Jewish Left,' *American Students for Israel*, n.d., n.p.

70 Interview with David Kaufman, 11 September 2000, Toronto.

71 Ibid.; interview with Mordechai Bar-On, 16 August 2001, Jerusalem; Mark Oppenheimer, *Knocking on Heaven's Door: American Religion in the Age of Counterculture* (New Haven: Yale University Press, 2003), 96–129.

72 Interview with Morton Weinfeld, 26 August 2008, Montreal (by telephone).

73 Interview with Steve Ain, 28 July 2003, Toronto.

74 JHC, CJC Papers, box 3518, file 10: Memorandum of Abe Arnold to Saul Hayes, Alan Rose, and Ben Kayfetz, re: Students for Israel and Arab Propaganda, 25 November1967.

75 OJA, MG 8/S, JCRC, 1970, box 44, file 136: Marvin Weintraub to Roy Waldman, 5 March 1970; Roy Waldman to Alan Rose, 6 March 1970; JHC, CJC Papers, box 14B, file 474: David A. Freedman to Kenneth Strand, 10 April 1970; interview with Marvin Weintraub, 12 August 2003, Vancouver.

76 Gene Colman, 'Jewish Students Arise and Unite: Let's Kick the Shit Out of the Jewish Establishment!' *Masada*, 6 January 1970, 1.

77 OJA, JCRC, MG 8/S, 1970, box 44, file 147: B.G. Kayfetz to Alan Rose, 23 January 1970.

78 Interview with Steve Ain, 28 July 2003.

Chapter 6: 'The Maddest and Most Passionate Fling'

1 Larry Zolf, *Just Watch Me: Remembering Pierre Trudeau* (Toronto: James Lorimer, 1984), 62.

2 Esther Delisle, *The Traitor and the Jew: Anti-Semitism and the Delirium of Extremist Right-Wing Nationalism in French Canada from 1929–1939* (Montreal: Robert Davis, 1993).

3 Interview with Allan Gotlieb, 22 September 2003, Toronto.

4 George Radwanski, *Trudeau* (Toronto: Macmillan, 1978), 38–57. Radwanski has not been alone in emphasizing the impact of Trudeau's offshore study and travel in shaping his world view. John English titled a biographical volume covering Trudeau's life to 1968 *Citizen of the World: The Life of Pierre Elliott Trudeau* (Toronto: Alfred A. Knopf, 2006).

5 Max Nemni and Monique Nemni, *Young Trudeau: 1919–1944: Son of Quebec, Father of Canada* (Toronto: Douglas Gibson Books, 2006), 311.

6 Interview with Harold Ashenmil, 11 March 2003, Montreal.

7 Martin Sullivan, *Mandate '68* (Doubleday: Toronto, 1968), 116–18; Radwanski, *Trudeau*, 80–1; Richard Cleroux, 'Former Speaker Took Secret to the Grave,' *CNEWS Politics*, 20 July 1999.

8 Interview with Harold Ashenmil, 11 March 2003, Montreal.

9 Garth Stevenson, *Community Besieged: The Anglophone Minority and the Politics of Quebec* (Montreal: McGill-Queen's University Press, 1999), 95.

10 John English, *The Worldly Years: The Life of Lester Pearson 1949–1972* (Toronto: Alfred A. Knopf, 1992), 383.

11 Interview with Hy Eiley, 19 September 2003, Toronto.

12 Interview with Jerry Grafstein, 10 June 2004, Toronto.

13 Ramsay Cook, *The Teeth of Time: Remembering Pierre Elliott Trudeau* (Montreal: McGill-Queen's University Press, 2006), 45–6.

14 OJA, MG 8/S, JCRC, 1968, box 5, file 44: Ben Kayfetz to file, n.d.

15 *Canadian Jewish News*, 28 June 1968, 1.

16 Zolf, *Just Watch Me*, 66.

17 Interview with Jerry Grafstein, 10 June 2004, Toronto.

18 Michel Vastel, *The Outsider: The Life of Pierre Elliott Trudeau* (Toronto: Macmillan, 1990).

19 Interview with Allan Gotlieb, 22 September 2003, Toronto.

20 John Porter, *The Vertical Mosaic: An Analysis of Social Class and Power in Canada* (Toronto: University of Toronto Press, 1965).

21 Merrijoy Sharon Kelner, 'The Elite Structure of Toronto: Ethnic Composition and Paths of Recruitment,' unpublished PhD diss., University of Toronto, 1969, 239.

22 Judith A. Klinghoffer, *Vietnam, Jews and the Middle East: Unintended Consequences* (New York: St Martin's Press, 1999), 4.

23 Interview with Nathan Glazer, 12 May 2001, Cambridge, MA; Jerald Podair, *The Strike That Changed New York* (New Haven, CT: Yale University Press, 2002); Cheryl Lynn Greenberg, *Troubling the Waters: Black-Jewish Relations in the American Century* (Princeton, NJ: Princeton University Press, 2006), 204–36.

24 Leonard Dinnerstein, *Ethnic Americans: A History of Immigration* (New York: Columbia University Press, 1999), 102.

25 Helen Davies, 'The Politics of Participation: A Study of Canada's Centennial Celebrations,' unpublished PhD diss., University of Manitoba, 1999, 227–30.

26 Interview with Harold Ashenmil, 11 March 2002, Montreal.

27 For a discussion of the historical origins of multiculturalism see Harold Troper, 'Multiculturalism,' in *The Oxford Companion to Canadian History* (Toronto: Oxford University Press, 2004), at http://www.oxfordreference.com/views/ENTRY.html?subview=Main&entry=t148.e1064. The Canadian Jewish community leadership were of mixed minds during the national debate that led to the govenment's multiculturalism policy statement. Some, particularly in Ontario and western Canada, regarded the possible government affirmation of cultural pluralism as a potential asset in the struggle against antisemitism and validation of the importance of

group identity maintenance in the Canadian context. What is more, they hoped the Jewish community would be able to tap into whatever financial support the government was intending to offer ethnic groups in support of ethnic-group identity maintenance. Others, particularly in Quebec, were concerned that any branding of Jews as an ethnic rather than a religious group would serve to undermine the position of Jews in Quebec, where as one of three faith groups – Catholic, Protestant, and Jewish – the Jewish community carried more weight than it might as one of many ethnic groups. Richard Menkis, 'A Case of Strategic Avoidance? The Canadian Jewish Congress and the Royal Commission on Bilingualism and Biculturalism,' delivered at the Biennial Conference in Canadian Studies, Jerusalem, 2 July 2004.

28 James Walker, 'The "Jewish Phase" in the Movement for Racial Equality in Canada,' *Canadian Ethnic Studies* 34 (2002), 1–29.

29 Harold M. Waller and Morton Weinfeld, 'The Jews of Quebec and "Le Fait français,"' in Morton Weinfeld et al., *The Canadian Jewish Mosaic* (Toronto: John Wiley, 1981), 415–39.

30 Daniel Elizar and Harold M. Waller, *Maintaining Consensus: The Canadian Jewish Polity in the Postwar World* (New York: University Press of America, 1990).

31 *Canadian Jewish News*, 12 April 1968, 4.

32 Ibid., 1.

33 *Canadian Jewish News*, 17 May 1968, 1.

34 Interview with Allan Gotlieb, 22 September 2003, Toronto.

35 Interview with Barney Danson, 29 October 2003, Toronto. If Trudeau was somewhat uneasy with Zionism, there were those among the Quebec sovereigntists Trudeau opposed (and in that opposition was embraced by most Jews in Quebec) who were sympathetic if not admiring of the Zionist enterprise. During the 1960s and 1970s some, such as René Lévesque, founder of the *Parti Québécois*, found inspiration for their cause in the narrative of Jewish national self-realization after two thousand years. They especially admired Israel's determination to ensure the survival of Hebrew as both a living language and symbol of Jewish continuity. What is more, as many in the sovereigntist camp in Quebec during that era came out of the left, they felt a kindred spirit with Israel's social democratic roots, the Histadrut and the kibbutz movement. Given this affinity for Israel and parallels to the situation in Quebec, some sovereigntists found it hard to understand why Quebec Jews neither sympathized with nor supported the nationalist cause in Quebec. René Lévesque was invited to address Montreal's Congregation Beth-El. During his speech he sympathetically

referred to Israel as a model for Quebec. If Israel could be a Jewish state, respectful of minority rights, why could not Quebec be a Québécois state respectful of minority rights? Interviews with Myer Bick, 12 March 2003, Montreal; Allan Langner, 13 December 2002, Montreal; Pierre Anctil, 13 December 2002, Montreal; and Manny Batshaw, 11 December 2002, Montreal.

36 Janice Gross Stein, 'Canadian Foreign Policy in the Middle East after the October War,' *Social Praxis* 4, nos. 3–4 (1977), 272. As if to underscore Canada's and Trudeau's overall disengagement from Middle East issues, a book by Trudeau and foreign policy adviser Ivan Head on Canada's foreign policy during the Trudeau years makes scarcely any reference to Israel or the Middle East. Ivan Head and Pierre Trudeau, *The Canadian Way: Shaping Canada's Foreign Policy, 1968–1984* (Toronto: McClelland & Stewart, 1995).

37 Mitchell Sharp, *Which Reminds Me: A Memoir* (Toronto: University of Toronto Press, 1994), 209; interview with Mitchell Sharp, 10 September 2003, Ottawa.

38 David Taras, 'From Passivity to Politics: Canada's Jewish Community and Political Support for Israel,' in David Taras and David H. Goldberg, eds., *The Domestic Battleground: Canada and the Arab-Israeli Conflict* (Kingston: McGill-Queen's University Press, 1989), 51–9.

39 Interview with Barney Danson, 28 October 2003, Toronto.

40 Interview with Naomi Alboim, 19 March 2007, Toronto.

41 Interview with Manny Weiner, 11 December 2002, Montreal; interview with Joe King, 2 December 2002, Montreal.

42 James Walker, 'Routes of Diversity: Strategies for Change, 1945–1970,' paper prepared for the Multiculturalism Program, Department of Canadian Heritage, 2001, and 'Human Rights in a Multicultural Framework: Defining Canadian Citizenship, 1945–1970,' *Canadian Issues/Thèmes Canadiens* (February 2002), 32–4; Harold Troper and Morton Weinfeld, *Old Wounds: Jews, Ukrainians and the Hunt for Nazi War Criminals in Canada* (Toronto: Viking, 1988); Harold Troper, *The Ransomed of God* (Toronto: Malcolm Lester, 1999).

43 David Taras, 'A Church Divided: A.C. Forrest and the United Church's Middle East Policy,' in Taras and Goldberg, eds., *The Domestic Battleground*, 86–101.

44 Sharp, *Which Reminds Me*, 210–11.

45 'Report from the Dark Ages,' *Near East Report*, 4 February 1969, 10, as quoted in Lorenzo Kent Kimball, *The Changing Pattern of Political Power in Iraq, 1958 to 1971* (New York: Robert Speller, 1972),148; Judith Miller and Laurie Mylroie, *Saddam Hussein and the Crisis in the Gulf* (New York: Random House, 1990), 34.

46 Shlomo Hillel, *Operation Babylon* (New York: Doubleday, 1987), 292–5; Mitchell Knisbacher, 'The Jews of Iraq and the International Protection of Rights of Minorities,' in David Sidorsky, ed., *Essays on Human Rights: Contemporary Issues and Jewish Perspectives* (Philadelphia: JPS, 1979), 170–6; Itamar Levin, *Locked Doors: The Seizure of Jewish Property in Arab Countries* (London: Praeger, 2001), 70–85.

47 'Evidence given by Raymond Muallem from Baghdad, Iraq,' in Malka Hillel Shulewitz, *The Forgotten Millions: The Modern Jewish Exodus from Arab Lands* (London: Cassell, 1999), 213.

48 Interview with Barney Danson, 28 October 2003, Toronto; interview with Donald Carr, 29 August 2003, Toronto; interview with Myer Bick, 26 March 2004.

49 LAC, External Affairs Department Papers (hereafter cited as EA), RG 25, 45-ME-13-3, vol. 2: Memorandum from G.G. Riddell to Consular Division, 5 February 1969, re: Possible Immigration of Jews from the Middle East.

50 Radwanski, *Trudeau*, 165–8; interview with Allan Gotlieb, 22 September 2003, Toronto.

51 Interview with Mitchell Sharp, 10 September 2003, Ottawa. Other instances of Canadian openness to refugees during Trudeau's tenure include the 1972 admission of 7000 Ugandans of South Asian heritage expelled from Uganda by Idi Amin and an approximately equal number of refugees from Pinochet's Chile following his 1973 coup. The latter refugee flow was, however, impeded for a time by concerns about the refugees' possible left-wing leanings. Ninette Kelly and Michael Trebilcock, *The Making of the Mosaic: A History of Canadian Immigration Policy* (Toronto: University of Toronto Press, 1998), 363–7.

52 Gerald Dirks, *Canada's Refugee Policy: Indifference or Opportunism?* (Montreal: McGill-Queen's University Press, 1977), 190–213, 233–5; Jean-Claude Lasry, 'A Francophone Diaspora in Quebec,' in Weinfeld et al., eds., *The Canadian Jewish Mosaic*, 221–40.

53 *Debates of the House of Commons*, 1968–9, vol. 5, 3 February 1969, 5045, and 10 February 1969, 5319.

54 LAC, EA, RG 25, 45-ME-13-3, vol. 2: Memorandum from G.G. Riddell to Consular Division, 5 February 1969; Cable from Mitchell Sharp to Tel Aviv/Tehran/Beirut/Cairo, 6 February 1969; *Globe and Mail*, 10 and 14 February 1969.

55 JHC, CJC Papers, box 3518, file 10: Draft letter, A.J. Arnold, re: Shloshim services for Iraq victims.

56 LAC, EA, RG 25, 45-ME-13-3, vol. 2: Memorandum to R.E. Collins from G.G. Riddell re: Jewish/Muslim Emigration from Iraq, 20 February 1969; Memorandum to Minister from M. Cadieux re: Jewish and Non-Jewish

Emigration from Iraq, 25 February 1969; Letter to A.J. MacEachen from Mitchell Sharp, 26 February 1969.

57 Ibid., vol. 2: Memorandum to the Minister from M. Cadieux re: Jewish and Non-Jewish emigration from Iraq, 28 February 1969; Memorandum to file from E.J. Bergbusch re: Emigration of Iraqi Jews, 5 March 1969.

58 Ibid., vol. 3: Mitchell Sharp to A.J. MacEachen, 9 May 1969.

59 Ibid.: Draft Memorandum to the Cabinet, 10 March 1969.

60 Ibid.: DM, Manpower and Immigration, to M. Cadieux, 14 March1969.

61 Ibid.: Allan MacEachen to Mitchell Sharp, 29 May 1969; Cabinet Committee on External Policy and Defense, Meeting of 24 June 1969, re: Jews in Iraq.

62 Marion Woolfson, *Prophets in Babylon: Jews in the Arab World* (London: Faber and Faber, 1980), 218–21.

63 Elie Wiesel, *The Jews of Silence: A Personal Report on Soviet Jewry* (New York: Holt, Rinehart and Winston, 1966).

64 Mindy B. Avrich-Skapinker, 'Canadian Jewish Involvement with Soviet Jewry, 1970–1990: The Toronto Case Study,' unpublished PhD diss., University of Toronto, 1993; Wendy Eisen, *Count on Us: The Struggle to Free Soviet Jews, A Canadian Perspective* (Toronto: Burgher, 1995); Zvi Gitelman, 'The Psychological and Political Consequences of the Six-Day War in the U.S.S.R.,' in Eli Lederhendler, ed., *The Six-Day War and World Jewry* (Bethesda: University of Maryland Press, 2000), 249–67.

65 CJA, ZA, 1970, box 2, file 15: Statement on Soviet Jewry Submitted by the Canadian Jewish Congress, n.d., n.p.

66 Ibid., file 20: Hy Hochberg to Alan Rose, 25 December 1970; LAC, B'nai Brith Canada Papers, MG 28, Series V 133, vol. 34: Memorandum from Sydney M. Harris to Community Leaders re: Activities Report #13, 5 January 1971, 3–4; CJA, ZA, 1971, box 1, file 4: Press release, Winnipeg Jewish Community Protests Harsh Leningrad Sentences, 7 January 1971.

67 CJA, ZA, 1971, box 7, file 65: Press release, St Catharines Protests Russian Show Trials, 11 1971; ibid., box 1, file 3: Sam Brownstone to IOI, 27 January 1971; *Hamilton Spectator*, 25 January 1971, 7; JHS/BC, CJC Papers, box 2, file 26: Rabbi Wilfred Solomon to J.R. Fisk, 8 January 1971.

68 CJA, ZA, 1971, box 7, file 65: Saul Hayes, Montreal, to Pierre Trudeau, Ottawa, 10 May 1971.

69 Barney Danson, *Not Bad for a Sergeant: The Memoirs of Barney Danson* (Toronto: Dundurn Press, 2002), 141.

70 Interview with Barney Danson, 29 October 2003, Toronto.

71 LAC, Lou Ronson Papers, MG 31, H 138, box 9: R.A.D. Ford, Moscow, to Herbert Levy, Toronto, 22 September 1971.

Chapter 7: 'Let Them Have It'

1 Larry Zeidel, as quoted in Stan Fischler, 'Chutzpah on Ice,' *The National Jewish Monthly*, February 1968, 18.
2 *Montreal Gazette*, 9 March 1968, 9; *Boston Globe*, 12 March 1968, 29. According to the former *New York Times* sportswriter Gerald Eskenazi, the actual insult hurled at Zeidel from the Bruins' bench was 'You're next for the ovens, Zeidel!' Asked by Eskenazi about the ovens comment, NHL president Clarence Campbell replied, 'The ethnic slur has always been part of hockey.' Gerald Eskenazi, 'Field of Dreams, Not Just Another Field,' *Forward*, 7 October 2005.
3 Editorial, *Toronto Star*, 13 March 1968.
4 *Toronto Star*, 13 March 1968, 22; *American Jewish Year Book, 1969* (New York: American Jewish Committee, 1969), 249.
5 LAC, B'nai Brith Canada Papers, MG 28, V 133, vol. 74: Louis Herman to Clarence Campbell, 14 March 1968.
6 *Toronto Star*, 20 March 1968. An irony of the *Toronto Star* report, if accurate, is that the Philadelphia Flyers owner, Ed Snider, who won the NHL expansion franchise for Philadelphia in 1966, is Jewish. The team started playing in 1967. In addition to his sports interests, Snider is a prominent member of the Philadelphia Jewish community, active on behalf of a number of Jewish and non-Jewish philanthropic causes. In 1999 Snider was awarded the Anti-Defamation League's Americanism Award. Zeidel left hockey at the end of the following season. Explaining Zeidel's departure, *Fischlers' Hockey Encyclopedia* made no reference to the on-ice antisemitic incident in Toronto. Rather, the publication explains that Flyers' manager Bud Poole 'wanted Zeidel to play [his next season] in Quebec of the American League, but Zeidel refused. He retired from hockey in 1969 and went into the investment counselling business.' Stan Fischler and Shirley Fischler, *Fischlers' Hockey Encyclopedia* (Toronto: Fitzhenry and Whiteside, 1975), 628.
7 LAC, B'nai Brith Canada Papers, MG 28, V 133, vol. 74: Draft letter, unsigned, to Campbell, n.d.
8 *Toronto Star*, 20 March 1968.
9 LAC, Lou Ronson Personal Papers, Richard D. Jones to Lou Ronson, 29 January 1987; Richard D. Jones to Editor, 24 April 1978.
10 John Porter, *The Vertical Mosaic: An Analysis of Social Class and Power in Canada* (Toronto: University of Toronto Press, 1965), 305.
11 Interview with Merrijoy Kelner, 17 June 2004, Toronto.
12 Merrijoy Sharon Kelner, 'The Elite Structure of Toronto: Ethnic Composition and Paths of Recruitment,' unpublished PhD diss., University of

Toronto, 1969, 217–19; 'Clubs, Too, Are Relevant,' *Monetary Times*, September 1969, 38–41.

13 Interview with Merrijoy Kelner, 17 June 2004, Toronto.

14 Peter C. Newman, *Titans: How the New Canadian Establishment Seized Power* (Toronto: Penguin, 1999), 80.

15 Charles Lynch, *Up from the Ashes: The Rideau Club Story* (Ottawa. University of Ottawa Press, 1990), 102.

16 Ibid., 100.

17 Lawrence Freiman, *Don't Fall Off the Rocking Horse: An Autobiography* (Toronto: McClelland and Stewart, 1978), 117–20; Bruce Muirhead, *Against the Odds: The Life and Times of Louis Rasminsky* (Toronto: University of Toronto Press, 1999), 220–1.

18 Lynch, *Up from the Ashes*, 103–15. Women were not admitted into membership until 1979.

19 *Official Report of the Debates of the Legislative Assembly*, Thursday, 3 May 1984, 4527–8.

20 Reginald H. Roy, *The Vancouver Club: First Century 1889–1989* (Vancouver: Vancouver Club, 1989), 85.

21 James Walker, 'The "Jewish Phase" in the Movement for Racial Equality in Canada,' *Canadian Ethnic Studies* 34 (2002), 1–29.

22 Sol I. Littman, 'The Problem of Social Discrimination in Canada,' n.d.

23 D. Rodwell Austin and Ted Barris, *Carved in Granite: 125 Years of Granite Club History* (Toronto: Macmillan, 1999), 279–84.

24 JHS/BC, CJC Papers, box 14, file14, General file: Sol I. Littman to Anne Zimmerman, 9 April 1968; interview with Sol Littman, 2 October 2003, Tucson (by telephone).

25 LAC, Lou R. Ronson Papers, MG 31, H 138, vol. 9, file 6: ADL District 22, Social Discrimination at the Granite Club 1965–1969, Memorandum, Max Shecter to National Cabinet, 21 November 1968. According to John Porter, in 1957 the three leading elite private clubs in Toronto were the York Club, the Toronto Club, and the National Club. John Porter, 'The Economic Elite and the Social Structure of Canada,' *Canadian Journal of Economics and Political Science* 23 (1957), 393.

26 LAC, B'nai Brith Canada Papers, MG 28, V 133, vol. 100, pt. 1: Sol Littman to Murray Chusid, 20 February 1969; *Toronto Telegram*, 25 February 1969.

27 LAC, William Morris Papers, MG 21, H 151: File Anti-Defamation League, 20 January 1969; Memorandum Louis Ronson to ADL Chairman and Presidents of Lodges and Chapters re: Social Discrimination, 4 March 1969.

28 LAC, B'nai Brith Canada Papers, MG 28, V 133, vol. 100, pt. 1: Sol Littman

to Harold Braverman, 17 April 1969; Austin and Barris, *Carved in Granite,* 288–9; *Toronto Telegram,* 28 March 1969; *Toronto Star,* 29 March 1969; *Chronicle Review,* 4 April 1969.

29 *Globe and Mail,* 25 February 1969; *Toronto Star,* 25 February 1969.

30 Interview with Robert Marshall, 10 October 2003, Toronto; Austin and Barris, *Carved in Granite,* 289.

31 *Toronto Star,* 26 September 1969.

32 LAC, B'nai Brith Canada Papers, MG 28, V 133, vol. 100, pt. 1: Memorandum from Harold Braverman to Sol Littman, 9 October 1969.

33 *Globe and Mail,* 16 October 1969.

34 Goodman and Goodman files, D-6455, Anti-Defamation League re: Granite Club Property; Borough of North York, Notice of Application re Section 30 of the Planning Act, 6 March 1969; LAC, B'nai Brith Canada Papers, MG 28, V 133, vol. 100, pt. 1: Memorandum from Sol Littman to Harold Braverman, 20 October 1969; LAC, W. Gunther Plaut Papers, MG 31, F 6, vol. 22: Minutes of Central Regional Cabinet Meeting, 4 November 1969; *Globe and Mail,* 16 October 1969; *Toronto Star,* 19 October 1969.

35 Interview with Lou Ronson, 12 November 2003, Toronto; *Toronto Telegram,* 4 December 1969.

36 LAC, B'nai Brith Canada Papers, MG 28, V 133, vol. 100, pt. 1: Sol Littman to R. Scott, 28 November 1969.

37 Goodman and Goodman files, D-6455, Anti-Defamation League re: Granite Club Property: Affidavit, 17 December 1969.

38 Ibid.: Handwritten notes, Edward Goodman, re: OMB Hearing, 19 December 1969; *Toronto Telegram,* 4 December 1969.

39 LAC, W. Gunther Plaut Papers, MG 31, F 6, vol. 22: Memorandum of Louis Ronson to National Cabinet and Central Regional Cabinet, 13 January 1970.

40 *Toronto Star,* 29 December 1969.

41 Austin and Barris, *Carved in Granite,* 289; interview with Lou Ronson, 12 November 2003.

42 Interview with Murray Koffler, 4 April 2004, Toronto. .

43 Goodman and Goodman files, D-6455, Anti-Defamation League re: Granite Club Property: Edward Goodman to D.R. Steeles, 6 January 1970; Louis Ronson to J. Kelley, 8 January 1970; Louis Ronson to McMaster Montgomery, 13 January 1970.

44 LAC, W. Gunther Plaut Papers, MG 31, F 6, vol. 22: Memorandum of Louis Ronson to National Cabinet and Central Regional Cabinet, 13 January 1970.

45 Interview with Robert Marshall, 10 October 2003, Toronto.

46 Interview with Lou Ronson, 12 November 2003, Toronto.

47 LAC, W. Gunther Plaut Papers, MG 31, F 6, vol. 22: Memorandum Sol I. Littman to Sydney Maislin, re: Granite Club, 15 January 1970; Louis Ronson to T. Millar Chase, 15 January 1970.

48 Goodman and Goodman files, D-6455, Anti-Defamation League re: Granite Club Property: Ontario Municipal Board, R. 1029-69, In the Matter of Section 30 of Planning Act; *Toronto Star*, 17 January 1970; *Toronto Telegram*, 17 January 1970.

49 *Toronto Telegram*, 19 January 1970.

50 *Toronto Star*, 19 January 1970; *Globe and Mail*, 19 January 1970.

51 Austin and Barris, *Carved in Granite*, 391.

52 Interview with Robert Marshall, October 10, 2003, Toronto.

53 LAC, B'nai Brith Canada Papers, MG 28, V 133, vol. 100, pt. 2: Memorandum, Sol Littman to Louis Ronson, n.d.; LAC, Lou R. Ronson Papers, MG 31, H 138, vol. 7, file 9: ADL District 22, Social Discrimination at the Granite Club 1970–1972.

54 Interview with Robert Marshall, 10 October 2003, Toronto; interview with Lou Ronson, 12 November 2003; interview with Murray Koffler, 3 April 2004, Toronto.

55 Goodman and Goodman files, D-6455, Anti-Defamation League re: Granite Club Property; Sol Littman to John A. Geller, 21 January 1970.

56 For a discussion of the roots and early days of the Soviet Jewish campaign see Yaacov Ro'i, *The Struggle for Soviet Jewish Emigration 1948–1967* (Cambridge: Cambridge University Press, 1991).

57 Moshe Decter, 'The Status of Jews in the Soviet Union,' *Foreign Affairs* 41 (1963), 430.

58 Gunther Lawrence, *Three Million More?* (New York: Doubleday, 1970), 10–12. Khrushchev's response to Bertrand Russell was republished by the Soviet embassy in Ottawa in its *Bulletin of Soviet News*, 12 December 1963.

59 Memorandum of A. Popov, CPSU Central Committee, Ottawa, 21 January 1964, in Boris Morozov, ed., *Documents on Soviet Jewish Emigration* (London: Frank Cass, 1999), 46–55.

60 For detail on the American Soviet Jewry movement see William W. Orbach, *The American Movement to Aid Soviet Jews* (Amherst: University of Massachusetts Press, 1979); Frederick A. Lazin, *The Struggle for Soviet Jewry in American Politics: Israel versus the American Jewish Establishment* (Lanham, MD: Lexington Books, 2005); Murray Friedman and Albert D. Chernin, eds., *A Second Exodus: The American Movement to Free Soviet Jews* (Waltham, MA: Brandeis University Press, 1999); Stuart Altshuler, *From Exodus to*

Freedom: The History of the Soviet Jewry Movement (Lanham, MD: Rowman and Littlefield, 2005).

61 LAC, Lavy M. Becker Papers, MG 31, H 81, vol.2: Resolution on Russian Jews Adopted by World Congress of Jewish Organizations, 4 March 1963; CJA, CJC Papers, CA, box 61, file 674: I. Rabbi S.M. Zambrowsky to Ambassador Ivan Shepedko, 1 November 1963; A. Popov to Rabbi S.M. Zambrowsky, 11 November 1963; Rabbi S.M. Zambrowsky to Ambassador Ivan Shepedko, 18 December 1963; A. Popov to Rabbi S.M. Zambrowsky, 4 January 1964.

62 CJA, CJC Papers, CA, box 61, file 574 H: All-Canadian Rabbinic Conference on Jews in Russia, *IOI* no. 2794, 9 January 9, 1964.; *Canadian Jewish News*, 17 January 1964, 4; LAC, W. Gunther Plaut Papers, MG 31, F 6, box 21: Rabbi S.M. Zambrowsky to Rabbi W.G. Plaut, 21 February 1964; S. Andhil Fineberg to W.G. Plaut, 27 February 1964.

63 Interview with Soviet Embassy on Position of Jews in Russia, *IOI* no. 2812, 11 March 1964; Wendy Eisen, *Count on Us: The Struggle to Free Soviet Jews, A Canadian Perspective* (Toronto: Burger, 1995), 19.

64 Cyril Levitt Papers, Minutes of Special JCRC Meeting, Toronto, 18 June 1965, 9; interview with Ben Kayfetz, 14 May 2001, Toronto.

65 OJA, MG 8/S, JCRC, 1966, box 18, file 52: Memorandum of Myer Sharzer to Harry L. Wolfson, re: Subcommittee on Foreign Affairs, 7 January 1966; CJC, ZA, 1969, box 2, file 2: Michael Garber to Leaders, 10 May 1966; OJA, CJC, Committee meetings etc., 1966, Foreign Affairs Committee: Memorandum of Myer Sharzer to Foreign Affairs Committee, Central Region, re: Proposal re Campaign for Soviet Jewry, 20 January 1966.

66 CJA, ZA, 1968, box 1, file 7: Resolutions Adopted at the Leadership Conference on Jews in the Soviet Union Held in Montreal, 29 May 1966.

67 Interview with Ben Kayfetz, 14 May 2001, Toronto.

68 LAC, W. Gunther Plaut Papers, MG 31, F 6, vol. 82: Charles A. Kent to Friend, 2 October 1967; interview with Donald Carr, 29 August 2003, Toronto.

69 For discussion of Soviet Jewish reaction to the Six Day War see Zvi Gitelman, 'The Psychological and Political Consequences of the Six-Day War in the USSR,' in Eli Lederhendler, ed., *The Six Day War and World Jewry* (Bethesda, MD: University of Maryland Press, 2000), 249–67; Ro'i, *The Struggle for Soviet Jewish Emigration*, 336–88.

70 Interview with David Kaufman, 11 September 2000, Toronto.

71 LAC, W. Gunther Plaut Papers, MG 31, F 6, vol. 82: Memorandum of Roz Fedder et al. to Friends re: Youth Rally on Soviet Jewry, 23 October 1967; OJA, MG 8/S, JCRC, 1966, box 27, file 77: Letter to Myer Sharzer, 17 September 1967.

72 'Canada,' in *American Jewish Yearbook 1969*, 390.
73 CJA, ZA, 1968, box 3, file 35: Sandor Frohlich to President, 25 September 1968; OJA, CJC, Committee meetings etc., 1968: Press release from Canadian Jewish Congress, Toronto, re: Youth to 'Dance in the Square' to Protest Soviet Policies, n.d. (1968); CJA, CJC Papers, CA, box 68, file 610-119: Murray Newman to Judaean and Parents, 30 September 1969; OJA, MG 8/S, JCRC, 1971, box 48, file 114: Hy Hochberg to Alan Rose, 8 October 1969; CJA, CJC Papers, CA, box 68, file 610-119: 'Canada' report – Soviet Jews.; Cape Breton Council of Hadassah-Wizo to Ben-Eliahu, 7 October 1969; CJA, CJC. Alan Rose Papers, DA5, vol. 13, file 38: Memorandum of Alan Rose to Monroe Abbey and Sydney M. Harris re: International Affairs, 30 December 1969.
74 JHC, CJC Papers, box P 3534, file 1: Demonstration for Soviet Jewry, Minutes of Meeting, Winnipeg, 11 September 1969; A.J. Arnold, Statement on the Winnipeg Demonstration of Solidarity with Soviet Jewry, 7 October 1969; *Winnipeg Free Press*, 6 October 1969, 1, 2.
75 CJA, Soviet Jewry Papers, DA 12, box 10, file 23: Memorandum of Ella Cohen to S. Lewin re: Kosygin's Visit to Canada, 17 September 1971.
76 OJA, CJC, Committee meetings etc., 1971, Soviet Union: Aide Memoire of a Meeting of a Delegation of the Canadian Jewish Congress with the Honourable Mitchell Sharp Secretary of State for External Affairs, Ottawa, 17 September 1971; LAC, William Morris Papers, MG 21, H 151, vol 2: Memorandum of Herbert S. Levy to Alexander Lipson, 23 September 1971.
77 Peter Worthington, 'A New Dialogue against Soviet Oppression,' *Toronto Telegram*, 23 July 1971.
78 Harold Troper and Morton Weinfeld, *Old Wounds: Jews, Ukrainians and the Hunt for Nazi War Criminals in Canada* (Toronto: Viking, 1988), 92–3.
79 *Ottawa Citizen*, 18 October 1971, 1.
80 LAC, W. Gunther Plaut Papers, MG 31, F 6, vol. 83: W. Gunther Plaut, 'Kosygin and the Jews of Canada,' 8–9; CJA, Soviet Jewry Papers, DA 12, box 10, file 11: Conference of Canadian Rabbis Text of Letter Addressed to Premier Kosygin, 18 October 1971.
81 LAC, W. Gunther Plaut Papers, MG 31, F 6, vol. 83: Rabbi Solomon J. Spiro to Rabbi W. Gunther Plaut, 24 October 1971.
82 *Canadian Jewish News*, 22 October 1971, 1.
83 Interview with Steve Ain, 28 July 2003, Toronto.
84 *Montreal Gazette*, 22 October 1971, 8; *Ottawa Citizen*, 23 October 1971, 22; *House of Commons Debates*, 21 October 1971, 8882.
85 *Montreal Gazette*, 'Mayor Drapeau's comments, a welcome surprise to

Jewish protesters, drew personal praise from Canadian Jewish Congress leaders,' 22 October 1971, 1; CJA, Soviet Jewry Papers, DA 12, box 10, file 6: Saul Hayes to Mayor Jean Drapeau, 25 October 1971.

86 *Montreal Star*, 22 October 1971, 3; *IOI* no. 639, 22 October 1971, 4.

87 *Vancouver Province*, 25 October 1971; *Vancouver Sun*, 25 October 1971, 15.

88 *Edmonton Journal*, 23 October 1971, 3; *Edmonton Journal*, 25 October 1971, 13.

89 LAC, W. Gunther Plaut Papers, MG 31, F 6, vol. 83: W. Gunther Plaut, 'Kosygin and the Jews of Canada,' 15.

90 Harold Troper and Lee Palmer, *Issues in Cultural Diversity* (Toronto: OISE, 1976), 87–95; *Globe and Mail*, 26 October 1971, 1–2; *Globe and Mail*, 27 October 1971, 1–2.

91 LAC, W. Gunther Plaut Papers, MG 31, F 6, vol. 83: Plaut, 'Kosygin and the Jews of Canada,' 17; Harold Troper, *The Ransomed of God: The Remarkable Story of One Woman's Role in the Rescue of Syrian Jews* (Toronto: Malcolm Lester Books, 1999), 19–22; *Montreal Gazette*, 29 October 1971, 1.

Conclusion

1 Thomas Beaudoin, 'Catholics, Jews and Vatican II,' *Historical Text Archives* (1991), at http://historicaltextarchive.com/sections.php?op=viewarticle&artid=76.

2 LAC, B'nai Brith Canada Papers, MG 28, series V 133, vol 86: Draft of Award Statement, Trudeau Dinner, 8 February 1970.

3 *Canadian Jewish News*, 12 February 1970, 1.

4 LAC, B'nai Brith Canada Papers, MG 28, V 133, vol 10: Transcript of the Prime Minister's Remarks at the Family of Man Award Banquet of the Anti-Defamation League of B'nai B'rith Montreal, 8 February 1970.

5 Ibid., vol. 86: Notes for Remarks by the Prime Minister at the Family of Man Award Banquet of the Anti-Defamation League of B'nai Brith, Montreal, 8 February 1970.

6 Ibid.: Draft of Award Statement, Trudeau Dinner, 8 February 1970.

7 Harold Waller and Morton Weinfeld, 'The Jews of Quebec and "Le Fait Français,"' in Morton Weinfeld et al., *The Canadian Jewish Mosaic* (Toronto: John Wiley, 1981), 422–35; Harold Waller, 'Canada,' in *American Jewish Yearbook, 1989* (New York: American Jewish Committee, 1989), 261.

8 *Globe and Mail*, 2 November 1970, 1.

9 *Canadian Jewish News*, 13 November 1970, 3.

10 *Canadian Jewish News*, 30 October 1970, 1.

11 *Canadian Jewish News*, 6 November 1970, 1.
12 LAC, B'nai Brith Canada Papers, MG 28, V 133, vol. 37: Saul Hayes, Montreal, to Ben Kayfetz, Toronto, 10 November 1970.
13 Ibid.: Transcript, Barry Callaghan–Golda Meir interview, Sunday, 1 November 1970, CBC 'Weekend.'
14 Michael Novak, *The Rise of the Unmeltable Ethnic* (New York: Macmillan, 1972), 8.

Interviews

Grafstein, Jerry	Toronto	10 June 2004
Greenspan, David	Toronto	24 November 2004
Greenspan, Louis	Toronto	1 August 2002
Gross, Bill	Tel Aviv	19 August 2001
Gross, Lisa	Tel Aviv	19 August 2001
Half, Shelly	Tel Aviv	21 August 2001
Kaplan, Irv	Tel Aviv	19 August 2001
Kaplan, Orah	Tel Aviv	19 August 2001
Kaufman, David	Toronto	11 September 2000
Kayfetz, Ben	Toronto	14 May 2001
Kelner, Merrijoy	Toronto	17 June 2004
King, Joe	Montreal	2 December 2002
Koffler, Murray	Toronto	3 April 2004
Kolber, Leo	Montreal	25 March 2004
Krell, Robert	Vancouver	2 November 2001
Langner, Rabbi Allan	Montreal	13 December 2002
Levitt, Cyril	Toronto	12 May 2002
Littman, Sol	Tucson	3 October 2003
Lowenthal, Gene	Jerusalem	8 August 2001
Lowenthal, Sue	Jerusalem	8 August 2001
Lucien, Lieherman	Vancouver	3 November 2001
Marshall, Robert	Toronto	10 October 2003
Oren, Michael	Jerusalem	15 August 2001
Pakes Allan	Jerusalem	10 August 2001
Plaut, Rabbi W. Gunther	Toronto	26 June 2002
Promislow, Barbara	Jerusalem	16 August 2001
Promislow, George	Jerusalem	16 August 2001
Reemer, Yehuda	Urim, Israel	18 August 2001
Rome, David	Montreal	18 June 1979
Ronson, Lou	Toronto	12 and 19 November 2003
Sable, Sam	Toronto	4 October 2004
Sarna, Jonathan	Jerusalem	14 August 2001
Schnoor, Toby	Winnipeg	1 June 2004
Sharp, Mitchell	Ottawa	10 September 2003
Shuchat, Rabbi Wilfred	Montreal	25 March 2004
Silver, Jerry	Toronto	7 August 2004
Solomon, Rabbi Wilfred	Jerusalem	15 August 2001
Solway, Herb	Toronto	7 April 2004
Stein, Michael	Toronto	19 February 2004

Steinberg, Moe	Vancouver	11 August 2003
Stern, Bill	Toronto	9 March 2007
Stilman, Harry	Toronto	29 December 2008
Usiskin, Roz	Winnipeg	3 June 2004
Vrba, Rudi	Vancouver	14 August 2003
Weiner, Manny	Montreal	11 December 2002
Weinfeld, Morton	Montreal	26 August 2008
Weintraub, Marvin	Vancouver	12 August 2003
Wisse, Ruth	Boston	21 October 2004
Zaslow, Marlene	Tel Aviv	21 August 2001
Zaslow, Motti	Tel Aviv	21 August 2001
Zetland, Dan	Tel Aviv	19 August 2001
Zetland, Fran	Tel Aviv	19 August 2001
Zolf, Larry	Toronto	1 August 2003

Sources

Abbreviations

CJA	Canadian Jewish Archives (Montreal)
CJC	Canadian Jewish Congress
CZA	Central Zionist Archives (Jerusalem)
JCRC	Joint Community Relations Committee
JHC	Jewish Heritage Centre of Western Canada (Winnipeg)
JHS/BC	Jewish Historical Society of British Columbia (Vancouver)
LAC	Library and Archives Canada (Ottawa)
OJA	Ontario Jewish Archives (Toronto)

Sources

Canadian Jewish Archives (CJA, Montreal), Canadian Jewish Congress
- Alan Rose Papers (DA 5)
- Central files (CA, CB)
- Chronological files (ZA)
- Soviet Jewry Papers (DA 12)
Central Zionist Archives (Jerusalem), Canadian Zionist Association Papers
Cyril Levitt Papers (personal papers, Toronto)
Goodman and Goodman files (Toronto), Anti-Defamation League, re: Granite
    Club Property (D-6455)
Jewish Heritage Centre of Western Canada (JHC, Winnipeg), CJC Papers
Jewish Historical Committee of Calgary, Mrs Eddie Cohen Papers (M-7744-15)
Jewish Historical Society of British Columbia (JHS/BC, Vancouver)
- CJC Papers, box 39, file 749
- CJC Western Region Papers

Library and Archives Canada (Ottawa)
- B'nai Brith Canada Papers (MG 28, V 133)
- Department of Foreign Affairs and International Trade Papers, Middle East, Syria Files (RG 25, 45-ME-13-3)
- Lavy M. Becker Papers (MG 31, H 81)
- Lou R. Ronson Papers (MG 31, H 138)
- W. Gunther Plaut Papers (MG 31, F6)
- William Morris Papers (MG 21, H 151)

Lou Ronson Papers (personal papers, Toronto)

Ontario Jewish Archives (Toronto)
- Canadian Jewish Congress (CJC), Committee meetings, agendas, minutes, reports, and correspondence, Fonds 17, Series 1:
- Box 226
- CA, CSA 92/1097
- 1966, Foreign Affairs Committee
- 1967, Israel Emergency Coordinating Committee, Minutes
- 1967, Israel Emergency Fund Raising
- 1967, Israel Emergency Publicity
- 1971, Soviet Union
- 1967, Zionist Organization of Canada

Canadian Jewish Congress (CJC), MG 8/S, Central Region, Joint Community Relations Committee Papers:
- 1965
- 1965/107
- 1966/52
- 1966/77
- 1967/77C
- 1969/127
- 1969/40/67
- 1970/136
- 1970/147
- 1970/168
- 1971/114
- Canadian Jewish Congress, General Files

Illustration Credits

Barney Danson Collection: Meeting between Canadian and Soviet political leaders.

Canadian Jewish Archives: Arrival of Moroccan family, PC2, Box 1, File 7C; Cardinal Paul-Émile Léger, PC1, Box 12, File 20C; Public hangings in Baghdad, PC1, Box 5, File 8; Twenty-four hour Soviet Jewry vigil, PC1, Box 10, File 24B-2; Sign left at Soviet Embassy, PC1, Box 8, File 21A; Soviet Jewry rally, PC1, Box 8, File 21B; Golda Meir, PC1, Box 2, File 21-A-5.

Granite Club Collection: T. Millar Chase.

Harry Stilman Personal Collection: Pavilion of Judaism at Expo 67.

JHSBC: Montreal Action Committee, CJC-Vancouver Papers, box 2, file 24.

Montreal Star: Israel Emergency Fund Day.

Ontario Jewish Archives: Governor General Georges Vanier, fonds 17, series 2, file 1308; Window of downtown Toronto store, fonds 17, series 2, file 1308; Actions Committee for Soviet Jewry, fonds 17, sub-series 3-5, file 7; Elie Weisel, fonds 17, series 3-5, file 7, photo 744-36A. Gabi Hoz photographer; Electric illuminated Star of David, fonds 17, series 3-5, file 7, photo 745-10. Gabi Hoz photographer.

United Church Observer Photo Collection: A.C. Forrest.

York University Library, Clara Thomas Archives & Special Collections:

Nazis parading in Allan Gardens, Toronto Telegram fonds, F0433, image no. ASC05586; Swastika daubing at Shomrai Shabos Synagogue, Toronto Telegram fonds, F0433, image no. ASC05584; Crowd gathered to protest Nazi rally, Toronto Telegram fonds, F0433, image no. ASC05587; Israel emergency meeting, Toronto Telegram fonds, F0433, image no. ASC05585; United Church of Canada Moderator, Robert B. McClure, Toronto Telegram fonds, F0433, image no. ASC05588; Students dancing around Torah, Toronto Telegram fonds, F0433, image no. ASC05589.

Zeidel Family Collection: Larry 'The Rock' Ziedel.

Index

327n6; Nazi (*see* Nazi Germany; neo-Nazi); in Quebec, 8, 50, 54, 57, 221 (*see also* Quebec); and social discrimination, 91–4, 218, 244–63, 307n23: –, at elite social clubs, 248–63 (*see also under* social clubs, elite); in Toronto, 84–6, 91–121, 262 (*see also under* Toronto Jewish community). *See also* Anti-Defamation League (ADL); Canada: anti-hate legislation; church relations
Arafat, Yasser, 294
Asbestos Strike, Quebec (1949), 209
assimilation, 14–21, 34, 43, 86–7, 127. *See also* intermarriage; 'vanishing Jew' debate
Association of Former Concentration Camp Inmates and Survivors of Nazi Oppression, 114. *See also* Holocaust survivors
Austin, Jack, 217
Avishai, Bernard, 164–5

Baghdad, hanging of Jews, 228–30
Bank of Canada, 216, 252
Bar-On, Mordechai, 168–9
Barrett, David, 252
Batshaw, Manny, 43
Beattie, John, 107–8, 110–11
Becker, Lavy, 10–11, 76
Berton, Pierre, 90
Beth Shalom Synagogue (Ottawa), 148
Beth Tzedec Synagogue (Toronto), 163, 268, 293
Bialystok, Franklin, 82, 98, 109
bicentenary celebrations. *See* Canadian Jewish Bicentenary
Bick, Myer, 157–9
Bikel, Theodore, 278

Bill 22 (Official Language Act of 1974), 290–1
'blackballing,' at social clubs, 251–2. *See also* antisemitism: social discrimination; social clubs, elite
B'nai Brith, 168, 177–8, 187–9, 213, 242, 254–60, 262; *Digest*, 187–8; libel case with Forrest, 187–90; Youth Organization, 168. *See also* Anti-Defamation League (ADL)
Booth, John Nicholls, 188–9
Boston Bruins, 244–5, 247. *See also* National Hockey League (NHL)
Brandeau, Esther, 10
British Columbia, 252. *See also* Vancouver Jewish community
British North America Act, 47, 55, 62. *See also* education: in Quebec
Bronfman, Allan, 292
Bronfman, Samuel, 4, 9, 31–2, 37–8, 42, 67–8; and Six Day War support, 131, 143–6, 155, 160–1; and philanthropy, 42, 77
Bruce, Lenny, 205

Callaghan, Barry, 294
Campbell, Clarence, 245
Canada, government of: and anti-hate legislation, 99, 106–7, 114, 227, 289, 250; Bank of Canada, 216, 252; Department of Immigration, 232; federal elections (1965), 209–18; foreign policy of (general), 230–1; human rights policy of, 5–6, 86–7, 89–90, 231–2, 234–5; Jewish members of, 210–12, 215–17, 219–20; Liberal Party, 209–18; multiculturalism, 68–70, 73, 86–7, 220–1, 295, 322–3n27; and Middle East policy, 124, 133–5, 160–1, 176–7, 179–80,